Florida Rules of Criminal Procedure 2014

Florida Evidence Code 2014

ALSO AVAILABLE FROM
SUAVE FISH PUBLISHING, LEGAL DIVISION

Florida Rules of Civil Procedure and Florida Evidence Code

Florida Standard Jury Instructions in Criminal Cases

Florida Probate Rules and Florida Probate Code

Other States

Illinois Code of Civil Procedure and Illinois Rules of Evidence

Illinois Code of Criminal Procedure and Illinois Rules of Evidence

Michigan Rules of Civil Procedure and Michigan Rules of Evidence

Michigan Rules of Criminal Procedure and Michigan Rules of Evidence

Michigan Rules of Probate Court and Michigan Rules of Evidence

Texas Rules of Civil Procedure and Texas Rules of Evidence

Florida Rules of Criminal Procedure
Table of Contents

CITATIONS TO OPINIONS 1

I. SCOPE, PURPOSE, AND CONSTRUCTION 5

    RULE 3.010. SCOPE 5

    RULE 3.020. PURPOSE AND CONSTRUCTION 5

    RULE 3.025. STATE AND PROSECUTING ATTORNEY DEFINED 5

II. GENERAL PROVISIONS 6

    RULE 3.030. SERVICE OF PLEADINGS AND PAPERS 6

    RULE 3.030. SERVICE AND FILING OF PLEADINGS, PAPERS AND DOCUMENTS 7

    RULE 3.040. COMPUTATION OF TIME 8

    RULE 3.050. ENLARGEMENT OF TIME 9

    RULE 3.060. TIME FOR SERVICE OF MOTIONS AND NOTICE OF HEARING 9

    RULE 3.070. ADDITIONAL TIME AFTER SERVICE BY MAIL 9

    RULE 3.070. ADDITIONAL TIME AFTER SERVICE BY MAIL, WHEN PERMITTED, OR ELECTRONIC MAIL 10

    RULE 3.080. NONVERIFICATION OF PLEADINGS 11

    RULE 3.090. PLEADING CAPTIONS 13

    RULE 3.111. PROVIDING COUNSEL TO INDIGENTS 14

    RULE 3.112. MINIMUM STANDARDS FOR ATTORNEYS IN CAPITAL CASES 19

    RULE 3.115. DUTIES OF STATE ATTORNEY; CRIMINAL INTAKE 24

III. PRELIMINARY PROCEEDINGS 24

    RULE 3.120. COMMITTING JUDGE... 24

    RULE 3.121. ARREST WARRANT 24

    RULE 3.125. NOTICE TO APPEAR 25

    RULE 3.130. FIRST APPEARANCE 32

    RULE 3.131. PRETRIAL RELEASE... 33

    RULE 3.132. PRETRIAL DETENTION 39

    RULE 3.133. PRETRIAL PROBABLE CAUSE DETERMINATIONS AND ADVERSARY PRELIMINARY HEARINGS 40

    RULE 3.134. TIME FOR FILING FORMAL CHARGES 44

    RULE 3.140. INDICTMENTS; INFORMATIONS.. 44

    RULE 3.150. JOINDER OF OFFENSES AND DEFENDANTS 53

    RULE 3.151. CONSOLIDATION OF RELATED OFFENSES 55

    RULE 3.152. SEVERANCE OF OFFENSES AND DEFENDANTS 56

    RULE 3.153. TIMELINESS OF DEFENDANT'S MOTION; WAIVER 58

IV. ARRAIGNMENT AND PLEAS 58

    RULE 3.160. ARRAIGNMENT 58

    RULE 3.170. PLEAS 60

    RULE 3.171. PLEA DISCUSSIONS AND AGREEMENTS 63

    RULE 3.172. ACCEPTANCE OF GUILTY OR NOLO CONTENDERE PLEA 66

    RULE 3.180. PRESENCE OF DEFENDANT 68

V. PRETRIAL MOTIONS AND DEFENSES 70

    RULE 3.190. PRETRIAL MOTIONS 70

    RULE 3.191. SPEEDY TRIAL 75

    RULE 3.192. MOTIONS FOR REHEARING 82

    RULE 3.200. NOTICE OF ALIBI 82

    RULE 3.201. BATTERED-SPOUSE SYNDROME DEFENSE 84

    RULE 3.202. EXPERT TESTIMONY OF MENTAL MITIGATION DURING PENALTY PHASE OF CAPITAL TRIAL: NOTICE AND EXAMINATION BY STATE EXPERT 84

    RULE 3.203. DEFENDANT'S MENTAL RETARDATION AS A BAR TO IMPOSITION OF THE DEATH PENALTY 85

    RULE 3.210. INCOMPETENCE TO PROCEED: PROCEDURE FOR RAISING THE ISSUE 87

    RULE 3.211. COMPETENCE TO PROCEED: SCOPE OF EXAMINATION AND REPORT 92

    RULE 3.212. COMPETENCE TO PROCEED: HEARING AND DISPOSITION 96

    RULE 3.213. CONTINUING INCOMPETENCY TO PROCEED, EXCEPT INCOMPETENCY TO PROCEED WITH SENTENCING: DISPOSITION 100

    RULE 3.214. INCOMPETENCY TO PROCEED TO SENTENCING: DISPOSITION . 102

    RULE 3.215. EFFECT OF ADJUDICATION OF INCOMPETENCY TO PROCEED: PSYCHOTROPIC MEDICATION 103

    RULE 3.216. INSANITY AT TIME OF OFFENSE OR PROBATION OR COMMUNITY CONTROL VIOLATION: NOTICE AND APPOINTMENT OF EXPERTS 104

    RULE 3.217. JUDGMENT OF NOT GUILTY BY REASON OF INSANITY: DISPOSITION OF DEFENDANT 107

    RULE 3.218. COMMITMENT OF A DEFENDANT FOUND NOT GUILTY BY REASON OF INSANITY 108

    RULE 3.219. CONDITIONAL RELEASE 109

VI. DISCOVERY 110

    RULE 3.220. DISCOVERY 110

VII. SUBSTITUTION OF JUDGE 127

    RULE 3.231. SUBSTITUTION OF JUDGE 127

VIII. CHANGE OF VENUE 127

    RULE 3.240. CHANGE OF VENUE 127

IX. THE TRIAL 130

    RULE 3.250. ACCUSED AS WITNESS 130

    RULE 3.251. RIGHT TO TRIAL BY JURY 130

    RULE 3.260. WAIVER OF JURY TRIAL 131

    RULE 3.270. NUMBER OF JURORS 131

    RULE 3.280. ALTERNATE JURORS 131

    RULE 3.281. LIST OF PROSPECTIVE JURORS 132

    RULE 3.290. CHALLENGE TO PANEL 132

    RULE 3.300. VOIR DIRE EXAMINATION, OATH, AND EXCUSING OF

    MEMBER 132

    RULE 3.310. TIME FOR CHALLENGE 133

    RULE 3.315. EXERCISE OF CHALLENGES 134

    RULE 3.320. MANNER OF CHALLENGE 134

    RULE 3.330. DETERMINATION OF CHALLENGE FOR CAUSE 134

    RULE 3.340. EFFECT OF SUSTAINING CHALLENGE 134

    RULE 3.350. PEREMPTORY CHALLENGES 135

    RULE 3.360. OATH OF TRIAL JURORS 136

    RULE 3.361. WITNESS ATTENDANCE AND SUBPOENAS 136

X. CONDUCT OF TRIAL; JURY INSTRUCTIONS 137

    RULE 3.370. REGULATION AND SEPARATION OF JURORS 137

    RULE 3.371. JUROR QUESTIONS OF WITNESSES 138

    RULE 3.372. JUROR NOTEBOOKS 138

    RULE 3.380. MOTION FOR JUDGMENT OF ACQUITTAL 138

    RULE 3.381. FINAL ARGUMENTS.. 139

    RULE 3.390. JURY INSTRUCTIONS 139

    RULE 3.391. SELECTION OF FOREPERSON OF JURY 140

    RULE 3.400. MATERIALS TO THE JURY ROOM 140

    RULE 3.410. JURY REQUEST TO REVIEW EVIDENCE OR FOR ADDITIONAL
    INSTRUCTIONS 141

    RULE 3.420. RECALL OF JURY FOR ADDITIONAL INSTRUCTIONS 141

    RULE 3.430. JURY NOT RECALLABLE TO HEAR ADDITIONAL EVIDENCE 141

XI. THE VERDICT 142

    RULE 3.440. RENDITION OF VERDICT; RECEPTION AND RECORDING 142

    RULE 3.450. POLLING THE JURY 142

    RULE 3.451. JUDICIAL COMMENT ON VERDICT 142

    RULE 3.470. PROCEEDINGS ON SEALED VERDICT 142

RULE 3.490. DETERMINATION OF DEGREE OF OFFENSE 143

RULE 3.500. VERDICT OF GUILTY WHERE MORE THAN ONE COUNT 143

RULE 3.505. INCONSISTENT VERDICTS 143

RULE 3.510. DETERMINATION OF ATTEMPTS AND LESSER INCLUDED OFFENSES 144

RULE 3.520. VERDICT IN CASE OF JOINT DEFENDANTS 144

RULE 3.530. RECONSIDERATION OF AMBIGUOUS OR DEFECTIVE VERDICT 144

RULE 3.540. WHEN VERDICT MAY BE RENDERED 145

RULE 3.550. DISPOSITION OF DEFENDANT 145

RULE 3.560. DISCHARGE OF JURORS 145

RULE 3.570. IRREGULARITY IN RENDITION, RECEPTION, AND RECORDING OF VERDICT 146

RULE 3.575. MOTION TO INTERVIEW JUROR 146

XII. POST-TRIAL MOTIONS 146

RULE 3.580. COURT MAY GRANT NEW TRIAL 146

RULE 3.590. TIME FOR AND METHOD OF MAKING MOTIONS; PROCEDURE; CUSTODY PENDING HEARING 147

RULE 3.600. GROUNDS FOR NEW TRIAL 148

RULE 3.610. MOTION FOR ARREST OF JUDGMENT; GROUNDS 149

RULE 3.620. WHEN EVIDENCE SUSTAINS ONLY CONVICTION OF LESSER OFFENSE 150

RULE 3.630. SENTENCE BEFORE OR AFTER MOTION FILED 150

RULE 3.640. EFFECT OF GRANTING NEW TRIAL 150

XIII. JUDGMENT 151

RULE 3.650. JUDGMENT DEFINED 151

RULE 3.670. RENDITION OF JUDGMENT 151

RULE 3.680. JUDGMENT ON INFORMAL VERDICT 152

RULE 3.690. JUDGMENT OF NOT GUILTY; DEFENDANT DISCHARGED AND SURETIES EXONERATED 152

RULE 3.691. POST-TRIAL RELEASE 152

RULE 3.692. PETITION TO SEAL OR EXPUNGE 153

XIV. SENTENCE 154

RULE 3.700. SENTENCE DEFINED; PRONOUNCEMENT AND ENTRY; SENTENCING JUDGE 154

RULE 3.701. SENTENCING GUIDELINES 155

RULE 3.702. SENTENCING GUIDELINES (1994) 161

RULE 3.703. SENTENCING GUIDELINES (1994 as amended) 166

RULE 3.704. THE CRIMINAL PUNISHMENT CODE 173

RULE 3.710. PRESENTENCE REPORT 180

RULE 3.711. PRESENTENCE REPORT: WHEN PREPARED 181

RULE 3.712. PRESENTENCE REPORT: DISCLOSURE 181

RULE 3.713. PRESENTENCE INVESTIGATION DISCLOSURE: PARTIES 182

RULE 3.720. SENTENCING HEARING 182

RULE 3.721. RECORD OF THE PROCEEDINGS 184

RULE 3.730. ISSUANCE OF CAPIAS WHEN NECESSARY TO BRING DEFENDANT
BEFORE COURT 184

RULE 3.750. PROCEDURE WHEN PARDON IS ALLEGED AS CAUSE FOR NOT
PRONOUNCING SENTENCE 184

RULE 3.760. PROCEDURE WHEN NONIDENTITY IS ALLEGED AS CAUSE FOR
NOT PRONOUNCING SENTENCE 184

RULE 3.770. PROCEDURE WHEN PREGNANCY IS ALLEGED AS CAUSE FOR NOT
PRONOUNCING DEATH SENTENCE 185

RULE 3.780. SENTENCING HEARING FOR CAPITAL CASES 185

RULE 3.790. PROBATION AND COMMUNITY CONTROL 186

RULE 3.800. CORRECTION, REDUCTION, AND MODIFICATION OF

SENTENCES 189

RULE 3.801. CORRECTION OF JAIL CREDIT... 189

XV. EXECUTION OF SENTENCE 193

RULE 3.810. COMMITMENT OF DEFENDANT; DUTY OF SHERIFF 193

RULE 3.811. INSANITY AT TIME OF EXECUTION: CAPITAL CASES 193

RULE 3.812. HEARING ON INSANITY AT TIME OF EXECUTION: CAPITAL

CASES 195

RULE 3.820. HABEAS CORPUS 195

XVI. CRIMINAL CONTEMPT 196

RULE 3.830. DIRECT CRIMINAL CONTEMPT 196

RULE 3.840. INDIRECT CRIMINAL CONTEMPT 196

XVII. POSTCONVICTION RELIEF 201

RULE 3.850. MOTION TO VACATE, SET ASIDE, OR CORRECT SENTENCE 201

RULE 3.851. COLLATERAL RELIEF AFTER DEATH SENTENCE HAS BEEN
IMPOSED AND AFFIRMED ON DIRECT APPEAL 209

RULE 3.852. CAPITAL POSTCONVICTION PUBLIC RECORDS PRODUCTION ... 221

RULE 3.853. MOTION FOR POSTCONVICTION DNA TESTING 228

XVIII. FORMS 230

RULE 3.992. CRIMINAL PUNISHMENT CODE SCORESHEET 230

FLORIDA EVIDENCE
CODE

TITLE VII
EVIDENCE

CHAPTER 90
EVIDENCE CODE

90.101	Short title.	Pg 243
90.102	Construction.	Pg 243
90.103	Scope; applicability.	Pg 243
90.104	Rulings on evidence.	Pg 243
90.105	Preliminary questions.	Pg 244
90.106	Summing up and comment by judge.	Pg 244
90.107	Limited admissibility.	Pg 244
90.108	Introduction of related writings or recorded statements.	Pg 244
90.201	Matters which must be judicially noticed.	Pg 245
90.202	Matters which may be judicially noticed.	Pg 245
90.203	Compulsory judicial notice upon request.	Pg 246
90.204	Determination of propriety of judicial notice and nature of matter noticed.	Pg 246
90.205	Denial of a request for judicial notice.	Pg 246
90.206	Instructing jury on judicial notice.	Pg 247
90.207	Judicial notice by trial court in subsequent proceedings.	Pg 247
90.301	Presumption defined; inferences.	Pg 247
90.302	Classification of rebuttable presumptions.	Pg 247
90.303	Presumption affecting the burden of producing evidence defined.	Pg 247
90.304	Presumption affecting the burden of proof defined.	Pg 248
90.401	Definition of relevant evidence.	Pg 248
90.402	Admissibility of relevant evidence.	Pg 248
90.4025	Admissibility of paternity determination in certain criminal prosecutions.	Pg 248
90.4026	Statements expressing sympathy; admissibility; definitions.	Pg 248
90.403	Exclusion on grounds of prejudice or confusion.	Pg 248
90.404	Character evidence; when admissible.	Pg 249
90.405	Methods of proving character.	Pg 250
90.406	Routine practice.	Pg 250
90.407	Subsequent remedial measures.	Pg 250
90.408	Compromise and offers to compromise.	Pg 250

90.409	Payment of medical and similar expenses.	Pg 251
90.410	Offer to plead guilty; nolo contendere; withdrawn pleas of guilty.	Pg 251
90.501	Privileges recognized only as provided.	Pg 251
90.5015	Journalist's privilege.	Pg 251
90.502	Lawyer-client privilege.	Pg 252
90.5021	Fiduciary lawyer-client privilege.	Pg 254
90.503	Psychotherapist-patient privilege.	Pg 254
90.5035	Sexual assault counselor-victim privilege.	Pg 256
90.5036	Domestic violence advocate-victim privilege.	Pg 257
90.504	Husband-wife privilege.	Pg 258
90.505	Privilege with respect to communications to clergy.	Pg 258
90.5055	Accountant-client privilege.	Pg 259
90.506	Privilege with respect to trade secrets.	Pg 260
90.507	Waiver of privilege by voluntary disclosure.	Pg 260
90.508	Privileged matter disclosed under compulsion or without opportunity to claim privilege.	Pg 260
90.509	Application of privileged communication.	Pg 260
90.510	Privileged communication necessary to adverse party.	Pg 261
90.601	General rule of competency.	Pg 261
90.603	Disqualification of witness.	Pg 261
90.604	Lack of personal knowledge.	Pg 261
90.605	Oath or affirmation of witness.	Pg 261
90.606	Interpreters and translators.	Pg 262
90.6063	Interpreter services for deaf persons.	Pg 262
90.607	Competency of certain persons as witnesses.	Pg 263
90.608	Who may impeach.	Pg 264
90.609	Character of witness as impeachment.	Pg 264
90.610	Conviction of certain crimes as impeachment.	Pg 264
90.611	Religious beliefs or opinions.	Pg 265
90.612	Mode and order of interrogation and presentation.	Pg 265
90.613	Refreshing the memory of a witness.	Pg 265
90.614	Prior statements of witnesses.	Pg 266
90.615	Calling witnesses by the court.	Pg 266
90.616	Exclusion of witnesses.	Pg 266
90.701	Opinion testimony of lay witnesses.	Pg 267

90.702	Testimony by experts.	Pg 267
90.703	Opinion on ultimate issue.	Pg 267
90.704	Basis of opinion testimony by experts.	Pg 267
90.705	Disclosure of facts or data underlying expert opinion.	Pg 268
90.706	Authoritativeness of literature for use in cross-examination.	Pg 268
90.801	Hearsay; definitions; exceptions.	Pg 268
90.802	Hearsay rule.	Pg 269
90.803	Hearsay exceptions; availability of declarant immaterial.	Pg 269
90.804	Hearsay exceptions; declarant unavailable.	Pg 274
90.805	Hearsay within hearsay.	Pg 276
90.806	Attacking and supporting credibility of declarant.	Pg 276
90.901	Requirement of authentication or identification.	Pg 276
90.902	Self-authentication.	Pg 276
90.903	Testimony of subscribing witness unnecessary.	Pg 278
90.91	Photographs of property wrongfully taken; use in prosecution, procedure; return of property to owner.	Pg 278
90.951	Definitions.	Pg 278
90.952	Requirements of originals.	Pg 279
90.953	Admissibility of duplicates.	Pg 279
90.954	Admissibility of other evidence of contents.	Pg 279
90.955	Public records.	Pg 280
90.956	Summaries.	Pg 280
90.957	Testimony or written admissions of a party.	Pg 280
90.958	Functions of court and jury.	Pg 280

CHAPTER 92
WITNESSES, RECORDS, AND DOCUMENTS

92.05	Final judgments and decrees of courts of record.	Pg 282
92.06	Judgments and decrees of United States District Courts.	Pg 282
92.07	Judgments and decrees of this state.	Pg 282
92.08	Deeds and powers of attorney of record for 20 years or more.	Pg 282
92.09	Effects of reversal, etc., of judgment or successful attack on deed.	Pg 283
92.13	Certified copies of records of certified copies.	Pg 283
92.14	United States deeds and patents and copies thereof.	Pg 283
92.141	Law enforcement employees; travel expenses; compensation as witness.	Pg 283

92.142	Witnesses; pay.	Pg 284
92.143	Compensation to traffic court witnesses.	Pg 284
92.15	Receipts in cases involving title from United States.	Pg 284
92.151	Witness compensation; payment; overcharges.	Pg 285
92.153	Production of documents by witnesses; reimbursement of costs.	Pg 285
92.16	Certificates of Board of Trustees of the Internal Improvement Trust Fund respecting the ownership, conveyance of, and other facts in connection with public lands.	Pg 286
92.17	Effect of seal of Board of Trustees of the Internal Improvement Trust Fund.	Pg 286
92.18	Certificate of state officer.	Pg 287
92.19	Portions of records.	Pg 287
92.20	Certificates issued under authority of Congress.	Pg 287
92.21	Certificate as to sanitary condition of buildings.	Pg 287
92.23	Rule of evidence in suits on fire policies for loss or damage to building.	Pg 287
92.231	Expert witnesses; fee.	Pg 287
92.233	Compensation of witness summoned in two or more criminal cases.	Pg 288
92.24	Certain tax deeds prima facie evidence of title.	Pg 288
92.25	Records destroyed by fire; use of abstracts.	Pg 288
92.251	Uniform Foreign Depositions Law.	Pg 289
92.26	Records destroyed by fire; use of sworn copies.	Pg 289
92.27	Records destroyed by fire; effect of abstracts in evidence.	Pg 289
92.28	Records destroyed by fire; land title suits; what may be received in evidence.	Pg 290
92.29	Photographic or electronic copies.	Pg 290
92.295	Copies of voter registration records.	Pg 290
92.30	Presumption of death; official findings.	Pg 290
92.31	Missing persons and persons imprisoned or interned in foreign countries; official reports.	Pg 291
92.32	Official findings and reports; presumption of authority to issue or execute.	Pg 291
92.33	Written statement concerning injury to person or property; furnishing copies; admission as evidence.	Pg 291
92.351	Prohibition against prisoners submitting nondocumentary physical evidence without authorization of court; prisoner mailings to courts.	Pg 291
92.38	Comparison of disputed writings.	Pg 292

92.39	Evidence of individual's claim against the state in suits between them.	Pg 292
92.40	Reports of buildings, housing, or health code violations; admissibility.	Pg 292
92.50	Oaths, affidavits, and acknowledgments; who may take or administer; requirements.	Pg 292
92.51	Oaths, affidavits, and acknowledgments; taken or administered by commissioned officer of United States Armed Forces.	Pg 293
92.52	Affirmation equivalent to oath.	Pg 294
92.525	Verification of documents; perjury by false written declaration, penalty.	Pg 294
92.53	Videotaping the testimony of a victim or witness under age 16 or who has an intellectual disability.	Pg 295
92.54	Use of closed circuit television in proceedings involving a victim or witness under the age of 16 or who has an intellectual disability.	Pg 296
92.55	Judicial or other proceedings involving victim or witness under the age of 16 or person who has an intellectual disability; special protections; use of registered service or therapy animals.	Pg 297
92.56	Judicial proceedings and court records involving sexual offenses.	Pg 298
92.561	Prohibition on reproduction of child pornography.	Pg 299
92.565	Admissibility of confession in sexual abuse cases.	Pg 299
92.57	Termination of employment of witness prohibited.	Pg 300
92.60	Foreign records of regularly conducted business activity.	Pg 300
92.605	Production of certain records by Florida businesses and out-of-state corporations.	Pg 301

Florida Rules of Criminal Procedure 2014

CITATIONS TO OPINIONS ADOPTING OR AMENDING RULES

ORIGINAL ADOPTION, effective 1-1-68: 196 So.2d 124

OTHER OPINIONS:

Effective 2-28-68:	207 So.2d 430.	Amended 1.840(a)(4).
Effective 9-30-68:	211 So.2d 203.	Amended 1.010, 1.120, 1.140(a)(2), 1.140(c)(2), 1.140(l), (o), 1.150, 1.200, 1.220(f), 1.790(b), 1.840(a)(6).
Effective 12-4-70:	241 So.2d 691.	Deleted 1.860.
Effective 2-24-71:	245 So.2d 33.	Added 1.191.
Effective 8-19-71:	251 So.2d 537.	Amended 1.191(i)(2).
Effective 12-13-71:	253 So.2d 421.	Renumbered rules 1.XXX to 3.XXX; added 3.025.
Effective 2-1-73:	272 So.2d 65.	Four-year-cycle revision.
Effective 2-1-73:	272 So.2d 513.	Amended 3.140, 3.170.
Effective 5-11-73:	281 So.2d 204.	Added 3.125.
Effective 1-16-74:	287 So.2d 678.	Amended 3.460.
Effective 3-1-74:	289 So.2d 3.	Amended 3.131(b).
Effective 7-18-74:	297 So.2d 301.	Amended 3.125(j).
Effective 3-31-75:	309 So.2d 544.	Amended 3.040, 3.131, 3.140(g).
Effective 7-11-75:	315 So.2d 172.	Added 3.986.
Effective 7-1-77:	343 So.2d 1247.	Four-year-cycle revision. Amended 3.125, 3.130, 3.131, 3.140, 3.151, 3.171, 3.190, 3.191, 3.210, 3.220, 3.280, 3.350, 3.390, 3.505, 3.691, 3.692, 3.800, 3.850; added 3.172, 3.780; deleted 3.722.
Effective 7-1-77:	347 So.2d 434.	Amended 3.125(m).
Effective 1-1-78:	353 So.2d 552.	Amended 3.850; added 3.987.
Effective 5-1-79:	370 So.2d 764.	Deleted 3.110.
Effective 7-1-79:	372 So.2d 449.	Amended 3.080; deleted 3.025, 3.090, 3.100.
Effective 10-9-79:	375 So.2d 855.	Former rules 3.210(a) and 3.210(e)(1)B(8) adopted as Transition Rules 23(a) and (b).
Effective 1-1-80:	376 So.2d 844.	Amended 3.111(e).
Effective 7-1-80:	389 So.2d 610.	Amended 3.210; added 3.211B3.219.
Effective 1-1-81:	389 So.2d 610.	Four-year-cycle revision. Amended 3.111, 3.191, 3.220, 3.300, 3.380, 3.590, 3.720, 3.800, 3.986; added 3.315; deleted 3.460.
Effective 10-1-81:	403 So.2d 979.	Added 3.490, 3.510.
Effective 11-1-81:	408 So.2d 207.	Amended 3.986.
Effective 10-1-83:	436 So.2d 60.	Amended 3.130, 3.131; added 3.132; renumbered 3.122 to 3.133.
Effective 10-1-83:	439 So.2d 848.	Added 3.701, 3.988.
Effective 7-1-84:	451 So.2d 824.	Amended 3.701, 3.988.
Effective 1-1-85:	460 So.2d 907.	Amended 3.850.
Effective 1-1-85:	462 So.2d 386.	Four-year-cycle revision. Amended 3.130, 3.160, 3.191, 3.390, 3.692, 3.989.
Effective 7-1-85:	468 So.2d 220.	Amended 3.701, 3.988.
Effective 12-19-85:	481 So.2d 480.	Amended 3.850.
Effective 10-1-86:	482 So.2d 311.	Amended 3.701, 3.988.
Effective 4-24-86:	487 So.2d 1045.	Amended 3.800(a).

Effective 7-17-86:	491 So.2d 1128.	Amended 3.988(e).
Effective 11-13-86:	497 So.2d 643.	Added 3.811.
Effective 11-26-86:	498 So.2d 875.	Amended 3.220(d).
Effective 4-1-87:	503 So.2d 320.	Added 3.851.
Effective 7-1-87:	509 So.2d 1088.	Amended 3.701, 3.988.
Effective 12-31-87:	518 So.2d 256.	Amended 3.010, 3.811; added 3.812.
Effective 7-1-88:	522 So.2d 374.	Amended 3.701, 3.988.
Effective 1-1-89:	536 So.2d 992.	Four-year-cycle revision. Amended 3.040, 3.133, 3.172, 3.210, 3.211, 3.212, 3.213, 3.216, 3.217, 3.218, 3.219, 3.390, 3.710, 3.790; added 3.214; renumbered 3.214 to 3.215; deleted 3.740.
Effective 7-1-89:	542 So.2d 1330.	Amended 3.191.
Effective 7-1-89:	544 So.2d 198.	Amended 3.710, 3.988.
Effective 7-1-89:	550 So.2d 1097.	Amended 3.220.
Effective 9-6-90, and 1-1-91:	566 So.2d 770.	Amended 3.701, 3.988.
Effective 4-1-91:	573 So.2d 826.	Amended 3.133(b)(6) and renumbered as 3.134.
Effective 3-7-91:	576 So.2d 1307.	Amended 3.701, 3.988.
Effective 11-7-91:	589 So.2d 271.	Amended 3.701, 3.988.
Effective 12-15-91:	591 So.2d 173.	Amended 3.130(a), 3.131(j).
Effective 3-26-92:	596 So.2d 1036.	Amended 3.370.
Effective 5-28-92:	603 So.2d 1144.	Amended 3.140, 3.986.
Effective 1-1-93:	606 So.2d 227.	Four-year-cycle revisions. Numerous changes.
Effective 1-1-93:	609 So.2d 465.	Deleted 3.230.
Effective 2-11-93:	613 So.2d 1307.	Amended 3.701(c), 3.988.
Effective 7-1-93:	615 So.2d 692.	Amended 3.191(b).
Effective 10-21-93:	630 So.2d 172.	Adopted emergency rule 3.201.
Effective 11-30-93:	628 So.2d 1084.	Amended 3.701(c), 3.988(b)B(c).
Effective 12-2-93:	628 So.2d 1102.	Amended 3.987.
Effective 1-1-94:	626 So.2d 198.	Amended 3.850, 3.851.
Effective 1-1-94:	628 So.2d 1084.	Added 3.702, 3.990, amended 3.701.
Effective 1-1-94:	630 So.2d 552.	Amended 3.133, 3.692, 3.986, 3.987, 3.989.
Effective 3-10-94:	633 So.2d 1056.	Amended 3.170, 3.700.
Effective 6-16-94:	639 So.2d 15.	Amended 3.692, 3.989.
Effective 6-1-95:	657 So.2d 1134.	Amended 3.400.
Effective 10-1-95:	660 So.2d 1374.	Adopted 3.703, 3.991.
Effective 1-1-96:	674 So.2d 83.	Adopted 3.202.
Effective 5-2-96:	654 So.2d 915.	Amended 3.202.
Effective 7-1-96:	675 So.2d 1374.	Amended 3.800.
Effective 10-1-96:	681 So.2d 666.	Amended 3.220.
Effective 10-1-96:	685 So.2d 1213	Amended 3.703.
Effective 10-31-96:	683 So.2d 475.	Adopted 3.852.
Effective 11-15-96:	684 So.2d 173.	Amended 3.986.
Effective 1-1-97:	685 So.2d 1213.	Amended 3.991.
Effective 1-1-97:	685 So.2d 1253.	Four-year-cycle revision. Adopted 3.090, 3.361; amended 3.170, 3.172, 3.180, 3.190, 3.212, 3.216, 3.780, 3.800, 3.850, 3.851, 3.986.
Effective 7-7-97:	696 So.2d 1171.	Amended 3.703, 3.991.

Effective 4-2-98:	710 So.2d 961.	Amended 3.220(h)(1).
Effective 4-2-98:	711 So.2d 27.	Amended 3.702(d)(9)B(10), 3991.
Effective 7-16-98:	719 So.2d 873.	Amended 3.111(d)(2)B(3).
Effective 10-1-98:	721 So.2d 265.	Adopted 3.704, 3.992.
Effective 10-1-98:	723 So.2d 163.	Adopted 3.993; amended 3.852.
Effective 12-3-98:	724 So.2d 1162.	Amended 3.220(h)(1), (3), 3.361.
Effective 12-10-98:	745 So.2d 319.	Amended 3.380(b).
Effective 2-18-99:	745 So.2d 319.	Amended 3.220(a).
Effective 5-27-99:	750 So.2d 592.	Amended 3.850.
Effective 5-27-99:	747 So.2d 931.	Amended 3.850(b).
Effective 7-1-99:	754 So.2d 640.	Amended 3.852, 3.993.
Effective 11-12-99:	760 So.2d 67.	Amended 3.670, 3.700(b).
Effective 11-12-99:	761 So.2d 1015.	Amended 3.111(e), 3.800.
Effective 12-9-99:	763 So.2d 997.	Amended 3.704(d).
Effective 1-1-00:	760 So.2d 67.	Amended 3.670.
Effective 1-14-00:	763 So.2d 273.	Readopted 3.850, 3.851, 3.852.
Effective 2-10-00:	763 So.2d 274	Amended 3.220(a).
Effective 7-1-00:	759 So.2d 610.	Adopted 3.112.
Effective 10-19-00:	779 So.2d 1290.	Amended 3.850(a).
Effective 11-22-00:	789 So.2d 262.	Amended 3.850(g).
Effective 1-1-01:	794 So.2d 457.	Four-year-cycle revision: Adopted 3.025; amended 3.030, 3.111, 3.125, 3.190, 3.191, 3.213, 3.217, 3.218, 3.219, 3.692, 3.800, 3.851, 3.986, 3.987, 3.989, 3.993.
Effective 9-26-01:	810 So.2d 826.	Amended 3.704 and 3.992(a).
Effective 10-1-01:	797 So.2d 1213.	Amended 3.851.
Effective 10-1-01:	802 So.2d 298.	Amended 3.851, 3.852.
Effective 10-18-01:	807 So.2d 633.	Adopted 3.853.
Effective 7-1-02:	820 So.2d 185.	Amended 3.112.
Effective 9-19-02:	828 So.2d 999.	Amended 3.851.
Effective 1-1-03:	837 So.2d 924.	Two-year-cycle revisions. Adopted 3.994; amended 3.111, 3.170, 3.190, 3.361.
Effective 2-27-03:	842 So.2d 110.	Committee note to 3.704(d)(14)(B).
Effective 9-30-03:	857 So.2d 190.	Suspended 3.853 deadline until further order of court.
Effective 9-15-04:	884 So.2d 934.	Amended 3.853.
Effective 10-1-04:	875 So.2d 563.	Adopted 3.203.
Effective 10-1-04:	887 So.2d 1090.	Amended 3.111, 3.120, 3.121, 3.125, 3.130, 3.131, 3.133, 3.220, 3.852.
Effective 1-1-05:	886 So.2d 197.	Amended 3.150, 3.191, 3.710, 3.800, 3.986; adopted 3.575, 3.995.
Effective 4-7-05:	900 So.2d 528.	Amended 3.111, 3.220, 3.670; adopted 3.984.
Effective 7-1-05:	910 So.2d 194.	Amended 3.984.
Effective 9-1-05:	911 So.2d 763.	Amended 3.172(c).
Effective 9-29-05:	935 So.2d 1218.	Amended 3.853(d).
Effective 9-21-06:	938 So.2d 977.	Amended 3.853.
Effective 9-21-06:	938 So.2d 978.	Amended 3.170, 3.172.
Effective 1-1-07	942 So.2d 407.	Amended 3.170, 3.180, 3.213, 3.640.
Effective 1-1-07:	945 So.2d 1124.	Amended 3.590, 3.851.
Effective 2-8-07:	949 So.2d 196.	Amended 3.800.
Effective 3-29-07:	953 So.2d 513.	Amended 3.170, 3.172.

3

Effective 4-1-07:	948 So.2d 731.	Amended 3.131, 3.132, 3.853.
Effective 4-19-07:	957 So.2d 1160.	Amended 3.704, 3.992.
Effective 5-3-07:	957 So.2d 1164.	Amended 3.250; adopted 3.381.
Effective 6-21-07:	959 So.2d 250.	Amended 3.131, 3.170.
Effective 7-5-07:	959 So.2d 1187.	Amended 3.790.
Effective 10-4-07:	967 So.2d 178.	Amended 3.390, 3.400; adopted 3.371, 3.372, 3.9855.
Effective 1-10-08:	972 So.2d 862.	Amended 3.992.
Effective 9-25-08:	992 So.2d 239.	Amended 3.992(a).
Effective 10-8-08:	993 So.2d 501.	Amended 3.112.
Effective 11-20-08:	998 So.2d 1128.	Amended 3.704, 3.986.
Effective 12-30-08:	1 So.3d 163.	Amended 3.851.
Effective 2-26-09:	3 So.3d 1175.	Amended 3.112.
Effective 3-19-09:	5 So.3d 662.	Amended 3.984.
Effective 5-28-09:	11 So.3d 341.	Amended 3.130.
Effective 7-16-09:	19 So.3d 274.	Amended 3.992.
Effective 8-28-09:	17 So.2d 272.	Amended 3.111.
Effective 9-10-09:	22 So.3d 1.	Amended 3.704 and 3.986.
Effective 10-1-09:	20 So.3d 376.	Amended 3.172, 3.985.
Effective 1-1-10:	19 So.3d 306.	Amended 3.132.
Effective 1-1-10:	26 So.3d 534.	Three-year-cycle revision. Adopted rule 3.192. Amended rules 3.131, 3.172, 3.190, 3.191, 3.203, 3.210, 3,211, 3.216, 3.220, 3.231, 3.240, 3.800, 3.851, 3.852, 3.853, form 3.986.
Effective 9-2-10:	43 So.3d 688.	Amended 3.853.
Effective 9-23-10:	48 So.3d 17.	Amended 3.111, 3.704, 3.720, form 3.986.
Effective 6-9-11:	66 So.3d 851.	Amended 3.191.
Effective 7-1-11:	72 So.3d 735.	Amended 3.850 and 3.851.
Effective 9-28-11:	73 So.3d 202.	Amended 3.992(a).
Effective 10-1-11:	80 So.3d 317.	Amended 3.140, 3.211, 3.212, 3.218 and 3.219.
Effective 12-8-11:	76 So.3d 913.	Amended 3.800(c).
Effective 3-8-11:	84 So.3d 254.	Amended 3.130.
Effective 9-1-12:	102 So.3d 505.	Amended 3.030, 3.070, 3.852.
Effective 10-1-12:	95 So.3d 96.	Amended 3.040.
Effective 10-11-12:	101 So.3d 1263.	Amended 3.992.
Effective 10-1-13:	102 So.3d 451.	Amended 3.030, 3.070, 3.080, 3.090, 3.240, 3.851.
Effective 12-20-12:	105 So. 3d 1275.	Amended 3.220(b)
Effective 1-1-13:	104 So. 3d 304.	Amended 3.111, 3.125, 3.140, 3.191, 3.220, 3.410, 3.590, 3.691, 3.800, 3.851.
Effective 5-23-13:	115 So.3d 207.	Amended 3.220(b).
Effective 7-1-13:	38 FLW S884.	Amended 3.800, 3.850, 3.851, and Adopted 3.801.
Effective 12-12-13:	38 FLW S890.	Amended 3.121, 3.203, 3.211, 3.212, 3.213, 3.851, and 3.852.

NOTE TO USERS: Rules in this pamphlet are current through 38 FLW S890. Subsequent amendments, if any, can be found at www.floridasupremecourt.org/decisions/rules.shtml. The Florida Bar also updates the rules on its website at www.FloridaBar.org (on the home page click —Rules Updatesl).

I. SCOPE, PURPOSE, AND CONSTRUCTION

RULE 3.010. SCOPE

These rules shall govern the procedure in all criminal proceedings in state courts including proceedings involving direct and indirect criminal contempt, proceedings under rule 3.850, and vehicular and pedestrian traffic offenses insofar as these rules are made applicable by the Florida Rules of Practice and Procedure for Traffic Courts. These rules shall not apply to direct or indirect criminal contempt of a court acting in any appellate capacity. These rules shall not apply to rules 3.811 and 3.812. These rules shall be known as the Florida Rules of Criminal Procedure and may be cited as Fla. R. Crim. P.

Committee Notes

1968 Adoption. These rules are not intended to apply to municipal courts, but are intended to apply to all state courts where "crimes" are charged.

1972 Amendment. Amended to provide for applicability of rules to vehicular traffic offenses, when made so by the traffic court rules.

1992 Amendment. The rule is amended to refer to "Florida Rules of Criminal Procedure" and "Fla. R. Crim. P." rather than to "Rules of Criminal Procedure" and "R. Crim. P." Although the Florida Bar Rules of Criminal Procedure already contains this language, the West publications, Florida Rules of Court (1991) and Florida Criminal Law and Rules (1991), do not. The published version of rule 3.010, In re Florida Rules of Criminal Procedure, 272 So.2d 65 (Fla. 1973), and the single published amendment to the rule, In re Amendments to the Florida Rules of Criminal Procedure, 518 So.2d 256 (Fla. 1987), also do not contain these additions. The Florida Bar publication, Florida Criminal Rules and Practice, in a commentary to rule 3.010, indicates that the Florida Supreme Court changed the citation form in an order effective January 1, 1977. The commentary indicates that the order stated in pertinent part:

In order to provide the clarity of citations in briefs filed in this court and other legal writings, the following amendments to the procedural rules adopted by this court pursuant to Article V, Section 2(a), of the Florida Constitution are hereby adopted.

* * *

The last sentence of Rule 3.010 of the Florida Rules of Criminal Procedure is amended as follows:
"These Rules shall be known as the Florida Rules of Criminal Procedure and may be cited as Fla. R. Crim. P."

However, these changes were apparently inadvertently omitted when the 1987 amendments were published. The proposed 1992 amendments again incorporate into the rule the language set out in the court's 1977 order.

The amendments would enable clearer identification of the rules and achieve consistency of style with other sets of court rules, in particular, rule 9.800(i), Fla. R. App. P., which provides that the proper citation to the Florida Rules of Criminal Procedure is Fla. R. Crim. P.

RULE 3.020. PURPOSE AND CONSTRUCTION

These rules are intended to provide for the just determination of every criminal proceeding. They shall be construed to secure simplicity in procedure and fairness in administration.

Committee Notes

1968 Adoption. Substantially the same as Federal Rule 2.

1972 Amendment. Same as prior rule.

RULE 3.025. STATE AND PROSECUTING ATTORNEY DEFINED

Whenever the terms "state," "state attorney," "prosecutor," "prosecution," "prosecuting officer," or "prosecuting attorney" are used in these rules, they shall be construed to mean the prosecuting authority representing the state of Florida.

Committee Notes

2000 Adoption. This provision is new. Its purpose is to include the Office of Statewide Prosecution as a prosecuting authority under these rules. No substantive changes are intended by the adoption of this rule.

II. GENERAL PROVISIONS

[Editor's Note: Email service, which becomes mandatory for criminal cases on October 1, 2013, is governed by this rule.]

RULE 3.030. SERVICE OF PLEADINGS AND PAPERS

Text of rule effective prior to amendment by Florida Supreme Court Opinion No. SC11-399. See also text of rule as amended by Florida Supreme Court Opinion SC11-399.

Every pleading subsequent to the initial indictment or information on which a defendant is to be tried unless the court otherwise orders, and every order not entered in open court, every written motion unless it is one about which a hearing ex parte is authorized, and every written notice, demand, and similar paper shall be served on each party in conformity with Florida Rule of Judicial Administration 2.516; however, nothing herein shall be construed to require that a plea of not guilty shall be in writing.

Committee Notes

1968 Adoption. Taken from the Florida Rules of Civil Procedure.

1972 Amendment. Same as prior rule; (a) amended by deleting reference to trial on affidavit.

2000 Amendment. Fraudulent manipulation of electronically transmitted service should be considered contemptuous and dealt with by appropriate sanctions by the court.

6

RULE 3.030. SERVICE AND FILING OF PLEADINGS, PAPERS, AND DOCUMENTS

Text of rule as amended by Florida Supreme Court Opinion SC11-399. See also text of rule prior to amendment by Florida Supreme Court Opinion SC11-399.

(a) Service. Every pleading subsequent to the initial indictment or information on which a defendant is to be tried unless the court otherwise orders, and every order not entered in open court, every written motion unless it is one about which a hearing ex parte is authorized, and every written notice, demand, and similar document shall be served on each party in conformity with Florida Rule of Judicial Administration 2.516; however, nothing herein shall be construed to require that a plea of not guilty shall be in writing.

(b) Filing. All documents that are "court records" as defined in the Florida Rules of Judicial Administration must be filed with the clerk in accordance with Florida Rules of Judicial Administration 2.520 and 2.525.

(c) Deposit with the Clerk. Any paper document that is a judgment and sentence or required by statute or rule to be sworn to or notarized shall be filed and deposited with the clerk immediately thereafter. The clerk shall maintain deposited original paper documents in accordance with Florida Rule of Judicial Administration 2.430, unless otherwise ordered by the court.

Committee Notes

1968 Adoption. Taken from the Florida Rules of Civil Procedure.

1972 Amendment. Same as prior rule; (a) amended by deleting reference to trial on affidavit.

2000 Amendment. Fraudulent manipulation of electronically transmitted service should be considered   contemptuous and dealt with by appropriate sanctions by the court.

Editor's Note

On October 18, 2012, the Supreme Court of Florida issued a revised opinion in case number SC11- 399, which was originally issued on June 21, 2012. See *In re Amendments to the Florida Rules of Judicial Administration*, 102 So. 3d 451(Fla. 2012). The opinion provides in relevant part:

"First, the new electronic filing requirements the Courts adopts will become effective in the civil, probate, small claims, and family law divisions of the trial courts, as well as for appeals to the circuit courts in these categories of cases, on April 1, 2013, at 12:01 a.m., except as may be otherwise provided by administrative order. Electronic filing will be mandatory in these divisions pursuant to rule 2.525 on that date. However, until the new rules take effect in these divisions, any clerk who is already accepting documents filed by electronic transmission under the current rules should continue to do so; attorneys in these counties are encouraged to file documents electronically under the current rules.

"Next, the new electronic filing requirements the Court adopts will become effective in the criminal,   traffic, and juvenile divisions of the trial courts, as well as for appeals to the circuit court in these categories of cases, on October 1, 2013, at 12:01 a.m., except as may be otherwise provided by administrative order. Electronic filing will be mandatory in these divisions under rule 2.525 on that date. The new e-filing requirements, as they apply in proceedings brought pursuant to the Florida Mental Health Act (Baker Act), Chapter 394, Part I, Florida Statutes, and the Involuntary Commitment of Sexually Violent Predators Act (Jimmy Ryce), Chapter 394, Part V, Florida Statutes, will also not be mandatory in these cases until October 1, 2013. As stated above, until the new rules take effect in these divisions and proceedings, any clerk who is already accepting electronically filed documents under the current rules should continue to do so; attorneys are again encouraged to utilize existing electronic filing procedures under the current rules.

"However, until the new rules and procedures take effect in the district courts, any clerk who is already accepting documents filed by electronic transmission may continue to do so; attorneys in these districts are encouraged to file documents electronically. Clerks will not be required to electronically transmit the record on appeal until July 1, 2013, at 12:01 a.m. Until July 1, we encourage clerks, whenever possible, to electronically transmit the record under the new rules and requirements.

"(W)e note that, in all types of cases, pursuant to amended rule 2.525(d) self-represented parties and self-represented nonparties, including nonparty governmental or public agencies, and attorneys excused from e- mail service under Florida Rule of Judicial Administration 2.516 will be permitted, but nor required, to file documents electronically.

By order of November 28, 2012, in case number SC11-399, the Court released a revised implementation schedule, which provides, in pertinent part: "The e-filing rules adopted in the October 2012 opinion will be mandatory in this (Supreme) Court on February 27, 2013, at 12:01 a.m.; and effective earlier on a voluntary basis as will be indicated by further administrative order of the chief justice.

"Thereafter, the e-filing rules will be mandatory in the Second District Court of Appeal on July 22, 2013, at 12:01 a.m.; in the Third District Court of Appeal on September 27, 2013, at 12:01 a.m.; in the Fourth District Court of Appeal on October 31, 2013, at 12:01 a.m.; in the Fifth District Court of Appeal on November 27, 2013 at 12:01 a.m.; and in the First District Court of Appeal on December 27, 2013, at 12:01 a.m., unless made mandatory earlier by the chief judge of the applicable district court of appeal. The e-filing rules will be effective earlier on a voluntary trial basis in the district courts of appeal as will be indicated by further administrative order by the chief judge of the applicable district court."

RULE 3.040. COMPUTATION OF TIME

Computation of time shall be governed by Florida Rule of Judicial Administration 2.514(a), except for the periods of time of less than 7 days contained in rules 3.130, 3.132(a) and (c), and 3.133(a).

Committee Notes

1968 Adoption. Taken from the Florida Rules of Civil Procedure.

1972 Amendment. Same as prior rule.

1988 Amendment. The 1983 amendments resulted in the reallocation of the time periods in rule 3.131 to rule 3.133, and also added an important 5 day period in the new rule regarding pretrial detention in rule 3.132.

Court Commentary

1975 Amendment. Underlined portion is the only change. The effect is to remove the 72 hour provision of proposed rule 3.131 from the Saturday, Sunday, and legal holiday exception.

RULE 3.050. ENLARGEMENT OF TIME

When by these rules or by a notice given thereunder or by order of court an act is required or allowed to be done at or within a specified time, the court for good cause shown may, at any time, in its discretion (1) with or without notice, order the period enlarged if a request therefor is made before the expiration of the period originally prescribed or extended by a previous order or (2) upon motion made and notice after the expiration of the specified period, permit the act to be done when the failure to act was the result of excusable neglect; but it may not, except as provided by statute or elsewhere in these rules, extend the time for making a motion for new trial, for taking an appeal, or for making a motion for a judgment of acquittal.

Committee Notes

1968 Adoption. Taken from the Florida Rules of Civil Procedure.

1972 Amendment. Same as prior rule.

RULE 3.060. TIME FOR SERVICE OF MOTIONS AND NOTICE OF HEARING

A copy of any written motion which may not be heard ex parte and a copy of the notice of the hearing thereof, shall be served on the adverse party a reasonable time before the time specified for the hearing.

Committee Notes

1968 Adoption. Taken from rules of civil procedure.

1972 Amendment. Same as prior rule.

[Editor's Note: Email service, which becomes mandatory for criminal cases on October 1, 2013, is governed by this rule.]

RULE 3.070. ADDITIONAL TIME AFTER SERVICE BY MAIL OR E-MAIL

Text of rule effective prior to amendment by Florida Supreme Court Opinion No. SC11-399. See also text of rule as amended by Florida Supreme Court Opinion SC11-399.

Whenever a party has the right or is required to do some act or take some proceedings within a prescribed period after the service of a notice or other paper on the party and the notice or paper is served on the party by mail or e- mail, 3 days shall be added to the prescribed period.

9

Committee Notes

1968 Adoption. This is the same as rule 1.6(e), Florida Rules of Civil Procedure, except for the omission of subdivision (c) of the civil rules, which appears to be inapplicable to criminal cases.

1972 Amendment. Same as prior rule.

RULE 3.070. ADDITIONAL TIME AFTER SERVICE BY MAIL, WHEN PERMITTED, OR ELECTRONIC MAIL

Text of rule as amended by Florida Supreme Court Opinion SC11-399. See also text of rule prior to amendment by Florida Supreme Court Opinion SC11-399.

Whenever a party has the right or is required to do some act or take some proceedings within a prescribed period after the service of a notice or other document on the party and the notice or document is served on the party by mail, when permitted, or electronic mail, 3 days shall be added to the prescribed period.

Committee Notes

1968 Adoption. This is the same as rule 1.6(e), Florida Rules of Civil Procedure, except for the omission of subdivision (c) of the civil rules, which appears to be inapplicable to criminal cases.

1972 Amendment. Same as prior rule.

Editor's Note

On October 18, 2012, the Supreme Court of Florida issued a revised opinion in case number SC11- 399, which was originally issued on June 21, 2012. See *In re Amendments to the Florida Rules of Judicial Administration*, 102 So. 3d 451(Fla. 2012). The opinion provides in relevant part:

"First, the new electronic filing requirements the Courts adopts will become effective in the civil, probate, small claims, and family law divisions of the trial courts, as well as for appeals to the circuit courts in these categories of cases, on April 1, 2013, at 12:01 a.m., except as may be otherwise provided by administrative order. Electronic filing will be mandatory in these divisions pursuant to rule 2.525 on that date. However, until the new rules take effect in these divisions, any clerk who is already accepting documents filed by electronic transmission under the current rules should continue to do so; attorneys in these counties are encouraged to file documents electronically under the current rules.

"Next, the new electronic filing requirements the Court adopts will become effective in the criminal, traffic, and juvenile divisions of the trial courts, as well as for appeals to the circuit court in these categories of cases, on October 1, 2013, at 12:01 a.m., except as may be otherwise provided by administrative order. Electronic filing will be mandatory in these divisions under rule 2.525 on that date. The new e-filing requirements, as they apply in proceedings brought pursuant to the Florida Mental Health Act (Baker Act), Chapter 394, Part I, Florida Statutes, and the Involuntary Commitment of Sexually Violent Predators Act (Jimmy Ryce), Chapter 394, Part V, Florida Statutes, will also not be mandatory in these cases until October 1, 2013. As stated above, until the new rules take

10

effect in these divisions and proceedings, any clerk who is already accepting electronically filed documents under the current rules should continue to do so; attorneys are again encouraged to utilize existing electronic filing procedures under the current rules.

"However, until the new rules and procedures take effect in the district courts, any clerk who is already accepting documents filed by electronic transmission may continue to do so; attorneys in these districts are encouraged to file documents electronically. Clerks will not be required to electronically transmit the record on appeal until July 1, 2013, at 12:01 a.m. Until July 1, we encourage clerks, whenever possible, to electronically transmit the record under the new rules and requirements.

"(W)e note that, in all types of cases, pursuant to amended rule 2.525(d) self-represented parties and self-represented nonparties, including nonparty governmental or public agencies, and attorneys excused from e- mail service under Florida Rule of Judicial Administration 2.516 will be permitted, but nor required, to file documents electronically.

By order of November 28, 2012, in case number SC11-399, the Court released a revised implementation schedule, which provides, in pertinent part: "The e-filing rules adopted in the October 2012 opinion will be mandatory in this (Supreme) Court on February 27, 2013, at 12:01 a.m.; and effective earlier on a voluntary basis as will be indicated by further administrative order of the chief justice.

"Thereafter, the e-filing rules will be mandatory in the Second District Court of Appeal on July 22, 2013, at 12:01 a.m.; in the Third District Court of Appeal on September 27, 2013, at 12:01 a.m.; in the Fourth District Court of Appeal on October 31, 2013, at 12:01 a.m.; in the Fifth District Court of Appeal on November 27, 2013 at 12:01 a.m.; and in the First District Court of Appeal on December 27, 2013, at 12:01 a.m., unless made mandatory earlier by the chief judge of the applicable district court of appeal. The e-filing rules will be effective earlier on a voluntary trial basis in the district courts of appeal as will be indicated by further administrative order by the chief judge of the applicable district court."

RULE 3.080. NONVERIFICATION OF PLEADINGS

Text of rule effective prior to amendment by Florida Supreme Court Opinion No. SC11-399. See also text of rule as amended by Florida Supreme Court Opinion SC11-399.

Except when otherwise specifically provided by these rules or an applicable statute, every written pleading or other paper of a party represented by an attorney need not be verified or accompanied by an affidavit.

Committee Notes

1968 Adoption. Taken from rules of civil procedure.

1972 Amendment. Same as prior rule.

RULE 3.080. NONVERIFICATION OF PLEADINGS

Text of rule as amended by Florida Supreme Court Opinion SC11-399. See also text of rule prior to amendment by Florida Supreme Court Opinion SC11-399.

Except when otherwise specifically provided by these rules or an applicable statute, every written pleading or other document of a party represented by an attorney need not be verified or accompanied by an affidavit.

Committee Notes

1968 Adoption. Taken from rules of civil procedure.

1972 Amendment. Same as prior rule.

Editor's Note

On October 18, 2012, the Supreme Court of Florida issued a revised opinion in case number SC11- 399, which was originally issued on June 21, 2012. See *In re Amendments to the Florida Rules of Judicial Administration*, 102 So. 3d 451(Fla. 2012). The opinion provides in relevant part:

"First, the new electronic filing requirements the Courts adopts will become effective in the civil, probate, small claims, and family law divisions of the trial courts, as well as for appeals to the circuit courts in these categories of cases, on April 1, 2013, at 12:01 a.m., except as may be otherwise provided by administrative order. Electronic filing will be mandatory in these divisions pursuant to rule 2.525 on that date. However, until the new rules take effect in these divisions, any clerk who is already accepting documents filed by electronic transmission under the current rules should continue to do so; attorneys in these counties are encouraged to file documents electronically under the current rules.

"Next, the new electronic filing requirements the Court adopts will become effective in the criminal, traffic, and juvenile divisions of the trial courts, as well as for appeals to the circuit court in these categories of cases, on October 1, 2013, at 12:01 a.m., except as may be otherwise provided by administrative order. Electronic filing will be mandatory in these divisions under rule 2.525 on that date. The new e-filing requirements, as they apply in proceedings brought pursuant to the Florida Mental Health Act (Baker Act), Chapter 394, Part I, Florida Statutes, and the Involuntary Commitment of Sexually Violent Predators Act (Jimmy Ryce), Chapter 394, Part V, Florida Statutes, will also not be mandatory in these cases until October 1, 2013. As stated above, until the new rules take effect in these divisions and proceedings, any clerk who is already accepting electronically filed documents under the current rules should continue to do so; attorneys are again encouraged to utilize existing electronic filing procedures under the current rules.

"However, until the new rules and procedures take effect in the district courts, any clerk who is already accepting documents filed by electronic transmission may continue to do so; attorneys in these districts are encouraged to file documents electronically. Clerks will not be required to electronically transmit the record on appeal until July 1, 2013, at 12:01 a.m. Until July 1, we encourage clerks, whenever possible, to electronically transmit the record under the new rules and requirements.

"(W)e note that, in all types of cases, pursuant to amended rule 2.525(d) self-represented parties and self-represented nonparties, including nonparty governmental or public agencies, and attorneys excused from e- mail service under Florida Rule of Judicial Administration 2.516 will be permitted, but nor required, to file documents electronically.

By order of November 28, 2012, in case number SC11-399, the Court released a revised implementation schedule, which provides, in pertinent part: "The e-filing rules adopted in the October 2012 opinion will be mandatory in this (Supreme) Court on February 27, 2013, at 12:01 a.m.; and effective earlier on a voluntary basis as will be indicated by further administrative order of the chief justice.

"Thereafter, the e-filing rules will be mandatory in the Second District Court of Appeal on July 22, 2013, at 12:01 a.m.; in the Third District Court of Appeal on September 27, 2013, at 12:01 a.m.; in the Fourth District Court of Appeal on October 31, 2013, at 12:01 a.m.; in the Fifth District Court of Appeal on November 27, 2013 at 12:01 a.m.; and in the First District Court of Appeal on December 27, 2013, at 12:01 a.m., unless made mandatory earlier by the chief judge of the applicable district court of appeal. The e-filing rules will be effective earlier on a voluntary trial basis in the district courts of appeal as will be indicated by further administrative order by the chief judge of the applicable district court."

RULE 3.090. PLEADING CAPTIONS

Text of rule effective prior to amendment by Florida Supreme Court Opinion No. SC11-399. See also text of rule as amended by Florida Supreme Court Opinion SC11-399.

Every pleading, motion, order, judgment, or other paper shall have a caption containing the name of the court, the file number, the name of the first party on each side with an appropriate indication of other parties, and a designation identifying the party filing it and its nature or the nature of the order, as the case may be. All papers filed in the action shall be styled in such a manner as to indicate clearly the subject matter of the paper and the party requesting or obtaining relief.

RULE 3.090. PLEADING CAPTIONS

Text of rule as amended by Florida Supreme Court Opinion SC11-399. See also text of rule prior to amendment by Florida Supreme Court Opinion SC11-399.

Every pleading, motion, order, judgment, or other document shall have a caption containing the name of the court, the file number, the name of the first party on each side with an appropriate indication of other parties, and a designation identifying the party filing it and its nature, to include if the pleading or document is sworn or the nature of the order, as the case may be. All documents filed in the action shall be styled in such a manner as to indicate clearly the subject matter of the document and the party requesting or obtaining relief.

Editor's Note

On October 18, 2012, the Supreme Court of Florida issued a revised opinion in case number SC11-399, which was originally issued on June 21, 2012. See *In re Amendments to the Florida Rules of Judicial Administration*, 102 So. 3d 451(Fla. 2012). The opinion provides in relevant part:

"First, the new electronic filing requirements the Courts adopts will become effective in the civil, probate, small claims, and family law divisions of the trial courts, as well as for appeals to the circuit courts in these categories of cases, on April 1, 2013, at 12:01 a.m., except as may be otherwise provided by administrative order. Electronic filing will be mandatory in these divisions pursuant to rule 2.525 on that date. However, until the new rules take effect in these divisions, any clerk who is already accepting documents filed by electronic transmission under the current rules should continue to do so; attorneys in these counties are encouraged to file documents electronically under the current rules.

"Next, the new electronic filing requirements the Court adopts will become effective in the criminal, traffic, and juvenile divisions of the trial courts, as well as for appeals to the circuit court in these categories of cases, on October 1, 2013, at 12:01 a.m., except as may be otherwise provided by administrative order. Electronic filing will be mandatory in these divisions under rule 2.525 on that date. The new e-filing requirements, as they apply in proceedings brought pursuant to the Florida Mental Health Act (Baker Act), Chapter 394, Part I, Florida Statutes, and the Involuntary Commitment of Sexually Violent Predators Act (Jimmy Ryce), Chapter 394, Part V, Florida Statutes, will also not be mandatory in these cases until October 1, 2013. As stated above, until the new rules take effect in these divisions and proceedings, any clerk who is already accepting electronically filed documents under the current rules should continue to do so; attorneys are again encouraged to utilize existing electronic filing procedures under the current rules.

"However, until the new rules and procedures take effect in the district courts, any clerk who is already accepting documents filed by electronic transmission may continue to do so; attorneys in these districts are encouraged to file documents electronically. Clerks will not be required to electronically transmit the record on appeal until July 1, 2013, at 12:01 a.m. Until July 1, we encourage clerks, whenever possible, to electronically transmit the record under the new rules and requirements.

"(W)e note that, in all types of cases, pursuant to amended rule 2.525(d) self-represented parties and self-represented nonparties, including nonparty governmental or public agencies, and attorneys excused from e- mail service under Florida Rule of Judicial Administration 2.516 will be permitted, but nor required, to file documents electronically.

By order of November 28, 2012, in case number SC11-399, the Court released a revised implementation schedule, which provides, in pertinent part: "The e-filing rules adopted in the October 2012 opinion will be mandatory in this (Supreme) Court on February 27, 2013, at 12:01 a.m.; and effective earlier on a voluntary basis as will be indicated by further administrative order of the chief justice.

"Thereafter, the e-filing rules will be mandatory in the Second District Court of Appeal on July 22, 2013, at 12:01 a.m.; in the Third District Court of Appeal on September 27, 2013, at 12:01 a.m.; in the Fourth District Court of Appeal on October 31, 2013, at 12:01 a.m.; in the Fifth District Court of Appeal on November 27, 2013 at 12:01 a.m.; and in the First District Court of Appeal on December 27, 2013, at 12:01 a.m., unless made mandatory earlier by the chief judge of the applicable district court of appeal. The e-filing rules will be effective earlier on a voluntary trial basis in the district courts of appeal as will be indicated by further administrative order by the chief judge of the applicable district court."

RULE 3.111. PROVIDING COUNSEL TO INDIGENTS

(a) **When Counsel Provided.** A person entitled to appointment of counsel as provided herein shall have counsel appointed when the person is formally charged with an offense, or as soon as feasible after custodial restraint, or at the first appearance before a committing judge, whichever occurs earliest.

(b)   **Cases Applicable.**

(1)   Counsel shall be provided to indigent persons in all prosecutions for offenses punishable by incarceration including appeals from the conviction thereof. In the discretion of the court, counsel does not have to be provided to an indigent person in a prosecution for a misdemeanor or violation of a municipal ordinance if the judge, at least 15 days prior to trial, files in the cause a written order of no incarceration certifying that the defendant will not be incarcerated in the case pending trial or probation violation hearing, or as part of a sentence after trial, guilty or nolo contendere plea, or probation revocation. This 15-day requirement may be waived by the defendant or defense counsel.

(A)   If the court issues an order of no incarceration after counsel has been appointed to represent the defendant, the court may discharge appointed counsel unless the defendant is incarcerated or the defendant would be substantially disadvantaged by the discharge of appointed counsel.

(B)   If the court determines that the defendant would be substantially disadvantaged by the discharge of appointed counsel, the court shall either:

(i)   not discharge appointed counsel; or

(ii)   discharge appointed counsel and allow the defendant a reasonable time to obtain private counsel, or if the defendant elects to represent himself or herself, a reasonable time to prepare for trial.

(C)   If the court withdraws its order of no incarceration, it shall immediately appoint counsel if the defendant is otherwise eligible for the services of the public defender. The court may not withdraw its order of no incarceration once the defendant has been found guilty or pled nolo contendere.

(2)   Counsel may be provided to indigent persons in all proceedings arising from the initiation of a criminal action against a defendant, including postconviction proceedings and appeals therefrom, extradition proceedings, mental competency proceedings, and other proceedings that are adversary in nature, regardless of the designation of the court in which they occur or the classification of the proceedings as civil or criminal.

(3)   Counsel may be provided to a partially indigent person on request, provided that the person shall defray that portion of the cost of representation and the reasonable costs of investigation as he or she is able without substantial hardship to the person or the person's family, as directed by the court.

(4)   "Indigent" shall mean a person who is unable to pay for the services of an attorney, including costs of investigation, without substantial hardship to the person or the person's family; "partially indigent" shall mean a person unable to pay more than a portion of the fee charged by an attorney, including costs of investigation, without substantial hardship to the person or the person's family.

(5)   Before appointing a public defender, the court shall:

(A)   inform the accused that, if the public defender or

other counsel is appointed, a lien for the services rendered by counsel may be imposed as provided by law;

(B)   make inquiry into the financial status of the accused in a manner not inconsistent with the guidelines established by section 27.52, Florida Statutes. The accused shall respond to the inquiry under oath;

(C)   require the accused to execute an affidavit of insolvency as required by section 27.52, Florida Statutes.

(c)   **Duty of Booking Officer.** In addition to any other duty, the officer who commits a defendant to custody has the following duties:

(1)   The officer shall immediately advise the defendant:

(A)   of the right to counsel;

(B)   that, if the defendant is unable to pay a lawyer, one will be provided immediately at no charge.

(2)   If the defendant requests counsel or advises the officer that he or she cannot afford counsel, the officer shall immediately and effectively place the defendant in communication with the (office of) public defender of the circuit in which the arrest was made.

(3)   If the defendant indicates that he or she has an attorney or is able to retain an attorney, the officer shall immediately and effectively place the defendant in communication with the attorney or the Lawyer Referral Service of the local bar association.

(4)   The public defender of each judicial circuit may interview a defendant when contacted by, or on behalf of, a defendant who is, or claims to be, indigent as defined by law.

(A)   If the defendant is in custody and reasonably appears to be indigent, the public defender shall tender such advice as is indicated by the facts of the case, seek the setting of a reasonable bail, and otherwise represent the defendant pending a formal judicial determination of indigency.

(B)   If the defendant is at liberty on bail or otherwise not in custody, the public defender shall elicit from the defendant only the information that may be reasonably relevant to the question of indigency and shall immediately seek a formal judicial determination of indigency. If the court finds the defendant indigent, it shall immediately appoint counsel to represent the defendant.

(d)   **Waiver of Counsel.**

(1)   The failure of a defendant to request appointment of counsel or the announced intention of a defendant to plead guilty shall not, in itself, constitute a waiver of counsel at any stage of the proceedings.

(2)   A defendant shall not be considered to have waived the

16

assistance of counsel until the entire process of offering counsel has been completed and a thorough inquiry has been made into both the accused's comprehension of that offer and the accused's capacity to make a knowing and intelligent waiver. Before determining whether the waiver is knowing and intelligent, the court shall advise the defendant of the disadvantages and dangers of self-representation.

(3)   Regardless of the defendant's legal skills or the complexity of the case, the court shall not deny a defendant's unequivocal request to represent himself or herself, if the court makes a determination of record that the defendant has made a knowing and intelligent waiver of the right to counsel, and does not suffer from severe mental illness to the point where the defendant is not competent to conduct trial proceedings by himself or herself.

(4)   A waiver of counsel made in court shall be of record; a waiver made out of court shall be in writing with not less than 2 attesting witnesses. The witnesses shall attest the voluntary execution thereof.

(5)   If a waiver is accepted at any stage of the proceedings, the offer of assistance of counsel shall be renewed by the court at each subsequent stage of the proceedings at which the defendant appears without counsel.

(e)   Withdrawal of Defense Counsel After Judgment and Sentence. The attorney of record for a defendant in a criminal proceeding shall not be relieved of any duties, nor be permitted to withdraw as counsel of record, except with approval of the lower tribunal on good cause shown on written motion, until after:

(1)   the filing of:

(A)   a notice of appeal;

(B)   a statement of judicial acts to be reviewed, if a transcript will require the expenditure of public funds;

(C)   directions to the clerk, if necessary; and

(D)   a designation of that portion of the reporter's transcript that supports the statement of judicial acts to be reviewed, if a transcript will require expenditure of public funds; or

(2)   substitute counsel has been obtained or appointed, or a statement has been filed with the appellate court that the appellant has exercised the right to self-representation. In publicly funded cases, the public defender for the local circuit court shall be appointed initially until the record is transmitted to the appellate court; or

(3)   the time has expired for filing of a notice of appeal, and no notice has been filed.

Orders allowing withdrawal of counsel are conditional, and counsel shall remain of record for the limited purpose of representing the defendant in the lower tribunal regarding any sentencing error that the lower tribunal is authorized to address during the pendency of the direct appeal under rule 3.800(b) (2).

Committee Notes

1972 Adoption. Part 1 of the ABA Standard relating to providing defense services deals with the general philosophy for providing criminal defense services and while the committee felt that the philosophy should apply to the Florida Rules of Criminal Procedure, the standards were not in such form to be the subject of that particular rule. Since the standards deal with the national situation, contained in them were alternative methods of providing defense services, i.e., assigned counsel vs. defender system; but, Florida, already having a defender system, need not be concerned with the assigned counsel system.

(a)   Taken from the first sentence of ABA Standard 5.1. There was considerable discussion within the committee concerning the time within which counsel should be appointed and who should notify defendant's counsel. The commentary in the ABA Standard under 5.1a, b, convinced the committee to adopt the language here contained.

(b)   Standard 4.1 provides that counsel should be provided in all criminal cases punishable by loss of liberty, except those types where such punishment is not likely to be imposed. The committee determined that the philosophy of such standard should be recommended to the Florida Supreme Court. The committee determined that possible deprivation of liberty for any period makes a case serious enough that the accused should have the right to counsel.

(c)   Based on the recommendation of ABA Standard 5.1b and the commentary thereunder which provides that implementation of a rule for providing the defendant with counsel should not be limited to providing a means for the accused to contact a lawyer.

(d)   From standard 7.2 and the commentaries thereunder.

1980 Amendment. Modification of the existing rule (the addition of (b)(5)(A)–(C)) provides a greater degree of uniformity in appointing counsel to indigent defendants. The defendant is put on notice of the lien for public defender services and must give financial information under oath.

A survey of Florida judicial circuits by the Committee on Representation of Indigents of the Criminal Law Section (1978–79) disclosed the fact that several circuits had no procedure for determining indigency and that there were circuits in which no affidavits of insolvency were executed (and no legal basis for establishing or collecting lien monies).

1992 Amendment. In light of *State v. District Court of Appeal of Florida, First District*, 569 So.2d 439 (Fla. 1990), in which the supreme court pronounced that motions seeking belated direct appeal based on ineffective assistance of counsel should be filed in the trial court pursuant to rule 3.850, the committee recommends that rule 3.111(e) be amended to detail with specificity defense counsel's duties to perfect an appeal prior to withdrawing after judgment and sentence. The present provision merely notes that such withdrawal is governed by Florida Rule of Appellate Procedure 9.140(b)(3).

1998 Amendment. The amendments to (d)   (2)–   (3) were adopted to reflect *State v. Bowen*, 698 So.2d 248 (Fla. 1997), which implicitly overruled *Cappetta v. State*, 204 So.2d 913 (Fla. 4th DCA 1967), rev'd on other grounds 216 So.2d 749 (Fla. 1968). See *Fitzpatrick v. Wainwright*, 800 F.2d 1057 (11th Cir. 1986), for a list of factors

18

the court may consider. See also *McKaskle v. Wiggins*, 465 U.S. 168, 104 S.Ct. 944, 79 L.Ed.2d 122 (1984), and *Savage v. Estelle*, 924 F.2d 1459 (9th Cir. 1990), cert. denied 501 U.S. 1255, 111 S.Ct. 2900, 115 L.Ed.2d 1064 (1992), which suggest that the defendant's right to self-representation is limited when the defendant is not able or willing to abide by the rules of procedure and courtroom protocol.

2000 Amendment. This rule applies only to judicial proceedings and is inapplicable to investigative proceedings and matters. See rule 3.010.

2002 Amendment. Indigent defendants are entitled to counsel if they are either currently in custody or might be incarcerated in their case. See *Alabama v. Shelton*, 122 S.Ct. 1764, 1767 (2002) (Sixth Amendment forbids imposition of suspended sentence that may "end up in the actual deprivation of a person's liberty" unless defendant accorded "the guiding hand of counsel"). See also *Tur v. State*, 797 So. 2d 4 (Fla. 3d DCA 2001) (uncounseled plea to criminal charge cannot result in jail sentence based on violation of probationary sentence for that charge); *Harris v. State*, 773 So.2d 627 (Fla. 4th DCA 2000).

Discharge of the public defender based on an order certifying no incarceration that is entered after the public defender has already spent considerable time and resources investigating the case and preparing a defense may leave the defendant "in a position worse than if no counsel had been appointed in the first place." *State v. Ull*, 642 So. 2d 721, 724 (Fla. 1994).

In determining whether a defendant's due process rights would be violated by the discharge of the public defender, the court should consider all of the relevant circumstances, including, but not limited to:

1. The stage of the proceedings at which the order of no incarceration is entered.

2. The extent of any investigation and pretrial preparation by the public defender.

3. Any prejudice that might result if the public defender is discharged.

4. The nature of the case and the complexity of the issues.

5. The relationship between the defendant and the public defender.

Counsel may be provided to indigent persons in all other proceedings in, or arising from, a criminal case and the court should resolve any doubts in favor of the appointment of counsel for the defendant. See *Graham v. State*, 372 So.2d 1363, 1365 (Fla. 1979).

See form found at Fla.R.Crim.P. 3.994.

2005 Amendment. See Affidavit of Indigent Status as provided by *In re Approval of Form for Use by Clerks of the Circuit Courts Pursuant to Rule 10-2.1(a) of the Rules Regulating the Florida Bar*, 877 So. 2d 720 (Fla. 2004).

RULE 3.112. MINIMUM STANDARDS FOR ATTORNEYS IN CAPITAL CASES

(a)   **Statement of Purpose.** The purpose of these rules is to set minimum

19

standards for attorneys in capital cases to help ensure that competent representation will be provided to capital defendants in all cases. Minimum standards that have been promulgated concerning representation for defendants in criminal cases generally and the level of adherence to such standards required for noncapital cases should not be adopted as sufficient for death penalty cases. Counsel in death penalty cases should be required to perform at the level of an attorney reasonably skilled in the specialized practice of capital representation, zealously committed to the capital case, who has had adequate time and resources for preparation. These minimum standards for capital cases are not intended to preclude any circuit from adopting or maintaining standards having greater requirements.

(b) **Definitions.** A capital trial is defined as any first-degree murder case in which the State has not formally waived the death penalty on the record. A capital appeal is any appeal in which the death penalty has been imposed. A capital postconviction proceeding is any postconviction proceeding where the defendant is still under a sentence of death.

(c) **Applicability.** This rule applies to all defense counsel handling capital trials and capital appeals, who are appointed or retained on or after July 1, 2002.

(d) **List of Qualified Conflict Counsel.**

(1) Every circuit shall maintain a list of conflict counsel qualified for appointment in capital cases in each of three categories:

(A) lead trial counsel;

(B) trial co-counsel; and

(C) appellate counsel.

(2) The chief judge for each circuit shall maintain a list of qualified counsel pursuant to section 27.40(3)(a), Florida Statutes.

(e) **Appointment of Counsel.** A court must appoint lead counsel and, upon written application and a showing of need by lead counsel, should appoint cocounsel to handle every capital trial in which the defendant is not represented by retained counsel. Lead counsel shall have the right to select cocounsel from attorneys on the lead counsel or cocounsel list. Both attorneys shall be reasonably compensated for the trial and sentencing phase. Except under extraordinary circumstances, only one attorney may be compensated for other proceedings. In capital cases in which the Public Defender or Criminal Conflict and Civil Regional Counsel is appointed, the Public Defender or Criminal Conflict and Civil Regional Counsel shall designate lead and co-counsel.

(f) **Lead Counsel.** Lead trial counsel assignments should be given to attorneys who:

(1) are members of the bar admitted to practice in the jurisdiction or admitted to practice pro hac vice; and

(2) are experienced and active trial practitioners with at least five years of litigation experience in the field of criminal law; and

(3)   have prior experience as lead counsel in no fewer than nine state or federal jury trials of serious and complex cases which were tried to completion, as well as prior experience as lead defense counsel or cocounsel in at least two state or federal cases tried to completion in which the death penalty was sought. In addition, of the nine jury trials which were tried to completion, the attorney should have been lead counsel in at least three cases in which the charge was murder; or alternatively, of the nine jury trials, at least one was a murder trial and an additional five were felony jury trials; and

(4)   are familiar with the practice and procedure of the criminal courts of the jurisdiction; and

(5)   are familiar with and experienced in the utilization of expert witnesses and evidence, including but not limited to psychiatric and forensic evidence; and

(6)   have demonstrated the necessary proficiency and commitment which exemplify the quality of representation appropriate to capital cases, including but not limited to the investigation and presentation of evidence in mitigation of the death penalty; and

(7)   have attended within the last two years a continuing legal education program of at least twelve hours' duration devoted specifically to the defense of capital cases.

(g)   **Co-counsel.** Trial co-counsel assignments should be given to attorneys who:

(1)   are members of the bar admitted to practice in the jurisdiction or admitted to practice pro hac vice; and

(2)   qualify as lead counsel under paragraph (f) of these standards or meet the following requirements:

(A)   are experienced and active trial practitioners with at least three years of litigation experience in the field of criminal law; and

(B)   have prior experience as lead counsel or cocounsel in no fewer than three state or federal jury trials of serious and complex cases which were tried to completion, at least two of which were trials in which the charge was murder; or alternatively, of the three jury trials, at least one was a murder trial and one was a felony jury trial; and

(C)   are familiar with the practice and procedure of the criminal courts of the jurisdiction; and

(D)   have demonstrated the necessary proficiency and commitment which exemplify the quality of representation appropriate to capital cases, and

(E)   have attended within the last two years a continuing legal education program of at least twelve hours' duration devoted specifically to the defense of capital cases.

(h)   **Appellate Counsel.** Appellate counsel assignments should be given to attorneys who:

   (1) are members of the bar admitted to practice in the jurisdiction or admitted to practice pro hac vice; and

   (2) are experienced and active trial or appellate practitioners with at least five years of experience in the field of criminal law; and

   (3) have prior experience in the appeal of at least one case where a sentence of death was imposed, as well as prior experience as lead counsel in the appeal of no fewer than three felony convictions in federal or state court, at least one of which was an appeal of a murder conviction; or alternatively, have prior experience as lead counsel in the appeal of no fewer than six felony convictions in federal or state court, at least two of which were appeals of a murder conviction; and

   (4) are familiar with the practice and procedure of the appellate courts of the jurisdiction; and

   (5) have demonstrated the necessary proficiency and commitment which exemplify the quality of representation appropriate to capital cases; and

   (6) have attended within the last two years a continuing legal education program of at least twelve hours' duration devoted specifically to the defense of capital cases.

  (i) **Notice of Appearance.** An attorney who is retained or appointed in place of the Public Defender or Criminal Conflict and Civil Regional Counsel to represent a defendant in a capital case shall immediately file a notice of appearance certifying that he or she meets the qualifications of this rule. If the office of the Public Defender or Criminal Conflict and Civil Regional Counsel is appointed to represent the defendant, the Public Defender or Criminal Conflict and Civil Regional Counsel shall certify that the individuals or assistants assigned as lead and co-counsel meet the requirements of this rule. A notice of appearance filed under this rule shall be served on the defendant.

  (j) **Limitation on Caseloads.**

   (1) **Generally.** As soon as practicable, the trial court should conduct an inquiry relating to counsel's availability to provide effective assistance of counsel to the defendant. In assessing the availability of prospective counsel, the court should consider the number of capital or other cases then being handled by the attorney and any other circumstances bearing on the attorney's readiness to provide effective assistance of counsel to the defendant in a timely fashion. No appointment should be made to an attorney who may be unable to provide effective legal representation as a result of an unrealistically high caseload. Likewise, a private attorney should not undertake the representation of a defendant in a capital case if the attorney's caseload is high enough that it might impair the quality of legal representation provided to the defendant.

   (2) **Public Defender.** If a Public Defender or Criminal Conflict and Civil Regional Counsel seeks to refuse appointment to a new capital case based on a claim of excessive caseload, the matter should be referred to the Chief Judge of the circuit or to the administrative judge as so designated by the Chief Judge. The Chief Judge or his or her designate should coordinate with the Public Defender or Criminal Conflict and Civil

Regional Counsel to assess the number of attorneys involved in capital cases, evaluate the availability of prospective attorneys, and resolve any representation issues.

(k)   **Exceptional Circumstances.** In the event that the trial court determines that exceptional circumstances require appointment of counsel not meeting the requirements of this rule, the trial court shall enter an order specifying, in writing, the exceptional circumstances requiring deviation from the rule and the court's explicit determination that counsel chosen will provide competent representation in accord with the policy concerns of the rule.

Committee Comments

These standards are based on the general premise that the defense of a capital case requires specialized skill and expertise. The Supreme Court has not only the authority, but the constitutional responsibility to ensure that indigent defendants are provided with competent counsel, especially in capital cases where the State seeks to take the life of the indigent defendant. The Supreme Court also has exclusive jurisdiction under Article V section 15 of the Florida Constitution to "[r]egulate the admission of persons to the practice of law and the discipline of persons admitted." Implied in this grant of authority is the power to set the minimum requirements for the admission to practice law, see *In re Florida Board of Bar Examiners*, 353 So. 2d 98 (Fla. 1977), as well as the minimum requirements for certain kinds of specialized legal work. The Supreme Court has adopted minimum educational and experience requirements for board certification in other specialized fields of the law.

The experience and continuing educational requirements in these standards are based on existing local standards in effect throughout the state as well as comparable standards in effect in other states. Specifically, the committee considered the standards for the appointment of counsel in capital cases in the Second, Sixth, Eleventh, Fifteenth, and Seventeenth Circuits, the statewide standards for appointing counsel in capital cases in California, Indiana, Louisiana, Ohio, and New York, and the American Bar Association standards for appointment of counsel in capital cases.

These standards are not intended to establish any independent legal rights. For example, the failure to appoint co-counsel, standing alone, has not been recognized as a ground for relief from a conviction or sentence. See *Ferrell v. State*, 653 So. 2d 367 (Fla. 1995); *Lowe v. State*, 650 So. 2d 969 (Fla. 1994); *Armstrong v. State*, 642 So. 2d 730 (Fla. 1994). Rather, these cases stand for the proposition that a showing of inadequacy of representation in the particular case is required. See *Strickland v. Washington*, 466 U.S. 668, 104 S.Ct. 2052, 80 L.Ed.2d 674 (1984). These rulings are not affected by the adoption of these standards. Any claims of ineffective assistance of counsel will be controlled by Strickland.

The American Bar Association Standards and many other state standards require the appointment of two lawyers at the trial level in every prosecution that could result in the imposition of the death penalty. The committee has modified this requirement by allowing the trial court some discretion as to the number of attorneys, and by eliminating certain provisions that may be unnecessary or economically unfeasible. Paragraph (e) minimizes the potential duplication of expenses by limiting the compensable participation of co-counsel. In addition, the standard adopted herein requires an initial showing by lead counsel of the need for co-counsel and, while the standard suggests that co-counsel should ordinarily be appointed, the ultimate decision is left to the discretion of the trial court.

The committee emphasizes that the right to appointed counsel is not enlarged by the application of these standards. The court should appoint conflict counsel only if there is a conflict and the defendant otherwise qualifies for representation by the Public Defender. A defendant who is represented by retained counsel is not entitled to the appointment of a second lawyer at public expense merely because that defendant is unable to bear the cost of retaining two lawyers.

RULE 3.115. DUTIES OF STATE ATTORNEY; CRIMINAL INTAKE

The state attorney shall provide the personnel or procedure for criminal intake in the judicial system. All sworn complaints charging the commission of a criminal offense shall be filed in the office of the clerk of the circuit court and delivered to the state attorney for further proceedings.

III. PRELIMINARY PROCEEDINGS

RULE 3.120. COMMITTING JUDGE

Each state and county judge is a committing judge and may issue a summons to, or a warrant for the arrest of, a person against whom a complaint is made in writing and sworn to before a person authorized to administer oaths, when the complaint states facts that show that such person violated a criminal law of this state within the jurisdiction of the judge to whom the complaint is presented. The judge may take testimony under oath to determine if there is reasonable ground to believe the complaint is true. The judge may commit the offender to jail, may order the defendant to appear before the proper court to answer the charge in the complaint, or may discharge the defendant from custody or from any undertaking to appear. The judge may authorize the clerk to issue a summons.

Committee Notes

1968 Adoption. This is substantially the same as part of section 901.01, Florida Statutes. (The remaining part should be retained as a statute.) It differs from the statute by requiring the complaint to be in writing and by identifying the initiating instrument as a "complaint," thus adopting the federal terminology which is more meaningful and modern. Some doubt was expressed as to whether the terms of the statute incorporated in the rule are within the rulemaking power of the Supreme Court.

1972 Amendment. Substantially same as former rule. Altered to incorporate the provision for testimony under oath formerly contained in rule 3.121(a), and authorize the execution of the affidavit before a notary or other person authorized to administer oaths.

RULE 3.121. ARREST WARRANT

     (a)   **Issuance.** An arrest warrant, when issued, shall:

          (1)   be in writing and in the name of the State of Florida;

          (2)   set forth substantially the nature of the offense;

          (3)   command that the person against whom the complaint was made be arrested and brought before a judge;

(4)   specify the name of the person to be arrested or, if the name is un-known to the judge, designate the person by any name or description by which the person can be identified with reasonable certainty;

(5)   state the date when issued and the county where issued;

(6)   be signed by the judge with the title of the office; or, may be electronically signed by the judge if the arrest warrant bears the affiant's signature, or electronic signature, is supported by an oath or affirmation administered by the judge, or other person authorized by law to administer oaths, and, if submitted electronically, is submitted by reliable electronic means; and

(7)   in all offenses bailable as of right be endorsed with the amount of bail and the return date.

(b)   **Amendment.** No arrest warrant shall be dismissed nor shall any person in custody be discharged because of any defect as to form in the warrant; but the warrant may be amended by the judge to remedy such defect.

Committee Notes

1968 Adoption. (a) This is substantially the same as section 901.02, Florida Statutes, except that the rule requires a written complaint. Also, the rule does not incorporate that seldom used part of the statute that permits the magistrate to issue an arrest warrant upon affidavits made before the prosecuting attorney.

(b)   This is the same as section 901.03, Florida Statutes.

(c)   This is the same as section 901.05, Florida Statutes, except for modernizing the language.

1972 Amendment. (a) of former rule has been deleted, as its substance is now contained in rules 3.120 and 3.130; (b) has been renumbered as (a); (c) has been renumbered as (b).

RULE 3.125. NOTICE TO APPEAR

(a)   **Definition.** Unless indicated otherwise, notice to appear means a written order issued by a law enforcement officer in lieu of physical arrest requiring a person accused of violating the law to appear in a designated court or governmental office at a specified date and time.

(b)   **By Arresting Officer.** If a person is arrested for an offense declared to be a misdemeanor of the first or second degree or a violation, or is arrested for violation of a municipal or county ordinance triable in the county, and demand to be taken before a judge is not made, notice to appear may be issued by the arresting officer unless:

(1)   the accused fails or refuses to sufficiently identify himself or herself or supply the required information;

(2)   the accused refuses to sign the notice to appear;

(3)   the officer has reason to believe that the continued liberty of the accused constitutes an unreasonable risk of bodily injury to the accused or others;

(4)   the accused has no ties with the jurisdiction reasonably sufficient to assure the accused's appearance or there is substantial risk that the accused will refuse to respond to the notice;

(5)   the officer has any suspicion that the accused may be wanted in any jurisdiction; or

(6)   it appears that the accused previously has failed to respond to a notice or a summons or has violated the conditions of any pretrial release program.

(c)   **By Booking Officer.** If the arresting officer does not issue notice to appear because of one of the exceptions listed in subdivision (b) and takes the accused to police headquarters, the booking officer may issue notice to appear if the officer determines that there is a likelihood that the accused will appear as directed, based on a reasonable investigation of the accused's:

(1)   residence and length of residence in the community;

(2)   family ties in the community;

(3)   employment record;

(4)   character and mental condition;

(5)   past record of convictions; or

(6)   past history of appearance at court proceedings.

(d)   **How and When Served.** If notice to appear is issued, it shall be prepared in quadruplicate. The officer shall deliver 1 copy of the notice to appear to the arrested person and the person, to secure release, shall give a written promise to appear in court by signing the 3 remaining copies: 1 to be retained by the officer and 2 to be filed with the clerk of the court. These 2 copies shall be sworn to by the arresting officer before a notary public or a deputy clerk. If notice to appear is issued under subdivision (b), the notice shall be issued immediately upon arrest. If notice to appear is issued under subdivision (c), the notice shall be issued immediately on completion of the investigation. The arresting officer or other duly authorized official then shall release from custody the person arrested.

(e)   **Copy to the Clerk of the Court.** With the sworn notice to appear, the arresting officer shall file with the clerk a list of witnesses and their addresses and a list of tangible evidence in the cause. One copy shall be retained by the officer and 2 copies shall be filed with the clerk of the court.

(f)   **Copy to State Attorney.** The clerk shall deliver 1 copy of the notice to appear and schedule of witnesses and evidence filed therewith to the state attorney.

(g)   **Contents.** If notice to appear is issued, it shall contain the:

(1)   name and address of the accused;

(2)   date of offense;

(3)   offense(s) charged — by statute and municipal ordinance if applicable;

(4)   counts of each offense;

(5)   time and place that the accused is to appear in court;

(6)   name and address of the trial court having jurisdiction to try the offense(s) charged;

(7)   name of the arresting officer;

(8)   name(s) of any other person(s) charged at the same time;

and

(9)   signature of the accused.

(h)   Failure to Appear. If a person signs a written notice to appear and fails to respond to the notice to appear, a warrant of arrest shall be issued under rule 3.121.

(i)   Traffic Violations Excluded. Nothing contained herein shall prevent the operation of a traffic violations bureau, the issuance of citations for traffic violations, or any procedure under chapter 316, Florida Statutes.

(j)   Rules and Regulations. Rules and regulations of procedure governing the exercise of authority to issue notices to appear shall be established by the chief judge of the circuit.

(k)   Procedure by Court.

(1)   When the accused appears before the court under the requirements of the notice to appear, the court shall advise the defendant as set forth in rule 3.130(b), and the provisions of that rule shall apply. The accused at such appearance may elect to waive the right to counsel and trial and enter a plea of guilty or nolo contendere by executing the waiver form contained on the notice to appear, and the court may enter judgment and sentence in the cause.

(2)   In the event the defendant enters a plea of not guilty, the court may set the cause for jury or nonjury trial on the notice to appear under the provisions of rules 3.140 and 3.160. When the court sets a trial date by the court, the clerk shall, without further praecipe, issue witness subpoenas to the law enforcement officer who executed the notice to appear and to the witnesses whose names and addresses appear on the list filed by the officer, requiring their attendance at trial.

(l)   Form of Notice to Appear and Schedule of Witnesses and Evidence. The notice to appear and schedule of witnesses and evidence shall be in substantially the following form:

IN THE COUNTY COURT, IN AND FOR
COUNTY, FLORIDA

NOTICE TO APPEAR

_____

Agency Case #

STATE OF FLORIDA, COUNTY OF

In the name of _____ County, Florida: The undersigned certifies that he or she has just
and reasonable grounds to believe, and does believe, that:

On .....(date)....., at _____ ( )a.m. ( )p.m.

_____

Last Name   First   M.I.   Aliases

_____

Street—City and State   Date and Place of Birth

_____ _____ _____ _____ ____ ____ _____

Phone   Race/Sex   Height   Weight   Hair   Eyes   Scars/Marks

_____ _____ _____

Occupation   Place of Employment   Employment Phone

_____ _____ _____

Complexion   Driver's License #   Yr./St. Social Security #

at (location) _____

in County, Florida, committed the following offense(s):

(1) _____ (2) _____

in violation of section(s): _____ : _____ ( ) State Statute
            _____   _____ ( ) Municipal Ord.

DID (Narrative):_____

_____

_____

_____

_____

_____

28

_____ _____ _____
Name of Officer   ID   Agency

[ ] Mandatory appearance in court, _____
                                        Location
on .....(date)....., at _____ ( )a.m. ( )p.m.

[ ] You need not appear in court, but must comply with instructions on back.

CO-DEFENDANTS:

                                                    [ ] Cited
1._____   [ ] Jailed
   Name   DOB   Address

                                                    [ ] Cited
2._____   [ ] Jailed
   Name   DOB   Address

If you are a person with a disability who needs any accommodation in order to participate in this proceeding, you are entitled, at no cost to you, to the provision of certain assistance. Please contact [identify applicable court personnel by name, address, and telephone number] at least 7 days before your scheduled court appearance, or immediately upon receiving this notification if the time before the scheduled appearance is less than 7 days; if you are hearing or voice impaired, call 711.

I AGREE TO APPEAR AT THE TIME AND PLACE DESIGNATED ABOVE TO ANSWER THE OFFENSE CHARGED OR TO PAY THE FINE SUBSCRIBED. I UNDERSTAND THAT SHOULD I WILLFULLY FAIL TO APPEAR BEFORE THE COURT AS REQUIRED BY THIS NOTICE TO APPEAR, I MAY BE HELD IN CONTEMPT OF COURT AND A WARRANT FOR MY ARREST SHALL BE ISSUED.

_____
Signature of Defendant

        I swear the above and reverse and attached statements are true and correct to the best of my knowledge and belief.

_____
Complainant

_____
Agency or Department

Sworn to and subscribed before me on .....(date)......

_____
Notary Public, State of Florida

[Editor's Note: Jurat should include identification information required by F.S. 117.05(13).]

WAIVER INFORMATION

If you desire to plead guilty or nolo contendere (no contest) and you need not appear in court as indicated on the face of this notice, you may present this notice at the county court named on the reverse of this page.

From .....(date)....., _____ to .....(date)....., _____

                  Hour   Hour

and pay a fine of _____ dollars in cash, money order, or certified check.

The waiver below must be completed and attached. Read carefully.

Your failure to answer this summons in the manner subscribed will result in a warrant being issued on a separate and additional charge.

"In consideration of my not appearing in court, I the undersigned, do hereby enter my appearance on the affidavit for the offense charged on the other side of this notice and waive the reading of the affidavit in the above named cause and the right to be present at the trial of said action. I hereby enter my plea of Guilty [ ] or Nolo Contendere [ ], and waive my right to prosecute appeal or error proceedings.

"I understand the nature of the charge against me; I understand my right to have counsel and waive this right and the right to a continuance. I waive my right to trial before a judge or jury. I plead Guilty [ ] or Nolo Contendere [ ] to the charge, being fully aware that my signature to this plea will have the same effect as a judgment of this court."

Total Fine and Cost _____
Defendant Signature _____
Address _____
_____

IN THE COUNTY COURT, IN AND FOR
_____ COUNTY, FLORIDA
SCHEDULE OF WITNESSES AND
EVIDENCE FOR NOTICE TO APPEAR

_____

Agency Case #

_____

Last Name   First   M.I.   Aliases

_____

Address

.....(date of notice to appear)..... Offense(s): (1) _____

Florida Rules of Criminal Procedure 2014

_____(2)_____

TANGIBLE EVIDENCE: (If none, write "None")

Item: _____

Obtained from (person and/or place): _____

first received by: _____

given to: _____

WITNESSES: (If none, write "None")

#1 Name: _____

Res. Tel. No. _____ Address: _____

Bus. Tel. No. _____ Business: _____

Testimony: _____

_____

#2 Name: _____

Res. Tel. No. _____ Address: _____

Bus. Tel. No. _____ Business: _____

Testimony: _____

_____

#3 Name: _____

Res. Tel. No. _____ Address: _____

Bus. Tel. No. _____ Business: _____

Testimony: _____

_____
I certify that the foregoing is a complete list of witnesses and evidence known to me.

_____

Investigating Officer

_____

Agency

Committee Notes

1992 Amendment. The amendment deletes subdivision (k) and reletters subdivisions (l) and (m). The elimination of subdivision (k) will entitle individuals charged with criminal violations to the same discovery, without regard to the nature of the charging instrument. As amended, persons charged by way of a notice to appear can obtain the same discovery as persons charged by way of either an information or an indictment. In this regard the committee also has proposed amendments to rule 3.220(b) (1), (b) (2), (c)(1), and (h)(1) to change the reference from "indictment or information" to "charging document."

RULE 3.130. FIRST APPEARANCE

(a) **Prompt First Appearance.** Except when previously released in a lawful manner, every arrested person shall be taken before a judicial officer, either in person or by electronic audiovisual device in the discretion of the court, within 24 hours of arrest. In the case of a child in the custody of juvenile authorities, against whom an information or indictment has been filed, the child shall be taken for a first appearance hearing within 24 hours of the filing of the information or indictment. The chief judge of the circuit for each county within the circuit shall designate 1 or more judicial officers from the circuit court, or county court, to be available for the first appearance and proceedings. The state attorney or an assistant state attorney and public defender or an assistant public defender shall attend the first appearance proceeding either in person or by other electronic means. First appearance hearings shall be held with adequate notice to the public defender and state attorney. An official record of the proceedings shall be maintained. If the defendant has retained counsel or ex- presses a desire to and is financially able, the attendance of the public defender or assistant public defender is not required at the first appearance, and the judge shall follow the procedure outlined in subdivision (c)(2).

(b) **Advice to Defendant.** At the defendant's first appearance the judge shall immediately inform the defendant of the charge, including an alleged violation of probation or community control and provide the defendant with a copy of the complaint. The judge shall also adequately advise the defendant that:

(1) the defendant is not required to say anything, and that anything the defendant says may be used against him or her;

(2) if unrepresented, that the defendant has a right to counsel, and, if financially unable to afford counsel, that counsel will be appointed; and

(3) the defendant has a right to communicate with counsel, family, or friends, and if necessary, will be provided reasonable means to do so.

(c) **Counsel for Defendant.**

(1) **Appointed Counsel.** If practicable, the judge should determine prior to the first appearance whether the defendant is financially able to afford counsel and whether the defendant desires representation. When the judge determines that the defendant is entitled to court-appointed counsel and desires counsel, the judge shall immediately appoint counsel. This determination must be made and, if required, counsel appointed no later than the time of the first appearance and before any other proceedings at the first appearance. If necessary, counsel may be appointed for the limited purpose of

representing the defendant only at first appearance or at subsequent proceedings before the judge.

    (2)   **Retained Counsel.** When the defendant has employed counsel or is financially able and desires to employ counsel to represent him or her at first appearance, the judge shall allow the defendant a reasonable time to send for counsel and shall, if necessary, postpone the first appearance hearing for that purpose. The judge shall also, on request of the defendant, require an officer to communicate a message to such counsel as the defendant may name. The officer shall, with diligence and without cost to the defendant if the counsel is within the county, perform the duty. If the postponement will likely result in the continued incarceration of the defendant beyond a 24-hour period, at the request of the defendant the judge may appoint counsel to represent the defendant for the first appearance hearing.

    (3)   **Opportunity to Confer.** No further steps in the proceedings should be taken until the defendant and counsel have had an adequate opportunity to confer, unless the defendant has intelligently waived the right to be represented by counsel.

    (4)   **Waiver of Counsel.** The defendant may waive the right to counsel at first appearance. The waiver, containing an explanation of the right to counsel, shall be in writing and signed and dated by the defendant. This written waiver of counsel shall, in addition, contain a statement that it is limited to first appearance only and shall in no way be construed to be a waiver of counsel for subsequent proceedings.

    (d)   **Pretrial Release.** The judicial officer shall proceed to determine conditions of release pursuant to rule 3.131. For a defendant who has been arrested for violation of his or her probation or community control by committing a new violation of law, the judicial officer:

    (1)   May order the offender to be taken before the court that granted the probation or community control if the offender admits the violation;

    (2)   If the offender does not admit the violation at first appearance hearing, the judicial officer may commit and order the offender to be brought before the court that granted probation or community control, or may release the offender with or without bail to await further hearing, notwithstanding section 907.041, Florida Statutes, relating to pretrial detention and release. In determining whether to require or set the amount of bail, the judicial officer may consider whether the offender is more likely than not to receive a prison sanction for the violation.

Committee Notes

1972 Amendment. Same as prior rule except (b), which is new.

RULE 3.131. PRETRIAL RELEASE

    (a)   **Right to Pretrial Release.** Unless charged with a capital offense or an offense punishable by life imprisonment and the proof of guilt is evident or the presumption is great, every person charged with a crime or violation of municipal or county ordinance shall be entitled to pretrial release on reasonable conditions. As a condition of pretrial release, whether such release is by surety bail bond or recognizance bond or in some other form, the defendant shall refrain from any contact of any type with the victim, except through pretrial discovery pursuant to the Florida Rules of Criminal Procedure and shall comply with all conditions of pretrial release as ordered by the court. Upon motion by the defendant when bail is set, or upon later motion properly noticed pursuant to law, the court may modify the condition precluding victim contact if good cause is shown and the interests of justice so require. The victim shall be permitted to be heard at any proceeding in which such modification is considered, and the state attorney shall notify the victim of the provisions of this subsection and of the pendency of any such proceeding. If no conditions of release can reasonably protect the community from risk of physical harm to persons, assure the presence of the accused at trial, or assure the integrity of the judicial process, the accused may be detained.

(b)   **Hearing at First Appearance—Conditions of Release.**

(1)   Unless the state has filed a motion for pretrial detention pursuant to rule 3.132, the court shall conduct a hearing to determine pretrial release. For the purpose of this rule, bail is defined as any of the forms of release stated below. Except as otherwise provided by this rule, there is a presumption in favor of release on nonmonetary conditions for any person who is granted pretrial release. The judicial officer shall impose the first of the following conditions of release that will reasonably protect the community from risk of physical harm to persons, assure the presence of the accused at trial, or assure the integrity of the judicial process; or, if no single condition gives that assurance, shall impose any combination of the following conditions:

(A)   personal recognizance of the defendant;

(B)   execution of an unsecured appearance bond in an amount specified by the judge;

(C)   placement of restrictions on the travel, association, or place of abode of the defendant during the period of release;

(D)   placement of the defendant in the custody of a designated person or organization agreeing to supervise the defendant;

(E)   execution of a bail bond with sufficient solvent sureties, or the deposit of cash in lieu thereof; provided, however, that any criminal defendant who is required to meet monetary bail or bail with any monetary component may satisfy the bail by providing an appearance bond; or

(F)   any other condition deemed reasonably necessary to assure appearance as required, including a condition requiring that the person return to custody after specified hours.

(2)   The judge shall at the defendant's first appearance consider all available relevant factors to determine what form of release is necessary to assure the defendant's appearance. If a monetary bail is required, the judge shall determine the amount. Any judge setting or granting monetary bond shall set a separate and specific bail amount for each charge or offense. When bail is posted each charge or offense requires a separate bond.

(3)   In determining whether to release a defendant on bail or other conditions, and what that bail or those conditions may be, the court may consider the nature

and circumstances of the offense charged and the penalty provided by law; the weight of the evidence against the defendant; the defendant's family ties, length of residence in the community, employment history, financial resources, need for substance abuse evaluation and/or treatment, and mental condition; the defendant's past and present conduct, including any record of convictions, previous flight to avoid prosecution, or failure to appear at court proceedings; the nature and probability of danger that the defendant's release poses to the community; the source of funds used to post bail; whether the defendant is already on release pending resolution of another criminal proceeding or is on probation, parole, or other release pending completion of sentence; and any other facts the court considers relevant.

(4)　　No person charged with a dangerous crime, as defined in section 907.041　(4)(a), Florida Statutes, shall be released on nonmonetary conditions under the supervision of a pretrial release service, unless the service certifies to the court that it has investigated or otherwise verified the conditions set forth in section 907.041(3)(b), Florida Statutes.

(5)　　All information provided by a defendant in connection with any application for or attempt to secure bail, to any court, court personnel, or individual soliciting or recording such information for the purpose of evaluating eligibility for or securing bail for the defendant, under circumstances such that the defendant knew or should have known that the information was to be used in connection with an application for bail, shall be accurate, truthful, and complete, without omissions, to the best knowledge of the defendant. Failure to comply with the provisions of this subdivision may result in the revocation or modification of bail. However, no defendant shall be compelled to provide information regarding his or her criminal record.

(6)　　Information stated in, or offered in connection with, any order entered pursuant to this rule need not strictly conform to the rules of evidence.

(c)　　Consequences of Failure to Appear.

(1)　　Any defendant who willfully and knowingly fails to appear and breaches a bond as specified in section 903.26, Florida Statutes, and who voluntarily appears or surrenders shall not be eligible for a recognizance bond.

(2)　　Any defendant who willfully and knowingly fails to appear and breaches a bond as specified in section 903.26, Florida Statutes, and who is arrested at any time following forfeiture shall not be eligible for a recognizance bond or any form of bond that does not require a monetary undertaking or commitment equal to or greater than $2,000 or twice the value of the monetary commitment or undertaking of the original bond, whichever is greater.

(d)　　Subsequent Application for Setting or Modification of Bail.

(1)　　When a judicial officer not possessing trial jurisdiction orders a defendant held to answer before a court having jurisdiction to try the defendant, and bail has been denied or sought to be modified, application by motion may be made to the court having jurisdiction to try the defendant or, in the absence of the judge of the trial court, to the circuit court. The motion shall be determined promptly. No judge or a court of equal or inferior jurisdiction may modify or set a condition of release, unless the judge:

(A)　　imposed the conditions of bail or set the amount of bond required;

(B)   is the chief judge of the circuit in which the defendant is to be tried;

(C)   has been assigned to preside over the criminal trial of the defendant; or

(D)   is the first appearance judge and was authorized by the judge initially setting or denying bail to modify or set conditions of release.

(2)   Applications by the defendant for modification of bail on any felony charge must be heard by a court in person at a hearing, with the defendant present and with at least 3 hours' notice to the state attorney and county attorney, if bond forfeiture proceedings are handled by the county attorney. The state may apply for modification of bail by showing good cause and with at least 3 hours' notice to the attorney for the defendant.

(3)   If any trial court fixes bail and refuses its reduction before trial, the defendant may institute habeas corpus proceedings seeking reduction of bail. If application is made to the supreme court or district court of appeal, notice and a copy of such application shall be given to the attorney general and the state attorney. Such proceedings shall be determined promptly.

(e)   **Bail Before Conviction; Condition of Undertaking.**

(1)   If a person is admitted to bail for appearance for a preliminary hearing or on a charge that a judge is empowered to try, the condition of the undertaking shall be that the person will appear for the hearing or to answer the charge and will submit to the orders and process of the judge trying the same and will not depart without leave.

(2)   If a person is admitted to bail after being held to answer by a judge or after an indictment or information on which the person is to be tried has been filed, the condition of the undertaking shall be that the person will appear to answer the charges before the court in which he or she may be prosecuted and submit to the orders and process of the court and will not depart without leave.

(f)   **Revocation of Bail.** The court in its discretion for good cause, any time after a defendant who is at large on bail appears for trial, may commit the defendant to the custody of the proper official to abide by the judgment, sentence, and any further order of the court.

(g)   **Arrest and Commitment by Court.** The court in which the cause is pending may direct the arrest and commitment of the defendant who is at large on bail when:

(1)   there has been a breach of the undertaking;

(2)   it appears that the defendant's sureties or any of them are dead or cannot be found or are insufficient or have ceased to be residents of the state; or

(3)   the court is satisfied that the bail should be increased or new

or additional security required.

The order for the commitment of the defendant shall recite generally the facts on which it is based and shall direct that the defendant be arrested by any official authorized to make arrests and that the defendant be committed to the official in whose custody he or she would be if he or she had not been given bail, to be detained by such official until legally discharged. The defendant shall be arrested pursuant to such order on a certified copy thereof, in any county, in the same manner as on a warrant of arrest. If the order provided for is made because of the failure of the defendant to appear for judgment, the defendant shall be committed. If the order is made for any other cause, the court may determine the conditions of release, if any.

(h) **Bail after Recommitment.** If the defendant applies to be admitted to bail after recommitment, the court that recommitted the defendant shall determine conditions of release, if any, subject to the limitations of (b) above.

(i) **Qualifications of Surety after Order of Recommitment.** If the defendant offers bail after recommitment, each surety shall possess the qualifications and sufficiency and the bail shall be furnished in all respects in the manner prescribed for admission to bail before recommitment.

(j) **Issuance of Capias; Bail Specified.** On the filing of either an indictment or information charging the commission of a crime, if the person named therein is not in custody or at large on bail for the offense charged, the judge shall issue or shall direct the clerk to issue, either immediately or when so directed by the prosecuting attorney, a capias for the arrest of the person. If the person named in the indictment or information is a child and the child has been served with a promise to appear under the Florida Rules of Juvenile Procedure, capias need not be issued. Upon the filing of the indictment or information, the judge shall endorse the amount of bail, if any, and may authorize the setting or modification of bail by the judge presiding over the defendant's first appearance hearing. This endorsement shall be made on the capias and signed by the judge.

(k) **Summons on Misdemeanor Charge.** When a complaint is filed charging the commission of a misdemeanor only and the judge deems that process should issue as a result, or when an indictment or information on which the defendant is to be tried charging the commission of a misdemeanor only, and the person named in it is not in custody or at large on bail for the offense charged, the judge shall direct the clerk to issue a summons instead of a capias unless the judge has reasonable ground to believe that the person will not appear in response to a summons, in which event an arrest warrant or a capias shall be issued with the amount of bail endorsed on it. The summons shall state substantially the nature of the offense and shall command the person against whom the complaint was made to appear before the judge issuing the summons or the judge having jurisdiction of the offense at a time and place stated in it.

(l) **Summons When Defendant Is Corporation.** On the filing of an indictment or information or complaint charging a corporation with the commission of a crime, whether felony or misdemeanor, the judge shall direct the clerk to issue or shall issue a summons to secure its appearance to answer the charge. If, after being summoned, the corporation does not appear, a plea of not guilty shall be entered and trial and judgment shall follow without further process.

Committee Notes

1968 Adoption. (a) Same as section 903.01, Florida Statutes.

(b)   Same as section 903.04, Florida Statutes.

(c)   Same as section 903.02, Florida Statutes.

(d)   Same as section 903.12, Florida Statutes.

(e)   Substantially same as section 903.13, Florida Statutes.

(f)   Same as section 903.19, Florida Statutes.

(g)   Same as section 918.01, Florida Statutes.

(h)   Substantially same as section 903.23, Florida Statutes.

(i)   Same as section 903.24, Florida Statutes.

(j)   Same as section 903.25, Florida Statutes.

(k) and (l)   Formerly rule 3.150(c). These proposals contain the essentials of present sections 907.01, 907.02, and 901.09(3), Florida Statutes, a change of some of the terminology being warranted for purpose of clarity.

(m)   Formerly rule 3.150(c). This proposal contains all of the essentials of section 907.03, Florida Statutes, and that part of section 901.14, Florida Statutes, pertaining to postindictment or postinformation procedure. A charge by affidavit is provided.
Although subdivision (g) is the same as section 918.01, Florida Statutes, its constitutionality was questioned by the subcommittee, constitutional right to bail and presumption of innocence.

1972 Amendment. Same as prior rule except (b), which is new. (k), (l), and (m) are taken from prior rule 3.150.

1977 Amendment. This proposal amends subdivision (b) (4) of the present rule [formerly rule 3.130(b) (4)] to expand the forms of pretrial release available to the judge. The options are the same as those available under the federal rules without the presumption in favor of release on personal recognizance or unsecured appearance.

This proposal leaves it to the sound discretion of the judge to determine the least onerous form of release which will still insure the defendant's appearance.

It also sets forth the specific factors the judge should take into account in making this determination.

1983 Amendment. Rule 3.131(d) is intended to replace former rule 3.130(f) and therefore contemplates all subsequent modifications of bail including all increases or reductions of monetary bail or any other changes sought by the state or by the defendant.

Court Comment

1977 Amendment. Subdivision (a) was repealed by Chapter 76-138, §2, Laws of Florida, insofar as it was inconsistent with the provision of that statute. Subdivision (a) has been amended so as to comply with the legislative act.

RULE 3.132. PRETRIAL DETENTION

(a) **Motion Filed at First Appearance.** A person arrested for an offense for which detention may be ordered under section 907.041, Florida Statutes, shall be taken before a judicial officer for a first appearance within 24 hours of arrest. The state may file with the judicial officer at first appearance a motion seeking pretrial detention, signed by the state attorney or an assistant, setting forth with particularity the grounds and the essential facts on which pretrial detention is sought and certifying that the state attorney has received testimony under oath supporting the grounds and the essential facts alleged in the motion. If no such motion is filed, the judicial officer may inquire whether the state intends to file a motion for pretrial detention, and if so, grant the state no more than three days to file a motion under this subdivision. Upon a showing by the state of probable cause that the defendant committed the offense and exigent circumstances, the defendant shall be detained in custody pending the filing of the motion. If, after inquiry, the State indicates it does not intend to file a motion for pretrial detention, or fails to establish exigent circumstances for holding defendant in custody pending the filing of the motion, or files a motion that is facially insufficient, the judicial officer shall proceed to determine the conditions of release pursuant to the provisions of rule 3.131(b). If the motion for pretrial detention is facially sufficient, the judicial officer shall proceed to determine whether there is probable cause that the person committed the offense. If probable cause is found, the person may be detained in custody pending a final hearing on pretrial detention. If probable cause is established after first appearance pursuant to the provisions of rule 3.133 and the person has been released from custody, the person may be recommitted to custody pending a final hearing on pretrial detention.

(b) **Motion Filed after First Appearance.** A motion for pretrial detention may be filed at any time prior to trial. The motion shall be made to the court with trial jurisdiction. On receipt of a facially sufficient motion and a determination of probable cause, unless otherwise previously established, that an offense eligible for pretrial detention has been committed, the following shall occur:

(1) In the event of exigent circumstances, the court shall issue a warrant for the arrest of the named person, if the person has been released from custody. The person may be detained in custody pending a final hearing on pretrial detention.

(2) In the absence of exigent circumstances, the court shall order a hearing on the motion as provided in (c) below.

(c) **Final Order.**

(1) **Hearing Required.** A final order of pretrial detention shall be entered only after a hearing in the court of trial jurisdiction. The hearing shall be held within 5 days of the filing of the motion or the date of taking the person in custody pursuant to a motion for pretrial detention, whichever is later. The state attorney has the burden of showing beyond a reasonable doubt the need for pretrial detention pursuant to the criteria in section 907.041, Florida Statutes. The defendant may request a continuance. The state shall

be entitled to 1 continuance for good cause. No continuance shall exceed 5 days unless there are extenuating circumstances. The defendant may be detained pending the hearing, but in no case shall the defendant be detained in excess of 10 days, unless the delay is sought by the defendant. The person sought to be detained is entitled to representation by counsel, to present witnesses and evidence, and to cross-examine witnesses. The court may admit relevant evidence and testimony under oath without complying with the rules of evidence, but evidence secured in violation of the United States Constitution or the Constitution of the State of Florida shall not be admissible. A final order of pretrial detention shall not be based exclusively on hearsay evidence. No testimony by the defendant shall be admissible to prove the guilt of the defendant at any other judicial proceeding, but may be admitted in an action for perjury based on the defendant's statements made at the pretrial detention hearing or for impeachment.

(2) **Findings and Conclusions to Be Recorded.** The court's pretrial detention order shall be based solely on evidence produced at the hearing and shall contain findings of fact and conclusions of law to support it. The order shall be made either in writing or orally on the record. The court shall render its findings within 24 hours of the pretrial detention hearing.

(3) **Dissolution of Order.** The defendant shall be entitled to dissolution of the pretrial detention order whenever the court finds that a subsequent event has eliminated the basis for detention.

(4) **Further Proceedings on Order.** If any trial court enters a final order of pretrial detention, the defendant may obtain review by motion to the appropriate appellate court. If motion for review is taken to the supreme court or the district court of appeal, notice and a copy of the motion shall be served on the attorney general and the state attorney; if review is taken to the circuit court, service shall be on the state attorney.

RULE 3.133. PRETRIAL PROBABLE CAUSE DETERMINATIONS AND ADVERSARY PRELIMINARY HEARINGS

(a) **Nonadversary Probable Cause Determination.**

(1) **Defendant in Custody.** In all cases in which the defendant is in custody, a nonadversary probable cause determination shall be held before a judge within 48 hours from the time of the defendant's arrest; provided, however, that this proceeding shall not be required when a probable cause determination has been previously made by a judge and an arrest warrant issued for the specific offense for which the defendant is charged. The judge after a showing of extraordinary circumstance may continue the proceeding for not more than 24 hours beyond the 48 hour period. The judge, after a showing that an extraordinary circumstance still exists, may continue the proceeding for not more than 24 additional hours following the expiration of the initial 24 hour continuance. This determination shall be made if the necessary proof is available at the time of the first appearance as required under rule 3.130, but the holding of this determination at that time shall not affect the fact that it is a nonadversary proceeding.

(2) **Defendant on Pretrial Release.** A defendant who has been released from custody before a probable cause determination is made and who is able to establish that the pretrial release conditions are a significant restraint on his or her liberty may file a written motion for a nonadversary probable cause determination setting forth with

specificity the items of significant restraint that a finding of no probable cause would eliminate. The motion shall be filed within 21 days from the date of arrest, and notice shall be given to the state. A judge who finds significant restraints on the defendant's liberty shall make a probable cause determination within 7 days from the filing of the motion.

(3)   **Standard of Proof.** Upon presentation of proof, the judge shall determine whether there is probable cause for detaining the arrested person pending further proceedings. The defendant need not be present. In determining probable cause to detain the defendant, the judge shall apply the standard for issuance of an arrest warrant, and the finding may be based on sworn complaint, affidavit, deposition under oath, or, if necessary, on testimony under oath properly recorded.

(4)   **Action on Determination.** If probable cause is found, the defendant shall be held to answer the charges. If probable cause is not found or the specified time periods are not complied with, the defendant shall be released from custody unless an information or indictment has been filed, in which event the defendant shall be released on recognizance subject to the condition that he or she appear at all court proceedings or shall be released under a summons to appear before the appropriate court at a time certain. Any release occasioned by a failure to comply with the specified time periods shall be by order of the judge on a written application filed by the defendant with notice sent to the state or by a judge without a written application but with notice to the state. The judge shall order the release of the defendant after it is determined that the defendant is entitled to release and after the state has a reasonable period of time, not to exceed 24 hours, in which to establish probable cause. A release required by this rule does not void further prosecution by information or indictment but does prohibit any restraint on liberty other than appearing for trial. A finding that probable cause does or does not exist shall be made in writing, signed by the judge, and filed, together with the evidence of such probable cause, with the clerk of the court having jurisdiction of the offense for which the defendant is charged.

(b)   Adversary Preliminary Hearing.

(1)   **When Applicable.** A defendant who is not charged in an information or indictment within 21 days from the date of arrest or service of the capias on him or her shall have a right to an adversary preliminary hearing on any felony charge then pending against the defendant. The subsequent filing of an information or indictment shall not eliminate a defendant's entitlement to this proceeding.

(2)   **Process.** The judge shall issue such process as may be necessary to secure attendance of witnesses within the state for the state or the defendant.

(3)   **Witnesses.** All witnesses shall be examined in the presence of the defendant and may be cross-examined. Either party may request that the witnesses be sequestered. At the conclusion of the testimony for the prosecution, the defendant who so elects shall be sworn and testify in his or her own behalf, and in such cases the defendant shall be warned in advance of testifying that anything he or she may say can be used against him or her at a subsequent trial. The defendant may be cross-examined in the same manner as other witnesses, and any witnesses offered by the defendant shall be sworn and examined.

(4)   **Record.** At the request of either party, the entire preliminary hearing, including all testimony, shall be recorded verbatim stenographically or by mechanical means and at the request of either party shall be transcribed. If the record of the

proceedings, or any part thereof, is transcribed at the request of the prosecuting attorney, a copy of this transcript shall be furnished free of cost to the defendant or the defendant's counsel.

(5)   Action on Hearing. If from the evidence it appears to the judge that there is probable cause to believe that an offense has been committed and that the defendant has committed it, the judge shall cause the defendant to be held to answer to the circuit court; otherwise, the judge shall release the defendant from custody unless an information or indictment has been filed, in which event the defendant shall be released on recognizance subject to the condition that he or she appear at all court proceedings or shall be released under a summons to appear before the appropriate court at a time certain. Such release does not, however, void further prosecution by information or indictment but does prohibit any restraint on liberty other than appearing for trial. A finding that probable cause does or does not exist shall be made in writing, signed by the judge, and, together with the evidence received in the cause, shall be filed with the clerk of the circuit court.

(c)   Additional Nonadversary Probable Cause Determinations and Preliminary Hearings. If there has been a finding of no probable cause at a nonadversary determination or adversary preliminary hearing, or if the specified time periods for holding a nonadversary probable cause determination have not been complied with, a judge may thereafter make a determination of probable cause at a nonadversary probable cause determination, in which event the defendant shall be retained in custody or returned to custody upon appropriate process issued by the judge. A defendant who has been retained in custody or returned to custody by such a determination shall be allowed an adversary preliminary hearing in all instances in which a felony offense is charged.

Committee Notes

1968 Adoption. (Notes are to former rule 1.122.)

(a)   Substantially the same as section 902.01, Florida Statutes; the word "examination" is changed to "hearing" to conform to modern terminology.

(b)   through (j)   Substantially the same as sections 902.02 through 902.10, 902.13, and 902.14, Florida Statutes, except for exchange of "hearing" for "examination."

(k)   Parts of section 902.11, Florida Statutes, and all of section 902.12, Florida Statutes, were omitted because of conflict with case law: *Escobedo v. Illinois*, 378 U.S. 478, 84 S.Ct. 1758, 12 L.Ed.2d 977 (1964); *White v. Maryland*, 373 U.S. 59, 83 S.Ct. 1050, 10 L.Ed.2d 193 (1963).

(l)   Taken from Federal Rule of Criminal Procedure 5(c). Previously Florida had no statute or rule defining what the magistrate should do at the conclusion of the preliminary hearing.

(m)   Substantially the same as section 902.18, Florida Statutes, except "without delay" changed to "within 7 days." Some specific time limit was felt necessary because of frequent delay by magistrates while defendants remain in jail.

1972 Amendment. The ABA Standards on Pre-Trial Release provide for a person arrested to be taken before a committing magistrate without unreasonable delay for immediate judicial consideration of the release decision. The committee determined that, since a determination of probable cause at this immediate hearing presents difficult logistical problems for the state and defense counsel, the question of probable cause should be decided at a later preliminary hearing. For this reason, subdivisions (c), (d), and (e) of the former rule have been deleted in favor of the hearing provision now contained in rule 3.130.

      (a)   A revised version of former rule 3.122(a).

      (b)   New. Establishes the time period in which the preliminary hearing must take place.

      (c)(1)   Substantially the same as former rule 3.122(b). Amended to provide for advice of counsel relative to waiver and for written waiver.

      (c)(2)   Amended to delete provisions relating to recording of proceedings as same are now contained in subdivision (h).

      (d)   Same as prior rule 3.122(g).

      (e)   Same as prior rule 3.122(h).

      (f)   Substantially the same as prior rule 3.122(i); language modernized by slight changes.

      (g)   Same as prior rule 3.122(j).

      (h)   New rule to provide for record of proceedings.

      (i)   Same as prior rule 3.122(l).

      (j)   Substantially the same as prior rule 3.122(m). Time period for transmission of papers is reduced. (2) provides for transmission of any transcript of proceedings.

1977 Amendment. The rule corrects several deficiencies in the prior rule:

      (1) In the prior rule no specific mechanism was provided to effect the release which is allowed. This revision provides such a mechanism and coordinates the mechanism with the additional procedures created by subdivision (c).

      (2) Once a determination of no probable cause was made and the defendant was released, no method was provided for reversing the process in those instances in which the determination is palpably in error or in instances in which it is later possible to establish probable cause.

      (3) The prior rule allowed the unconditioned release of a defendant without the possibility of recapture simply because of a technical failure to abide by the rather arbitrary time limits established for the conduct of a nonadversary probable cause determination and regardless of the ability to establish probable cause. The new rule allows a determination or redetermination of probable cause to be made in instances in which to do so is sensible. The defendant is protected by the provision allowing an adversary preliminary

hearing as a check against any possible abuse.

Court Comment

1975 Amendment. This is a complete rewrite of the preliminary hearing rule.

RULE 3.134. TIME FOR FILING FORMAL CHARGES

The state shall file formal charges on defendants in custody by information, or indictment, or in the case of alleged misdemeanors by whatever documents constitute a formal charge, within 30 days from the date on which defendants are arrested or from the date of the service of capiases upon them. If the defendants remain uncharged, the court on the 30th day and with notice to the state shall:

(1) Order that the defendants automatically be released on their own recognizance on the 33rd day unless the state files formal charges by that date; or

(2) If good cause is shown by the state, order that the defendants automatically be released on their own recognizance on the 40th day unless the state files formal charges by that date.

In no event shall any defendants remain in custody beyond 40 days unless they have been formally charged with a crime.

RULE 3.140. INDICTMENTS; INFORMATIONS

(a) **Methods of Prosecution.**

(1) **Capital Crimes.** An offense that may be punished by death shall be prosecuted by indictment.

(2) **Other Crimes.** The prosecution of all other criminal offenses shall be as follows:

In circuit courts and county courts, prosecution shall be solely by indictment or information, except that prosecution in county courts for violations of municipal ordinances and metropolitan county ordinances may be by affidavit or docket entries and prosecutions for misdemeanors, municipal ordinances, and county ordinances may be by notice to appear issued and served pursuant to rule 3.125. A grand jury may indict for any offense. When a grand jury returns an indictment for an offense not triable in the circuit court, the circuit judge shall either issue a summons returnable in the county court or shall bail the accused for trial in the county court, and the judge, or at the judge's direction, the clerk of the circuit court, shall certify the indictment and file it in the records of the county court.

(b) **Nature of Indictment or Information.** The indictment or information on which the defendant is to be tried shall be a plain, concise, and definite written statement of the essential facts constituting the offense charged.

(c) **Caption, Commencement, Date, and Personal Statistics.**

(1) **Caption.** No formal caption is essential to the validity of an indictment or information on which the defendant is to be tried. Upon objection made as to

its absence a caption shall be prefixed in substantially the following manner:

In the (name of court)

State of Florida versus (name of defendant)

or, in the case of municipal ordinance cases in county court,

City of _____ / _____ County versus (name of defendant).

Any defect, error, or omission in a caption may be amended as of course, at any stage of the proceeding, whether before or after a plea to the merits, by court order.

(2) **Commencement.** All indictments or informations on which the defendant is to be tried shall expressly state that the prosecution is brought in the name and by the authority of the State of Florida. Indictments shall state that the defendant is charged by the grand jury of the county. Informations shall state that the appropriate prosecuting attorney makes the charge.

(3) **Date.** Every indictment or information on which the defendant is to be tried shall bear the date (day, month, year) that it is filed in each court in which it is so filed.

(4) **Personal Statistics.** Every indictment or information shall include the defendant's race, gender, and date of birth when any of these facts are known. Failure to include these facts shall not invalidate an otherwise sufficient indictment or information.

(d) **The Charge.**

(1) **Allegation of Facts; Citation of Law Violated.** Each count of an indictment or information on which the defendant is to be tried shall allege the essential facts constituting the offense charged. In addition, each count shall recite the official or customary citation of the statute, rule, regulation, or other provision of law that the defendant is alleged to have violated. Error in or omission of the citation shall not be ground for dismissing the count or for a reversal of a conviction based thereon if the error or omission did not mislead the defendant to the defendant's prejudice.

(2) **Name of Accused.** The name of the accused person shall be stated, if known, and if not known, the person may be described by any name or description by which the person can be identified with reasonable certainty. If the grand jury, prosecuting attorney, or affiant making the charge does not know either the name of the accused or any name or description by which the accused can be identified with reasonable certainty, the indictment or information, as the case may be, shall so allege and the accused may be charged by a fictitious name.

(3) **Time and Place.** Each count of an indictment or information on which the defendant is to be tried shall contain allegations stating as definitely as possible the time and place of the commission of the offense charged in the act or transaction or on 2 or more acts or transactions connected together, provided the court in which the indictment or information is filed has jurisdiction to try all of the offenses charged.

(4) **Allegation of Intent to Defraud.** If an intent to defraud is required as an element of the offense to be charged, it shall be sufficient to allege an intent to defraud, without naming therein the particular person or body corporate intended to be defrauded.

(e) **Incorporation by Reference.** Allegations made in 1 count shall not be incorporated by reference in another count.

(f) **Endorsement and Signature; Indictment.** An indictment shall be signed by the foreperson or the acting foreperson of the grand jury returning it. The state attorney or acting state attorney or an assistant state attorney shall make and sign a statement on the indictment to the effect that he or she has advised the grand jury returning the indictment as authorized and required by law. No objection to the indictment on the ground that the statement has not been made shall be entertained after the defendant pleads to the merits.

(g) **Signature, Oath, and Certification; Information.** An information charging the commission of a felony shall be signed by the state attorney, or a designated assistant state attorney, under oath stating his or her good faith in instituting the prosecution and certifying that he or she has received testimony under oath from the material witness or witnesses for the offense. An information charging the commission of a misdemeanor shall be signed by the state attorney, or a designated assistant state attorney, under oath stating his or her good faith in instituting the prosecution. No objection to an information on the ground that it was not signed or verified, as herein provided, shall be entertained after the defendant pleads to the merits.

(h) **Conclusion.** An indictment or information on which the defendant is to be tried need contain no formal conclusion.

(i) **Surplusage.** An unnecessary allegation may be disregarded as surplusage and, on motion of the defendant, may be stricken from the pleading by the court.

(j) **Amendment of Information.** An information on which the defendant is to be tried that charges an offense may be amended on the motion of the prosecuting attorney or defendant at any time prior to trial because of formal defects.

(k) **Form of Certain Allegations.** Allegations concerning the following items may be alleged as indicated below:

(1) **Description of Written Instruments.** Instruments consisting wholly or in part of writing or figures, pictures, or designs may be described by any term by which they are usually known or may be identified, without setting forth a copy or facsimile thereof.

(2) **Words; Pictures.** Necessary averments relative to spoken or written words or pictures may be made by the general purport of such words or pictures without setting forth a copy or facsimile thereof.

(3) **Judgments; Determinations; Proceedings.** A judgment, determination, or proceeding of any court or official, civil or military, may be alleged generally in such a manner as to identify the judgment, determination, or proceeding, without alleging facts conferring jurisdiction on the court or official.

(4)   Exceptions; Excuses; Provisos. Statutory exceptions, excuses, or provisos relative to offenses created or defined by statute need not be negatived by allegation.

(5)   Alternative or Disjunctive Allegations. For an offense that may be committed by doing 1 or more of several acts, or by 1 or more of several means, or with 1 or more of several intents or results, it is permissible to allege in the disjunctive or alternative such acts, means, intents, or results.

(6)   Offenses Divided into Degrees. For an offense divided into degrees it is sufficient to charge the commission of the offense without specifying the degree.

(7)   Felonies. It shall not be necessary to allege that the offense charged is a felony or was done feloniously.

(l)   Custody of Indictment or Information. Unless the defendant named therein has been previously released on a citation, order to appear, personal recognizance, or bail, or has been summoned to appear, or unless otherwise ordered by the court having jurisdiction, all indictments or informations and the records thereof shall be in the custody of the clerk of the court to which they are presented and shall not be inspected by any person other than the judge, clerk, attorney general, and prosecuting attorney until the defendant is in custody or until 1 year has elapsed between the return of an indictment or the filing of an information, after which time they shall be opened for public inspection.

(m)   Defendant's Right to Copy of Indictment or Information. Each person who has been indicted or informed against for an offense shall, on application to the clerk, be furnished a copy of the indictment or information and the endorsements thereon, at least 24 hours before being required to plead to the indictment or information if a copy has not been so furnished. A failure to furnish a copy shall not affect the validity of any subsequent proceeding against the defendant if he or she pleads to the indictment or information.

(n)   Statement of Particulars. The court, on motion, shall order the prosecuting attorney to furnish a statement of particulars when the indictment or information on which the defendant is to be tried fails to inform the defendant of the particulars of the offense sufficiently to enable the defendant to prepare a defense. The statement of particulars shall specify as definitely as possible the place, date, and all other material facts of the crime charged that are specifically requested and are known to the prosecuting attorney, including the names of persons intended to be defrauded. Reasonable doubts concerning the construction of this rule shall be resolved in favor of the defendant.

(o)   Defects and Variances. No indictment or information, or any count thereof, shall be dismissed or judgment arrested, or new trial granted on account of any defect in the form of the indictment or information or of misjoinder of offenses or for any cause whatsoever, unless the court shall be of the opinion that the indictment or information is so vague, indistinct, and indefinite as to mislead the accused and embarrass him or her in the preparation of a defense or expose the accused after conviction or acquittal to substantial danger of a new prosecution for the same offense.

Committee Notes

1968 Adoption. Introductory Statement: The contention may be made that the authority of the Supreme Court of Florida to govern practice and procedure in all courts by court rule does not include the power to vary in any way from present statutory law governing the work product of the grand jury, viz., the indictment. Such a contention must, of necessity, be based in part, at least, upon the assumption that the grand jury is not an integral part of the judicial system of Florida but is a distinct entity which serves that system. The Supreme Court of Florida, in State v. Clemons, 150 So.2d 231 (Fla. 1963), seems to have taken a position contrary to such an assumption.

Regardless of whether such a contention is valid, it seems beyond controversy that the essentials of the indictment, as in the case of an information, are so intimately associated with practice and procedure in the courts that the individual or group having the responsibility of determining its makeup and use is thus empowered to govern a substantial segment of such practice and procedure. The conclusion seems to be inescapable, therefore, that, since the constitution grants to the supreme court authority over this phase of the judicial scheme, the following material is appropriate for consideration as a part of the proposed rules:

(a)(1) **Capital Crimes.** This recommendation is consistent with present Florida law. See §10 DR, Fla. Const. (1885, as amended) (now Art. I, §15, Fla. Const. (1968 as amended)); § 904.01, Fla. Stat. (1963). The terminology "which may be punished by death" is deemed preferable to the terminology "capital crime" of the constitution and "capital offenses" of the statute because of its definitive nature. The recommended terminology is utilized in Federal Rule of Criminal Procedure 7(a) and in the American Law Institute's Code of Criminal Procedure, section 115. The terminology used in the 1963 Code of Criminal Procedure of Illinois is "when death is a possible punishment." See §110 4.

Section 10, DR, Florida Constitution, provides: "No person shall be tried for a capital crime unless on presentment or indictment by a grand jury." No provision is made in the recommendation for prosecution by presentment. This omission is consistent with the apparent legislative construction placed on this section.
Section 904.01, Florida Statutes, provides "All capital offenses shall be tried by indictment by a grand jury." Since presentments traditionally have not been used as trial accusatorial writs in Florida, there seems little reason, at this date, to question that the constitution authorizes the implementing authority, be it the legislature or the supreme court, to use one of the specified methods of prosecution to the exclusion of the other.

(a)(2) **Other Crimes.** In criminal courts of record and the Court of Record of Escambia County, the constitution of Florida requires that prosecutions be by information. (§§9 (5) & 10, Art. V). In county judges' courts having elective prosecuting attorneys, present statutory law permits prosecutions by indictment (§904.02) and affidavit (Ch. 937). The additional method of prosecution by information is provided as a step toward attaining uniformity with other courts in the prosecution of noncapital offenses, at least to the extent that a prosecutor desires to use an information. This addition involved consideration of whether a nonelected prosecutor serving in a county judge's court, which often is the case, has the authority to use an information as an accusatorial writ. Since this question has not been definitely resolved under present law, caution dictated the specification that the prosecuting attorney be elected as a prerequisite to the use of an information.

48

In all courts not hereinabove mentioned that have elective prosecuting attorneys, trial by indictment or information is consistent with present Florida constitutional law and most of the statutory law. (See §10, DR, Fla. Const., §§904.01 & 904.02, Fla. Stat.; cf. §932.56, where an affidavit may be used in cases appealed from a justice of the peace court and which is tried de novo in a circuit court.) In specially created courts having elective prosecutors and which are not otherwise provided for in foregoing provisions of this rule, it was felt that prosecution by indictment or information should be allowed, even though present statutory authority may limit prosecutions in such courts to the use of an information, e.g., the Court of Record of Alachua County.

In courts not having elective prosecutors, prosecution by information is not recommended because of the aforementioned doubt as to the authority of a nonelected prosecutor to use an information as an accusatorial writ. With reference to the present court structure of Florida this part of the proposal applies only to county judges' courts and justice of the peace courts. The only variation from present procedure contemplated by this part of the proposal is the use of an indictment as a basis for prosecution in a justice of the peace court.

Under this proposal a grand jury may indict for any criminal offense. This recommendation is based on the premise that a grand jury's power to indict should not be limited by virtue of levels in a state court structure. A grand jury should be considered as a guardian of the public peace against all criminal activity and should be in a position to act directly with reference thereto. While practicalities dictate that most non-capital felonies and misdemeanors will be tried by information or affidavit, if appropriate, even if an indictment is permissible as an alternative procedure, it is well to retain the grand jury's check on prosecutors in this area of otherwise practically unrestricted discretion.

The procedure proposed for the circuit judge to follow if a grand jury returns an indictment for an offense not triable in the circuit court applies, with appropriate variations, much of the procedure presently used when a grand jury returns an indictment triable in a criminal court of record. See §32.18, Fla. Stat.

(b) **Nature of Indictment or Information.** This provision appears in rule 7(c) of the Rules of Criminal Procedure for the United States District Court (hereafter referred to as the federal rules for purposes of brevity). It may be deemed appropriate for incorporation into the recommendations since it preserves to the defendant expressly the right to a formal written accusation and at the same time permits the simplification of the form of the accusation and the elimination of unnecessary phraseology.

(c) **Caption, Commencement, and Date.**

(1) Caption. Section 906.02, Florida Statutes, contains the essentials of this proposal. It is well settled at common law that the caption is no part of the indictment and that it may be amended. The caption may be considered as serving the purpose of convenience by making more readily identifiable a particular accusatorial writ. The proposal makes it possible for this convenience to be served if either party wishes it, yet does not provide that the caption be a matter of substance. The essentials of this recommendation also appear in section 149 of the American Law Institute's Code of Criminal Procedure.

(2) Commencement. This proposal apparently is directly contrary to section 906.02(1), Florida Statutes, which treats the caption and the commencement in the same manner, i.e., that neither is necessary to the validity of the indictment or information but may be present as mere matters of convenience. This legislative assumption may not be a correct one and caution dictates that a meaningful commencement be included. Section 20, article V, of the Constitution of Florida provides that the style of all process shall be: "The State of Florida' and all prosecutions shall be conducted in the name and by the authority of the State." As contemplated in the proposal, the commencement expressly states the sovereign authority by which the accusatorial writ is issued and the agent of that authority. Section 906.02 (2), Florida Statutes, seems to contemplate that there will be included in the indictment an express provision concerning the agency of the state responsible for its presentation, viz., the grand jury, by stating, "It is unnecessary to allege that the grand jurors were empaneled, sworn or charged, or that they present the indictment upon their oaths or affirmations." The American Law Institute's commentary on the commencement (A.L.I. Code of Criminal Procedure, p. 529 et seq.) indicates that there is much confusion between what information should be in the commencement as distinguished from the caption.

(3) **Date.** Since in many cases the beginning of the prosecution is co-existent with the issuance of the indictment or information, the date the writ bears may be of great significance, particularly with reference to the tolling of a statute of limitations. If the date of a grand jury's vote of a true bill or a prosecutor's making
oath to an information differs from the date of filing of the indictment or information with the appropriate clerk, it seems the date of filing is the preferable date for a writ to bear since until the filing transpires there is no absolute certainty that the prosecution actually will leave the province of the grand jury or prosecutor.

(d)   **The Charge.**

(1) **Allegation of Facts; Citation of Law Violated.** This proposal is consistent with various sections of chapter 906, Florida Statutes, in that the charge is adequately alleged when based on the essentials of the offense; surplusage should be guarded against. The citation of the law allegedly violated contributes to defining the charge and conserves time in ascertaining the exact nature of the charge. The 1963 Illinois Criminal Code, section 111-3(a)(2), and Federal Rule of Criminal Procedure 7(c) contain similar provisions.

(2) **Name of Accused.** The provision concerning the method of stating the name of the accused is consistent with the very elaborate section 906.08, Florida Statutes, which seems unnecessarily long. It is deemed desirable that when a fictitious name is used the necessity therefor should be indicated by allegation.

(3) **Time and Place.** This provision is consistent with present Florida law. (See Morgan v. State, 51 Fla. 76, 40 So. 828 (1906), as to "time"; see Rimes v. State, 101 Fla. 1322, 133 So. 550 (1931), as to "place".) The provision is patterned after section 111-3(4) of the 1963 Illinois Code of Criminal Procedure.

(4) **Joinder of Offenses.** The essence of this proposal is presently found in section 906.25, Florida Statutes, federal rule 8(a), and section 111-4(a) of the 1963 Illinois Code of Criminal Procedure.

(5) **Joinder of Defendants.** This proposal is taken from federal rule 8(b). Its substance also appears in section 111-4(b) of the Illinois Code of Criminal Procedure. Although section 906.25, Florida Statutes, does not expressly contain this provision, there is little doubt that its broad language includes it.

(6) Allegation of Intent to Defraud. The language of this proposal presently appears in section 906.18, Florida Statutes, except for the provision concerning affidavit. Its continuation seems advisable as an aid to drawing allegations in charging instruments, although such information if known to the prosecutor may be required to be given in a bill of particulars upon motion of the defendant. (See subdivision (n) of this rule.) At times such information may be unknown to the prosecutor. A part of the statute is purposely not included in the proposal. The excluded part states "and on the trial it shall be sufficient, and shall not be deemed a variance, if there appear to be an intent to defraud the United States or any state, county, city, town or parish, or any body corporate, or any public officer in his official capacity, or any copartnership or members thereof, or any particular person." It seems that this part of the statute is stated in terms of the law of evidence rather than practice and procedure and should not be included in the rules, although apparently being a logical conclusion from the part included in the proposal.

(e)   Incorporation by Reference. Although provision for incorporation by reference appears in federal rule 7(c), the prohibition of such incorporation is recommended with the thought that even though repetition may be minimized by incorporation, confusion, vagueness, and misunderstanding may be fostered by such procedure.

(f)   Endorsement and Signature; Indictment. The requirement that the indictment be endorsed "A true bill" and be signed by the foreman or acting foreman of the grand jury presently appears in section 905.23, Florida Statutes. There apparently is no valid reason for changing this requirement since it serves the useful purpose of lending authenticity to the indictment as a legal product of the grand jury. The requirement of the foreman's signature also appears in federal rule 6(c), 1963, Illinois CCP section 111-3(b), and A.L.I. Model Code of Criminal Procedure section 125.

The provision pertaining to the statement and signature of the prosecuting attorney varies from present Florida law and is offered in alternative form. Florida statutes presently provide that an indictment shall be signed by a state attorney (§§27.21 & 27.22). Federal rule 7(c) also provides for the signature of the attorney for the government.

No requirement presently is made in Florida necessitating an express explanatory statement preceding such signature. Presumably the justification for the signature appears in the Florida statutes that require the aforementioned officers to wait upon the grand jury as advisors, as examiners of witnesses, and to draw indictments. (See §§905.16, 905.17, 905.19, 905.22, 27.02, 27.16, 27.21, & 27.22, Fla. Stat.)

Vagueness remains concerning the significance of the signature, however. Since the prosecuting attorney cannot be present while the grand jury is deliberating or voting (see section 905.17, Florida Statutes) and has no voice in the decision of whether an indictment is found (see section 905.26, Florida Statutes), a logical question arises concerning the necessity for the prosecuting attorney's signature on the indictment. The provision for the statement is made for the purpose of clarifying the reason for the signature.

(g)   Signature, Oath, and Certification; Information. Section 10, DR, Florida Constitution, requires that informations be under oath of the prosecuting attorney of the court in which the information is filed. Article V, section 9   (5),   Florida Constitution, contains the same requirement concerning informations filed by the prosecuting attorney in a criminal court of record. This proposal also does not deviate from present Florida statutory law as found in section 906.04, Florida Statutes. This statute has received judicial approval. (See *Champlin v. State*, 122 So.2d 412 (Fla. 2d DCA 1960).) It should be noted here that the prosecutor's statement under oath is defined as to the purpose served by the signature.

(h)　　**Conclusion.** A similar provision currently appears in section 906.03, Florida Statutes, and should be included in the rules because of its tendency to minimize unnecessary statements in accusatorial writs. Provision is added for the affidavit as an accusatorial writ.

(i)　　**Surplusage.** The first part of the proposal, providing for the disregarding of unnecessary allegations as surplusage, is similar to section 906.24, Florida Statutes. The part concerned with striking such material is patterned after federal rule 7(d). The parts are properly complementary.

(j)　　**Amendment of Information.** This proposal contains no provision for an amendment of an indictment since, presumably, a grand jury may not amend an indictment which it has returned and which is pending, although it may return another indictment and the first indictment may be disposed of by a nolle prosequi. (See 17 Fla. Jur. Indictments and Informations, 9 (1958).) A federal indictment cannot be amended without reassembling the grand jury (*see Ex parte Bain*, 121 U.S. 1 (1887)); consequently the federal rules contain no provision for the amendment of an indictment. (It may be that the Supreme Court of Florida will feel inclined to include in the rules an express statement concerning amendments of an indictment. None is included here, however.)

The proposal is patterned after section 111-5 of the 1963 Illinois Code of Criminal Procedure, with one exception. The exception arises due to the fact that the Illinois Code provision applies to indictments as well as informations, the position in Illinois apparently being assumed that an indictment may be amended, at least with reference to specified items listed in the statute, as well as other formalities.

(k)　　**Form of Certain Allegations.** Several statutes in chapter 906, Florida Statutes, are concerned with the manner of making allegations in indictments and informations. Some of these sections are of such general application that it seems advisable to include their substance in the rules; others are so restricted that it may be deemed appropriate to recommend other disposition of them.

The proposals made in (1) through (7) here are based on the substance of the designated Florida

Proposal (1):　　section 906.09.

Proposal (2):　　section 906.10.

Proposal (3):　　section 906.11.

Proposal (4):　　section 906.12.

Proposal (5):　　section 906.13.

Proposal (6):　　section 906.23.

Proposal (7):　　section 906.17.

(l) **Custody and Inspection.** The proposal is taken verbatim from section 906.27, Florida Statutes. The necessity for specific provision for the custody and inspection of accusatorial writs seems to be proper to include here.

(m) **Defendant's Right to Copy of Indictment or Information.** The procedure contained in this proposal is presently required under section 906.28, Florida Statutes, and seems to be unobjectionable.

(n) **Statement of Particulars.** The phrase, "bill of particulars," has been modernized by changing
"bill" to "statement." Historically, a "bill" is a written statement. The first sentence of this proposal is taken from section 906.27, Florida Statutes, the only change being the narrowing of the scope of the judicial discretion now granted by the statute. The latter part of the proposal is recommended in order to clarify the requirements of the rule. Provision for the accusatorial affidavit has been added.

(o) **Defects and Variances.** This proposal presently appears in Florida law in the form of section 906.25, Florida Statutes. The statute has been the object of much judicial construction and it seems inadvisable to divide it into parts merely for convenience in placing these parts under more appropriate titles, such as "Pre- Trial Motions," "Motion for New Trial," etc.

The intimate relation the statute has with indictments and informations justifies its inclusion here. The useful purposes served by the court constructions dictate the use of the statutory language without change.

1972 Amendment. Substantially the same as prior rule. References to trial by affidavit have been deleted throughout this rule and all Florida Rules of Criminal Procedure because of the passage of the 1972 amendment to article V of the Florida Constitution.

(a) (2) Amended to refer only to circuit courts and county courts. Reference to trial of vehicular traffic offenses transferred to rule 3.010 and made applicable to all rules of criminal procedure.

Former rule (d)(4) and (d)(5) transferred to new rule 3.150. Former rule (d)(6) renumbered as (d)(4).

1973 Amendment. The purpose of the amendment is to provide the same method for prosecution of violations of metropolitan county ordinances as for violations of municipal ordinances.

RULE 3.150. JOINDER OF OFFENSES AND DEFENDANTS

(a) **Joinder of Offenses.** Two or more offenses that are triable in the same court may be charged in the same indictment or information in a separate count for each offense, when the offenses, whether felonies or misdemeanors, or both, are based on the same act or transaction or on 2 or more connected acts or transactions.

(b) **Joinder of Defendants.** Two or more defendants may be charged in the same indictment or information on which they are to be tried when:

(1)   each defendant is charged with accountability for each offense charged;

(2)   each defendant is charged with conspiracy and some of the defendants are also charged with 1 or more offenses alleged to have been committed in furtherance of the conspiracy; or

(3)   even if conspiracy is not charged and all defendants are not charged in each count, it is alleged that the several offenses charged were part of a common scheme or plan.

Such defendants may be charged in 1 or more counts together or separately, and all of the defendants need not be charged in each count.

(c)   **Joint Representation.** When 2 or more defendants have been jointly charged under rule 3.150(b) or have been joined for trial and are represented by the same attorney or by attorneys who are associated in the practice of law, the court shall, as soon as practicable, inquire into such joint representation and shall personally advise each defendant of the right to effective assistance of counsel, including separate representation. The court shall take such measures as are necessary to protect each defendant's right to counsel.

Committee Notes

1968 Adoption. (Notes are to rule 1.140(d)(4) and (5).)

(4)   **Joinder of Offenses.** The essence of this proposal is presently found in section 906.25, Florida Statutes, federal rule 8(a), and section 111-4(a) of the 1963 Illinois Code of Criminal Procedure.

(5)   **Joinder of Defendants.** This proposal is taken from federal rule 8(b). Its substance also appears in section 111-4(b) of the Illinois Code of Criminal Procedure. While section 906.25, Florida Statutes, does not expressly contain this provision, there is little doubt that its broad language includes it.

1972 Amendment. Provisions of former rule 3.150 are transferred to and incorporated in rule 3.130, Pretrial Release.

(a)   Substantially the same as former rule 3.140(d)(4) except that it omits proviso that the court have jurisdiction to try all offenses charged. The proviso seems redundant.

(b)   Substantially the same as ABA Standard 1.2 of ABA Standards Relating to Joinder and Severance but omits sub-paragraph (c)(2) which would permit joinder of charges "so closely connected in respect to time, place, and occasion that it would be difficult to separate proof of one charge from proof of the others." The ABA commentary on this standard concedes that in such cases the chances are considerable that defendants would have a right to severance. Difficulty of separating proof is a good reason for denying a right to join charges. The committee is of the opinion that defendants not connected in the commission of an act and not connected by conspiracy or by common scheme or plan should not, under any circumstances, be joined. The suggested rule omits the provision of former rule 3.140(d)(4) permitting joinder of 2 or more defendants in a single indictment or information, if they are alleged to have participated in the same series of acts or transactions constituting more than 1 offense. If all defendants participated in a series of connected acts or transactions constituting 2 or more offenses, the offenses can be joined under rule 3.150(a).

The last sentence of the suggested rule is the last sentence of former rule 3.140(d)(5).

2004 Amendment. This rule is intended to provide a uniform procedure for judges to follow when codefendants are represented by the same attorney, by the same law firm, or by attorneys who are associated in the practice of law. This provision is substantially derived from Rule 44, Fed. R. Crim. P. See also *Larzelere v. State*, 676 So. 2d 394 (Fla. 1996).

Court Commentary

2004 Amendment. Like Federal Rule of Criminal Procedure 44(c), new subdivision (c) does not specify the particular measures that the court must take to protect a defendant's right to counsel. Because the measures that will best protect a defendant's right to counsel can vary from case to case, this determination is left within the court's discretion. One possible course of action is to advise the defendant of the possible conflict of interest that could arise from dual representation and to obtain a voluntary, knowing, and intelligent waiver of the right to obtain separate representation. See *Larzelere v. State*, 676 So. 2d 394 (Fla. 1996). Another option is to require separate representation. See Fed. R. Crim. P. 44(c) advisory committee notes 1979 amendment.

RULE 3.151. CONSOLIDATION OF RELATED OFFENSES

(a)   **Related Offenses.** For purposes of these rules, 2 or more offenses are related offenses if they are triable in the same court and are based on the same act or transaction or on 2 or more connected acts or transactions.

(b)   **Consolidation of Indictments or Informations.** Two or more indictments or informations charging related offenses shall be consolidated for trial on a timely motion by a defendant or by the state. The procedure thereafter shall be the same as if the prosecution were under a single indictment or information. Failure to timely move for consolidation constitutes a waiver of the right to consolidation.

(c)   **Dismissal of Related Offenses after Trial.** When a defendant has been tried on a charge of 1 of 2 or more related offenses, the charge of every other related offense shall be dismissed on the defendant's motion unless a motion by the defendant for consolidation of the charges has been previously denied, or unless the defendant has waived the right to consolidation, or unless the prosecution has been unable, by due diligence, to obtain sufficient evidence to warrant charging the other offense or offenses.

(d)   **Plea.** A defendant may plead guilty or nolo contendere to a charge of 1 offense on the condition that other charges of related offenses be dismissed or that no charges of other related offenses be instituted. Should the court find that the condition cannot be fulfilled, the plea shall be considered withdrawn.

Committee Notes

1968 Adoption. This rule is almost the same as federal rule 13, with provisions added for trial by affidavit.

1972 Amendment. (a) To same general effect as ABA Standard with changes to conform to rules 3.150(a) and 3.190(k).

(b)　　　Limits motion for consolidation to defendant and provides that defendant waives his or her right to consolidation by failing to file a timely motion. Under standards relating to joinder of offenses and defendants, the prosecution may avoid the necessity for consolidation by charging offenses and defendants in a single indictment or information where consolidation is permissible. Omits provision of ABA Standard authorizing denial of consolidation if prosecuting attorney does not have "sufficient evidence to warrant trying" 1 of the "offenses" or if the court finds that the ends of justice would be defeated by consolidation. The lack of "sufficient evidence to warrant" trial of 1 of several charges of "related offenses" would be quite rare. In the rare case in which there is such a lack of evidence, the appropriate remedy would be a motion for continuance of all pending charges of related offenses, showing that the lack of evidence could probably be cured by a reasonable delay. The committee does not favor separate trials of charges of related offenses over the defendant's objection.

(c)　　　Florida has no similar rule. Omits exception in ABA Standard in case "the prosecuting attorney did not have sufficient evidence to warrant trying (the) offense" or upon a finding that "the ends of justice would be defeated if the motion was granted." See comment on (b). The rule is not intended to restrict defendant's substantive rights.

(d)　　　Florida has no similar rule. The first sentence of ABA Standard is considered by the committee to state a rule of substantive law and is omitted as unnecessary.

1977 Amendment. The changes from the prior rule are intended to provide equal treatment for both the state and the defendant.

RULE 3.152. SEVERANCE OF OFFENSES AND DEFENDANTS

(a)　　　Severance of Offenses.

(1)　　　In case 2 or more offenses are improperly charged in a single indictment or information, the defendant shall have a right to a severance of the charges on timely motion.

(2)　　　In case 2 or more charges of related offenses are joined in a single indictment or information, the court nevertheless shall grant a severance of charges on motion of the state or of a defendant:

(A)　　　before trial on a showing that the severance is appropriate to promote a fair determination of the defendant's guilt or innocence of each offense; or

(B)　　　during trial, only with defendant's consent, on a showing that the severance is necessary to achieve a fair determination of the defendant's guilt or innocence of each offense.

(b)　　　Severance of Defendants.

(1)　　　On motion of the state or a defendant, the court shall order a severance of defendants and separate trials:

      (A)   before trial, on a showing that the order is necessary to protect a defendant's right to a speedy trial, or is appropriate to promote a fair determination of the guilt or innocence of 1 or more defendants; or

      (B)   during trial, only with defendant's consent and on a showing that the order is necessary to achieve a fair determination of the guilt or innocence of 1 or more defendants.

      (2)   If a defendant moves for a severance of defendants on the ground that an oral or written statement of a codefendant makes reference to him or her but is not admissible against him or her, the court shall determine whether the state will offer evidence of the statement at the trial. If the state intends to offer the statement in evidence, the court shall order the state to submit its evidence of the statement for consideration by the court and counsel for defendants and if the court determines that the statement is not admissible against the moving defendant, it shall require the state to elect 1 of the following courses:

      (A)   a joint trial at which evidence of the statement will not be admitted;

      (B)   a joint trial at which evidence of the statement will be admitted after all references to the moving defendant have been deleted, provided the court determines that admission of the evidence with deletions will not prejudice the moving defendant; or

      (C)   severance of the moving defendant.

      (3)   In cases in which, at the close of the state's case or at the close of all of the evidence, the evidence is not sufficient to support a finding that allegations on which the joinder of a defendant is based have been proved, the court shall, on motion of that defendant, grant a severance unless the court finds that severance is unnecessary to achieve a fair determination of that defendant's guilt or innocence.

Committee Notes

1968 Adoption. This subdivision rewords and adds to federal rule 14. It covers subject matter of section 918.02, Florida Statutes.

1972 Amendment. (a)(1) Severance on timely motion by defendant is mandatory if multiple offenses are improperly joined.

(a)(2) Provides for severance of offenses before trial on showing that severance will promote a fair determination of guilt or innocence substantially as provided by former rule 3.190(j)(2) and, unlike any Florida rule, distinguishes motion during trial.

(b)(1)Based on ABA Standard 2.3(b). Expands rule 3.190(j) to include defendant's right to speedy trial as ground for severance and, unlike any Florida rule, distinguishes between motion before and motion during trial.

(b)(2)   Based on ABA Standard 2.3, subparagraphs (a) and (c). Requires court to determine whether the statement will be offered as distinguished from asking the state its intention. Requires production of evidence of the statement in the event it will be offered so that the court and counsel can intelligently deal with the problem. Florida has no similar rule.

(b)(3)   Substantially the same as ABA Standard, except that the proposed rule requires severance unless the court affirmatively finds that severance is unnecessary. Florida has no similar rule.

RULE 3.153. TIMELINESS OF DEFENDANT'S MOTION; WAIVER

(a)   **Timeliness; Waiver.** A defendant's motion for severance of multiple offenses or defendants charged in a single indictment or information shall be made before trial unless opportunity therefor did not exist or the defendant was not aware of the grounds for such a motion, but the court in its discretion may entertain such a motion at the trial. The right to file such a motion is waived if it is not timely made.

(b)   **Renewal of Motion.** If a defendant's pretrial motion for severance is overruled, the defendant may renew the motion on the same grounds at or before the close of all the evidence at the trial.

Committee Notes

1972 Adoption. (a) Relates solely to defendant's motion for severance. Florida has no similar rule.

(b)   Florida has no similar rule.

IV.   ARRAIGNMENT AND PLEAS

RULE 3.160. ARRAIGNMENT

(a)   **Nature of Arraignment.** The arraignment shall be conducted in open court or by audiovisual device in the discretion of the court and shall consist of the judge or clerk or prosecuting attorney reading the indictment or information on which the defendant will be tried to the defendant or stating orally to the defendant the substance of the charge or charges and calling on the defendant to plead thereto. The reading or statement as to the charge or charges may be waived by the defendant. If the defendant is represented by counsel, counsel may file a written plea of not guilty at or before arraignment and thereupon arraignment shall be deemed waived.

(b)   **Effect of Failure to Arraign or Irregularity of Arraignment.** Neither a failure to arraign nor an irregularity in the arraignment shall affect the validity of any proceeding in the cause if the defendant pleads to the indictment or information on which the defendant is to be tried or proceeds to trial without objection to such failure or irregularity.

(c)   **Plea of Guilty after Indictment or Information Filed.** If a person who has been indicted or informed against for an offense, but who has not been arraigned, desires to plead guilty thereto, the person may so inform the court having jurisdiction of the offense, and the court shall, as soon as convenient, arraign the defendant and permit the defendant to plead guilty to the indictment or information.

(d)   Time to Prepare for Trial. After a plea of not guilty the defendant is entitled to a reasonable time in which to prepare for trial.

(e)   Defendant Not Represented by Counsel. Prior to arraignment of any person charged with the commission of a crime, if he or she is not represented by counsel, the court shall advise the person of the right to counsel and, if he or she is financially unable to obtain counsel, of the right to be assigned court-appointed counsel to represent him or her at the arraignment and at all subsequent proceedings. The person shall execute an affidavit that he or she is unable financially or otherwise to obtain counsel, and if the court shall determine the reason to be true, the court shall appoint counsel to represent the person.

If the defendant, however, understandingly waives representation by counsel, he or she shall execute a written waiver of such representation, which shall be filed in the case. If counsel is appointed, a reasonable time shall be accorded to counsel before the defendant shall be required to plead to the indictment or information on which he or she is to be arraigned or tried, or otherwise to proceed further.

Committee Notes

1968 Adoption. (a) A combination of section 908.01, Florida Statutes, and Federal Rule of Criminal Procedure 10.

(b)   Same as section 908.02, Florida Statutes.

(c)   Same as section 909.15, Florida Statutes, except provision is made for trial by affidavit.

(d)   Same as section 909.20, Florida Statutes.

(e)   Federal rule 44 provides:

"If the defendant appears in court without counsel the court shall advise him of his right to counsel and assign counsel to represent him at every stage of the proceeding unless he elects to proceed without counsel or is able to obtain counsel."

A presently proposed amendment to such rule provides:

"(a)   Right to Assigned Counsel. Every defendant who is unable to obtain counsel shall be entitled to have counsel assigned to represent him at every stage of the proceedings from his initial appearance before the commissioner or the court through appeal, unless he waives such appointment.

"(b)   Assignment Procedure. The procedures for implementing the right set out in subdivision (a) shall be those provided by law or by local rules of district courts of appeal."

In lieu of such latter, blanket provision, it is suggested that the rule provide, as stated, for inquiry of the defendant and determination by the court as to the defendant's desire for and inability to obtain counsel, after being advised of entitlement thereto. Many defendants, of course, will waive counsel.

In view of *Harvey v. Mississippi*, 340 F.2d 263 (5th Cir. 1965), and *White v. Maryland*, 373 U.S. 59, 83 S.Ct. 1050, 10 L.Ed.2d 193 (1963), holding that entitlement to counsel does not depend upon whether the offense charged is a felony or misdemeanor, it is suggested that the word "crime" be used instead of "felony" only in the first sentence of the proposed rule.

In *Hamilton v. Alabama*, 368 U.S. 52, 82 S.Ct. 157, 7 L.Ed.2d 114 (1961), involving breaking and entering with intent to commit rape, the Supreme Court held the defendant was entitled to counsel at the arraignment, if the arraignment be deemed a part of the trial, as apparently it is under Alabama law. *In Ex parte Jeffcoat*, 109 Fla. 207, 146 So. 827 (1933), the Supreme Court of Florida held the arraignment to be a mere formal preliminary step to an answer or plea. However, in *Sardinia v. State*, 168 So.2d 674 (Fla. 1964), the court recognized the accused's right to counsel upon arraignment. Section 909.21, Florida Statutes, provides for appointment of counsel in capital cases.

1972 Amendment. Substantially the same as prior rule. The committee considered changes recommended by The Florida Bar and incorporated the proposed change relating to written plea of not guilty and waiver of arraignment.

1992 Amendment. The amendment allows the judge to participate in the arraignment process by including the judge as one of the designated individuals who may advise the defendant of the pending charges. Apparently, the 1988 amendment to rule 3.160(a) inadvertently eliminated the judge from the arraignment procedure. *In re Rule 3.160(a), Florida Rules of Criminal Procedure*, 528 So.2d 1179, 1180 (Fla. 1988). The prior amendment did include the judge. *The Florida Bar Re: Amendment to Rules — Criminal Procedure*, 462 So.2d 386 (Fla. 1984). While the language of rule 3.160(a) as presently set out in the Florida Bar pamphlet, Florida Rules of Criminal Procedure, is identical to the language of this proposed amendment (that is, it includes the judge in the arraignment process), the West publications, Florida Criminal Laws and Rules (1991) and Florida Rules of Court (1991), nevertheless follow the language set out in 528 So.2d at 1180.

RULE 3.170. PLEAS

(a) **Types of Plea; Court's Discretion.** A defendant may plead not guilty, guilty, or, with the consent of the court, nolo contendere. Except as otherwise provided by these rules, all pleas to a charge shall be in open court and shall be entered by the defendant. If the sworn complaint charges the commission of a misdemeanor, the defendant may plead guilty to the charge at the first appearance under rule 3.130, and the judge may thereupon enter judgment and sentence without the necessity of any further formal charges being filed. A plea of not guilty may be entered in writing by counsel. Every plea shall be entered of record, but a failure to enter it shall not affect the validity of any proceeding in the cause.

(b) **Pleading to Other Charges.** Having entered a plea in accordance with this rule, the defendant may, with the court's permission, enter a plea of guilty or nolo contendere to any and all charges pending against him or her in the State of Florida over which the court would have jurisdiction and, when authorized by law, to charges pending in a court of lesser jurisdiction, if the prosecutor in the other case or cases gives written consent thereto. The court accepting such a plea shall make a disposition of all such charges by judgment, sentence, or otherwise. The record of the plea and its disposition shall be filed in the court of original jurisdiction of the offense. If a defendant secures permission to plead to other pending charges and does so plead, the entry of such a plea shall constitute a waiver by the defendant of venue and all nonjurisdictional defects relating to such charges.

(c)   **Standing Mute or Pleading Evasively.** If a defendant stands mute, or pleads evasively, a plea of not guilty shall be entered.

(d)   **Failure of Corporation to Appear.** If the defendant is a corporation and fails to appear, a plea of not guilty shall be entered of record.

(e)   **Plea of Not Guilty; Operation in Denial.** A plea of not guilty is a denial of every material allegation in the indictment or information on which the defendant is to be tried.

(f)   **Withdrawal of Plea of Guilty or No Contest.** The court may in its discretion, and shall on good cause, at any time before a sentence, permit a plea of guilty or no contest to be withdrawn and, if judgment of conviction has been entered thereon, set aside the judgment and allow a plea of not guilty, or, with the consent of the prosecuting attorney, allow a plea of guilty or no contest of a lesser included offense, or of a lesser degree of the offense charged, to be substituted for the plea of guilty or no contest. The fact that a defendant may have entered a plea of guilty or no contest and later withdrawn the plea may not be used against the defendant in a trial of that cause.

(g)   **Vacation of Plea and Sentence Due to Defendant's Noncompliance.**

(1)   Whenever a plea agreement requires the defendant to comply with some specific terms, those terms shall be expressly made a part of the plea entered into in open court.

(2)   Unless otherwise stated at the time the plea is entered:

(A)   The state may move to vacate a plea and sentence within 60 days of the defendant's noncompliance with the specific terms of a plea agreement.

(B)   When a motion is filed pursuant to subdivision (g)(2)(A) of this rule, the court shall hold an evidentiary hearing on the issue unless the defendant admits noncompliance with the specific terms of the plea agreement.

(C)   No plea or sentence shall be vacated unless the court finds that there has been substantial noncompliance with the express plea agreement.

(D)   When a plea and sentence is vacated pursuant to this rule, the cause shall be set for trial within 90 days of the order vacating the plea and sentence.

(h)   **Plea of Guilty to Lesser Included Offense or Lesser Degree.** The defendant, with the consent of the court and of the prosecuting attorney, may plead guilty to any lesser offense than that charged that is included in the offense charged in the indictment or information or to any lesser degree of the offense charged.

(i)   **Plea of Guilty to an Offense Divided into Degrees; Determination of the Degree.** When an indictment or information charges an offense that is divided into degrees without specifying the degree, if the defendant pleads guilty, generally the court shall, before accepting the plea, examine witnesses to determine the degree of the offense of which the defendant is guilty.

(j)   Time and Circumstances of Plea. No defendant, whether represented by counsel or otherwise, shall be called on to plead unless and until he or she has had a reasonable time within which to deliberate thereon.

(k)   Responsibility of Court on Pleas. No plea of guilty or nolo contendere shall be accepted by a court without the court first determining, in open court, with means of recording the proceedings stenographically or mechanically, that the circumstances surrounding the plea reflect a full understanding of the significance of the plea and its voluntariness and that there is a factual basis for the plea of guilty. A complete record of the proceedings at which a defendant pleads shall be kept by the court.

(l)   Motion to Withdraw the Plea after Sentencing. A defendant who pleads guilty or nolo contendere without expressly reserving the right to appeal a legally dispositive issue may file a motion to withdraw the plea within thirty days after rendition of the sentence, but only upon the grounds specified in Florida Rule of Appellate Procedure 9.140(b)(2)(A)(ii)(a)–(e) except as provided by law.

(m)   Motion to Withdraw the Plea after Drug Court Transfer. A defendant who pleads guilty or nolo contendere to a charge for the purpose of transferring the case, pursuant to section 910.035, Florida Statutes, may file a motion to withdraw the plea upon successful completion of the drug court treatment program.

Committee Notes

1968 Adoption. (a) Patterned after the major portion of Federal Rule of Criminal Procedure 11.

(b)   Same as section 909.07, Florida Statutes, except the word "made" is substituted for "pleaded."

(c)   Taken from a part of section 908.03, Florida Statutes.

(d)   Taken from a part of section 908.03, Florida Statutes.

(e)   Same as section 909.16, Florida Statutes, except that provision is added for trial by affidavit.

(f)   Essentially the same as section 909.13, Florida Statutes.

(g)   Essentially the same as section 909.09, Florida Statutes, except for the addition of the charge by affidavit.

(h)   Same as section 909.11, Florida Statutes, except provision is made for a charge by affidavit.

1972 Amendment. This general topic is found in ABA Standard relating to pleas of guilty. The Standards are divided into 3 parts: receiving and acting upon a plea; withdrawal of the plea; and plea discussions and plea agreements. The first and second parts are considered under this rule.

(a)   Same as first part of existing rule; substance of second sentence of existing rule transferred to new subdivision (j); new provision permits, with court approval, plea of not guilty to be made in writing.

(b)   From ABA Standard 1.2; the purpose of this rule is to permit a defendant to plead guilty or nolo contendere to all cases pending against the defendant, thus avoiding multiple judicial and prosecutorial labors. New concept of permitting this procedure even though the other cases are pending in other counties is taken from Federal Rule of Criminal Procedure 20 which has successfully met the purpose explained above.

(c)   Same as prior rule.

(d)   Same as prior rule.

(e)   Same as prior rule.

(f)   Last sentence added from ABA Standard 2.2.

(g)   Same as prior rule.

(h)   Same as prior rule.

(i)   This should be done in accordance with *Boykin v. Alabama*, 395 U.S. 238, 89 S.Ct. 1709, 23 L.Ed.2d 274 (1969), and Garcia v. State, 228 So.2d 300 (Fla. 1969). This should also include advising a defendant so pleading of the possibility of an action or charge against him or her as a multiple felon if the circumstances so warrant.

(j)   From first sentence of present rule 3.170(a) with addition of requirement of determination of factual basis for a plea of guilty as provided by last sentence of federal rule 11. While requiring the presence of a court reporter, the proposed rule does not require that the reporter transcribe and file a transcript of the proceedings on a plea of guilty or nolo contendere, although the committee considers that such a requirement by the trial judge is desirable.

1973 Amendment. The purpose of this amendment is to provide a method whereby a defendant may plead guilty to a misdemeanor at first appearance without the necessity of the state attorney subsequently filing an information.

RULE 3.171. PLEA DISCUSSIONS AND AGREEMENTS

(a)   **In General.** Ultimate responsibility for sentence determination rests with the trial judge. However, the prosecuting attorney and the defense attorney, or the defendant when representing himself or herself, are encouraged to discuss and to agree on pleas that may be entered by a defendant. The discussion and agreement must be conducted with the defendant's counsel. If the defendant represents himself or herself, all discussions between the defendant and the prosecuting attorney shall be of record.

(b)   **Responsibilities of the Prosecuting Attorney.**

(1)   A prosecuting attorney may:

(A)   engage in discussions with defense counsel or a defendant who is without counsel with a view toward reaching an agreement that, upon the defendant's entering a plea of guilty or nolo contendere to a charged offense or to a lesser or related offense, the prosecuting attorney will do any of the following:

(i)   abandon other charges; or

(ii)   make a recommendation, or agree not to oppose the defendant's request for a particular sentence, with the understanding that such recommendation or request shall not be binding on the trial judge; or

(iii)   agree to a specific sentence; and

(B)   consult with the victim, investigating officer, or other interested persons and advise the trial judge of their views during the course of plea discussions.

(2)   The prosecuting attorney shall:

(A)   apprise the trial judge of all material facts known to the attorney regarding the offense and the defendant's background prior to acceptance of a plea by the trial judge; and

(B)   maintain the record of direct discussions with a defendant who represents himself or herself and make the record available to the trial judge upon the entry of a plea arising from these discussions.

(c)   Responsibilities of Defense Counsel.

(1)   Defense counsel shall not conclude any plea agreement on behalf of a defendant-client without the client's full and complete consent thereto, being certain that any decision to plead guilty or nolo contendere is made by the defendant.

(2)   Defense counsel shall advise defendant of:

(A)   all plea offers; and

(B)   all pertinent matters bearing on the choice of which plea to enter and the particulars attendant upon each plea and the likely results thereof, as well as any possible alternatives that may be open to the defendant.

(d)   Responsibilities of the Trial Judge. After an agreement on a plea has been reached, the trial judge may have made known to him or her the agreement and reasons therefor prior to the acceptance of the plea. Thereafter, the judge shall advise the parties whether other factors (unknown at the time) may make his or her concurrence impossible.

Committee Notes

1972 Amendment. New in Florida. Most criminal cases are disposed of by pleas of guilty arrived at by negotiations between prosecutor and defense counsel, but there was no record of the "plea negotiations," "plea bargaining," or "compromise." The result has been a flood of postconviction claims which require evidentiary hearings and frequently conflicting testimony concerning the plea negotiations. There has also been criticism of the practice of requiring a defendant, upon a negotiated guilty plea, to give a negative reply to the court's inquiry concerning any "promise" made to the defendant. This is designed to avoid the foregoing pitfalls and criticisms by having the negotiations made of record and permitting some control of them. See Commentary to Standard 3.1 ABA Standards relating to pleas of guilty.

(a)   From Standard 3.1a.

(b)   From Standard 3.2.

(c)   From Standard 3.3 except for omission of that part of standard which prohibits trial judge from participating in plea discussions.

(d)   From Standard 3.4.

1977 Amendment. This is a rewording of the prior rule in order to set out the responsibilities of the participants. The rule recognizes the ultimate responsibility of the trial judge, but it encourages prosecution and defense counsel to assist the trial judge in this regard. When the circumstances of the case so merit, it is the responsibility of each respective party to discuss a fair disposition in lieu of trial. For protection of the prosecutor and the defendant, plea discussions between the state and a pro se defendant should be recorded, in writing or electronically.

(b)   New in Florida.

(1)(i)   Restatement of policy followed by extensive revision in the form of Federal Rule of Criminal Procedure 11(e)(1).

(1)(ii)   The rule sets out discretionary minimum professional prosecutorial procedure where either victim or law enforcement officers are involved to better guide the trial judge.

(2)(i)   Mandatory responsibility of prosecutor contemplates disposition with no presentence investigation.

(2)(ii)   Mandatory record protects both the prosecutor and the pro se defendant.

(c)(1)   Renumbering subdivision (b) of prior rule.

(2)(i)   New in Florida. This proposed language makes it mandatory for defense counsel to advise fully defendant of all plea offers by the state. Defense counsel should also discuss and explain to the defendant those matters which trial judge will inquire about before accepting a plea.

(2)(ii)   Same as prior rule 3.171(b), paragraph 2.

(d)   Now embraces and renumbers former rule 3.171(c). The content of former rule 3.171(d) now appears as part of new rule 3.172.

RULE 3.172. ACCEPTANCE OF GUILTY OR NOLO CONTENDERE PLEA

(a) **Voluntariness; Factual Basis.** Before accepting a plea of guilty or nolo contendere, the trial judge shall determine that the plea is voluntarily entered and that a factual basis for the plea exists. Counsel for the prosecution and the defense shall assist the trial judge in this function.

(b) **Open Court.** All pleas shall be taken in open court, except that when good cause is shown a plea may be taken in camera.

(c) **Determination of Voluntariness.** Except when a defendant is not present for a plea, pursuant to the provisions of rule 3.180(d), the trial judge should, when determining voluntariness, place the defendant under oath and shall address the defendant personally and shall determine that he or she understands:

(1) the nature of the charge to which the plea is offered, the maximum possible penalty, and any mandatory minimum penalty provided by law;

(2) if not represented by an attorney, that the defendant has the right to be represented by an attorney at every stage of the proceeding and, if necessary, an attorney will be appointed to represent him or her;

(3) the right to plead not guilty or to persist in that plea if it has already been made, the right to be tried by a jury, and at that trial a defendant has the right to the assistance of counsel, the right to compel attendance of witnesses on his or her behalf, the right to confront and cross-examine witnesses against him or her, and the right not to testify or be compelled to incriminate himself or herself;

(4) that upon a plea of guilty, or nolo contendere without express reservation of the right to appeal, he or she gives up the right to appeal all matters relating to the judgment, including the issue of guilt or innocence, but does not impair the right to review by appropriate collateral attack;

(5) that if the defendant pleads guilty or is adjudged guilty after a plea of nolo contendere there will not be a further trial of any kind, so that by pleading guilty or nolo contendere he or she waives the right to a trial;

(6) that if the defendant pleads guilty or nolo contendere, the trial judge may ask the defendant questions about the offense to which he or she has pleaded, and if the defendant answers these questions under oath, on the record, and in the presence of counsel, the answers may later be used against him or her in a prosecution for perjury;

(7) the complete terms of any plea agreement, including specifically all obligations the defendant will incur as a result;

(8) that if he or she pleads guilty or nolo contendere, if he or she is not a United States citizen, the plea may subject him or her to deportation pursuant to the laws and regulations governing the United States Immigration and Naturalization Service. It shall not be necessary for the trial judge to inquire as to whether the defendant is a United States citizen, as this admonition shall be given to all defendants in all cases; and

(9) that if the defendant pleads guilty or nolo contendere, and the

offense to which the defendant is pleading is a sexually violent offense or a sexually motivated offense, or if the defendant has been previously convicted of such an offense, the plea may subject the defendant to involuntary civil commitment as a sexually violent predator upon completion of his or her sentence. It shall not be necessary for the trial judge to determine whether the present or prior offenses were sexually motivated, as this admonition shall be given to all defendants in all cases.

(10)　　that if the defendant pleads guilty or nolo contendre and the offense to which the defendant is pleading is one for which automatic, mandatory driver's license suspension or revocation is required by law to be imposed (either by the court or by a separate agency), the plea will provide the basis for the suspension or revocation of the defendant's driver's license.

(d)　　**DNA Evidence Inquiry.** Before accepting a defendant's plea of guilty or nolo contendere to a felony, the judge must inquire whether counsel for the defense has reviewed the discovery disclosed by the state, whether such discovery included a listing or description of physical items of evidence, and whether counsel has reviewed the nature of the evidence with the defendant. The judge must then inquire of the defendant and counsel for the defendant and the state whether physical evidence containing DNA is known to exist that could exonerate the defendant. If no such physical evidence is known to exist, the court may accept the defendant's plea and impose sentence. If such physical evidence is known to exist, upon defendant's motion specifying the physical evidence to be tested, the court may postpone the proceeding and order DNA testing.

(e)　　**Acknowledgment by Defendant.** Before the trial judge accepts a guilty or nolo contendere plea, the judge must determine that the defendant either (1) acknowledges his or her guilt or (2) acknowledges that he or she feels the plea to be in his or her best interest, while maintaining his or her innocence.

(f)　　**Proceedings of Record.** The proceedings at which a defendant pleads guilty or nolo contendere shall be of record.

(g)　　**Withdrawal of Plea Offer or Negotiation.** No plea offer or negotiation is binding until it is accepted by the trial judge formally after making all the inquiries, advisements, and determinations required by this rule. Until that time, it may be withdrawn by either party without any necessary justification.

(h)　　**Withdrawal of Plea When Judge Does Not Concur.** If the trial judge does not concur in a tendered plea of guilty or nolo contendere arising from negotiations, the plea may be withdrawn.

(i)　　**Evidence.** Except as otherwise provided in this rule, evidence of an offer or a plea of guilty or nolo contendere, later withdrawn, or of statements made in connection therewith, is not admissible in any civil or criminal proceeding against the person who made the plea or offer.

(j)　　**Prejudice.** Failure to follow any of the procedures in this rule shall not render a plea void absent a showing of prejudice.

Committee Notes

1977 Adoption. New in Florida. In view of the supreme court's emphasis on the importance of this procedure as set forth in *Williams v. State*, 316 So.2d 267 (Fla. 1975), the committee felt it appropriate to expand the language of former rule 3.170(j) (deleted) and establish a separate rule. Incorporates Federal Rule of Criminal Procedure 11(c) and allows for pleas of convenience as provided in *North Carolina v. Alford*, 400 U.S. 25, 91 S.Ct. 160, 27 L.Ed.2d 162 (1970).

(a), (b) Mandatory record of voluntariness and factual predicate is proper responsibility of counsel as well as the court.

(c)(iv) This waiver of right to appeal is a change from the proposed amendments to the rules of criminal procedure now pending. A sentence if lawful is not subject to appellate review; a judgment, however, is. The committee was of the opinion that the proposed rule should be expanded to include a waiver of appeal from the judgment as well as the sentence. Waivers of appeal have been approved. *United States ex rel. Amuso v. LaValle*, 291 F.Supp. 383 (E.D.N.Y. 1968), aff'd 427 F.2d 328 (2d Cir. 1970); State v. Gibson, 68 N.J. 499, 348 A.2d 769 (1975); *People v. Williams*, 36 N.Y.2d 829, 370 N.Y.S.2d 904, 331 N.E.2d 684 (1975).

(vii) Requires the court to explain the plea agreement to the defendant, including conditions subsequent such as conditions of probation.

(e) Provides a readily available record (either oral or by use of standard forms) in all cases where a felony is charged.

(h) Rewording of federal rule 11(e)(6).

2005 Amendment. Rule 3.172(c)(9) added. See section 394.910, et seq., Fla. Stat.; and *State v. Harris*, 881 So.2d 1079 (Fla. 2004).

RULE 3.180. PRESENCE OF DEFENDANT

(a) **Presence of Defendant.** In all prosecutions for crime the defendant shall be present:

(1) at first appearance;

(2) when a plea is made, unless a written plea of not guilty shall be made in writing under the provisions of rule 3.170(a);

(3) at any pretrial conference, unless waived by the defendant in writing;

(4) at the beginning of the trial during the examination, challenging, impanelling, and swearing of the jury;

(5) at all proceedings before the court when the jury is present;

(6) when evidence is addressed to the court out of the presence of the jury for the purpose of laying the foundation for the introduction of evidence before the jury;

(7) at any view by the jury;

(8)   at the rendition of the verdict; and

(9)   at the pronouncement of judgment and the imposition of sentence.

(b)   Presence; Definition. A defendant is present for purposes of this rule if the defendant is physically in attendance for the courtroom proceeding, and has a meaningful opportunity to be heard through counsel on the issues being discussed.

(c)   Defendant Absenting Self.

(1)   **Trial.** If the defendant is present at the beginning of the trial and thereafter, during the progress of the trial or before the verdict of the jury has been returned into court, voluntarily absents himself or herself from the presence of the court without leave of court, or is removed from the presence of the court because of his or her disruptive conduct during the trial, the trial of the cause or the return of the verdict of the jury in the case shall not thereby be postponed or delayed, but the trial, the submission of the case to the jury for verdict, and the return of the verdict thereon shall proceed in all respects as though the defendant were present in court at all times.

(2)   **Sentencing.** If the defendant is present at the beginning of the trial and thereafter absents himself or herself as described in subdivision (1), or if the defendant enters a plea of guilty or no contest and thereafter absents himself or herself from sentencing, the sentencing may proceed in all respects as though the defendant were present at all times.

(d)   Defendant May Be Tried in Absentia for Misdemeanors. Persons prosecuted for misdemeanors may, at their own request, by leave of court, be excused from attendance at any or all of the proceedings aforesaid.

(e)   Presence of Corporation. A corporation may appear by counsel at all times and for all purposes.

Committee Notes

1968 Adoption. (a) The suggested rule is in great part a recopying of section 914.01, Florida Statutes:

In (3) the words "at the beginning of the trial" are recommended for inclusion to avoid questions arising as to the necessity for the defendant's presence at times other than upon trial, such as when the jury venire is ordered, etc.

Subdivision (a)(8) is not in the present statute. However, it is deemed advisable to include it, as the several sections of chapter 921, Florida Statutes, particularly section 921.07, appear to impliedly or expressly require the defendant's presence at such times.

(c)   The statute and the suggested rule make no distinction between capital and other cases. In all probability, however, were a person on trial for a capital case to escape during trial, a mistrial should be ordered if such person were not captured within a reasonable time.

(d)   It is suggested that this language be used rather than the all-inclusive general language of the   present statute as to misdemeanor cases.

(e)   This provision does not appear in section 914.01, Florida Statutes, but it is a part of Federal   Rule of Criminal Procedure 43. It is deemed useful to include it.

1972 Amendment. Same as prior rule except   (3) added to conform to rule 3.220(k); other subdivisions   renumbered.

V.   PRETRIAL MOTIONS AND DEFENSES

RULE 3.190. PRETRIAL MOTIONS

(a)   **In General.** Every pretrial motion and pleading in response to a motion shall be in writing and signed by the party making the motion or the attorney for the party. This requirement may be waived by the court for good cause shown. Each motion or other pleading shall state the ground or grounds on which it is based. A copy shall be served on the adverse party. A certificate of service must accompany the filing of any pleading.

(b)   **Motion to Dismiss; Grounds.** All defenses available to a defendant by plea, other than not guilty, shall be made only by motion to dismiss the indictment or information, whether the same shall relate to matters of form, substance, former acquittal, former jeopardy, or any other defense.

(c)   **Time for Moving to Dismiss.** Unless the court grants further time, the defendant shall move to dismiss the indictment or information either before or at arraignment. The court in its discretion may permit the defendant to plead and thereafter to file a motion to dismiss at a time to be set by the court. Except for objections based on fundamental grounds, every ground for a motion to dismiss that is not presented by a motion to dismiss within the time hereinabove provided shall be considered waived. However, the court may at any time entertain a motion to dismiss on any of the following grounds:

(1)   The defendant is charged with an offense for which the defendant has been pardoned.

(2)   The defendant is charged with an offense for which the defendant previously has been placed in jeopardy.

(3)   The defendant is charged with an offense for which the defendant previously has been granted immunity.

(4)   There are no material disputed facts and the undisputed facts do not establish a prima facie case of guilt against the defendant. The facts on which the motion is based should be alleged specifically and the motion sworn to.

(d)   **Traverse or Demurrer.** The state may traverse or demur to a motion to dismiss that alleges factual matters. Factual matters alleged in a motion to dismiss under subdivision (c)   (4) of this rule shall be considered admitted unless specifically denied by the state in the traverse. The court may receive evidence on any issue of fact necessary to the decision on the motion. A motion to dismiss under subdivision (c) (4) of this rule shall be denied if the state files a traverse that, with specificity, denies under oath the material fact or facts alleged in the motion to dismiss. The demurrer or traverse shall be filed a reasonable time before the hearing on the motion to dismiss.

(e)   **Effect of Sustaining a Motion to Dismiss.** If the motion to dismiss is sustained, the court may order that the defendant be held in custody or admitted to bail for a reasonable specified time pending the filing of a new indictment or information. If a new indictment or information is not filed within the time specified in the order, or within such additional time as the court may allow for good cause shown, the defendant, if in custody, shall be discharged therefrom, unless some other charge justifies a continuation in custody. If the defendant has been released on bail, the defendant and the sureties shall be exonerated; if money or bonds have been deposited as bail, the money or bonds shall be refunded.

(f)   **Motion for Continuance.**

      (1)   **Definition.** A continuance within the meaning of this rule is the postponement of a cause for any period of time.

      (2)   **Cause.** On motion of the state or a defendant or on its own motion, the court may grant a continuance, in its discretion for good cause shown.

      (3)   **Time for Filing.** A motion for continuance may be made only before or at the time the case is set for trial, unless good cause for failure to so apply is shown or the ground for the motion arose after the cause was set for trial.

      (4)   **Certificate of Good Faith.** A motion for continuance shall be accompanied by a certificate of the movant's counsel that the motion is made in good faith.

      (5)   **Affidavits.** The party applying for a continuance may file affidavits in support of the motion, and the adverse party may file counter- affidavits in opposition to the motion.

(g)   **Motion to Suppress Evidence in Unlawful Search.**

      (1)   **Grounds.** A defendant aggrieved by an unlawful search and seizure may move to suppress anything so obtained for use as evidence because:

      (A)   the property was illegally seized without a warrant;

      (B)   the warrant is insufficient on its face;

      (C)   the property seized is not the property described in the warrant.

      (D)   there was no probable cause for believing the existence of the grounds on which the warrant was issued; or

      (E)   the warrant was illegally executed.

      (2)   **Contents of Motion.** Every motion to suppress evidence shall

state clearly the particular evidence sought to be suppressed, the reasons for suppression, and a general statement of the facts on which the motion is based.

(3)   **Hearing.** Before hearing evidence, the court shall determine if the motion is legally sufficient. If it is not, the motion shall be denied. If the court hears the motion on its merits, the defendant shall present evidence supporting the defendant's position and the state may offer rebuttal evidence.

(4) **Time for Filing.** The motion to suppress shall be made before trial unless opportunity therefor did not exist or the defendant was not aware of the grounds for the motion, but the court may entertain the motion or an appropriate objection at the trial.

(h) Motion to Suppress a Confession or Admission Illegally Obtained.

(1)   **Grounds.** On motion of the defendant or on its own motion, the court shall suppress any confession or admission obtained illegally from the defendant.

(2)   **Contents of Motion.** Every motion made by a defendant to suppress a confession or admission shall identify with particularity any statement sought to be suppressed, the reasons for suppression, and a general statement of the facts on which the motion is based.

(3)   **Time for Filing.** The motion to suppress shall be made before trial unless opportunity therefor did not exist or the defendant was not aware of the grounds for the motion, but the court in its discretion may entertain the motion or an appropriate objection at the trial.

(4)   **Hearing.** The court shall receive evidence on any issue of fact necessary to be decided to rule on the motion.

(i)   Motion to Take Deposition to Perpetuate Testimony.

(1)   After the filing of an indictment or information on which a defendant is to be tried, the defendant or the state may apply for an order to perpetuate testimony. The application shall be verified or supported by the affidavits of credible persons that a prospective witness resides beyond the territorial jurisdiction of the court or may be unable to attend or be prevented from attending a trial or hearing, that the witness's testimony is material, and that it is necessary to take the deposition to prevent a failure of justice. The court shall order a commission to be issued to take the deposition of the witnesses to be used in the trial and that any nonprivileged designated books, papers, documents, or tangible objects be produced at the same time and place. If the application is made within 10 days before the trial date, the court may deny the application.

(2)   If the defendant or the state desires to perpetuate the testimony of a witness living in or out of the state whose testimony is material and necessary to the case, the same proceedings shall be followed as provided in subdivision (i)(1), but the testimony of the witness may be taken before an official court reporter, transcribed by the reporter, and filed in the trial court.

(3)   If the deposition is taken on the application of the state, the defendant and the defendant's attorney shall be given reasonable notice of the time and place set for the deposition. The officer having custody of the defendant shall be notified of

the time and place and shall produce the defendant at the examination and keep the defendant in the presence of the witness during the examination. A defendant not in custody may be present at the examination, but the failure to appear after notice and tender of expenses shall constitute a waiver of the right to be present. The state shall pay to the defendant's attorney and to a defendant not in custody the expenses of travel and subsistence for attendance at the examination. The state shall make available to the defendant for examination and use at the deposition any statement of the witness being deposed that is in the possession of the state and that the state would be required to make available to the defendant if the witness were testifying at trial.

(4)   The application and order to issue the commission may be made either in term time or in vacation. The commission shall be issued at a time to be fixed by the court.

(5)   Except as otherwise provided, the rules governing the taking and filing of oral depositions, the objections thereto, the issuing, execution, and return of the commission, and the opening of the depositions in civil actions shall apply in criminal cases.

(6)   No deposition shall be used or read into evidence when the attendance of the witness can be procured. If the court determines that any person whose deposition has been taken is absent because of procurement, inducement, or threats of any person on behalf of the state or of the defendant or of any person on the defendant's behalf, the deposition shall not be read in evidence on behalf of the defendant.

(j)   Motion to Expedite. On motion by the state, the court, in the exercise of its discretion, shall take into consideration the dictates of sections 825.106 and 918.0155, Florida Statutes (1995).

Committee Notes

1968 Adoption. (a) New; devised by committee.

(b)   Substantially the same as section 909.02, Florida Statutes, except changes name of "motion to quash" to "motion to dismiss." This conforms to the terminology of the Federal Rules of Criminal Procedure. The statute authorizing the state to appeal from certain orders, section 924.07, Florida Statutes, should be amended by substituting the words "motion to dismiss" for "motion to quash."

(c)   Combines the substance of sections 909.01 and 909.06, Florida Statutes. Subdivision (4) affords a new remedy to an accused. Although there is now a conclusive presumption of probable cause once an indictment or information is filed (see *Sullivan v. State*, 49 So.2d 794 (Fla. 1951)), it is felt that this rule is necessary. Primarily, this procedure will permit a pretrial determination of the law of the case when the facts are not in dispute. In a sense, this is somewhat similar to summary judgment proceedings in civil cases, but a dismissal under this rule is not a bar to a subsequent prosecution.

(d)   New; based on *Marks v. State*, 115 Fla. 497, 155 So. 727 (1934), and what is generally regarded as the better practice. Hearing provision based on federal rule 41(e).

(e)   Combines federal rule 12(b)(5) and section 909.05, Florida Statutes.

With reference to the maximum time that a defendant will be held in custody or on bail pending the filing of a new indictment or information, the trial court is given discretion in setting such time as to both the indictment and information. This proposal differs from section 909.05, Florida Statutes, with reference to the filing of a new indictment in that the statute requires that the new indictment be found by the same grand jury or the next grand jury having the authority to inquire into the offense. If the supreme court has the authority to deviate from this statutory provision by court rule, it seems that the trial court should be granted the same discretion with reference to the indictment that it is granted concerning the information. The statute is harsh in that under its provisions a person can be in custody or on bail for what may be an unreasonable length of time before a grand jury is required to return an indictment in order that the custody or bail be continued.

(g)(1)   This subdivision is almost the same as section 916.02   (1),   Florida Statutes.

(g)(2)   This subdivision is almost the same as section 916.02   (2),   Florida Statutes.

(g)(3)   This subdivision is almost the same as section 916.03, Florida Statutes.

(g)(4)   This subdivision rewords a portion of section 916.04, Florida Statutes.

(g)(5)   This subdivision rewords section 916.07, Florida Statutes.

(h)   Same as federal rule 41(e) as to the points covered.

(i)   This rule is based on 38-144-11 of the Illinois Code of Criminal Procedure and federal rule 41(e).

(j)   This subdivision rewords and adds to federal rule 14. It covers the subject matter of section 918.02, Florida Statutes.

(k)   This rule is almost the same as federal rule 13, with provision added for trial by affidavit.

(l)   Substantially same as section 916.06, Florida Statutes, with these exceptions: application cannot be made until indictment, information, or trial affidavit is filed; application must be made at least 10 days before trial; oral deposition in addition to written interrogatories is permissible.

1972 Amendment. Subdivision (h) is amended to require the defendant to specify the factual basis behind the grounds for a motion to suppress evidence. Subdivision (l) is amended to permit the state to take depositions under the same conditions that the defendant can take them. Former subdivisions (j) and (k) transferred to rules 3.150, 3.151, and 3.152. Subdivisions (l) and (m) renumbered (j) and (k) respectively. Otherwise, same as prior rule.

1977 Amendment. This amendment resolves any ambiguity in the rule as to whether the state must file a general or a specific traverse to defeat a motion to dismiss filed under the authority of rule 3.190(c)(4).

See *State v. Kemp*, 305 So.2d 833 (Fla. 3d DCA 1974).

74

The amendment clearly now requires a specific traverse to specific material fact or facts.

1992 Amendment. The amendments, in addition to gender neutralizing the wording of the rule, make a minor grammatical change by substituting the word "upon" for "on" in several places. The amendments also delete language from subdivision (a) to eliminate from the rule any reference as to when pretrial motions are to be served on the adverse party. Because rule 3.030 addresses the service of pleadings and papers, such language was removed to avoid confusion and reduce redundancy in the rules.

2002 Amendment. If the trial court exercises its discretion to consider the motion to suppress during trial, the court may withhold ruling on the merits of the motion, and motion for a judgment of acquittal, and allow the case to be submitted to the jury. If the defendant is acquitted, no further proceedings regarding the motion to suppress or motion for a judgment of acquittal would be necessary. However, if the jury finds the defendant guilty of the crime charged, the trial court could then consider the motion to suppress post-trial in conjunction with the defendant's renewed motion for a judgment of acquittal or motion for new trial.

RULE 3.191. SPEEDY TRIAL

(a) **Speedy Trial without Demand.** Except as otherwise provided by this rule, and subject to the limitations imposed under subdivisions (e) and (f), every person charged with a crime shall be brought to trial within 90 days of arrest if the crime charged is a misdemeanor, or within 175 days of arrest if the crime charged is a felony. If trial is not commenced within these time periods, the defendant shall be entitled to the appropriate remedy as set forth in subdivision (p). The time periods established by this subdivision shall commence when the person is taken into custody as defined under subdivision (d). A person charged with a crime is entitled to the benefits of this rule whether the person is in custody in a jail or correctional institution of this state or a political subdivision thereof or is at liberty on bail or recognizance or other pretrial release condition. This subdivision shall cease to apply whenever a person files a valid demand for speedy trial under subdivision (b).

(b) **Speedy Trial upon Demand.** Except as otherwise provided by this rule, and subject to the limitations imposed under subdivisions (e) and (g), every person charged with a crime by indictment or information shall have the right to demand a trial within 60 days, by filing with the court a separate pleading entitled "Demand for Speedy Trial," and serving a copy on the prosecuting authority.

(1) No later than 5 days from the filing of a demand for speedy trial, the court shall hold a calendar call, with notice to all parties, for the express purposes of announcing in open court receipt of the demand and of setting the case for trial.

(2) At the calendar call the court shall set the case for trial to commence at a date no less than 5 days nor more than 45 days from the date of the calendar call.

(3) The failure of the court to hold a calendar call on a demand that has been properly filed and served shall not interrupt the running of any time periods under this subdivision.

(4)   If the defendant has not been brought to trial within 50 days of the filing of the demand, the defendant shall have the right to the appropriate remedy as set forth in subdivision (p).

(c)   Commencement of Trial. A person shall be considered to have been brought to trial if the trial commences within the time herein provided. The trial is considered to have commenced when the trial jury panel for that specific trial is sworn for voir dire examination or, on waiver of a jury trial, when the trial proceedings begin before the judge.

(d)   Custody. For purposes of this rule, a person is taken into custody (1) when the person is arrested as a result of the conduct or criminal episode that gave rise to the crime charged, or (2) when the person is served with a notice to appear in lieu of physical arrest.

(e)   Prisoners outside Jurisdiction. A person who is in federal custody or incarcerated in a jail or correctional institution outside the jurisdiction of this state or a subdivision thereof, and who is charged with a crime by indictment or information issued or filed under the laws of this state, is not entitled to the benefit of this rule until that person returns or is returned to the jurisdiction of the court within which the Florida charge is pending and until written notice of the person's return is filed with the court and served on the prosecutor. For these persons, the time period under subdivision (a) commences on the date the last act required under this subdivision occurs. For these persons the time period under subdivision (b) commences when the demand is filed so long as the acts required under this subdivision occur before the filing of the demand. If the acts required under this subdivision do not precede the filing of the demand, the demand is invalid and shall be stricken upon motion of the prosecuting attorney. Nothing in this rule shall affect a prisoner's right to speedy trial under law.

(f)   Consolidation of Felony and Misdemeanor. When a felony and a misdemeanor are consolidated for disposition in circuit court, the misdemeanor shall be governed by the same time period applicable to the felony.

(g)   Demand for Speedy Trial; Accused Is Bound. A demand for speedy trial binds the accused and the state. No demand for speedy trial shall be filed or served unless the accused has a bona fide desire to obtain a trial sooner than otherwise might be provided. A demand for speedy trial shall be considered a pleading that the accused is available for trial, has diligently investigated the case, and is prepared or will be prepared for trial within 5 days. A demand filed by an accused who has not diligently investigated the case or who is not timely prepared for trial shall be stricken as invalid on motion of the prosecuting attorney. A demand may not be withdrawn by the accused except on order of the court, with consent of the state or on good cause shown. Good cause for continuances or delay on behalf of the accused thereafter shall not include nonreadiness for trial, except as to matters that may arise after the demand for trial is filed and that reasonably could not have been anticipated by the accused or counsel for the accused. A person who has demanded speedy trial, who thereafter is not prepared for trial, is not entitled to continuance or delay except as provided in this rule.

(h)   Notice of Expiration of Time for Speedy Trial; When Timely. A notice of expiration of speedy trial time shall be timely if filed and served after the expiration of the periods of time for trial provided in this rule. However, a notice of expiration of speedy trial time filed before expiration of the period of time for trial is invalid and shall be stricken on motion of the prosecuting attorney.

      (i)   **When Time May Be Extended.** The periods of time established by this rule may be extended, provided the period of time sought to be extended has not expired at the time the extension was procured. An extension may be procured by:

      (1)   stipulation, announced to the court or signed in proper person or by counsel, by the party against whom the stipulation is sought to be enforced;

      (2)   written or recorded order of the court on the court's own motion or motion by either party in exceptional circumstances as hereafter defined in subdivision (l);

      (3)   written or recorded order of the court with good cause shown by the accused;

      (4)   written or recorded order of the court for a period of reasonable and necessary delay resulting from proceedings including but not limited to an examination and hearing to determine the mental competency or physical ability of the defendant to stand trial, for hearings on pretrial motions, for appeals by the state, for DNA testing ordered on the defendant's behalf upon defendant's motion specifying the physical evidence to be tested pursuant to section 925.12 (2), Florida Statutes, and for trial of other pending criminal charges against the accused; or

      (5)   administrative order issued by the chief justice, under Florida Rule of Judicial Administration 2.205(a)(2)(B)(iv), suspending the speedy trial procedures as stated therein.

      (j)   **Delay and Continuances; Effect on Motion.** If trial of the accused does not commence within the periods of time established by this rule, a pending motion for discharge shall be granted by the court unless it is shown that:

      (1)   a time extension has been ordered under subdivision (i) and that extension has not expired;

      (2)   the failure to hold trial is attributable to the accused, a codefendant in the same trial, or their counsel;

      (3)   the accused was unavailable for trial under subdivision (k);

or

      (4)   the demand referred to in subdivision (g) is invalid.

If the court finds that discharge is not appropriate for reasons under subdivisions (j) (2), (3), or (4), the pending motion for discharge shall be denied, provided, however, that trial shall be scheduled and commence within 90 days of a written or recorded order of denial.

      (k)   **Availability for Trial.** A person is unavailable for trial if the person or the person's counsel fails to attend a proceeding at which either's presence is required by these rules, or the person or counsel is not ready for trial on the date trial is scheduled. A person who has not been available for trial during the term provided for in this rule is not entitled to be discharged. No presumption of nonavailability attaches, but if the state objects to discharge and presents any evidence tending to show nonavailability, the accused must establish, by competent proof, availability during the term.

(l) **Exceptional Circumstances.** As permitted by subdivision (i) of this rule, the court may order an extension of the time periods provided under this rule when exceptional circumstances are shown to exist. Exceptional circumstances shall not include general congestion of the court's docket, lack of diligent preparation, failure to obtain available witnesses, or other avoidable or foreseeable delays. Exceptional circumstances are those that, as a matter of substantial justice to the accused or the state or both, require an order by the court. These circumstances include:

(1) unexpected illness, unexpected incapacity, or unforeseeable and unavoidable absence of a person whose presence or testimony is uniquely necessary for a full and adequate trial;

(2) a showing by the state that the case is so unusual and so complex, because of the number of defendants or the nature of the prosecution or otherwise, that it is unreasonable to expect adequate investigation or preparation within the periods of time established by this rule;

(3) a showing by the state that specific evidence or testimony is not available despite diligent efforts to secure it, but will become available at a later time;

(4) a showing by the accused or the state of necessity for delay grounded on developments that could not have been anticipated and that materially will affect the trial;

(5) a showing that a delay is necessary to accommodate a codefendant, when there is reason not to sever the cases to proceed promptly with trial of the defendant; and

(6) a showing by the state that the accused has caused major delay or disruption of preparation of proceedings, as by preventing the attendance of witnesses or otherwise.

(m) **Effect of Mistrial; Appeal; Order of New Trial.** A person who is to be tried again or whose trial has been delayed by an appeal by the state or the defendant shall be brought to trial within 90 days from the date of declaration of a mistrial by the trial court, the date of an order by the trial court granting a new trial, the date of an order by the trial court granting a motion in arrest of judgment, or the date of receipt by the trial court of a mandate, order, or notice of whatever form from a reviewing court that makes possible a new trial for the defendant, whichever is last in time. If a defendant is not brought to trial within the prescribed time periods, the defendant shall be entitled to the appropriate remedy as set forth in subdivision (p).

(n) **Discharge from Crime; Effect.** Discharge from a crime under this rule shall operate to bar prosecution of the crime charged and of all other crimes on which trial has not commenced nor conviction obtained nor adjudication withheld and that were or might have been charged as a result of the same conduct or criminal episode as a lesser degree or lesser included offense.

(o) **Nolle Prosequi; Effect.** The intent and effect of this rule shall not be avoided by the state by entering a nolle prosequi to a crime charged and by prosecuting a new crime grounded on the same conduct or criminal episode or otherwise by prosecuting new and different charges based on the same conduct or criminal episode whether or not the pending charge is suspended, continued, or is the subject of entry of a nolle prosequi.

(p) **Remedy for Failure to Try Defendant within the Specified Time.**

(1) No remedy shall be granted to any defendant under this rule until the court has made the required inquiry under subdivision (j).

(2) At any time after the expiration of the prescribed time period, the defendant may file a separate pleading entitled "Notice of Expiration of Speedy Trial Time," and serve a copy on the prosecuting authority.

(3) No later than 5 days from the date of the filing of a notice of expiration of speedy trial time, the court shall hold a hearing on the notice and, unless the court finds that one of the reasons set forth in subdivision (j) exists, shall order that the defendant be brought to trial within 10 days. A defendant not brought to trial within the 10-day period through no fault of the defendant, on motion of the defendant or the court, shall be forever discharged from the crime.

Committee Notes

1972 Amendment. Same as prior rule. The schedule is omitted as being unnecessary.

1977 Amendment. An appeal by the state from an order dismissing the case constitutes an interlocutory appeal and should be treated as such. The additional phrase removes any ambiguities in the existing rule.

1980 Amendment.

(a)(1). Speedy Trial without Demand.

1. Prisoners in Florida institutions are now treated like any other defendant [formerly (b)(1)].

2. Federal prisoners and prisoners outside Florida may claim the benefit of this subdivision once special prerequisites are satisfied under (b)(1).

3. Before a court can discharge a defendant, the court must make complete inquiry to ensure that discharge is appropriate.

(a)(2). Speedy Trial upon Demand.

1. Trial cannot be scheduled within 5 days of the filing of the demand without the consent of both the state and the defendant.

2. Before a court can discharge a defendant, the court must make complete inquiry to ensure that discharge is appropriate.

3.   Prisoners in Florida are now treated like any other defendant [formerly (b)(2)].

4.   Federal prisoners and prisoners outside Florida may claim the benefit of this subdivision once special prerequisites are satisfied under (b)(1).

(a)   (3). Commencement of Trial.

1.   Minor change in language to reflect case law.

(a)(4).   Custody. [NEW]

1.   Custody is defined in terms tantamount to arrest. This definition was formerly contained in (a)(1).

2.   Where a notice to appear is served in lieu of arrest, custody results on the date the notice is served.

(b)(1).   Prisoners outside Jurisdiction. [NEW]

1.   Prisoners outside the jurisdiction of Florida may claim benefit under (a)(1) and (a)(2) after the prisoner returns to the jurisdiction of the court where the charge is pending and after the prisoner files and serves a notice of this fact.

2.   As an alternative, certain prisoners may claim the benefit of sections 941.45–941.50, Florida Statutes (1979).

3.   Former (b)(1) is repealed.

(b)(2).   [NEW]

1.   Where a misdemeanor and felony are consolidated for purposes of trial in circuit court, the misdemeanor is governed by the same time period applicable to the felony. To claim benefit under this provision, the crimes must be consolidated before the normal time period applicable to misdemeanors has expired.

2.   Former (b)(2) is repealed.

(b)   (3). Repealed and superseded by (b)(1).

(c).   Demand for Speedy Trial.

1.   The subdivision recognizes that an invalid (spurious) demand must be stricken.

2.   The subdivision now puts a 5-day limit on the time when a defendant must be prepared.

(d)(1).   Motion for Discharge.
1.   Under the amended provision, a prematurely filed motion is invalid and may be stricken.

(d)(2).   When Time May Be Extended.
1.   The terms "waiver," "tolling," or "suspension" have no meaning within the context of the   subdivision as amended. The subdivision addresses extensions for a specified period of time.

2.   Except for stipulations, all extensions require an order of the court.

3.   The term "recorded order" refers to stenographic recording and not recording of a written   order by the clerk.

(d)(3).   Delay and Continuances.

1.   Even though the normal time limit has expired under (a)(1) or (a)(2), a trial court may not   properly discharge a defendant without making a complete inquiry of possible reasons to deny discharge. If the   court finds that the time period has been properly extended and the extension has not expired, the court must   simply deny the motion. If the court finds that the delay is attributable to the accused, that the accused was unavailable for trial, or that the demand was invalid, the court must deny the motion and schedule trial within   90 days. If the court has before it a valid motion for discharge and none of the above circumstances are present,   the court must grant the motion.

(e).   Availability for Trial.

1.   Availability for trial is now defined solely in terms of required attendance and readiness for trial.

(f).   Exceptional Circumstances.

1.   The 2 extension limit for unavailable evidence has been discarded.

2.   The new trial date paragraph was eliminated because it simply was unnecessary.

(g).   Effect of Mistrial; Appeal; Order of New Trial.

1.   Makes uniform a 90-day period within which a defendant must be brought to trial after a   mistrial, order of new trial, or appeal by the state or defendant.

(h)(1).   Discharge from Crime.

1.   No change.

(h)(2).   Nolle Prosequi.

1.   No change.

1984 Amendment.

(a)(1).   Repeals the remedy of automatic discharge from the crime and refers instead to the new   subdivision on remedies.

(a)(2).   Establishes the calendar call for the demand for speedy trial when filed.

This provision, especially sought by prosecutors, brings the matter to the attention of both the court and the prosecution. The subdivision again repeals the automatic discharge for failure to meet the mandated time limit, referring to the new subdivision on remedies for the appropriate remedy.

(i). The intent of (i)(4) is to provide the state attorney with 15 days within which to bring a defendant to trial from the date of the filing of the motion for discharge. This time begins with the filing of the motion and continues regardless of whether the judge hears the motion.

This subdivision provides that, upon failure of the prosecution to meet the mandated time periods, the defendant shall file a motion for discharge, which will then be heard by the court within 5 days. The court sets trial of the defendant within 10 additional days. The total 15-day period was chosen carefully by the committee, the consensus being that the period was long enough that the system could, in fact, bring to trial a defendant not yet tried, but short enough that the pressure to try defendants within the prescribed time period would remain. In other words, it gives the system a chance to remedy a mistake; it does not permit the system to forget about the time constraints. It was felt that a period of 10 days was too short, giving the system insufficient time in which to bring a defendant to trial; the period of 30 days was too long, removing incentive to maintain strict docket control in order to remain within the prescribed time periods.

The committee further felt that it was not appropriate to extend the new remedy provisions to misdemeanors, but only to more serious offenses.

1992 Amendment. The purpose of the amendments is to gender neutralize the wording of the rule. In addition, the committee recommends the rule be amended to differentiate between 2 separate and distinct pleadings now referred to as "motion for discharge." The initial "motion for discharge" has been renamed "notice of expiration of speedy trial time."

RULE 3.192. MOTIONS FOR REHEARING

When an appeal by the state is authorized by Florida Rule of Appellate Procedure 9.140, or sections 924.07 or 924.071, Florida Statutes, the state may file a motion for rehearing within 10 days of an order subject to appellate review. A motion for rehearing shall state with particularity the points of law or fact that, in the opinion of the state, the court has overlooked or misapprehended in its decision, and shall not present issues not previously raised in the proceeding. A response may be filed within 10 days of service of the motion. The trial court's order disposing of the motion for rehearing shall be filed within 15 days of the response but not later than 40 days from the date of the order of which rehearing is sought. If no order is filed within 40 days, the motion is deemed denied. A timely filed motion for rehearing shall toll rendition of the order subject to appellate review and the order shall be deemed rendered 40 days from the order of which rehearing is sought, or upon the filing of a written order denying the motion for rehearing, whichever is earlier. This rule shall not apply to post-conviction proceedings pursuant to rule 3.800(a), 3.850, 3.851, or 3.853. Nothing in this rule precludes the trial court from exercising its inherent authority to reconsider a ruling while the court has jurisdiction of the case.

RULE 3.200. NOTICE OF ALIBI

On the written demand of the prosecuting attorney, specifying as particularly as is known to the prosecuting attorney the place, date, and time of the commission of the crime charged, a defendant in a criminal case who intends to offer evidence of an alibi in defense shall, not less than 10 days before trial or such other time as the court may direct, file and serve on the prosecuting attorney a notice in writing of an intention to claim an alibi, which notice shall contain specific information as to the place at which the defendant claims to have been at the time of the alleged offense and, as particularly as is known to the defendant or the defendant's attorney, the names and addresses of the witnesses by whom the defendant proposes to establish the alibi. Not more than 5 days after receipt of defendant's witness list, or any other time as the court may direct, the prosecuting attorney shall file and serve on the defendant the names and addresses (as particularly as are known to the prosecuting attorney) of the witnesses the state proposes to offer in rebuttal to discredit the defendant's alibi at the trial of the cause. Both the defendant and the prosecuting attorney shall be under a continuing duty to promptly disclose the

names and addresses of additional witnesses who come to the attention of either party subsequent to filing their respective witness lists as provided in this rule. If a defendant fails to file and serve a copy of the notice as herein required, the court may exclude evidence offered by the defendant for the purpose of providing an alibi, except the defendant's own testimony. If the notice is given by a defendant, the court may exclude the testimony of any witness offered by the defendant for the purpose of proving an alibi if the name and address of the witness as particularly as is known to the defendant or the defendant's attorney is not stated in the notice. If the prosecuting attorney fails to file and serve a copy on the defendant of a list of witnesses as herein provided, the court may exclude evidence offered by the state in rebuttal to the defendant's alibi evidence. If notice is given by the prosecuting attorney, the court may exclude the testimony of any witness offered by the prosecuting attorney for the purpose of rebutting the defense of alibi if the name and address of the witness as particularly as is known to the prosecuting attorney is not stated in the notice.

For good cause shown the court may waive the requirements of this rule.

Committee Notes

1968 Adoption. The rule is completely new in Florida. Fourteen states have adopted notice of alibi statutes or rules: Arizona Supreme Court Rules of Criminal Procedure 192 (enacted in 1940); Ind.Ann.Stat. 9- 1631, 9-1632, 9-1633 (1956) (enacted in 1935); Iowa Code Ann. 777 18 (1958) (enacted in 1941); Kan.Gen.Stat. Ann. 62-1341 (1949) (enacted in 1935); Mich.Stat.Ann. 630.14 (1947) (enacted in 1935); N.J. Superior and County Court Criminal Practice Rule 3:5-9 (1948) (enacted in 1934); N.Y. Code of Crim. Proc. 295-L (1935) (enacted in 1935); Ohio Rev. Code Ann. 2945.58 (1953) (enacted in 1929); Okla.Stat.Ann. 22-585 (1937) (enacted in 1935); S.D. Code 34.2801 (1939) (enacted in 1935); Utah Code Ann. 77-22-17 (1953) (enacted in 1935); Vt.Stat.Ann. 13-6561, 6562 (1958) (enacted in 1935); Wis.Stat.Ann. 955.07 (1958) (enacted in 1935).

The rule is modeled after the Ohio, New York, and New Jersey statutes:

(1) The requirement of notice in writing is taken from the Ohio statute.

(2) The requirement of an initial demand by the prosecuting attorney is based on the New York and New Jersey statutes.

(3) The requirement of a mutual exchange of witness lists is based on those statutes which require the defendant to disclose alibi witnesses. In the interest of mutuality, the requirement of a reciprocal exchange of witness lists has been added. The

enforcement provision is based on the Ohio and New York statutes. In New York, a defendant who fails to give advance notice of alibi may still give alibi testimony himself. *People v. Rakiec*, 23 N.Y.S.2d 607, aff'd 45 N.E.2d 812 (1942).

For an excellent article on notice of alibi statutes, court decisions thereunder, and some empirical data on the practical effect of the rules, see David M. Epstein, "Advance Notice of Alibi," 55 J. Crim. L. & Criminology 29 (1964).

1972 Amendment. Same as prior rule.

1992 Amendment. The purpose of the amendments is to gender neutralize the wording of the rule.

RULE 3.201. BATTERED-SPOUSE SYNDROME DEFENSE

(a) **[Notice of] Battered-Spouse Syndrome [Defense].** When in any criminal case it shall be intention of the defendant to rely on the defense of battered-spouse syndrome at trial, no evidence offered by the defendant for the purpose of establishing that defense shall be admitted in the case unless advance notice in writing of the defense shall have been given by the defendant as hereinafter provided.

(b) **Time for Filing Notice.** The defendant shall give notice of intent to rely on the defense of battered-spouse syndrome no later than 30 days prior to trial. The notice shall contain a statement of particulars showing the nature of the defense the defendant expects to prove and the names and addresses of the witnesses by whom the defendant expects to show battered-spouse syndrome, insofar as possible.

RULE 3.202. EXPERT TESTIMONY OF MENTAL MITIGATION DURING PENALTY PHASE OF CAPITAL TRIAL: NOTICE AND EXAMINATION BY STATE EXPERT

(a) **Notice of Intent to Seek Death Penalty.** The provisions of this rule apply only in those capital cases in which the state gives written notice of its intent to seek the death penalty within 45 days from the date of arraignment. Failure to give timely written notice under this subdivision does not preclude the state from seeking the death penalty.

(b) **Notice of Intent to Present Expert Testimony of Mental Mitigation.** When in any capital case, in which the state has given notice of intent to seek the death penalty under subdivision (a) of this rule, it shall be the intention of the defendant to present, during the penalty phase of the trial, expert testimony of a mental health professional, who has tested, evaluated, or examined the defendant, in order to establish statutory or nonstatutory mental mitigating circumstances, the defendant shall give written notice of intent to present such testimony.

(c) **Time for Filing Notice; Contents.** The defendant shall give notice of intent to present expert testimony of mental mitigation not less than 20 days before trial. The notice shall contain a statement of particulars listing the statutory and nonstatutory mental mitigating circumstances the defendant expects to establish through expert testimony and the names and addresses of the mental health experts by whom the defendant expects to establish mental mitigation, insofar as is possible.

(d) **Appointment of State Expert; Time of Examination.** After the filing

84

of such notice and on the motion of the state indicating its desire to seek the death penalty, the court shall order that, within 48 hours after the defendant is convicted of capital murder, the defendant be examined by a mental health expert chosen by the state. Attorneys for the state and defendant may be present at the examination. The examination shall be limited to those mitigating circumstances the defendant expects to establish through expert testimony.

(e) **Defendant's Refusal to Cooperate.** If the defendant refuses to be examined by or fully cooperate with the state's mental health expert, the court may, in its discretion:

(1) order the defense to allow the state's expert to review all mental health reports, tests, and evaluations by the defendant's mental health expert; or

(2) prohibit defense mental health experts from testifying concerning mental health tests, evaluations, or examinations of the defendant.

RULE 3.203. DEFENDANT'S INTELLECTUAL DISABILITY AS A BAR TO IMPOSITION OF THE DEATH PENALTY

(a) **Scope.** This rule applies in all first-degree murder cases in which the state attorney has not waived the death penalty on the record and the defendant's intellectual disability becomes an issue.

(b) **Definition of Intellectual Disability.** As used in this rule, the term "intellectual disability" means significantly subaverage general intellectual functioning existing concurrently with deficits in adaptive behavior and manifested during the period from conception to age 18. The term "significantly subaverage general intellectual functioning," for the purpose of this rule, means performance that is two or more standard deviations from the mean score on a standardized intelligence test authorized by the Department of Children and Family Services in rule 65G-4.011 of the Florida Administrative Code. The term "adaptive behavior," for the purpose of this rule, means the effectiveness or degree with which an individual meets the standards of personal independence and social responsibility expected of his or her age, cultural group, and community.

(c) **Motion for Determination of Intellectual Disability as a Bar to Execution: Contents; Procedures.**

(1) A defendant who intends to raise intellectual disability as a bar to execution shall file a written motion to establish intellectual disability as a bar to execution with the court.

(2) The motion shall state that the defendant is intellectually disabled and, if the defendant has been tested, evaluated, or examined by one or more experts, the names and addresses of the experts. Copies of reports containing the opinions of any experts named in the motion shall be attached to the motion. The court shall appoint an expert chosen by the state attorney if the state attorney so requests. The expert shall promptly test, evaluate, or examine the defendant and shall submit a written report of any findings to the parties and the court.

(3) If the defendant has not been tested, evaluated, or examined by one or more experts, the motion shall state that fact and the court shall appoint two

experts who shall promptly test, evaluate, or examine the defendant and shall submit a written report of any findings to the parties and the court.

(4)   Attorneys for the state and defendant may be present at the examinations conducted by court-appointed experts.

(5)   If the defendant refuses to be examined or fully cooperate with the court appointed experts or the state's expert, the court may, in the court's discretion:

(A)   order the defense to allow the court-appointed experts to review all mental health reports, tests, and evaluations by the defendant's expert;

(B)   prohibit the defense experts from testifying concerning any tests, evaluations, or examinations of the defendant regarding the defendant's intellectual disability; or

(C)   order such relief as the court determines to be appropriate.

(d)   Time for filing Motion for Determination of Intellectual Disability as a Bar to Execution. The motion for a determination of intellectual disability as a bar to execution shall be filed not later than 90 days prior to trial, or at such time as is ordered by the court.

(e)   Hearing on Motion to Determine Intellectual Disability. The circuit court shall conduct an evidentiary hearing on the motion for a determination of intellectual disability. At the hearing, the court shall consider the findings of the experts and all other evidence on the issue of whether the defendant is intellectually disabled. The court shall enter a written order prohibiting the imposition of the death penalty and setting forth the court's specific findings in support of the court's determination if the court finds that the defendant is intellectually disabled as defined in subdivision (b) of this rule. The court shall stay the proceedings for 30 days from the date of rendition of the order prohibiting the death penalty or, if a motion for rehearing is filed, for 30 days following the rendition of the order denying rehearing, to allow the state the opportunity to appeal the order. If the court determines that the defendant has not established intellectual disability, the court shall enter a written order setting forth the court's specific findings in support of the court's determination.

(f)   Waiver. A claim authorized under this rule is waived if not filed in accord with the time requirements for filing set out in this rule, unless good cause is shown for the failure to comply with the time requirements.

(g)   Finding of Intellectual Disability; Order to Proceed. If, after the evidence presented, the court is of the opinion that the defendant is intellectually disabled, the court shall order the case to proceed without the death penalty as an issue.

(h)   Appeal. An appeal may be taken by the state if the court enters an order finding that the defendant is intellectually disabled, which will stay further proceedings in the trial court until a decision on appeal is rendered. Appeals are to proceed according to Florida Rule of Appellate Procedure 9.140(c).

(i) **Motion to Establish Intellectual Disability as a Bar to Execution; Stay of Execution.** The filing of a motion to establish intellectual disability as a bar to execution shall not stay further proceedings without a separate order staying execution.

RULE 3.210. INCOMPETENCE TO PROCEED: PROCEDURE FOR RAISING THE ISSUE

(a) **Proceedings Barred during Incompetency.** A person accused of an offense or a violation of probation or community control who is mentally incompetent to proceed at any material stage of a criminal proceeding shall not be proceeded against while incompetent.

(1) A "material stage of a criminal proceeding" shall include the trial of the case, pretrial hearings involving questions of fact on which the defendant might be expected to testify, entry of a plea, violation of probation or violation of community control proceedings, sentencing, hearings on issues regarding a defendant's failure to comply with court orders or conditions, or other matters where the mental competence of the defendant is necessary for a just resolution of the issues being considered. The terms "competent," "competence," "incompetent," and "incompetence," as used in rules 3.210– 3.219, shall refer to mental competence or incompetence to proceed at a material stage of a criminal proceeding.

(2) The incompetence of the defendant shall not preclude such judicial action, hearings on motions of the parties, discovery proceedings, or other procedures that do not require the personal participation of the defendant.

(b) **Motion for Examination.** If, at any material stage of a criminal proceeding, the court of its own motion, or on motion of counsel for the defendant or for the state, has reasonable ground to believe that the defendant is not mentally competent to proceed, the court shall immediately enter its order setting a time for a hearing to determine the defendant's mental condition, which shall be held no later than 20 days after the date of the filing of the motion, and may order the defendant to be examined by no more than 3 experts, as needed, prior to the date of the hearing. Attorneys for the state and the defendant may be present at any examination ordered by the court.

(1) A written motion for the examination made by counsel for the defendant shall contain a certificate of counsel that the motion is made in good faith and on reasonable grounds to believe that the defendant is incompetent to proceed. To the extent that it does not invade the lawyer-client privilege, the motion shall contain a recital of the specific observations of and conversations with the defendant that have formed the basis for the motion.

(2) A written motion for the examination made by counsel for the state shall contain a certificate of counsel that the motion is made in good faith and on reasonable grounds to believe the defendant is incompetent to proceed and shall include a recital of the specific facts that have formed the basis for the motion, including a recitation of the observations of and statements of the defendant that have caused the state to file the motion.

(3) If the defendant has been released on bail or other release provision, the court may order the defendant to appear at a designated place for evaluation at a specific time as a condition of such release. If the court determines that the defendant

will not submit to the evaluation or that the defendant is not likely to appear for the scheduled evaluation, the court may order the defendant taken into custody until the determination of the defendant's competency to proceed. A motion made for evaluation under this subdivision shall not otherwise affect the defendant's right to release.

(4)   The order appointing experts shall:

(A)   identify the purpose or purposes of the evaluation, including the nature of the material proceeding, and specify the area or areas of inquiry that should be addressed by the evaluator;

(B)   specify the legal criteria to be applied; and

(C)   specify the date by which the report should be submitted and to whom the report should be submitted.

Committee Notes

1968 Adoption. (a) Same as section 917.01, Florida Statutes, except it was felt that court cannot by rule direct institution officials. Thus words, "he shall report this fact to the court which conducted the hearing. If the officer so reports" and concluding sentence, "No defendant committed by a court to an institution, by reason of the examination referred to in this paragraph, shall be released therefrom, without the consent of the court committing him," should be omitted from the rule but retained by statute.

(b)   Same as section 909.17, Florida Statutes.

(c)   Same as section 917.02, Florida Statutes.

1972 Amendment. Subdivision (a)   (3) refers to *Jackson v. Indiana*, 406 U.S. 715, 730, 92 S.Ct. 1845, 32 L.Ed.2d 435 (1972); also, *United States v. Curry*, 410 F.2d 1372 (4th Cir. 1969). Subdivision (d) is added to give the court authority to confine an insane person who is likely to cause harm to others even if the person is otherwise entitled to bail. The amendment does not apply unless the defendant contends that he or she is insane at the time of trial or at the time the offense was committed. The purpose of the amendment is to prevent admittedly insane persons from being at large when there is a likelihood they may injure themselves or others.

1977 Amendment. This language is taken, almost verbatim, from existing rule 3.210(a). The word "insane" is changed to reflect the new terminology, "competence to stand trial." The definition of competence to stand trial is taken verbatim from the United States Supreme Court formulation of the test in *Dusky v. United States*, 362 U.S. 402, 80 S.Ct. 788, 4 L.Ed.2d 824 (1960).

(a)   (2) The first part of this paragraph is taken, almost verbatim, from the existing rule. The right of counsel for the state to move for such examination has been added.

(b)   (1) In order to confine the defendant as incompetent to stand trial, the defendant must be confined under the same standards as those used for civil commitment. These criteria were set forth in the recent U.S. Supreme Court case of *Jackson v. Indiana*, 406 U.S. 715, 92 S.Ct. 1845, 32 L.Ed.2d 435 (1972), in which it was held to be a denial of equal protection to subject a criminal defendant to a more lenient commitment standard than would be applied to one not charged with a crime. Therefore, the criteria for involuntary civil commitment should be incorporated as the criteria for commitment for incompetence to stand trial.

In this subdivision is found the most difficult of the problems to resolve for the rule. The head-on conflict between the Department of Health and Rehabilitative Services, a part of the executive branch of the government, and the courts occurs when the administrator determines that a defendant no longer should be confined, but the trial judge does not wish the defendant released because the trial judge feels that further commitment is necessary. Under the civil commitment model, the administrator has the power to release a committed patient at such time as the administrator feels the patient no longer meets the standards for commitment. Obviously, since a defendant in a criminal case is under the jurisdiction of the court, such immediate release is unwarranted.

The time period of the initial commitment parallels that of civil commitment.

(b)   (2) treats the problem of what the court should do with a defendant who is not competent to stand trial, but who fails to meet the criteria for commitment. If incompetent, but not in need of treatment and not dangerous, then the defendant cannot be committed. The present rule provides for dismissal of the charges immediately. There appears to be no reason why someone in this situation should not be released pending trial on bail, as would other defendants.

The finding of "not guilty by reason of insanity," required under the present rule when a defendant cannot be tried by reason of incompetence, seems inappropriate since such a defense admits the commission of the fact of the crime but denies the defendant's mental state. Since no such finding has been made (and cannot be made), the verdict entered of not guilty by reason of insanity is not appropriate. Further, it would give a defendant, later competent, a res judicata or double jeopardy defense, the verdict being a final determination of guilt or innocence. It would seem far more appropriate to withdraw the charges. A defendant who regains competence within the period of the statute of limitations could still be tried for the offense, if such trial is warranted.

One of the major problems confronting the institution in which an incompetent person is being held is that of obtaining consent for medical procedures and treatment, not necessarily mental treatment. Generally, under the statute, the patient civilly committed is not thereby deemed incompetent to consent. At the commitment hearing in the civil proceedings, the judge may make the general competency determination. It is recommended that the same process apply in the hearing on competency to stand trial, and that, if the trial judge does not find the defendant incompetent for other purposes, the defendant be legally considered competent for such other purposes.

1980 Amendment.

(a)   This provision is identical to that which has been contained in all prior rules and statutes relating to competence to stand trial. No change is suggested.

(b)   In order to ensure that the proceedings move quickly the court is required to set a hearing within 20 days. This subdivision should be read in conjunction with rule 3.211 which requires the experts to submit their report to the court at such time as the court shall specify. The court therefore determines the time on which the report is to be submitted. The provision requiring at least 2 but no more than 3 experts is meant to coincide with section 394.02, Florida Statutes (1979), in which the legislature provides for the number of experts to be appointed and that at least 1 of such experts be appointed from a group of certain designated state- related professionals. This legislative restriction on appointment will ensure that the Department of Health and Rehabilitative Services will, to some extent, be involved in the hospitalization decision-making process. Other possible procedures were discussed at great length both among members of the committee and with representatives of the legislature, but it was decided that any more specific procedures should be developed on the local level in the individual circuits and that it would be inappropriate to mandate such specific procedures in a statewide court rule. Since it was felt by the committee to be a critical stage in the proceedings and subject to Sixth Amendment provisions, and since no psychiatrist-patient privilege applies to this stage of the proceeding, the committee felt that attorneys for both sides should have the right to be present at such examinations.

(1) and (2) A motion for examination relative to competency to stand trial should not be a "boiler plate" motion filed in every case. The inclusion of specific facts in the motion will give the trial judge a basis on which to determine whether there is sufficient indication of incompetence to stand trial that experts should be appointed to examine the defendant. Provision was made that conversations and observations need not be disclosed if they were felt to violate the lawyer-client privilege. Observations of the defendant were included in this phrase in that these may, in some cases, be considered "verbal acts."

(3) The mere filing of a motion for examination to determine competence to stand trial should not affect in any way the provision for release of a defendant on bail or other pretrial release provision. If a defendant has been released on bail, the judgment already having been made that he or she is so entitled, and as long as the defendant will continue to appear for appropriate evaluations, the mere fact that the motion was filed should not abrogate the right to bail. Obviously, if other factors would affect the defendant's right to release or would affect the right to release on specific release conditions, those conditions could be changed or the release revoked. By making the requirement that the defendant appear for evaluation a condition of release, the court can more easily take back into custody a defendant who has refused to appear for evaluation, and the defendant can then be evaluated in custody.

1988 Amendment. Title. The title is amended to reflect change in subdivision (a)(1), which broadens the issue of competency in criminal proceedings from the narrow issue of competency to stand trial to competency to proceed at any material stage of a criminal proceeding.

(a) This provision is broadened to prohibit proceeding against a defendant accused of a criminal offense or a violation of probation or community control and is broadened from competency to stand trial to competency to proceed at any material stage of a criminal proceeding as defined in subdivision (1).

(1) This new provision defines a material stage of a criminal proceeding when an incompetent defendant may not be proceeded against. This provision includes competence to be sentenced, which was previously addressed in rule 3.740 and is now addressed with more specificity in the new rule 3.214. Under the Florida Supreme Court decision of *Jackson v. State*, 452 So.2d 533 (Fla. 1984), this definition would not apply to a motion under rule 3.850.

(2)   This new provision allows certain matters in a criminal case to proceed, even if a defendant is determined to be incompetent, in areas not requiring the personal participation of the defendant.

(b)   This provision is amended to reflect the changes in subdivision (a) above.

(1)   Same as above.

(2)   Same as above.

(3)   Same as above. This provision also changes the phrase "released from custody" on a pre-trial release provision" to "released on bail or other release provision" because the term "custody" is subject to several interpretations.

(4)   This new provision is designed to specify and clarify in the order appointing experts, the matters the appointed experts are to address, and to specify when and to whom their reports are to be submitted. Court-appointed experts often do not understand the specific purpose of their examination or the specifics of the legal criteria to be applied. Specifying to whom the experts' reports are to be submitted is designed to avoid confusion.

1992 Amendment. The purpose of the amendment is to gender neutralize the wording of the rule.

Introductory Note Relating to Amendments to Rules 3.210 to 3.219. In 1985, the Florida Legislature enacted amendments to part I of chapter 394, the "Florida Mental Health Act," and substantial amendments to chapter 916 entitled "Mentally Deficient and Mentally Ill Defendants." The effect of the amendments is to avoid tying mentally ill or deficient defendants in the criminal justice system to civil commitment procedures in the "Baker Act." Reference to commitment of a criminal defendant found not guilty by reason of insanity has been removed from section 394.467, Florida Statutes. Chapter 916 now provides for specific commitment criteria of mentally ill or mentally retarded criminal defendants who are either incompetent to proceed or who have been found not guilty by reason of insanity in criminal proceedings.

In part, the following amendments to rules 3.210 to 3.219 are designed to reflect the 1985 amendments to chapters 394 and 916.

Florida judges on the criminal bench are committing and the Department of Health and Rehabilitative Services (HRS) mental health treatment facilities are admitting and treating those mentally ill and mentally retarded defendants in the criminal justice system who have been adjudged incompetent to stand trial and defendants found to be incompetent to proceed with violation of probation and community control proceedings. Judges are also finding such defendants not guilty by reason of insanity and committing them to HRS for treatment, yet there were no provisions for such commitments in the rules.

Some of the amendments to rules 3.210 to 3.219 are designed to provide for determinations of whether a defendant is mentally competent to proceed in any material stage of a criminal proceeding and provide for community treatment or commitment to HRS when a defendant meets commitment criteria under the provisions of chapter 916 as amended in 1985.

RULE 3.211. COMPETENCE TO PROCEED: SCOPE OF EXAMINATION AND REPORT

(a) **Examination by Experts.** Upon appointment by the court, the experts shall examine the defendant with respect to the issue of competence to proceed, as specified by the court in its order appointing the experts to evaluate the defendant, and shall evaluate the defendant as ordered.

(1) The experts shall first consider factors related to the issue of whether the defendant meets the criteria for competence to proceed; that is, whether the defendant has sufficient present ability to consult with counsel with a reasonable degree of rational understanding and whether the defendant has a rational, as well as factual, understanding of the pending proceedings.

(2) In considering the issue of competence to proceed, the examining experts shall consider and include in their report:

(A) the defendant's capacity to:

(i) appreciate the charges or allegations against the defendant.

(ii) appreciate the range and nature of possible penalties, if applicable, that may be imposed in the proceedings against the defendant;

(iii) understand the adversary nature of the legal process.

(iv) disclose to counsel facts pertinent to the proceedings at issue;

(v) manifest appropriate courtroom behavior;

(vi) testify relevantly; and

(B) any other factors deemed relevant by the experts.

(b) **Factors to Be Evaluated.** If the experts should find that the defendant is incompetent to proceed, the experts shall report on any recommended treatment for the defendant to attain competence to proceed. In considering the issues relating to treatment, the examining experts shall report on:

(1) the mental illness or intellectual disability causing the incompetence;

(2) the treatment or treatments appropriate for the mental illness or intellectual disability of the defendant and an explanation of each of the possible treatment alternatives in order of choices;

(3) the availability of acceptable treatment. If treatment is

92

available in the community, the expert shall so state in the report; and

        (4)   the likelihood of the defendant attaining competence under the treatment recommended, an assessment of the probable duration of the treatment required to restore competence, and the probability that the defendant will attain competence to proceed in the foreseeable future.

      (c)   **Written Findings of Experts.** Any written report submitted by the experts shall:

        (1)   identify the specific matters referred for evaluation;

        (2)   describe the evaluative procedures, techniques, and tests used in the examination and the purpose or purposes for each;

        (3)   state the expert's clinical observations, findings, and opinions on each issue referred for evaluation by the court, and indicate specifically those issues, if any, on which the expert could not give an opinion; and

        (4)   identify the sources of information used by the expert and present the factual basis for the expert's clinical findings and opinions.

      The procedure for determinations of the confidential status of reports is governed by Rule of Judicial Administration 2.420.

      (d)   **Limited Use of Competency Evidence.**

        (1)   The information contained in any motion by the defendant for determination of competency to proceed or in any report of experts filed under this rule insofar as the report relates solely to the issues of competency to proceed and commitment, and any information elicited during a hearing on competency to proceed or commitment held pursuant to this rule, shall be used only in determining the mental competency to proceed or the commitment or other treatment of the defendant.

        (2)   The defendant waives this provision by using the report, or portions thereof, in any proceeding for any other purpose, in which case disclosure and use of the report, or any portion thereof, shall be governed by applicable rules of evidence and rules of criminal procedure. If a part of the report is used by the defendant, the state may request the production of any other portion of that report that, in fairness, ought to be considered.

Committee Notes

      1980 Adoption. This rule provides for appointment of experts and for the contents of the report which the experts are to render. Since the issue of competency has been raised, the experts will, of course, report on this issue. If there is reason to believe that involuntary hospitalization is also required, the court should order the experts to make this evaluation as well during their initial examination. It was felt, however, that the experts should not inquire into involuntary hospitalization as a matter of course, but only if sufficient reasonable grounds to do so were alleged in the motion, comparing the procedure to that required by the civil commitment process.

(a)   Certain factors relating to competency to stand trial have been determined to be appropriate for analysis by examining experts. Often, with different experts involved, the experts do not use the same   criteria in reaching their conclusions. The criteria used by experts who testify at the competency and commitment hearings may not be the same as those used by persons involved in the treatment process or later hearings after treatment. This subdivision, therefore, addresses those factors which, at least, should be considered by experts at both ends of the spectrum. Additional factors may be considered, and these factors listed may be addressed in different ways. At least the requirement that these specific factors be addressed will give a common basis of understanding for the experts at the competency hearing, the trial judge, and the experts who will later receive a defendant who is found to be incompetent to stand trial and in need of involuntary hospitalization. The test for determining competency to stand trial is that which has been contained in both the prior rules and statutes developed from *Dusky v. United States*, 362 U.S. 402, 80 S.Ct. 788, 4 L.Ed.2d 824 (1960).

(1)   The factors set forth in this section have been developed by the Department of Health and Rehabilitative Services (HRS) in its Competency Evaluation Instrument, a refinement of the McGarry Competency Evaluation Procedure.

(b)   The issue of involuntary hospitalization is to be considered only if the court has ordered the experts to consider this issue; the court would do so if it found that there existed reasonable grounds to believe that the defendant met the criteria for involuntary hospitalization. The factors set forth in order to determine this issue are those that have been developed through prior statutes relating to involuntary hospitalization, from the case of *Jackson v. Indiana*, 406 U.S. 715, 92 S.Ct. 1845, 32 L.Ed.2d 435 (1972), and *In Re: Beverly*, 342 So.2d 481 (Fla. 1977).

As to criteria for involuntary hospitalization, see chapter 394, Florida Statutes, or, in the case of mental retardation, see chapter 393, Florida Statutes.

Section 394.467(1), Florida Statutes (1979), prescribes criteria for involuntary hospitalization or placement. In case of mental retardation, section 393.11, Florida Statutes (1979), governs.

(c)   In most instances, the issues of incompetency at time of trial and insanity at time of the offense will be raised at the same time or, at least, in the same case. In the event that the 2 are not raised in the same case, there would be no reason for the examining experts to inquire into the mental status of the defendant at the time of the offense itself at the incompetency examination. However, if insanity as a defense is raised, it would be most appropriate for judicial efficiency to have the examining experts inquire into all issues at the same time. This provision permits such inquiry by the experts in the event that notice of intent to rely on the defense of insanity has been filed by the defendant.

(d)   This provision is meant to permit local circuits to develop their own forms for such reports if they feel that such forms are appropriate. It does not preclude HRS from suggesting a form that would be of particular assistance to them and requesting its adoption, but adoption is not mandated.

(e)   This subdivision provides for the confidentiality of the information obtained by virtue of an examination of the defendant pursuant to this subdivision. Cf. §90.108, Fla.Stat. (1979); Fla.R.Civ.P. 1.330(6).

Section 916.12, Florida Statutes is a companion statute relating to mental competence to stand trial.

1988 Amendment. Title. The title is amended to reflect changes in rule 3.210.

(a)   This subdivision, which was originally an introductory paragraph, is amended to reflect changes in rule 3.210. The deletions related to the extent of the evaluation and when and to whom the experts' reports are to be submitted have been placed in rule 3.210(4) above.

(1)   This subdivision, which was formerly subdivision (a), has been amended to reflect changes in rule 3.210 above.

(2)   This provision has been amended to reflect the changes to rule 3.210. In addition, the 11 factors previously numbered (i) through (xi) have been reduced to 6 factors. Numbers (v), (vi), (vii), (x), and (xi) have been removed. Those 5 factors were felt to not be directly related to the issue of a defendant having the mental capacity to communicate with his or her attorney or to understand the proceedings against him or her and may have had the effect of confusing the issues the experts are to address in assessing a defendant's competency to proceed. The terms "ability" and "capacity" which were used interchangeably in the prior version of this provision have been changed to the single term "capacity" for continuity. A provision has been added which allows the appointed expert to also include any other factors deemed relevant to take into account different techniques and points of view of the experts.

(b)   This subdivision, including its 4 subdivisions, is amended to reflect the changes in rule 3.210. It also expands the determination from the limited area of whether an incompetent defendant should be voluntarily committed to treatment to recommended treatment options designed to restore or maintain competence. Subdivision (v) has been deleted because consideration of less restrictive alternatives is addressed in other amendments. [See rule 3.212(c)(3)(iv).] The amendments further reflect 1985 legislative amendments to chapters 394 and 916, Florida Statutes.

(ii)   Appropriate treatment may include maintaining the defendant on psychotropic or other medication. See rule 3.215.

(c)   This provision is amended to take into account the defense of insanity both at trial and in violation of probation/community control hearings.

(d)   This provision deletes the old language relating to the use of standardized forms. The new provision, with its 4 subdivisions, outlines in detail what the written report of an expert is to include, to ensure the appointed expert understands what issues are to be addressed, and that the report identifies sources of information, tests or evaluation techniques used, and includes the findings and observations upon which the expert's opinion is based. It requires the expert to specify those issues on which the expert could not render an opinion.

(e)   This provision is amended to comply with changes in rule 3.210. In addition, the second paragraph has been expanded to clarify under what circumstances the reports of experts in a competency evaluation may be discovered by the prosecution and used as evidence in a hearing other than the hearing on the issue of a defendant's competency to proceed.

1992 Amendment. The purpose of the amendments is to gender neutralize the wording of the rule.

Introductory Note Relating to Amendments to Rules 3.210 to 3.219. See notes following rule 3.210 for the text of this note.

RULE 3.212. COMPETENCE TO PROCEED: HEARING AND DISPOSITION

(a)   **Admissibility of Evidence.** The experts preparing the reports may be called by either party or the court, and additional evidence may be introduced by either party. The experts appointed by the court shall be deemed court witnesses whether called by the court or either party and may be examined as such by either party.

(b)   **Finding of Competence.** The court shall first consider the issue of the defendant's competence to proceed. If the court finds the defendant competent to proceed, the court shall enter its order so finding and shall proceed.

(c)   **Commitment on Finding of Incompetence.** If the court finds the defendant is incompetent to proceed, or that the defendant is competent to proceed but that the defendant's competence depends on the continuation of appropriate treatment for a mental illness or intellectual disability, the court shall consider issues relating to treatment necessary to restore or maintain the defendant's competence to proceed.

(1)   The court may order the defendant to undergo treatment if the court finds that the defendant is mentally ill or intellectually disabled and is in need of treatment and that treatment appropriate for the defendant's condition is available. If the court finds that the defendant may be treated in the community on bail or other release conditions, the court may make acceptance of reasonable medical treatment a condition of continuing bail or other release conditions.

(2)   If the defendant is incarcerated, the court may order treatment to be administered at the custodial facility or may order the defendant transferred to another facility for treatment or may commit the defendant as provided in subdivision (3).

(3)   A defendant may be committed for treatment to restore a defendant's competence to proceed if the court finds that:

(A)   the defendant meets the criteria for commitment as set forth by statute;

(B)   there is a substantial probability that the mental illness or intellectual disability causing the defendant's incompetence will respond to treatment and that the defendant will regain competency to proceed in the reasonably foreseeable future;

(C)   treatment appropriate for restoration of the defendant's competence to proceed is available; and

(D)   no appropriate treatment alternative less restrictive than that involving commitment is available.

96

(4)   If the court commits the defendant, the order of commitment shall contain:

(A)   findings of fact relating to the issues of competency and commitment addressing the factors set forth in rule 3.211 when applicable;

(B)   copies of the reports of the experts filed with the court pursuant to the order of examination;

(C)   copies of any other psychiatric, psychological, or social work reports submitted to the court relative to the mental state of the defendant; and

(D)   copies of the charging instrument and all supporting affidavits or other documents used in the determination of probable cause.

(5)   The treatment facility shall admit the defendant for hospitalization and treatment and may retain and treat the defendant. No later than 6 months from the date of admission, the administrator of the facility shall file with the court a report that shall address the issues and consider the factors set forth in rule 3.211, with copies to all parties. If, at any time during the 6- month period or during any period of extended commitment that may be ordered pursuant to this rule, the administrator of the facility determines that the defendant no longer meets the criteria for commitment or has become competent to proceed, the administrator shall notify the court by such a report, with copies to all parties.

(A)   If, during the 6-month period of commitment and treatment or during any period of extended commitment that may be ordered pursuant to this rule, counsel for the defendant shall have reasonable grounds to believe that the defendant is competent to proceed or no longer meets the criteria for commitment, counsel may move for a hearing on the issue of the defendant's competence or commitment. The motion shall contain a certificate of counsel that the motion is made in good faith and on reasonable grounds to believe that the defendant is now competent to proceed or no longer meets the criteria for commitment. To the extent that it does not invade the attorney-client privilege, the motion shall contain a recital of the specific observations of and conversations with the defendant that have formed the basis for the motion.

(B)   If, upon consideration of a motion filed by counsel for the defendant or the prosecuting attorney and any information offered the court in support thereof, the court has reasonable grounds to believe that the defendant may have regained competence to proceed or no longer meets the criteria for commitment, the court shall order the administrator of the facility to report to the court on such issues, with copies to all parties, and shall order a hearing to be held on those issues.

(6)   The court shall hold a hearing within 30 days of the receipt of any such report from the administrator of the facility on the issues raised thereby. If, following the hearing, the court determines that the defendant continues to be incompetent to proceed and that the defendant meets the criteria for continued commitment or treatment, the court shall order continued commitment or treatment for a period not to exceed 1 year. When the defendant is retained by the facility, the same procedure shall be repeated prior to the expiration of each additional 1-year period of extended commitment.

(7)   If, at any time after such commitment, the court decides, after

hearing, that the defendant is competent to proceed, it shall enter its order so finding and shall proceed.

(8) If, after any such hearing, the court determines that the defendant remains incompetent to proceed but no longer meets the criteria for commitment, the court shall proceed as provided in rule 3.212(d).

(d) **Release on Finding of Incompetence.** If the court decides that a defendant is not mentally competent to proceed but does not meet the criteria for commitment, the defendant may be released on appropriate release conditions for a period not to exceed 1 year. The court may order that the defendant receive outpatient treatment at an appropriate local facility and that the defendant report for further evaluation at specified times during the release period as conditions of release. A report shall be filed with the court after each evaluation by the persons appointed by the court to make such evaluations, with copies to all parties. The procedure for determinations of the confidential status of reports is governed by Rule of Judicial Administration 2.420.

Committee Notes

1980 Adoption. This rule sets forth the procedure for the hearing itself. If other experts have been involved who were not appointed pursuant to this rule, provision is made that such experts may then be called by either party. Those experts appointed by the court to conduct the examination, if called by the court or by either party to testify at the hearing, will be regarded as court experts. Either party may then examine such experts by leading questions or may impeach such experts. If a party calls an expert witness other than those appointed by the court pursuant to these rules, the usual evidentiary rules of examining such witnesses shall then apply. Following the hearing, the court may come to one of 3 conclusions: (a) the defendant is competent to stand trial, rule 3.212(a); (b) the defendant is incompetent to stand trial and is in need of involuntary hospitalization, rule 3.212(b); or (c) the defendant is incompetent to stand trial but is not in need of involuntary hospitalization, rule 3.212(c).

(a) This provision has been contained in every prior rule or statute relating to the issues of competency to stand trial and provides that if the defendant is competent the trial shall commence. No change is recommended.

(b) This subdivision provides for the second possible finding of the court, namely that the defendant is found incompetent to stand trial and is in need of involuntary hospitalization. It is designed to track the provisions of chapter 394, Florida Statutes, relating to involuntary hospitalization and the provisions of chapter 393 relating to residential services insofar as they may apply to the defendant under criminal charges. In this way, the procedures to be set up by the institution to which a criminal defendant is sent should not vary greatly from procedures common to the institution in the involuntary hospitalization or residential treatment of those not subject to criminal charges.

The criteria for involuntary hospitalization are set forth in section 394.467(1), Florida Statutes (1979). As to involuntary hospitalization for mental retardation, see section 393.11, Florida Statutes (1979); definition of treatment facility, see section 394.455, Florida Statutes (1979); involuntary admission to residential services, see section 393.11, Florida Statutes (1979).

(2) The requirement that there be certain contents to the order of

commitment is set forth in order to give greater assistance to the personnel of the treatment facility. The information to be included in the order should give them the benefit of all information that has been before the trial judge and has been considered by that judge in making the decision to involuntarily hospitalize the defendant. This information should then assist the personnel of the receiving institution in making their initial evaluation and in instituting appropriate treatment more quickly. The last requirement, that of supporting affidavits or other documents used in the determination of probable cause, is to give some indication of the nature of the offense to the examining doctors to enable them to determine when the defendant has reached a level of improvement that he or she can discuss the charge with "a reasonable degree of rational understanding."

(3) This subdivision is designed to correspond with a complementary section of the Florida Statutes. It mandates, as does the statute, that the treatment facility must admit the defendant for hospitalization and treatment. The time limitations set forth in this subdivision are designed to coincide with those set forth in chapter 394, Florida Statutes. If, however, the defendant should regain competence or no longer meets hospitalization criteria prior to the expiration of any of the time periods set, the administrator of the facility may report to the court and cause a re-evaluation of the defendant's mental status. At the end of the 6-month period, and every year thereafter, the administrator must report to the court. These time periods are set forth so as to coincide with chapter 394, Florida Statutes.

(i) Permits the defendant's attorney, in an appropriate case, to request a hearing if the attorney believes the defendant to have regained competency. The grounds for such belief are to be contained in the motion, as is a certificate of the good faith of counsel in filing it. If the motion is sufficient to give the court reasonable grounds to believe that the defendant may be competent or no longer meets the criteria for hospitalization, the court can order a report from the administrator and hold a hearing on the issues.

(4) The rule is meant to mandate that the court hold a hearing as quickly as possible, but the hearing must be held at least within 30 days of the receipt of the report from the administrator of the facility.

(c) This rule provides for the disposition of the defendant who falls under the third of the alternatives listed above, that is, one who is incompetent to stand trial but does not meet the provisions for involuntary hospitalization. It is meant to provide as great a flexibility as possible for the trial judge in handling such defendant.

As to criteria for involuntary hospitalization, see section 394.467 (1), Florida Statutes (1979).

Section 916.13, Florida Statutes complements this rule and provides for the hospitalization of defendants adjudicated incompetent to stand trial.

1988 Amendment. Title. The title has been amended to reflect changes in rules 3.210 and 3.211.

(a) This provision was formerly the introductory paragraph to this rule. It has been labeled subdivision (a) for consistency in form.

(b) This provision was former subdivision (a). It has been amended to reflect changes in rules 3.210 and 3.211. The former subdivisions (b) and (b) (1) have been deleted because similar language is now found in new subdivision (c).

(c)   This new provision, including all its subdivisions, is designed to reflect the commitment criteria in section 916.13   (1), Florida Statutes, and to reflect that commitment to the Department of Health and Rehabilitative Services is to be tied to specific commitment criteria when no less restrictive treatment alternative is available.

(1)   This provision provides for available community treatment when appropriate.

(2)   This provision provides for treatment in a custodial facility or other available community residential program.

(3)   This provision, and its subdivisions, outlines when a defendant may be committed and refers to commitment criteria under the provisions of section 916.13 (1), Florida Statutes.

(4)   This provision, and its subdivisions, was formerly subdivision (b)(2). The language has been amended to reflect changes in chapter 916 relating to the commitment of persons found incompetent to proceed and changes in rules 3.210 and 3.211.

(5)   This provision, and its subdivisions, was formerly subdivision (b)(3). The amendments are for the same reasons as (4) above.

(6)   This provision was formerly subdivision (b)(4). The amendments are for the same reasons as (4) above.

(7)   This provision was formerly subdivision (b)(5). The amendments are for the same reasons as (4) above.

(8)   This provision was formerly subdivision (b)(6). The amendments are for the same reasons as (4) above.

(d)   The amendments to the provision are for the same reasons as (4) above.

1992 Amendment. The amendments substitute "shall" in place of "may" in subdivision (c)(5)(B) to require the trial court to order the administrator of the facility where an incompetent defendant has been committed to report to the court on the issue of competency when the court has reasonable grounds to believe that the defendant may have regained competence to proceed or no longer meets the criteria for commitment. The amendments also gender neutralize the wording of the rule.

Introductory Note Relating to Amendments to Rules 3.210 to 3.219. See notes following rule 3.210 for the text of this note.

RULE 3.213. CONTINUING INCOMPETENCY TO PROCEED, EXCEPT INCOMPETENCY TO PROCEED WITH SENTENCING: DISPOSITION

(a)   **Dismissal without Prejudice during Continuing Incompetency.**

(1)   If at any time after 5 years following a determination that a person is incompetent to stand trial or proceed with a probation or community control violation hearing when charged with a felony, or 1 year when charged with a misdemeanor, the court, after hearing, determines that the defendant remains incompetent to stand trial or proceed with a probation or community control violation hearing, that there is no substantial probability that the defendant will become mentally competent to stand trial or proceed with a probation or community control violation hearing in the foreseeable future, and that the defendant does not meet the criteria for commitment, it shall dismiss the charges against the defendant without prejudice to the state to refile the charges should the defendant be declared competent to proceed in the future.

(2)   If the incompetency to stand trial or to proceed is due to intellectual disability or autism, the court shall dismiss the charges within a reasonable time after such determination, not to exceed 2 years for felony charges and 1 year for misdemeanor charges, unless the court specifies in its order the reasons for believing that the defendant will become competent within the foreseeable future and specifies the time within which the defendant is expected to become competent. The dismissal shall be without prejudice to the state to refile should the defendant be declared competent to proceed in the future.

(b)   Commitment or Treatment during Continuing Incompetency.

(1)   If at any time after 5 years following a determination that a person is incompetent to stand trial or proceed with a probation or community control violation hearing when charged with a felony, or 1 year when charged with a misdemeanor, the court, after hearing, determines that the defendant remains incompetent to stand trial or proceed with a probation or community control violation hearing, that there is no substantial probability that the defendant will become mentally competent to stand trial or proceed with a probation or community control violation hearing in the foreseeable future, and that the defendant does meet the criteria for commitment, the court shall dismiss the charges against the defendant and commit the defendant to the Department of Children and Family Services for involuntary hospitalization or residential services solely under the provisions of law or may order that the defendant receive outpatient treatment at any other facility or service on an outpatient basis subject to the provisions of those statutes. In the order of commitment, the judge shall order that the administrator of the facility notify the state attorney of the committing circuit no less than 30 days prior to the anticipated date of release of the defendant. If charges are dismissed pursuant to this subdivision, the dismissal shall be without prejudice to the state to refile the charges should the defendant be declared competent to proceed in the future.

(2)   If the continuing incompetency is due to intellectual disability or autism, and the defendant either lacks the ability to provide for his or her well-being or is likely to physically injure himself or herself, or others, the defendant may be involuntarily admitted to residential services as provided by law.

(c)   Applicability. This rule shall not apply to defendants determined to be incompetent to proceed with sentencing, which is addressed in rule 3.214.

Committee Notes

1980 Adoption. As to involuntary hospitalization, see section 394.467   (1), Florida Statutes (1979); as to involuntary admission to residential services, see chapter 393,

101

Florida Statutes (1979).

(b)   This provision is meant to deal with the defendant who remains incompetent after 5 years, and who does meet the criteria for involuntary hospitalization. It provides that the criminal charges will be   dismissed and the defendant will be involuntarily hospitalized. It further provides that the administrator of the facility must notify the state attorney prior to any release of a defendant committed pursuant to this subdivision.

As to criteria for involuntary hospitalization, see section 394.467(1), Florida Statutes (1979); in case of retardation, see chapter 393, Florida Statutes (1979).

(c)   Since commitment criteria for a defendant determined to be incompetent to stand trial are the   same as for civil hospitalization, there is no need to continue the difference between felony and misdemeanor   procedure.

Section 916.14, Florida Statutes, makes the statute of limitations and defense of former jeopardy inapplicable to criminal charges dismissed because of incompetence of defendant to stand trial.

1988 Amendment. Title. The title has been amended to comply with changes in rule 3.210, but specifically excludes competency to proceed with sentencing, which is addressed in the new rule 3.214.

(a)   This provision was amended to reflect changes in rules 3.210 and 3.211. New language is added which specifies that, if charges are dismissed under this rule, it is without prejudice to the state to refile if the defendant is declared competent to proceed in the future. Similar language was previously found in rule   3.214(d), but is more appropriate under this rule.

(b)   This provision has been amended for the same reasons as (a) above.

(c)   This new provision specifically exempts this rule from being used against a defendant determined to be incompetent to be sentenced, which is now provided in the new rule 3.214. It is replaced by the new rule 3.214.

1992 Amendment. The purpose of the amendment is to gender neutralize the wording of the rule.

Introductory Note Relating to Amendments to Rules 3.210 to 3.219. See notes following rule 3.210 for the text of this note.

RULE 3.214. INCOMPETENCY TO PROCEED TO SENTENCING: DISPOSITION

If a defendant is determined to be incompetent to proceed after being found guilty of an offense or violation of probation or community control or after voluntarily entering a plea to an offense or violation of probation or community control, but prior to sentencing, the court shall postpone the pronouncement of sentence and proceed pursuant to rule 3.210 (et seq.) and the following rules.

Committee Note

1988 Amendment. Title. This new rule replaces the former rule 3.740. It was felt to be more appropriately addressed in this sequence. The former rule 3.214 is now renumbered 3.215. The former rule 3.740 used the inappropriate phrase "(p)rocedures when insanity is alleged as cause for not pronouncing sentence." Insanity is an affirmative defense to a criminal charge. The more correct term is "incompetence to proceed to sentencing."

(a)   This new provision reiterates amendments to rule 3.210 and provides that sentencing shall be postponed for a defendant incompetent to proceed with disposition of a criminal matter—to include a finding of guilt at trial, after entry of a voluntary plea, or after a violation of probation or community control proceeding.

Introductory Note Relating to Amendments to Rules 3.210 to 3.219. See notes following rule 3.210 for the text of this note.

RULE 3.215. EFFECT OF ADJUDICATION OF INCOMPETENCY TO PROCEED: PSYCHOTROPIC MEDICATION

(a)   **Former Jeopardy.** If the defendant is declared incompetent to stand trial during trial and afterwards declared competent to stand trial, the defendant's other uncompleted trial shall not constitute former jeopardy.

(b)   **Limited Application of Incompetency Adjudication.** An adjudication of incompetency to proceed shall not operate as an adjudication of incompetency to consent to medical treatment or for any other purpose unless such other adjudication is specifically set forth in the order.

(c)   **Psychotropic Medication.** A defendant who, because of psychotropic medication, is able to understand the proceedings and to assist in the defense shall not automatically be deemed incompetent to proceed simply because the defendant's satisfactory mental condition is dependent on such medication, nor shall the defendant be prohibited from proceeding solely because the defendant is being administered medication under medical supervision for a mental or emotional condition.

(1)   Psychotropic medication is any drug or compound affecting the mind, behavior, intellectual functions, perception, moods, or emotion and includes anti-psychotic, anti-depressant, anti-manic, and anti-anxiety drugs.

(2)   If the defendant proceeds to trial with the aid of medication for a mental or emotional condition, on the motion of defense counsel, the jury shall, at the beginning of the trial and in the charge to the jury, be given explanatory instructions regarding such medication.

Committee Notes

1980 Adoption. (c) As to psychotropic medications, see section 916.12 (2), Florida Statutes (1980).

(d)   This subdivision is intended to provide specific exceptions to the speedy trial rule.

1988 Amendment. Title. This rule was formerly rule 3.214.

The amendments to this rule, including the title, are designed to reflect amendments to rules 3.210 and 3.211.

(d)   Matters contained in former subsection (d) are covered by the provisions of rule 3.191. That subsection has therefore been deleted.

1992 Amendment. The purpose of the amendment is to gender neutralize the wording of the rule.

Introductory Note Relating to Amendments to Rules 3.210 to 3.219. See notes following rule 3.210 for the text of this note.

RULE 3.216. INSANITY AT TIME OF OFFENSE OR PROBATION OR COMMUNITY CONTROL VIOLATION: NOTICE AND APPOINTMENT OF EXPERTS

(a)   **Expert to Aid Defense Counsel.** When in any criminal case a defendant is adjudged to be indigent or partially indigent, and is not represented by the public defender or regional counsel, and counsel has reason to believe that the defendant may be incompetent to proceed or that the defendant may have been insane at the time of the offense or probation or community control violation, counsel may so inform the court who shall appoint 1 expert to examine the defendant in order to assist counsel in the preparation of the defense. The expert shall report only to the attorney for the defendant and matters related to the expert shall be deemed to fall under the lawyer-client privilege.

(b)   **Notice of Intent to Rely on Insanity Defense.** When in any criminal case it shall be the intention of the defendant to rely on the defense of insanity either at trial or probation or community control violation hearing, no evidence offered by the defendant for the purpose of establishing that defense shall be admitted in the case unless advance notice in writing of the defense shall have been given by the defendant as hereinafter provided.

(c)   **Time for Filing Notice.** The defendant shall give notice of intent to rely on the defense of insanity no later than 15 days after the arraignment or the filing of a written plea of not guilty in the case when the defense of insanity is to be relied on at trial or no later than 15 days after being brought before the appropriate court to answer to the allegations in a violation of probation or community control proceeding. If counsel for the defendant shall have reasonable grounds to believe that the defendant may be incompetent to proceed, the notice shall be given at the same time that the motion for examination into the defendant's competence is filed. The notice shall contain a statement of particulars showing the nature of the insanity the defendant expects to prove and the names and addresses of the witnesses by whom the defendant expects to show insanity, insofar as is possible.

(d)   **Court-Ordered Evaluations.** On the filing of such notice and on motion of the state, the court shall order the defendant to be examined by the state's mental health expert(s) as to the sanity or insanity of the defendant at the time of the commission of the alleged offense or probation or community control violation. Attorneys for the state and defendant may be present at the examination.

(e)   Time for Filing Notice of Intent to Rely on a Mental Health Defense Other than Insanity. The defendant shall give notice of intent to rely on any mental health defense other than insanity as soon as a good faith determination has been made to utilize the defense but in no event later than 30 days prior to trial. The notice shall contain a statement of particulars showing the nature of the defense the defendant expects to prove and the names and addresses of the witnesses by whom the defendant expects to prove the defense, insofar as possible. If expert testimony will be presented, the notice shall indicate whether the expert has examined the defendant.

(f)   Court-Ordered Experts for Other Mental Health Defenses. If the notice to rely on any mental health defense other than insanity indicates the defendant will rely on the testimony of an expert who has examined the defendant, the court shall upon motion of the state order the defendant be examined by one qualified expert for the state as to the mental health defense raised by the defendant. Upon a showing of good cause, the court may order additional examinations upon motion by the state or the defendant. Attorneys for the state and defendant may be present at the examination. When the defendant relies on the testimony of an expert who has not examined the defendant, the state shall not be entitled to a compulsory examination of the defendant.

(g)   Waiver of Time to File. On good cause shown for the omission of the notice of intent to rely on the defense of insanity, or any mental health defense, the court may in its discretion grant the defendant 10 days to comply with the notice requirement. If leave is granted and the defendant files the notice, the defendant is deemed unavailable to proceed. If the trial has already commenced, the court, only on motion of the defendant, may declare a mistrial in order to permit the defendant to raise the defense of insanity pursuant to this rule. Any motion for mistrial shall constitute a waiver of the defendant's right to any claim of former jeopardy arising from the uncompleted trial.

(h)   Evaluating Defendant after Pretrial Release. If the defendant has been released on bail or other release conditions, the court may order the defendant to appear at a designated place for evaluation at a specific time as a condition of the release provision. If the court determines that the defendant will not submit to the evaluation provided for herein or that the defendant is not likely to appear for the scheduled evaluation, the court may order the defendant taken into custody until the evaluation is completed. A motion made for evaluation under this subdivision shall not otherwise affect the defendant's right to pretrial release.

(i)   Evidence. Any experts appointed by the court may be summoned to testify at the trial, and shall be deemed court witnesses whether called by the court or by either party. Other evidence regarding the defendant's insanity or mental condition may be introduced by either party. At trial, in its instructions to the jury, the court shall include an instruction on the consequences of a verdict of not guilty by reason of insanity.

Committee Notes

1980 Adoption.

(a)   This subdivision is based on *Pouncy v. State*, 353 So.2d 640 (Fla. 3d DCA 1977), and provides that an expert may be provided for an indigent defendant. The appointment of the expert will in this way allow the public defender or court-appointed attorney to screen possible incompetency or insanity cases and give a basis for determining whether issues of incompetency or insanity ought to be raised before the court; it will also permit the defense attorney to specify in greater detail in the statement of particulars the nature of the insanity that attorney expects to prove, if any, and the basis for the raising of that defense.

(b)   Essentially the same as in prior rules; provides that written notice must be given in advance by the defendant.

(c)   Since counsel for indigents often are not appointed until arraignment and since it is sometimes difficult for a defendant to make a determination on whether the defense of insanity should be raised prior to arraignment, a 15-day post-arraignment period is provided for the filing of the notice. The defendant must raise incompetency at the same time as insanity, if at all possible. With the appointment of the expert to assist, the defendant should be able to raise both issues at the same time if grounds for both exist. The remainder of the rule, providing for the statement to be included in the notice, is essentially the same as that in prior rules.

(d)   The appointment of experts provision is designed to track, insofar as possible, the provisions for appointment of experts contained in the rules relating to incompetency to stand trial and in the Florida Statutes relating to appointment of expert witnesses. Insofar as possible, the single examination should include incompetency, involuntary commitment issues where there are reasonable grounds for their consideration, and issues of insanity at time of the offense. Judicial economy would mandate such a single examination where possible.

(g)   In order to obtain more standardized reports, specific items relating to the examination are required of the examining experts. See note to rule 3.211(a).

(h)   Essentially the substance of prior rule 3.210(e)(4) and (5), with some changes. Both prior provisions are combined into a single provision; speedy trial time limits are no longer set forth, but waiver of double jeopardy is mandated.

(i)   Same as rule 3.210(b)   (3), relating to incompetency to stand trial. See commentary to that rule.

(j)   A restatement of former rule 3.210(e)   (7). The provision that experts called by the court shall be deemed court witnesses is new. The former provision relating to free access to the defendant is eliminated as unnecessary.

As to appointment of experts, see section 912.11, Florida Statutes.

1988 Amendment. The amendments to this rule, including the title, provide for the affirmative defense of insanity in violation of probation or community control proceedings as well as at trial.

1992 Amendment. The purpose of the amendment is to gender neutralize the wording of the rule.

1996 Amendment. Subdivisions (e) and (f) were added to conform to State v. Hickson, 630 So.2d 172 (Fla. 1993). These amendments are not intended to expand existing case law.

Introductory Note Relating to Amendments to Rules 3.210 to 3.219. See notes following rule 3.210 for the text of this note.

RULE 3.217. JUDGMENT OF NOT GUILTY BY REASON OF INSANITY: DISPOSITION OF DEFENDANT

(a) **Verdict of Not Guilty by Reason of Insanity.** When a person is found by the jury or the court not guilty of the offense or is found not to be in violation of probation or community control by reason of insanity, the jury or judge, in giving the verdict or finding of not guilty judgment, shall state that it was given for that reason.

(b) **Treatment, Commitment, or Discharge after Acquittal.** When a person is found not guilty of the offense or is found not to be in violation of probation or community control by reason of insanity, if the court then determines that the defendant presently meets the criteria set forth by law, the court shall commit the defendant to the Department of Children and Family Services or shall order outpatient treatment at any other appropriate facility or service, or shall discharge the defendant. Any order committing the defendant or requiring outpatient treatment or other outpatient service shall contain:

(1)   findings of fact relating to the issue of commitment or other court-ordered treatment;

(2)   copies of any reports of experts filed with the court; and

(3)   any other psychiatric, psychological, or social work report submitted to the court relative to the mental state of the defendant.

Committee Notes

1980 Adoption.

(a)   Same substance as in prior rule.

(b)   The criteria for commitment are set forth in chapter 394, Florida Statutes. This rule incorporates those statutory criteria by reference and then restates the other alternatives available to the judge under former rule 3.210.

See section 912.18, Florida Statutes, for criteria.

(1) This subdivision is equivalent to rule 3.212(b) (2); see commentary to that rule.

1988 Amendment. The amendments to this rule provide for evaluation of a defendant found not guilty by reason of insanity in violation of probation or community control proceedings as well as at trial. The amendments further reflect 1985 amendments to chapter 916, Florida Statutes.

1992 Amendment. The purpose of the amendment is to gender neutralize the wording of the rule.

Introductory Note Relating to Amendments to Rules 3.210 to 3.219. See notes following rule 3.210 for the text of this note.

RULE 3.218. COMMITMENT OF A DEFENDANT FOUND NOT GUILTY BY REASON OF INSANITY

(a) **Commitment; 6-Month Report.** The Department of Children and Family Services shall admit to an appropriate facility a defendant found not guilty by reason of insanity under rule 3.217 and found to meet the criteria for commitment for hospitalization and treatment and may retain and treat the defendant. No later than 6 months from the date of admission, the administrator of the facility shall file with the court a report, and provide copies to all parties, which shall address the issues of further commitment of the defendant. If at any time during the 6 month period, or during any period of extended hospitalization that may be ordered under this rule, the administrator of the facility shall determine that the defendant no longer meets the criteria for commitment, the administrator shall notify the court by such a report and provide copies to all parties. The procedure for determinations of the confidential status of reports is governed by Rule of Judicial Administration 2.420.

(b) **Right to Hearing if Committed upon Acquittal.** The court shall hold a hearing within 30 days of the receipt of any report from the administrator of the facility on the issues raised thereby, and the defendant shall have a right to be present at the hearing. If the court determines that the defendant continues to meet the criteria for continued commitment or treatment, the court shall order further commitment or treatment for a period not to exceed 1 year. The same procedure shall be repeated before the expiration of each additional 1 year period in which the defendant is retained by the facility.

(c) **Evidence to Determine Continuing Insanity.** Before any hearing held under this rule, the court may, on its own motion, and shall, on motion of counsel for the state or defendant, appoint no fewer than 2 nor more than 3 experts to examine the defendant relative to the criteria for continued commitment or placement of the defendant and shall specify the date by which the experts shall report to the court on these issues and provide copies to all parties.

Committee Notes

1980 Adoption. This provision provides for hospitalization of a defendant found not guilty by reason of insanity and is meant to track similar provisions in the rules relating to competency to stand trial and the complementary statutes. It provides for an initial 6 month period of commitment with successive 1-year periods; it provides for reports to the court and for the appointment of experts to examine the defendant when such hearings are necessary. The underlying rationale of this rule is to make standard, insofar as possible, the commitment process, whether it be for incompetency to stand trial or following a judgment of not guilty by reason of insanity.

For complementary statute providing for hospitalization of defendant adjudicated not guilty by reason of insanity, see section 912.15, Florida Statutes.

1988 Amendment. The amendments to this rule, including the title, provide for commitment of defendants found not guilty by reason of insanity in violation of probation or community control proceedings, as well as those so found at trial. The amendments further reflect 1985 amendments to chapter 916, Florida Statutes.

Introductory Note Relating to Amendments to Rules 3.210 to 3.219. See notes following rule 3.210 for the text of this note.

RULE 3.219. CONDITIONAL RELEASE

(a)   **Release Plan.** The committing court may order a conditional release of any defendant who has been committed according to a finding of incompetency to proceed or an adjudication of not guilty by reason of insanity based on an approved plan for providing appropriate outpatient care and treatment. When the administrator shall determine outpatient treatment of the defendant to be appropriate, the administrator may file with the court, and provide copies to all parties, a written plan for outpatient treatment, including recommendations from qualified professionals. The plan may be submitted by the defendant. The plan shall include:

(1)   special provisions for residential care, adequate supervision of the defendant, or both;

(2)   provisions for outpatient mental health services; and

(3)   if appropriate, recommendations for auxiliary services such as vocational training, educational services, or special medical care.

In its order of conditional release, the court shall specify the conditions of release based on the release plan and shall direct the appropriate agencies or persons to submit periodic reports to the court regarding the defendant's compliance with the conditions of the release, and progress in treatment, and provide copies to all parties. The procedure for determinations of the confidential status of reports is governed by Rule of Judicial Administration 2.420.

(b)   **Defendant's Failure to Comply.** If it appears at any time that the defendant has failed to comply with the conditions of release, or that the defendant's condition has deteriorated to the point that inpatient care is required, or that the release conditions should be modified, the court, after hearing, may modify the release conditions or, if the court finds the defendant meets the statutory criteria for commitment, may order that the defendant be recommitted to the Department of Children and Family Services for further treatment.

(c)   **Discharge.** If at any time it is determined after hearing that the defendant no longer requires court-supervised follow-up care, the court shall terminate its jurisdiction in the cause and discharge the defendant.

Committee Notes

1980 Adoption. This rule implements the prior statutory law permitting conditional release.

For complementary statute providing for conditional release, see section 916.17, Florida Statutes.

1988 Amendment. The amendments to this rule are designed to reflect amendments to rules 3.210, 3.211, and 3.218 as well as 1985 amendments to chapter 916, Florida Statutes.

(b)   This provision has been amended to permit the court to recommit a conditionally released defendant to HRS under the provisions of chapter 916 only if the court makes a finding that the defendant currently meets the statutory commitment criteria found in section 916.13 (1), Florida Statutes.

1992 Amendment. The purpose of the amendment is to gender neutralize the wording of the rule.

Introductory Note Relating to Amendments to Rules 3.210 to 3.219. See notes following rule 3.210 for the text of this note.

VI. DISCOVERY

RULE 3.220. DISCOVERY

    (a)   **Notice of Discovery.** After the filing of the charging document, a defendant may elect to participate in the discovery process provided by these rules, including the taking of discovery depositions, by filing with the court and serving on the prosecuting attorney a "Notice of Discovery" which shall bind both the prosecution and defendant to all discovery procedures contained in these rules. Participation by a defendant in the discovery process, including the taking of any deposition by a defendant or the filing of a public records request under chapter 119, Florida Statutes, for law enforcement records relating to the defendant's pending prosecution, which are nonexempt as a result of a codefendant's participation in discovery, shall be an election to participate in discovery and triggers a reciprocal discovery obligation for the defendant. If any defendant knowingly or purposely shares in discovery obtained by a codefendant, the defendant shall be deemed to have elected to participate in discovery.

    (b)   **Prosecutor's Discovery Obligation.**

        (1)   Within 15 days after service of the Notice of Discovery, the prosecutor shall serve a written Discovery Exhibit which shall disclose to the defendant and permit the defendant to inspect, copy, test, and photograph the following information and material within the state's possession or control, except that any property or material that portrays sexual performance by a child or constitutes child pornography may not be copied, photographed, duplicated, or otherwise reproduced so long as the state attorney makes the property or material reasonably available to the defendant or the defendant's attorney:

            (A)   a list of the names and addresses of all persons known to the prosecutor to have information that may be relevant to any offense charged or any defense thereto, or to any similar fact evidence to be presented at trial under section 90.404 (2), Florida Statutes. The names and addresses of persons listed shall be clearly designated in the following categories:

                (i)   Category A. These witnesses shall include (1) eye witnesses, (2) alibi witnesses and rebuttal to alibi witnesses, (3) witnesses who were present when a recorded or unrecorded statement was taken from or made by a defendant or codefendant, which shall be separately identified within this category, (4) investigating officers, (5) witnesses known by the prosecutor to have any material information that tends to negate the guilt of the defendant as to any offense charged, (6) child hearsay witnesses, and (7) expert witnesses who have not provided a written report and a curriculum vitae or who are going to testify.

(ii)   Category B. All witnesses not listed in either Category A or Category C.

(iii)   Category C. All witnesses who performed only ministerial functions or whom the prosecutor does not intend to call at trial and whose involvement with and knowledge of the case is fully set out in a police report or other statement furnished to the defense;

(B)   the statement of any person whose name is furnished in compliance with the preceding subdivision. The term "statement" as used herein includes a written statement made by the person and signed or otherwise adopted or approved by the person and also includes any statement of any kind or manner made by the person and written or recorded or summarized in any writing or recording. The term "statement" is specifically intended to include all police and investigative reports of any kind prepared for or in connection with the case, but shall not include the notes from which those reports are compiled;

(C)   any written or recorded statements and the substance of any oral statements made by the defendant, including a copy of any statements contained in police reports or report summaries, together with the name and address of each witness to the statements;

(D)   any written or recorded statements and the substance of any oral statements made by a codefendant;

(E)   those portions of recorded grand jury minutes that contain testimony of the defendant;

(F)   any tangible papers or objects that were obtained from or belonged to the defendant;

(G)   whether the state has any material or information that has been provided by a confidential informant;

(H)   whether there has been any electronic surveillance, including wiretapping, of the premises of the defendant or of conversations to which the defendant was a party and any documents relating thereto;

(I)   whether there has been any search or seizure and any documents relating thereto;

(J)   reports or statements of experts made in connection with the particular case, including results of physical or mental examinations and of scientific tests, experiments, or comparisons; and

(K)   any tangible papers or objects that the prosecuting attorney intends to use in the hearing or trial and that were not obtained from or that did not belong to the defendant.

(L)   any tangible paper, objects or substances in the possession of law enforcement that could be tested for DNA.

(2)   If the court determines, in camera, that any police or investigative report contains irrelevant, sensitive information or information interrelated with other crimes or criminal activities and the disclosure of the contents of the police report may seriously impair law enforcement or jeopardize the investigation of those other crimes or activities, the court may prohibit or partially restrict the disclosure.

(3)   The court may prohibit the state from introducing into evidence any of the foregoing material not disclosed, so as to secure and maintain fairness in the just determination of the cause.

(4)   As soon as practicable after the filing of the charging document the prosecutor shall disclose to the defendant any material information within the state's possession or control that tends to negate the guilt of the defendant as to any offense charged, regardless of whether the defendant has incurred reciprocal discovery obligations.

(c)   Disclosure to Prosecution.

(1)   After the filing of the charging document and subject to constitutional limitations, the court may require a defendant to:

(A)   appear in a lineup;

(B)   speak for identification by witnesses to an offense;

(C)   be fingerprinted;

(D)   pose for photographs not involving re-enactment of a scene;

(E)   try on articles of clothing;

(F)   permit the taking of specimens of material under the defendant's fingernails;

(G)   permit the taking of samples of the defendant's blood, hair, and other materials of the defendant's body that involves no unreasonable intrusion thereof;

(H)   provide specimens of the defendant's handwriting; and

(I)   submit to a reasonable physical or medical inspection of the defendant's body.

(2)   If the personal appearance of a defendant is required for the foregoing purposes, reasonable notice of the time and location of the appearance shall be given by the prosecuting attorney to the defendant and his or her counsel. Provisions may be made for appearances for such purposes in an order admitting a defendant to bail or providing for pretrial release.

(d)   Defendant's Obligation.

(1)   If a defendant elects to participate in discovery, either through filing the appropriate notice or by participating in any discovery process, including the taking of a discovery deposition, the following disclosures shall be made:

(A)   Within 15 days after receipt by the defendant of the Discovery Exhibit furnished by the prosecutor pursuant to subdivision (b)   (1)(A) of this rule, the defendant shall furnish to the prosecutor a written list of the names and addresses of all witnesses whom the defendant expects to call as witnesses at the trial or hearing. When the prosecutor subpoenas a witness whose name has been furnished by the defendant, except for trial subpoenas,   the rules applicable to the taking of depositions shall apply.

(B)   Within 15 days after receipt of the prosecutor's Discovery Exhibit the defendant shall serve a written Discovery Exhibit which shall disclose to and permit the prosecutor to inspect, copy, test, and photograph the following information and material that is in the defendant's possession or control:

(i)   the statement of any person listed in subdivision (d)(1)   (A), other than that of the defendant;

(ii)   reports or statements of experts made in connection with the particular case, including results of physical or mental examinations and of scientific tests, experiments, or comparisons; and

(iii)   any tangible papers or objects that the defendant intends to use in the hearing or trial.

(2)   The prosecutor and the defendant shall perform their obligations under this rule in a manner mutually agreeable or as ordered by the court.

(3)   The filing of a motion for protective order by the prosecutor will automatically stay the times provided for in this subdivision. If a protective order is granted, the defendant may, within 2 days thereafter, or at any time before the prosecutor furnishes the information or material that is the subject of the motion for protective order, withdraw the defendant's notice of discovery and not be required to furnish reciprocal discovery.

(e)   **Restricting Disclosure.** The court on its own initiative or on motion of counsel shall deny or partially restrict disclosures authorized by this rule if it finds there is a substantial risk to any person of physical harm, intimidation, bribery, economic reprisals, or unnecessary annoyance or embarrassment resulting from the disclosure, that outweighs any usefulness of the disclosure to either party.

(f)   **Additional Discovery.** On a showing of materiality, the court may require such other discovery to the parties as justice may require.

(g)   **Matters Not Subject to Disclosure.**

(1)   **Work Product.** Disclosure shall not be required of legal research or of records, correspondence, reports, or memoranda to the extent that they contain the opinions, theories, or conclusions of the prosecuting or defense attorney or members of their legal staffs.

(2)   **Informants.** Disclosure of a confidential informant shall not be required unless the confidential informant is to be produced at a hearing or trial or a failure to disclose the informant's identity will infringe the constitutional rights of the defendant.

(h)   Discovery Depositions.

(1)   **Generally.** At any time after the filing of the charging document any party may take the deposition upon oral examination of any person authorized by this rule. A party taking a deposition shall give reasonable written notice to each other party and shall make a good faith effort to coordinate the date, time, and location of the deposition to accommodate the schedules of other parties and the witness to be deposed. The notice shall state the time and the location where the deposition is to be taken, the name of each person to be examined, and a certificate of counsel that a good faith effort was made to coordinate the deposition schedule. After notice to the parties the court may, for good cause shown, extend or shorten the time and may change the location of the deposition. Except as provided herein, the procedure for taking the deposition, including the scope of the examination, and the issuance of a subpoena (except a subpoena duces tecum) for deposition by an attorney of record in the action, shall be the same as that provided in the Florida Rules of Civil Procedure. Any deposition taken pursuant to this rule may be used by any party for the purpose of contradicting or impeaching the testimony of the deponent as a witness. The trial court or the clerk of the court may, upon application by a pro se litigant or the attorney for any party, issue subpoenas for the persons whose depositions are to be taken. In any case, including multiple defendants or consolidated cases, no person shall be deposed more than once except by consent of the parties or by order of the court issued on good cause shown. A witness who refuses to obey a duly served subpoena may be adjudged in contempt of the court from which the subpoena issued.

(A)   The defendant may, without leave of court, take the deposition of any witness listed by the prosecutor as a Category A witness or listed by a co-defendant as a witness to be called at a joint trial or hearing. After receipt by the defendant of the Discovery Exhibit, the defendant may, without leave of court, take the deposition of any unlisted witness who may have information relevant to the offense charged. The prosecutor may, without leave of court, take the deposition of any witness listed by the defendant to be called at a trial or hearing.

(B)   No party may take the deposition of a witness listed by the prosecutor as a Category B witness except upon leave of court with good cause shown. In determining whether to allow a deposition, the court should consider the consequences to the defendant, the complexities of the issues involved, the complexity of the testimony of the witness (e.g., experts), and the other opportunities available to the defendant to discover the information sought by deposition.

(C)   A witness listed by the prosecutor as a Category C witness shall not be subject to deposition unless the court determines that the witness should be listed in another category.

(D)   No deposition shall be taken in a case in which the defendant is charged only with a misdemeanor or a criminal traffic offense when all other discovery provided by this rule has been complied with unless good cause can be shown to the trial court. In determining whether to allow a deposition, the court should consider the consequences to the defendant, the complexity of the issues involved, the complexity of the witness' testimony (e.g., experts), and the other opportunities available to the defendant to discover the information sought by deposition. However, this prohibition against the taking of depositions shall not be applicable if following the furnishing of discovery by the defendant the state then takes the statement of a listed defense witness pursuant to section 27.04, Florida Statutes.

(2)   **Transcripts.** No transcript of a deposition for which the state may be obligated to expend funds shall be ordered by a party unless it is in compliance with general law.

(3)   **Location of Deposition.** Depositions of witnesses residing in the county in which the trial is to take place shall be taken in the building in which the trial shall be held, such other location as is agreed on by the parties, or a location designated by the court. Depositions of witnesses residing outside the county in which the trial is to take place shall be taken in a court reporter's office in the county or state in which the witness resides, such other location as is agreed on by the parties, or a location designated by the court.

(4)   **Depositions of Sensitive Witnesses.** Depositions of children under the age of 16 shall be videotaped unless otherwise ordered by the court. The court may order the videotaping of a deposition or the taking of a deposition of a witness with fragile emotional strength to be in the presence of the trial judge or a special magistrate.

(5)   **Depositions of Law Enforcement Officers.** Subject to the general provisions of subdivision (h)   (1), law enforcement officers shall appear for deposition, without subpoena, upon written notice of taking deposition delivered at the address of the law enforcement agency or department, or an address designated by the law enforcement agency or department, five days prior to the date of the deposition. Law enforcement officers who fail to appear for deposition after being served notice as required by the rule may be adjudged in contempt of court.

(6)   **Witness Coordinating Office/Notice of Taking Deposition.** If a witness coordinating office has been established in the jurisdiction pursuant to applicable Florida Statutes, the deposition of any witness should be coordinated through that office. The witness coordinating office should attempt to schedule the depositions of a witness at a time and location convenient for the witness and acceptable to the parties.

(7)   **Defendant's Physical Presence.** A defendant shall not be physically present at a deposition except on stipulation of the parties or as provided by this rule. The court may order the physical presence of the defendant on a showing of good cause. The court may consider   (A) the need for the physical presence of the defendant to obtain effective discovery,   (B) the intimidating effect of the defendant's presence on the witness, if any, (C) any cost or inconvenience which may result, and   (D) any alternative electronic or audio/visual means available.

(8)   **Telephonic Statements.** On stipulation of the parties and the consent of the witness, the statement of any witness may be taken by telephone in lieu of the deposition of the witness. In such case, the witness need not be under oath. The statement, however, shall be recorded and may be used for impeachment at trial as a prior inconsistent statement pursuant to the Florida Evidence Code.

(i)   **Investigations Not to Be Impeded.** Except as is otherwise provided as to matters not subject to disclosure or restricted by protective orders, neither the counsel for the parties nor other prosecution or defense personnel shall advise persons having relevant material or information (except the defendant) to refrain from discussing the case with opposing counsel or showing opposing counsel any relevant material, nor shall they otherwise impede opposing counsel's investigation of the case.

(j) **Continuing Duty to Disclose.** If, subsequent to compliance with the rules, a party discovers additional witnesses or material that the party would have been under a duty to disclose or produce at the time of the previous compliance, the party shall promptly disclose or produce the witnesses or material in the same manner as required under these rules for initial discovery.

(k) **Court May Alter Times.** The court may alter the times for compliance with any discovery under these rules on good cause shown.

(l) **Protective Orders.**

(1) **Motion to Restrict Disclosure of Matters.** On a showing of good cause, the court shall at any time order that specified disclosures be restricted, deferred, or exempted from discovery, that certain matters not be inquired into, that the scope of the deposition be limited to certain matters, that a deposition be sealed and after being sealed be opened only by order of the court, or make such other order as is appropriate to protect a witness from harassment, unnecessary inconvenience, or invasion of privacy, including prohibiting the taking of a deposition. All material and information to which a party is entitled, however, must be disclosed in time to permit the party to make beneficial use of it.

(2) **Motion to Terminate or Limit Examination.** At any time during the taking of a deposition, on motion of a party or of the deponent, and upon a showing that the examination is being conducted in bad faith or in such manner as to unreasonably annoy, embarrass, or oppress the deponent or party, the court in which the action is pending or the circuit court where the deposition is being taken may (1) terminate the deposition, (2) limit the scope and manner of the taking of the deposition, (3) limit the time of the deposition, (4) continue the deposition to a later time, (5) order the deposition to be taken in open court, and, in addition, may (6) impose any sanction authorized by this rule. If the order terminates the deposition, it shall be resumed thereafter only upon the order of the court in which the action is pending. Upon demand of any party or deponent, the taking of the deposition shall be suspended for the time necessary to make a motion for an order.

(m) **In Camera and Ex Parte Proceedings.**

(1) Any person may move for an order denying or regulating disclosure of sensitive matters. The court may consider the matters contained in the motion in camera.

(2) Upon request, the court shall allow the defendant to make an ex parte showing of good cause for taking the deposition of a Category B witness.

(3) A record shall be made of proceedings authorized under this subdivision. If the court enters an order granting relief after an in camera inspection or ex parte showing, the entire record of the proceeding shall be sealed and preserved and be

116

made available to the appellate court in the event of an appeal.

(n) **Sanctions.**

(1)   If, at any time during the course of the proceedings, it is brought to the attention of the court that a party has failed to comply with an applicable discovery rule or with an order issued pursuant to an applicable discovery rule, the court may order the party to comply with the discovery or inspection of materials not previously disclosed or produced, grant a continuance, grant a mistrial, prohibit the party from calling a witness not disclosed or introducing in evidence the material not disclosed, or enter such other order as it deems just under the circumstances.

(2)   Willful violation by counsel or a party not represented by counsel of an applicable discovery rule, or an order issued pursuant thereto, shall subject counsel or the unrepresented party to appropriate sanctions by the court. The sanctions may include, but are not limited to, contempt proceedings against the attorney or unrepresented party, as well as the assessment of costs incurred by the opposing party, when appropriate.

(3)   Every request for discovery or response or objection, including a notice of deposition made by a party represented by an attorney, shall be signed by at least 1 attorney of record in the attorney's individual name, whose address shall be stated. A party who is not represented by an attorney shall sign the request, response, or objection and list his or her address. The signature of the attorney or party constitutes a certification that the signer has read the request, response, or objection and that to the best of the signer's knowledge, information, or belief formed after a reasonable inquiry it is:

(A)   consistent with these rules and warranted by existing law or a good faith argument for the extension, modification, or reversal of existing law;

(B)   not interposed for any improper purpose, such as to harass or to cause unnecessary delay or needless increase in the cost of litigation; and

(C)   not unreasonable or unduly burdensome or expensive, given the needs of the case and the importance of the issues at stake in the litigation.

If a request, response, or objection is not signed, it shall be stricken unless it is signed promptly after the omission is called to the attention of the party making the request, response, or objection, and a party shall not be obligated to take any action with respect to it until it is signed.

If a certification is made in violation of this rule, the court, on motion or on its own initiative, shall impose on the person who made the certification, the firm or agency with which the person is affiliated, the party on whose behalf the request, response, or objection is made, or any or all of the above an appropriate sanction, which may include an order to pay the amount of the reasonable expenses incurred because of the violation, including a reasonable attorney's fee.

(o) **Pretrial Conference.**

(1)   The trial court may hold 1 or more pretrial conferences, with

trial counsel present, to consider such matters as will promote a fair and expeditious trial. The defendant shall be present unless the defendant waives this in writing.

(2)   The court may set, and upon the request of any party shall set, a discovery schedule, including a discovery cut-off date, at the pretrial conference.

Committee Notes

1968 Adoption.

(a)(1)   This is substantially the same as section 925.05, Florida Statutes.

(a)(2)   This is new and allows a defendant rights which he did not have, but must be considered in light of subdivision (c).

(a)(3)   This is a slight enlargement upon the present practice; however, from a practical standpoint, it is not an enlargement, but merely a codification of section 925.05, Florida Statutes, with respect to the defendant's testimony before a grand jury.

(b)   This is a restatement of section 925.04, Florida Statutes, except for the change of the word
"may" to "shall."

(c)   This is new and affords discovery to the state within the trial judge's discretion by allowing the trial judge to make discovery under (a)   (2)   and   (b) conditioned upon the defendant giving the state some information if the defendant has it. This affords the state some area of discovery which it did not previously have with respect to (b). A question was raised concerning the effect of (a)   (2) on FBI reports and other reports which are submitted to a prosecutor as "confidential" but it was agreed that the interests of justice would be better served by allowing this rule and that, after the appropriate governmental authorities are made aware of the fact that their reports may be subject to compulsory disclosure, no harm to the state will be done.

(d)and (e) This gives the defendant optional procedures. (d) is simply a codification of section 906.29, Florida Statutes, except for the addition of "addresses." The defendant is allowed this procedure in any event. (e) affords the defendant the additional practice of obtaining all of the state's witnesses, as distinguished from merely those on whose evidence the information, or indictment, is based, but only if the defendant is willing to give the state a list of all defense witnesses, which must be done to take advantage of this rule. The confidential informant who is to be used as a witness must be disclosed; but it was expressly viewed that this should not otherwise overrule present case law on the subject of disclosure of confidential informants, either where disclosure is required or not required.

(f)   This is new and is a compromise between the philosophy that the defendant should be allowed unlimited discovery depositions and the philosophy that the defendant should not be allowed any discovery depositions at all. The purpose of the rule is to afford the defendant relief from situations when witnesses refuse to "cooperate" by making pretrial disclosures to the defense. It was determined to be necessary that the written signed statement be a criterion because this is the only way witnesses can be impeached by prior contradictory statements. The word "cooperate" was intentionally left in the rule, although the word is a loose one, so that it can be given a liberal interpretation, i.e., a witness may claim to be available and yet never actually submit to an interview. Some express the view that the defendant is not being afforded adequate protection because the cooperating witness will not have been under oath, but the subcommittee felt that the only alternative would be to make unlimited discovery depositions available to the defendant which was a view not approved by a majority of the subcommittee. Each minority is expressed by the following alternative proposals:

Alternative Proposal (1): When a person is charged with an offense, at any time after the filing of the indictment, information, or affidavit upon which the defendant is to be tried, such person may take the deposition of any person by deposition upon oral examination for the purpose of discovery. The attendance of witnesses may be compelled by the use of subpoenas as provided by law. The deposition of a person confined in prison may be taken only by leave of court on such terms as the court prescribes. The scope of examination and the manner and method of taking such deposition shall be as provided in the Florida Rules of Civil Procedure and the deposition may be used for the purpose of contradicting or impeaching the testimony of a deponent as a witness.

Alternative Proposal (2): If a defendant signs and files a written waiver of his or her privilege against self-incrimination and submits to interrogation under oath by the prosecuting attorney, then the defendant shall be entitled to compulsory process for any or all witnesses to enable the defendant to interrogate them under oath, before trial, for discovery purposes.

A view was expressed that some limitation should be placed on the state's rights under sections 27.04 and 32.20, Florida Statutes, which allow the prosecutor to take all depositions unilaterally at any time. It was agreed by all members of the subcommittee that this right should not be curtailed until some specific time after the filing of an indictment, information, or affidavit, because circumstances sometimes require the filing of the charge and a studied marshalling of evidence thereafter. Criticism of the present practice lies in the fact that any time up to and during the course of the trial the prosecutor can subpoena any person to the privacy of the prosecutor's office without notice to the defense and there take a statement of such person under oath. The subcommittee was divided, however, on the method of altering this situation and the end result was that this subcommittee itself should not undertake to change the existing practice, but should make the Supreme Court aware of this apparent imbalance.

(g) This is new and is required in order to make effective the preceding rules.

(h) This is new and, although it encompasses relief for both the state and the defense, its primary purpose is to afford relief in situations when witnesses may be intimidated and a prosecuting attorney's heavy docket might not allow compliance with discovery within the time limitations set forth in the rules. The words, "sufficient showing" were intentionally included in order to permit the trial judge to have discretion in granting the protective relief. It would be impossible to specify all possible grounds which can be the basis of a protective order. This verbiage also permits a possible abuse by a prosecution-minded trial judge, but the subcommittee felt that the appellate court would remedy any such abuse in the course of making appellate decisions.

(i) This is new and, although it will entail additional expense to counties, it was determined that it was necessary in order to comply with the recent trend of federal decisions which hold that due process is violated when a person who has the money with which to resist criminal prosecution gains an advantage over the person who is not so endowed. Actually, there is serious doubt that the intent of this subdivision can be accomplished by a rule of procedure; a statute is needed. It is recognized that such a statute may be unpopular with the legislature and not enacted. But, if this subdivision has not given effect there is a likelihood that a constitutional infirmity (equal protection of the law) will be found and either the entire rule with all subdivisions will be held void or confusion in application will result.

(j)   This provision is necessary since the prosecutor is required to assume many responsibilities under the various subdivisions under the rule. There are no prosecuting attorneys, either elected or regularly assigned, in justice of the peace courts. County judge's courts, as distinguished from county courts, do not have elected prosecutors. Prosecuting attorneys in such courts are employed by county commissions and may be handicapped in meeting the requirements of the rule due to the irregularity and uncertainty of such employment. This subdivision is inserted as a method of achieving as much uniformity as possible in all of the courts of Florida having jurisdictions to try criminal cases.

1972 Amendment. The committee studied the ABA Standards for Criminal Justice relating to discovery and procedure before trial. Some of the standards are incorporated in the committee's proposal, others are not. Generally, the standards are divided into 5 parts:

Part I deals with policy and philosophy and, while the committee approves the substance of Part I, it was determined that specific rules setting out this policy and philosophy should not be proposed.

Part II provides for automatic disclosures (avoiding judicial labor) by the prosecutor to the defense of almost everything within the prosecutor's knowledge, except for work product and the identity of confidential informants. The committee adopted much of Part II, but felt that the disclosure should not be automatic in every case; the disclosure should be made only after request or demand and within certain time limitations. The ABA Standards do not recommend reciprocity of discovery, but the committee deemed that a large degree of reciprocity is in order and made appropriate recommendations.

Part III of the ABA Standards recommends some disclosure by the defense (not reciprocal) to which the state was not previously entitled. The committee adopted Part III and enlarged upon it.

Part IV of the Standards sets forth methods of regulation of discovery by the court. Under the Standards the discovery mentioned in Parts II and III would have been automatic and without the necessity of court orders or court intervention. Part III provides for procedures of protection of the parties and was generally incorporated in the recommendations of the committee.

Part V of the ABA Standards deals with omnibus hearings and pretrial conferences. The committee rejected part of the Standards dealing with omnibus hearings because it felt that it was superfluous under Florida procedure. The Florida committee determined that a trial court may, at its discretion, schedule a hearing for the purposes enumerated in the ABA Omnibus Hearing and that a rule authorizing it is not necessary. Some of the provisions of the ABA Omnibus Hearing were rejected by the Florida committee, i.e., stipulations as to issues, waivers by defendant, etc. A modified form of pretrial conference was provided in the proposals by the Florida committee.

(a)(1)(i)   Same as ABA Standard 2.1(a)(i) and substance of Standard 2.1(e). Formerly Florida Rule of Criminal Procedure 3.220(e) authorized exchange of witness lists. When considered with proposal 3.220(a)(3), it is seen that the proposal represents no significant change.

(ii)   This rule is a modification of Standard 2.1(a)(ii) and is new in Florida, although some such statements might have been discoverable under rule 3.220(f). Definition of "statement" is derived from 18 U.S.C. § 3500.

Requiring law enforcement officers to include irrelevant or sensitive material in their disclosures to the defense would not serve justice. Many investigations overlap and information developed as a byproduct of one investigation may form the basis and starting point for a new and entirely separate one. Also, the disclosure of any information obtained from computerized records of the Florida Crime Information Center and the National Crime Information Center should be subject to the regulations prescribing the confidentiality of such information so as to safeguard the right of the innocent to privacy.

(iii)   Same as Standard 2.1(a)(ii) relating to statements of accused; words "known to the prosecutor, together with the name and address of each witness to the statement" added and is new in Florida.

(iv)   From Standard 2.1(a)(ii). New in Florida.

(v)   From Standard 2.1(a)(iii) except for addition of words, "that have been recorded" which were inserted to avoid any inference that the proposed rule makes recording of grand jury testimony mandatory. This discovery was formerly available under rule 3.220(a)   (3).

(vi)   From Standard 2.1(a)(v). Words, "books, papers, documents, photographs" were condensed to "papers or objects" without intending to change their meaning. This was previously available under rule 3.220(b).

(vii)   From Standard 2.1(b)(i) except word "confidential" was added to clarify meaning. This is new in this form.

(viii)   From Standard 2.1(b)(iii) and is new in Florida in this form. Previously this was disclosed upon motion and order.

(ix)   From Standard 2.3(a), but also requiring production of "documents relating thereto" such as search warrants and affidavits. Previously this was disclosed upon motion and order.

(x)   From Standard 2.1(a)(iv). Previously available under rule 3.220(a)(2). Defendant must reciprocate under proposed rule 3.220(b)   (4).

(xi)   Same committee note as (b) under this subdivision.

(2)   From Standard 2.1(c) except omission of words "or would tend to reduce his punishment therefor" which should be included in sentencing.

(3)   Based upon Standard 2.2(a) and (b) except Standards required

prosecutor to furnish voluntarily and without demand while this proposal requires defendant to make demand and permits prosecutor 15 days in which to respond.

(4)   From Standards 2.5(b) and 4.4. Substance of this proposal previously available under rule 3.220(h).

(5)   From Standard 2.5. New in Florida.

(b)(1)   From Standard 3.1(a). New in Florida.

(2)   From Standard 3.1(b). New in Florida.

(3)   Standards did not recommend that defendant furnish prosecution with reciprocal witness list; however, formerly, rule 3.220(e) did make such provision. The committee recommended continuation of reciprocity.

(4)   Standards did not recommend reciprocity of discovery. Previously, Florida rules required some reciprocity. The committee recommended continuation of former reciprocity and addition of exchanging witness' statement other than defendants'.

(c)   From Standard 2.6. New in Florida, but generally recognized in decisions.

(d)   Not recommended by Standards. Previously permitted under rule 3.220(f) except for change limiting the place of taking the deposition and eliminating requirement that witness refuse to give voluntary signed statement.

(e)   From Standard 4.1. New in Florida.

(f)   Same as rule 3.220(g).

(g)   From Standard 4.4 and rule 3.220(h).

(h)   From Standard 4.4 and rule 3.220(h).

(i)   From Standard 4.6. Not previously covered by rule in Florida, but permitted by decisions.

(j)(1)   From Standard 4.7(a). New in Florida except court discretion permitted by rule 3.220(g).

(2)   From Standard 4.7(b). New in Florida.

(k)   Same as prior rule.

(l)   Modified Standard 5.4. New in Florida.

1977 Amendment. The proposed change only removes the comma which currently appears after (a)   (1).

1980 Amendment. The intent of the rule change is to guarantee that the accused will receive those portions of police reports or report summaries which contain any written, recorded, or oral statements made by the accused.

1986 Amendment. The showing of good cause under (d)(2) of this rule may be presented ex parte or in camera to the court.

1989 Amendment. 3.220(a). The purpose of this change is to ensure reciprocity of discovery. Under the previous rule, the defendant could tailor discovery, demanding only certain items of discovery with no requirement to reciprocate items other than those demanded. A defendant could avoid reciprocal discovery by taking depositions, thereby learning of witnesses through the deposition process, and then deposing those witnesses without filing a demand for discovery. With this change, once a defendant opts to use any discovery device, the defendant is required to produce all items designated under the discovery rule, whether or not the defendant has specifically requested production of those items.

Former subdivision (c) is relettered (b). Under (b) (1) the prosecutor's obligation to furnish a witness list is conditioned upon the defendant filing a "Notice of Discovery."

Former subdivision (a)(1)(i) is renumbered (b)(1)(i) and, as amended, limits the ability of the defense to take depositions of those persons designated by the prosecutor as witnesses who should not be deposed because of their tangential relationship to the case. This does not preclude the defense attorney or a defense investigator from interviewing any witness, including a police witness, about the witness's knowledge of the case.

This change is intended to meet a primary complaint of law enforcement agencies that depositions are frequently taken of persons who have no knowledge of the events leading to the charge, but whose names are disclosed on the witness list. Examples of these persons are transport officers, evidence technicians, etc.

In order to permit the defense to evaluate the potential testimony of those individuals designated by the prosecutor, their testimony must be fully set forth in some document, generally a police report.

(a)(1)(ii) is renumbered (b)(1)(ii). This subdivision is amended to require full production of all police incident and investigative reports, of any kind, that are discoverable, provided there is no independent reason for restricting their disclosure. The term "statement" is intended to include summaries of statements of witnesses made by investigating officers as well as statements adopted by the witnesses themselves.

The protection against disclosure of sensitive information, or information that otherwise should not be disclosed, formerly set forth in (a) (1)(i), is retained, but transferred to subdivision (b)(1)(xii).

The prohibition sanction is not eliminated, but is transferred to subdivision (b)(1)(xiii). "Shall" has been changed to "may" in order to reflect the procedure for imposition of sanctions specified in Richardson v. State, 246 So.2d 771 (Fla. 1971).

The last phrase of renumbered subdivision (b)(2) is added to emphasize that constitutionally required Brady material must be produced regardless of the defendant's election to participate in the discovery process.

Former subdivision (b) is relettered (c).

Former subdivisions (b)(3) and (4) are now included in new subdivision (d). An introductory phrase has been added to subdivision (d). Subdivision (d) reflects the change in nomenclature from a "Demand for Discovery" to the filing of a "Notice of Discovery."

As used in subdivision (d), the word "defendant" is intended to refer to the party rather than to the person. Any obligations incurred by the "defendant" are incurred by the defendant's attorney if the defendant is represented by counsel and by the defendant personally if the defendant is not represented.

The right of the defendant to be present and to examine witnesses, set forth in renumbered subdivision (d)(1), refers to the right of the defense, as party to the action. The term refers to the attorney for the defendant if the defendant is represented by counsel. The right of the defendant to be physically present at the deposition is controlled by new subdivision (h)(6).

Renumbered subdivision (d)(2), as amended, reflects the new notice of discovery procedure. If the defendant elects to participate in discovery, the defendant is obligated to furnish full reciprocal disclosure.

Subdivision (e) was previously numbered (a)(4). This subdivision has been modified to permit the remedy to be sought by either prosecution or defense.

Subdivision (f) was previously numbered (a)(5) and has been modified to permit the prosecutor, as well as the defense attorney, to seek additional discovery.

Former subdivision (c) is relettered (g).

Former subdivision (d) is relettered (h). Renumbered subdivision (h)(1) has been amended to reflect the restrictions on deposing a witness designated by the prosecution under (b)(1)(i) (designation of a witness performing ministerial duties only or one who will not be called at trial).

(h) (1)(i) is added to provide that a deposition of a witness designated by the prosecutor under (b)(1)(i) may be taken only upon good cause shown by the defendant to the court.

(h)(1)(ii) is added to provide that abuses by attorneys of the provisions of (b)(1)(i) are subject to stringent sanctions.

New subdivision (h)(1)(iii) abolishes depositions in misdemeanor cases except when good cause is shown.

A portion of former subdivision (d)(1) is renumbered (h)(3). This subdivision now permits the administrative judge or chief judge, in addition to the trial judge, to designate the place for taking the deposition.

New subdivision (h)(4) recognizes that children and some adults are especially vulnerable to intimidation tactics. Although it has been shown that such tactics are infrequent, they should not be tolerated because of the traumatic effect on the witness. The videotaping of the deposition will enable the trial judge to control such tactics. Provision is also made to protect witnesses of fragile emotional strength because of their vulnerability to intimidation tactics.

New subdivision (h)(5) emphasizes the necessity for the establishment, in each jurisdiction, of an effective witness coordinating office. The Florida Legislature has authorized the establishment of such office through section 43.35, Florida Statutes. This subdivision is intended to make depositions of witnesses and law enforcement officers as convenient as possible for the witnesses and with minimal disruption of law enforcement officers' official duties.

New subdivision (h)(6) recognizes that one of the most frequent complaints from child protection workers and from rape victim counselors is that the presence of the defendant intimidates the witnesses. The trauma to the victim surpasses the benefit to the defense of having the defendant present at the deposition. Since there is no right, other than that given by the rules of procedure, for a defendant to attend a deposition, the Florida Supreme Court Commission on Criminal Discovery believes that no such right should exist in those cases. The "defense," of course, as a party to the action, has a right to be present through counsel at the deposition. In this subdivision, the word "defendant" is meant to refer to the person of the defendant, not to the defense as a party. See comments to rules 3.220(d) and 3.220(d)(1).

Although defendants have no right to be present at depositions and generally there is no legitimate reason for their presence, their presence is appropriate in certain cases. An example is a complex white collar fraud prosecution in which the defendant must explain the meaning of technical documents or terms. Cases requiring the defendant's presence are the exception rather than the rule. Accordingly, (h)(6)(i)–(ii) preclude the presence of defendants at depositions unless agreed to by the parties or ordered by the court. These subdivisions set forth factors that a court should take into account in considering motions to allow a defendant's presence.

New subdivision (h)(7) permits the defense to obtain needed factual information from law enforcement officers by informal telephone deposition. Recognizing that the formal deposition of a law enforcement officer is often unnecessary, this procedure will permit such discovery at a significant reduction of costs.

Former subdivisions (e), (f), and (g) are relettered (i), (j), and (k), respectively.

Former subdivision (h) is relettered (l) and is modified to emphasize the use of protective orders to protect witnesses from harassment or intimidation and to provide for limiting the scope of the deposition as to certain matters.

Former subdivision (i) is relettered (m). Former subdivision (j) is relettered (n).
Renumbered (n)(2) is amended to provide that sanctions are mandatory if the court finds willful abuse of discovery. Although the amount of sanction is discretionary, some sanction must be imposed.

(n)(3) is new and tracks the certification provisions of federal procedure. The very fact of signing such a certification will make counsel cognizant of the effect of that action.

Subdivision (k) is relettered (o). Subdivision (l) is relettered (p).
1992 Amendment. The proposed amendments change the references to "indictment or information" in subdivisions (b)(1), (b)(2), (c)(1), and (h)(1) to "charging document." This amendment is proposed in conjunction with amendments to rule 3.125 to

provide that all individuals charged with a criminal violation would be entitled to the same discovery regardless of the nature of the charging document (i.e., indictment, information, or notice to appear).

1996 Amendment. This is a substantial rewording of the rule as it pertains to depositions and pretrial case management. The amendment was in response to allegations of discovery abuse and a call for a more cost conscious approach to discovery by the Florida Supreme Court. In felony cases, the rule requires prosecutors to list witnesses in categories A, B, and C. Category A witnesses are subject to deposition as under the former rule.

Category B witnesses are subject to deposition only upon leave of court. Category B witnesses include, but are not limited to, witnesses whose only connection to the case is the fact that they are the owners of property; transporting officers; booking officers; records and evidence custodians; and experts who have filed a report and curriculum vitae and who will not offer opinions subject to the Frye test. Category C witnesses may not be deposed. The trial courts are given more responsibility to regulate discovery by pretrial conference and by determining which category B witnesses should be deposed in a given case.

The rule was not amended for the purpose of prohibiting discovery. Instead, the rule recognized that many circuits now have "early resolution" or "rocket dockets" in which "open file discovery" is used to resolve a substantial percentage of cases at or before arraignment. The committee encourages that procedure. If a case cannot be resolved early, the committee believes that resolution of typical cases will occur after the depositions of the most essential witnesses (category A) are taken. Cases which do not resolve after the depositions of category A, may resolve if one or more category B witnesses are deposed. If the case is still unresolved, it is probably going to be a case that needs to be tried. In that event, judges may determine which additional depositions, if any, are necessary for pretrial preparation. A method for making that determination is provided in the rule.

Additionally, trial judges may regulate the taking of depositions in a number of ways to both facilitate resolution of a case and protect a witness from unnecessary inconvenience or harassment. There is a provision for setting a discovery schedule, including a discovery cut-off date as is common in civil practice. Also, a specific method is provided for application for protective orders.

One feature of the new rule relates to the deposition of law enforcement officers. Subpoenas are no longer required.

The rule has standardized the time for serving papers relating to discovery at fifteen days. Discovery in misdemeanor cases has not been changed.

(b)(1)(A)(i) An investigating officer is an officer who has directed the collection of evidence, interviewed material witnesses, or who was assigned as the case investigator.

(h)(1) The prosecutor and defense counsel are encouraged to be present for the depositions of essential witnesses, and judges are encouraged to provide calendar time for the taking of depositions so that counsel for all parties can attend. This will 1) diminish the potential for the abuse of witnesses, 2) place the parties in a position to timely and effectively avail themselves of the remedies and sanctions established in this rule, 3) promote an expeditious and timely resolution of the cause, and 4) diminish the need to order transcripts of the deposition, thereby reducing costs.

1998 Amendment. This rule governs only the location of depositions. The procedure for procuring out-of-state witnesses for depositions is governed by statute.

Court Commentary

1996 Amendment. The designation of a witness who will present similar fact evidence will be dependent upon the witness's relationship to the similar crime, wrong, or act about which testimony will be given rather than the witness's relationship to the crime with which the defendant is currently charged.

1999/2000 Amendment. This rule does not affect requests for nonexempt law enforcement records as provided in chapter 119, Florida Statutes, other than those that are nonexempt as a result of a codefendant's participation in discovery. See *Henderson v. State*, 745 So.2d 319 (Fla. Feb. 18, 1999).

VII. SUBSTITUTION OF JUDGE

RULE 3.231. SUBSTITUTION OF JUDGE

If by reason of death or disability the judge before whom a trial has commenced is unable to proceed with the trial, or posttrial proceedings, another judge, certifying that he or she has become familiar with the case, may proceed with the disposition of the case, except in death penalty sentencing proceedings. In death penalty sentencing proceedings, a successor judge who did not hear the evidence during the penalty phase of the trial shall conduct a new sentencing proceeding before a new jury.

Committee Notes

1972 Adoption. New. Follows ABA Standard 4.3, Trial by Jury. Inserted to provide for substitution of trial judge in specified instances.

VIII. CHANGE OF VENUE

RULE 3.240. CHANGE OF VENUE

(a) **Grounds for Motion.** The state or the defendant may move for a change of venue on the ground that a fair and impartial trial cannot be had in the county where the case is pending for any reason other than the interest and prejudice of the trial judge.

(b) **Contents of Motion.** Every motion for change of venue shall be in writing and be accompanied by:

(1) affidavits of the movant and 2 or more other persons setting forth facts on which the motion is based; and

(2) a certificate by the movant's counsel that the motion is made in good faith.

127

(c) **Time for Filing.** A motion for change of venue shall be filed no less than 10 days before the time the case is called for trial unless good cause is shown for failure to file within such time.

(d) **Action on Motion.** The court shall consider the affidavits filed by all parties and receive evidence on every issue of fact necessary to its decision. If the court grants the motion it shall make an order removing the cause to the court having jurisdiction to try such offense in some other convenient county where a fair and impartial trial can be had.

(e) **Defendant in Custody.** If the defendant is in custody, the order shall direct that the defendant be forthwith delivered to the custody of the sheriff of the county to which the cause is removed.

(f) **Transmittal of Documents.** The clerk shall enter on the minutes the order of removal and transmit to the court to which the cause is removed a certified copy of the order of removal and of the record and proceedings and of the undertakings of the witnesses and the accused.

(g) **Attendance by Witnesses.** When the cause is removed to another court, witnesses who have been lawfully subpoenaed or ordered to appear at the trial shall, on notice of such removal, attend the court to which the cause is removed at the time specified in the order of removal. A witness who refuses to obey a duly served subpoena may be adjudged in contempt of court.

(h) **Multiple Defendants.** If there are several defendants and an order is made removing the cause on the application of one or more but not all of them, the other defendants shall be tried and all proceedings had against them in the county in which the cause is pending in all respects as if no order of removal had been made as to any defendant.

(i) **Action of Receiving Court.**

Text of rule effective prior to amendment by Florida Supreme Court Opinion No. SC11-399. See also text of rule as amended by Florida Supreme Court Opinion SC11-399.

The court to which the cause is removed shall proceed to trial and judgment therein as if the cause had originated in that court. If it is necessary to have any of the original pleadings or other papers before that court, the court from which the cause is removed shall at any time on application of the prosecuting attorney or the defendant order such papers or pleadings to be transmitted by the clerk, a certified copy thereof being retained.

(i) **Action of Receiving Court.**

Text of rule as amended by Florida Supreme Court Opinion SC11-399. See also text of rule prior to amendment by Florida Supreme Court Opinion SC11-399.

The court to which the cause is removed shall proceed to trial and judgment therein as if the cause had originated in that court. If it is necessary to have any of the original pleadings or other documents before that court, the court from which the cause is removed shall at any time on application of the prosecuting attorney or the defendant order such documents or pleadings to be transmitted by the clerk, a certified copy thereof being retained.

(j) **Prosecuting Attorney's Obligation.** The prosecuting attorney of the court to which the cause is removed may amend the information, or file a new information, and such new information shall be entitled in the county in which the trial is had, but the allegations as to the place of commission of the crime shall refer to the county in which the crime was actually committed.

Committee Notes

1968 Adoption. (a) through (d) substantially same as sections 911.02 through 911.05, Florida Statutes. Language is simplified and requirement pertaining to cases in criminal courts of record that removal be to adjoining county is omitted. Modern communications and distribution of television and press makes old requirements impractical. Designation of county left to discretion of the trial judge.

(e) through (i) same as corresponding sections 911.06 through 911.10, Florida Statutes.

1972 Amendment. Same as prior rule.

Editor's Note

On October 18, 2012, the Supreme Court of Florida issued a revised opinion in case number SC11- 399, which was originally issued on June 21, 2012. See *In re Amendments to the Florida Rules of Judicial Administration*, 102 So. 3d 451(Fla. 2012). The opinion provides in relevant part:

"First, the new electronic filing requirements the Courts adopts will become effective in the civil, probate, small claims, and family law divisions of the trial courts, as well as for appeals to the circuit courts in these categories of cases, on April 1, 2013, at 12:01 a.m., except as may be otherwise provided by administrative order. Electronic filing will be mandatory in these divisions pursuant to rule 2.525 on that date. However, until the new rules take effect in these divisions, any clerk who is already accepting documents filed by electronic transmission under the current rules should continue to do so; attorneys in these counties are encouraged to file documents electronically under the current rules.

"Next, the new electronic filing requirements the Court adopts will become effective in the criminal, traffic, and juvenile divisions of the trial courts, as well as for appeals to the circuit court in these categories of cases, on October 1, 2013, at 12:01 a.m., except as may be otherwise provided by administrative order. Electronic filing will be mandatory in these divisions under rule 2.525 on that date. The new e-filing requirements, as they apply in proceedings brought pursuant to the Florida Mental Health Act (Baker Act), Chapter 394, Part I, Florida Statutes, and the Involuntary Commitment of Sexually Violent Predators Act (Jimmy Ryce), Chapter 394, Part V, Florida Statutes, will also not be mandatory in these cases until October 1, 2013. As stated above, until the new rules take effect in these divisions and proceedings, any clerk who is already accepting electronically filed documents under the current rules should continue to do so; attorneys are again encouraged to utilize existing electronic filing procedures under the current rules.

"However, until the new rules and procedures take effect in the district courts, any clerk who is already accepting documents filed by electronic transmission may continue to do so; attorneys in these districts are encouraged to file documents electronically. Clerks will not be required to electronically transmit the record on appeal until July 1, 2013, at 12:01 a.m. Until July 1, we encourage clerks, whenever possible, to electronically transmit the record under the new rules and requirements.

"(W)e note that, in all types of cases, pursuant to amended rule 2.525(d) self-represented parties and self-represented nonparties, including nonparty governmental or public agencies, and attorneys excused from e- mail service under Florida Rule of Judicial Administration 2.516 will be permitted, but nor required, to file documents electronically.

By order of November 28, 2012, in case number SC11-399, the Court released a revised implementation schedule, which provides, in pertinent part: "The e-filing rules adopted in the October 2012 opinion will be mandatory in this (Supreme) Court on February 27, 2013, at 12:01 a.m.; and effective earlier on a voluntary basis as will be indicated by further administrative order of the chief justice.

"Thereafter, the e-filing rules will be mandatory in the Second District Court of Appeal on July 22, 2013, at 12:01 a.m.; in the Third District Court of Appeal on September 27, 2013, at 12:01 a.m.; in the Fourth District Court of Appeal on October 31, 2013, at 12:01 a.m.; in the Fifth District Court of Appeal on November 27, 2013 at 12:01 a.m.; and in the First District Court of Appeal on December 27, 2013, at 12:01 a.m., unless made mandatory earlier by the chief judge of the applicable district court of appeal. The e-filing rules will be effective earlier on a voluntary trial basis in the district courts of appeal as will be indicated by further administrative order by the chief judge of the applicable district court."

IX. THE TRIAL

RULE 3.250. ACCUSED AS WITNESS

In all criminal prosecutions the accused may choose to be sworn as a witness in the accused's own behalf and shall in that case be subject to examination as other witnesses, but no accused person shall be compelled to give testimony against himself or herself, nor shall any prosecuting attorney be permitted before the jury or court to comment on the failure of the accused to testify in his or her own behalf.

Committee Notes

1968 Adoption. Same as section 918.09, Florida Statutes.

1972 Amendment. Same as prior rule. The committee considered The Florida Bar proposed amendment to this rule, but makes no recommendation with respect thereto.

RULE 3.251. RIGHT TO TRIAL BY JURY

In all criminal prosecutions the accused shall have the right to a speedy and public trial by an impartial jury in the county where the crime was committed.

1972 Adoption. Substance of Art. I, §16, Florida Constitution.

RULE 3.260. WAIVER OF JURY TRIAL

A defendant may in writing waive a jury trial with the consent of the state.

1968 Adoption. This is the same as Federal Rule of Criminal Procedure 23(a). This changes existing law by providing for consent of state.

1972 Amendment. Changes former rule by deleting "the approval of the Court," thus making trial by judge mandatory where both parties agree. The committee felt that the matter of withdrawal of a waiver was a matter within the inherent discretion of the trial judge and that no rule is required.

RULE 3.270. NUMBER OF JURORS

Twelve persons shall constitute a jury to try all capital cases, and 6 persons shall constitute a jury to try all other criminal cases.

1968 Adoption. Except for substituting the word "persons" for "men," the suggested rule is a transcription of section 913.10, Florida Statutes. The standing committee on Florida court rules raised the question as to whether this rule is procedural or substantive and directed the subcommittee to call this fact to the attention of the Supreme Court.

1972 Amendment. Same as prior rule.

RULE 3.280. ALTERNATE JURORS

(a) **Selection.** The court may direct that jurors, in addition to the regular panel, be called and impanelled to sit as alternate jurors. Alternate jurors, in the order in which they are impanelled, shall replace jurors who, prior to the time the jury retires to consider its verdict, become unable or disqualified to perform their duties. Alternate jurors shall be drawn in the same manner, have the same qualifications, be subject to the same examination, take the same oath, and have the same functions, powers, facilities, and privileges as the principal jurors. Except as hereinafter provided regarding capital cases, an alternate juror who does not replace a principal juror shall be discharged at the same time the jury retires to consider its verdict.

(b) **Responsibilities.** At the conclusion of the guilt or innocence phase of the trial, each alternate juror will be excused with instructions to remain in the courtroom. The jury will then retire to consider its verdict, and each alternate will be excused with appropriate instructions that the alternate juror may have to return for an additional hearing should the defendant be convicted of a capital offense.

Committee Notes

1968 Adoption. Save for certain rewording, the suggested rule is a transcription of section 913.10(2), Florida Statutes, except that the provisions for the challenging of the alternate jurors has been included more appropriately in the rule relating to challenges.

1972 Amendment. Same as prior rule.

1977 Amendment. This rule clarifies any ambiguities as to what should be done with alternate jurors at the conclusion of a capital case and whether they should be available for the penalty phase of the trial. The change specifies that they will not be instructed as to any further participation until the other jurors who are deliberating on guilt or innocence are out of the courtroom, in order not to influence the deliberating jurors or in any way convey that the trial judge feels that a capital conviction is imminent.

RULE 3.281. LIST OF PROSPECTIVE JURORS

Upon request, any party shall be furnished by the clerk of the court with a list containing names and addresses of prospective jurors summoned to try the case together with copies of all jury questionnaires returned by the prospective jurors.

Committee Note

1972 Adoption. ABA Standard 2.2. The furnishing of such a list should result in considerable time being saved at voir dire. Also includes those questionnaires authorized by section 40.101, Florida Statutes, although the statute itself provides for such disclosure.

RULE 3.290. CHALLENGE TO PANEL

The state or defendant may challenge the panel. A challenge to the panel may be made only on the ground that the prospective jurors were not selected or drawn according to law. Challenges to the panel shall be made and decided before any individual juror is examined, unless otherwise ordered by the court. A challenge to the panel shall be in writing and shall specify the facts constituting the ground of the challenge. Challenges to the panel shall be tried by the court. Upon the trial of a challenge to the panel the witnesses may be examined on oath by the court and may be so examined by either party. If the challenge to the panel is sustained, the court shall discharge the panel. If the challenge is not sustained, the individual jurors shall be called.

Committee Notes

1968 Adoption. This is a transcription of section 913.01, Florida Statutes.

1972 Amendment. Same as prior rule 3.300; order of rule changed to improve chronology.

RULE 3.300. VOIR DIRE EXAMINATION, OATH, AND EXCUSING OF MEMBER

(a) **Oath.** The prospective jurors shall be sworn collectively or individually, as the court may decide. The form of oath shall be as follows:

"Do you solemnly swear (or affirm) that you will answer truthfully all questions asked of you as prospective jurors, so help you God?"

If any prospective juror affirms, the clause "so help you God" shall be omitted.

(b)   Examination. The court may then examine each prospective juror individually or may examine the prospective jurors collectively. Counsel for both the state and defendant shall have the right to examine jurors orally on their voir dire. The order in which the parties may examine each juror shall be determined by the court. The right of the parties to conduct an examination of each juror orally shall be preserved.

(c)   Prospective Jurors Excused. If, after the examination of any prospective juror, the court is of the opinion that the juror is not qualified to serve as a trial juror, the court shall excuse the juror from the trial of the cause. If, however, the court does not excuse the juror, either party may then challenge the juror, as provided by law or by these rules.

Committee Notes

1968 Adoption.

(a)   Save for the inclusion of the form of oath, the suggested rule is a transcription of a part of section 913.02(1), Florida Statutes. The form of oath paraphrases in pertinent part the oath set out in section 913.11, Florida Statutes.

(b)   The suggested rule is a transcription of the remainder of section 913.02 (1), Florida Statutes.

(c)   Substantially same as section 913.02   (2), Florida Statutes.

1972 Amendment. (a) The language relating to competence to serve as jurors deleted as superfluous, (c)   amended for clarification by inserting the clause "that such juror is not qualified to serve as a trial juror" for the clause "that such juror is incompetent."

1980 Amendment. As to examination by parties, this brings rule 3.300(b) into conformity with Florida Rule of Civil Procedure 1.431(b). This rule also allows the court to examine each prospective juror individually or collectively.

RULE 3.310. TIME FOR CHALLENGE

The state or defendant may challenge an individual prospective juror before the juror is sworn to try the cause; except that the court may, for good cause, permit a challenge to be made after the juror is sworn, but before any evidence is presented.

Committee Notes

1968 Adoption. Save for the heading and for the inclusion of the phrase, "for cause or peremptorily,"   the suggested rule is a transcription of the provisions of section 913.04, Florida Statutes.

1972 Amendment. Prior rule amended only by deleting some language felt by the committee to be superfluous.

RULE 3.315. EXERCISE OF CHALLENGES

On the motion of any party, all challenges shall be addressed to the court outside the hearing of the jury panel in a manner selected by the court so that the jury panel is not aware of the nature of the challenge, the party making the challenge, or the basis of the court's ruling on the challenge, if for cause.

Committee Notes

1980 Adoption. With the exception of "Upon the motion of any party," the language is taken directly from Florida Rule of Civil Procedure 1.431(c)   (3). This rule had no counterpart in the criminal rules.

RULE 3.320. MANNER OF CHALLENGE

A challenge to an individual juror may be oral. When a juror is challenged for cause the ground of the challenge shall be stated.

Committee Notes

1968 Adoption. Save for the heading and the insertion of the word "the," the suggested rule is a transcription of the pro\visions of section 913.05, Florida Statutes. The phrase "for cause or peremptorily" has been added.

1972 Amendment. Same as prior rule [but some terminology has been changed].

RULE 3.330. DETERMINATION OF CHALLENGE FOR CAUSE

The court shall determine the validity of a challenge of an individual juror for cause. In making such determination the juror challenged and any other material witnesses, produced by the parties, may be examined on oath by either party. The court may consider also any other evidence material to such challenge.

Committee Notes

1968 Adoption. The suggested rule is essentially a transcription of sections 913.06 and 913.07, Florida Statutes, except for the first and last sentences.

1972 Amendment. Same as prior rule [but some terminology has been changed].

RULE 3.340. EFFECT OF SUSTAINING CHALLENGE

If a challenge for cause of an individual juror is sustained, the juror shall be discharged from the trial of the cause. If a peremptory challenge to an individual juror is made, the juror shall be discharged likewise from the trial of the cause.

Committee Notes

1968 Adoption. The first sentence of the suggested rule except for the inclusion of the words "for cause" is a transcription of section 913.09, Florida Statutes. The last sentence has been added.

1972 Amendment. Same as prior rule.

RULE 3.350. PEREMPTORY CHALLENGES

(a) **Number.** Each party shall be allowed the following number of peremptory challenges:

    (1) **Felonies Punishable by Death or Imprisonment for Life.** Ten, if the offense charged is punishable by death or imprisonment for life.

    (2) **All Other Felonies.** Six, if the offense charged is a felony not punishable by death or imprisonment for life.

    (3) **Misdemeanors.** Three, if the offense charged is a misdemeanor.

(b) **Codefendants.** If 2 or more defendants are jointly tried, each defendant shall be allowed the number of peremptory challenges specified above, and in such case the state shall be allowed as many challenges as are allowed to all of the defendants.

(c) **Multiple Counts and Multiple Charging Documents.** If an indictment or information contains 2 or more counts or if 2 or more indictments or informations are consolidated for trial, the defendant shall be allowed the number of peremptory challenges that would be permissible in a single case, but in the interest of justice the judge may use judicial discretion in extenuating circumstances to grant additional challenges to the accumulated maximum based on the number of charges or cases included when it appears that there is a possibility that the state or the defendant may be prejudiced. The state and the defendant shall be allowed an equal number of challenges.

(d) **Alternate Jurors.** If 1 or 2 alternate jurors are called, each party is entitled to 1 peremptory challenge, in addition to those otherwise allowed by law, for each alternate juror so called. The additional peremptory challenge may be used only against the alternate juror and the other peremptory challenges allowed by law shall not be used against the alternate juror.

(e) **Additional Challenges.** The trial judge may exercise discretion to allow additional peremptory challenges when appropriate.

Committee Notes

1968 Adoption. The suggested rule is a transcription of section 913.08, Florida Statutes, excluding subdivision (5), which is lifted from section 913.10(2), Florida Statutes, and included since the several provisions relate to peremptory challenges. The question was raised regarding multiple counts or consolidation in their relation to the number of challenges. It was decided not to imply approval of multiple counts or consolidation. The standing committee on Florida court rules raised the question as to whether or not this rule is procedural or substantive and directed the subcommittee to call this fact to the attention of the supreme court.

1972 Amendment. Substantially same as prior rule; introductory language modernized.

1977 Amendment. This proposed rule amends rule 3.350(e) to allow the defendant and the state an equal number of peremptory challenges and to permit the court to grant additional challenges to both parties where it appears that the state would otherwise be prejudiced.

1992 Amendment. The amendment adds (e) that specifically sets out the trial court's discretion to allow peremptory challenges in addition to those provided for in the rule. This amendment was one of several proposed by the jury management committee that provided for a reduction in the number of peremptory challenges allowed by the rule. The majority of the criminal procedure rules committee, while recommending against adoption of the remaining proposals of the jury management committee, nevertheless felt it would be appropriate to add (e) to clarify that the trial court's discretion is not limited to those situations set out in (c) of the rule (i.e., multiple counts or informations or indictments consolidated for trial).

RULE 3.360. OATH OF TRIAL JURORS

The following oath shall be administered to the jurors:

"Do you solemnly swear (or affirm) that you will well and truly try the issues between the State of Florida and the defendant and render a true verdict according to the law and the evidence, so help you God?"

If any juror affirms, the clause "so help you God" shall be omitted.

Committee Notes

1968 Adoption. The suggested rule is a transcription of section 913.11, Florida Statutes.

1972 Adoption. Language of prior rule amended slightly to modernize.

RULE 3.361. WITNESS ATTENDANCE AND SUBPOENAS

(a) **Subpoenas generally.** Subpoenas for testimony before the court and subpoenas for production of tangible evidence before the court may be issued by the clerk of the court or by any attorney of record in an action.

(b) **Subpoena for testimony or production of tangible evidence.**

(1) A subpoena for testimony or production of tangible evidence before the court shall state the name of the court and the title of the action and shall command each person to whom it is directed to attend and give testimony or produce the evidence at a time and place specified in the subpoena.

(2) On oral request of an attorney, the clerk shall issue a subpoena for testimony before the court or a subpoena for the production of tangible evidence before the court, signed and sealed but otherwise in blank, and the subpoena shall be filled in by the attorney before service.

(c) **For production of tangible evidence.**

(1)　　　If a subpoena commands a person or entity to produce books, papers, documents, or tangible things, the person or entity may move the court to quash or modify the subpoena before the time specified in the subpoena for compliance.

(2)　　　The court may (A) quash or modify the subpoena if it is unreasonable and oppressive, or (B) require the person in whose behalf the subpoena is issued to advance the reasonable cost of producing the books, papers, documents, or tangible things.

(d)　　**Attendance and enforcement.** A witness subpoenaed for testimony before the court or for production of tangible evidence before the court shall appear and remain in attendance until excused by the court or by all parties. A witness who refuses to obey a subpoena or who departs without being excused properly may be held in contempt.

X. CONDUCT OF TRIAL; JURY INSTRUCTIONS

RULE 3.370. REGULATION AND SEPARATION OF JURORS

(a)　　**During Trial.** After the jurors have been sworn they shall hear the case as a body and, within the discretion of the trial judge, may be sequestered. In capital cases, absent a showing of prejudice, the trial court may order that between the guilt and penalty phases of the trial the jurors may separate for a definite time to be fixed by the court and then reconvene before the beginning of the penalty phase.

(b)　　**After Submission of Cause.** Unless the jurors have been kept together during the trial the court may, after the final submission of the cause, order that the jurors may separate for a definite time to be fixed by the court and then reconvene in the courtroom before retiring for consideration of their verdict.

(c)　　**During Deliberations.** Absent exceptional circumstances of emergency, accident, or other special necessity or unless sequestration is waived by the state and the defendant, in all capital cases in which the death penalty is sought by the state, once the jurors have retired for consideration of their verdict, they must be sequestered until such time as they have reached a verdict or have otherwise been discharged by the court. In all other cases, the court, in its discretion, either on the motion of counsel or on the court's initiative, may order that the jurors be permitted to separate. If jurors are allowed to separate, the trial judge shall give appropriate cautionary instructions.

Committee Notes

1968 Adoption. (a) Taken from section 919.01, Florida Statutes.

(b)　　Taken from section 919.02, Florida Statutes.

1972 Amendment. (a) and (b) substantially the same as former rule 3.380, except that some language has been modernized. New provision permits nonsequestered jury to separate after receiving case for consideration.

Former rule 3.370 has been deleted as its substance is now contained in new Rules 3.150 through 3.153 on Joinder and Severance.

RULE 3.371. JUROR QUESTIONS OF WITNESSES

(a) **Judicial Discretion.** At the discretion of the presiding trial judge, jurors may be allowed to submit questions of witnesses during the trial.

(b) **Procedure.** The trial judge shall utilize the following procedure if a juror indicates that the juror wishes to ask a question:

(1) the questions must be submitted in writing;

(2) the trial judge shall review the question outside the presence of the jury;

(3) counsel shall have an opportunity to object to the question outside the presence of the jury;

(4) counsel shall be allowed to ask follow up questions; and

(5) the jury must be advised that if a question submitted by a juror is not allowed for any reason, the juror must not discuss it with the other jurors and must not hold it against either party.

RULE 3.372. JUROR NOTEBOOKS

In its discretion, the court may authorize documents and exhibits to be included in notebooks for use by the jurors during trial to aid them in performing their duties.

RULE 3.380. MOTION FOR JUDGMENT OF ACQUITTAL

(a) **Timing.** If, at the close of the evidence for the state or at the close of all the evidence in the cause, the court is of the opinion that the evidence is insufficient to warrant a conviction, it may, and on the motion of the prosecuting attorney or the defendant shall, enter a judgment of acquittal.

(b) **Waiver.** A motion for judgment of acquittal is not waived by subsequent introduction of evidence on behalf of the defendant. The motion must fully set forth the grounds on which it is based.

(c) **Renewal.** If the jury returns a verdict of guilty or is discharged without having returned a verdict, the defendant's motion may be made or renewed within 10 days after the reception of a verdict and the jury is discharged or such further time as the court may allow.

Committee Notes

1968 Adoption. Substantially same as section 918.08, Florida Statutes, except as follows:

(a) The existing statutory practice of granting directed verdicts is abolished in favor of the federal practice of having the judge enter a judgment of acquittal.

(b) The wording was changed to comply with the judgment of acquittal theory. A majority of the committee felt that the substance of the existing statute was all right, but a minority felt that the language should be changed so that a defendant would waive an erroneous denial of his motion for judgment of acquittal by introducing evidence. This point was raised in Wiggins v. State, 101 So.2d 833 (Fla. 1st DCA 1958), wherein the court said that this statute is "ineptly worded."

1972 Amendment. (a) and (b) same as prior rule 3.660, transferred to better follow trial chronology. (c) provides time period for renewal of motion and is new.

1980 Amendment. This brings rule 3.380(c) into conformity with Florida Rule of Civil Procedure 1.480(b) as it relates to the number of days (10) within which a party, either in a civil or criminal case, may make or renew a motion for judgment of acquittal. There appears to be no sound reason for the distinction between the criminal rule (4 days or such greater time as the court may allow, not to exceed 15 days) and the civil rule (10 days).

RULE 3.381. FINAL ARGUMENTS

In all criminal trials, excluding the sentencing phase of a capital case, at the close of all the evidence, the prosecuting attorney shall be entitled to an initial closing argument and a rebuttal closing argument before the jury or the court sitting without a jury. Failure of the prosecuting attorney to make a closing argument shall not deprive the defense of its right to make a closing argument or the prosecuting attorney's right to then make a rebuttal argument. If the defendant does not present a closing argument, the prosecuting attorney will not be permitted a rebuttal argument.

RULE 3.390. JURY INSTRUCTIONS

(a)   **Subject of Instructions.** The presiding judge shall instruct the jury only on the law of the case before or after the argument of counsel and may provide appropriate instructions during the trial. If the instructions are given prior to final argument, the presiding judge shall give the jury final procedural instructions after final arguments are concluded and prior to deliberations. Except in capital cases, the judge shall not instruct the jury on the sentence that may be imposed for the offense for which the accused is on trial.

(b)   **Form of Instructions.** The instruction to a jury shall be orally delivered and shall also be in writing. All written instructions shall also be filed in the cause.

(c)   **Written Request.** At the close of the evidence, or at such earlier time during the trial as the court reasonably directs, any party may file written requests that the court instruct the jury on the law as set forth in the requests. The court shall inform counsel of its proposed action on the request and of the instructions that will be given prior to their argument to the jury.

(d)   **Objections.** No party may raise on appeal the giving or failure to give an instruction unless the party objects thereto before the jury retires to consider its verdict, stating distinctly the matter to which the party objects and the grounds of the objection. Opportunity shall be given to make the objection out of the presence of the jury.

(e)   **Transcript and Review.** When an objection is made to the giving of or failure to give an instruction, no exception need be made to the court's ruling thereon in order to have the ruling reviewed, and the grounds of objection and ruling thereon shall be taken by the court reporter and, if the jury returns a verdict of guilty, transcribed by the court reporter and filed in the cause.

Committee Notes

1972 Adoption. The committee adopted section 918.10, Florida Statutes, with only minor modification as to terminology.

1988 Amendment. To assist the jury in understanding the jury instructions.

1992 Amendment. Suggested change in wording to make (d) clearer and easier to understand and also so it more closely follows its federal counterpart, Federal Rule of Criminal Procedure 30.

RULE 3.391. SELECTION OF FOREPERSON OF JURY

The court shall instruct the jurors to select one of their number foreperson.

Committee Notes

1968 Adoption. This rule was inserted in order to clarify the system of selecting jury foreman.

1972 Amendment. Same as former rule 3.390.

RULE 3.400. MATERIALS TO THE JURY ROOM

(a)   **Discretionary Materials.** The court may permit the jury, upon retiring for deliberation, to take to the jury room:

(1)   a copy of the charges against the defendant;

(2)   forms of verdict approved by the court, after being first submitted to counsel;

(3)   all things received in evidence other than depositions. If the thing received in evidence is a public record or a private document which, in the opinion of the court, ought not to be taken from the person having it in custody, a copy shall be taken or sent instead of the original.

(b)   **Mandatory Materials.** The court must provide the jury, upon retiring for deliberation, with a written copy of the instructions given to take to the jury room.

Committee Notes

1968 Adoption. (1) and (2) same as section 919.04(1) and (2), Florida Statutes.

Section (3) was changed from the existing section 919.04(3) by adding to the things which should not be taken with or sent to the jury, written or recorded statements or confessions. It was felt by the committee that the present practice of allowing such things to be taken with the jury is unfair and emphasizes such statements or confessions to the jury. Since they are always read to the jury they should receive no additional emphasis than the testimony of any witness from the stand. [Court did not approve this change; the proposal was not adopted; and F.S.A. § 919.04(3) was transferred unchanged to Rule 1.400(c).]

1972 Amendment. (a) permits a copy of the indictment or information to be taken to the jury room. The committee deliberated at length about this provision but finally approved same. (b), (c), and (d) are same as former rule 3.400(a), (b), and (c) [but some terminology has been changed].

RULE 3.410. JURY REQUEST TO REVIEW EVIDENCE OR FOR ADDITIONAL INSTRUCTIONS

After the jurors have retired to consider their verdict, if they request additional instructions or to have any testimony read or played back to them they may be conducted into the courtroom by the officer who has them in charge and the court may give them the additional instructions or may order the testimony read or played back to them. The instructions shall be given and the testimony presented only after notice to the prosecuting attorney and to counsel for the defendant. All testimony read or played back must be done in open court in the presence of all parties. In its discretion, the court may respond in writing to the inquiry without having the jury brought before the court, provided the parties have received the opportunity to place objections on the record and both the inquiry and response are made part of the record.

Committee Notes

1968 Adoption. Same as section 919.05, Florida Statutes.

1972 Amendment. This is the same as former rule 3.410, except that the former rule made it mandatory for the trial judge to give additional instructions upon request. The committee feels that this should be discretionary.

RULE 3.420. RECALL OF JURY FOR ADDITIONAL INSTRUCTIONS

The court may recall the jurors after they have retired to consider their verdict to give them additional instructions or to correct any erroneous instructions given them. The additional or corrective instructions may be given only after notice to the prosecuting attorney and to counsel for the defendant.

Committee Notes

1968 Adoption. Same as section 919.06, Florida Statutes.

1972 Amendment. Same as former rule.

RULE 3.430. JURY NOT RECALLABLE TO HEAR ADDITIONAL EVIDENCE

After the jurors have retired to consider their verdict the court shall not recall the jurors to hear additional evidence.

Committee Notes

1968 Adoption. Same as section 919.07, Florida Statutes.

1972 Amendment. Same as prior rule.

XI. THE VERDICT

RULE 3.440. RENDITION OF VERDICT; RECEPTION AND RECORDING

When the jurors have agreed upon a verdict they shall be conducted into the courtroom by the officer having them in charge. The court shall ask the foreperson if an agreement has been reached on a verdict. If the foreperson answers in the affirmative, the judge shall call on the foreperson to deliver the verdict in writing to the clerk. The court may then examine the verdict and correct it as to matters of form with the unanimous consent of the jurors. The clerk shall then read the verdict to the jurors and, unless disagreement is expressed by one or more of them or the jury is polled, the verdict shall be entered of record, and the jurors discharged from the cause. No verdict may be rendered unless all of the trial jurors concur in it.

Committee Notes

1968 Adoption. Same as section 919.09, Florida Statutes.

1972 Amendment. Same as prior rule.

RULE 3.450. POLLING THE JURY

On the motion of either the state or the defendant or on its own motion, the court shall cause the jurors to be asked severally if the verdict rendered is their verdict. If a juror dissents, the court must direct that the jury be sent back for further consideration. If there is no dissent the verdict shall be entered of record and the jurors discharged. However, no motion to poll the jury shall be entertained after the jury is discharged or the verdict recorded.

Committee Notes

1968 Adoption. Same as section 919.10, Florida Statutes, except elimination of polling jury after directed verdict in view of innovation of "judgment of acquittal."

1972 Amendment. Same as prior rule.

RULE 3.451. JUDICIAL COMMENT ON VERDICT

While it is appropriate for the court to thank jurors at the conclusion of a trial for their public service, the court shall not praise or criticize their verdict.

Committee Notes

1972 Adoption. From ABA Standard 5.6, Trial by Jury.

RULE 3.470. PROCEEDINGS ON SEALED VERDICT

The court may, with the consent of the prosecuting attorney and the defendant, direct the jurors that if they should agree upon a verdict during a temporary adjournment of the court, the foreperson and each juror shall sign the same, and the verdict shall be sealed in an envelope and delivered to the officer having charge of the jury, after which the jury may separate until the next convening of the court. When the court authorizes the rendition of a sealed verdict, it shall admonish the jurors not to make any disclosure concerning it or to speak with other persons concerning the cause, until their verdict shall have been rendered in open court. The officer shall, forthwith, deliver the sealed verdict to the clerk. When the jurors have reassembled in open court, the envelope shall be opened by the court or clerk and the same proceedings shall be had as in the receiving of other verdicts.

Committee Notes

1968 Adoption of Rule 3.470. Same as section 919.12, Florida Statutes.

1968 Adoption of Rule 3.480. Same as section 919.13, Florida Statutes.

1972 Amendment. Former rule 3.480 has been deleted, its substance now contained in rule 3.470. Substantially same as former rules 3.470 and 3.480.

RULE 3.490. DETERMINATION OF DEGREE OF OFFENSE

If the indictment or information charges an offense divided into degrees, the jury may find the defendant guilty of the offense charged or any lesser degree supported by the evidence. The judge shall not instruct on any degree as to which there is no evidence.

Committee Notes

1968 Adoption. Same as 919.14.

1972 Amendment. Same as prior rule except references to affidavit have been deleted.

RULE 3.500. VERDICT OF GUILTY WHERE MORE THAN ONE COUNT

If different offenses are charged in the indictment or information on which the defendant is tried, the jurors shall, if they convict the defendant, make it appear by their verdict on which counts or of which offenses they find the defendant guilty.

Committee Notes

1968 Adoption. Same as section 919.15, Florida Statutes.

1972 Amendment. Amended to modernize the language of the rule. Substantially the same as prior rule.

RULE 3.505. INCONSISTENT VERDICTS

The state need not elect between inconsistent counts, but the trial court shall submit to the jury verdict forms as to each count with instructions applicable to returning its verdicts from the inconsistent counts.

Committee Notes

1977 Adoption. Although there appears to be no rule or statute relating to "election," many Florida cases refer to the fact that the trial court is required to make the state elect, before or during trial, between inconsistent counts. Many times the circumstances show conclusively that the accused is guilty of one or the other of inconsistent offenses. Since the evidence is then inconsistent with any reasonable hypothesis of innocence, the circumstantial rule is satisfied and the evidence should support a verdict of guilty as to either offense. In such a case the state should not be required to elect. This new rule is intended to lead to uniformity throughout the state on this issue and is more consonant with rule 3.140(k)(5).

RULE 3.510. DETERMINATION OF ATTEMPTS AND LESSER INCLUDED OFFENSES

On an indictment or information on which the defendant is to be tried for any offense the jury may convict the defendant of:

(a) an attempt to commit the offense if such attempt is an offense and is supported by the evidence. The judge shall not instruct the jury if there is no evidence to support the attempt and the only evidence proves a completed offense; or

(b) any offense that as a matter of law is a necessarily included offense or a lesser included offense of the offense charged in the indictment or information and is supported by the evidence. The judge shall not instruct on any lesser included offense as to which there is no evidence.

Committee Notes

1968 Adoption. Same as section 919.16, Florida Statutes. The standing committee on Florida court rules raised the question as to whether this rule is procedural or substantive and directed the subcommittee to call this fact to the attention of the supreme court.

1972 Amendment. Same as prior rule except that references to affidavit have been deleted.

RULE 3.520. VERDICT IN CASE OF JOINT DEFENDANTS

On the trial of 2 or more defendants jointly the jurors may render a verdict as to any defendant in regard to whom the jurors agree.

Committee Notes

1968 Adoption. Same as section 919.17, Florida Statutes.

1972 Amendment. Same as prior rule.

RULE 3.530. RECONSIDERATION OF AMBIGUOUS OR DEFECTIVE VERDICT

If a verdict is so defective that the court cannot determine from it whether the jurors intended to acquit the defendant or to convict the defendant of an offense for which judgment could be entered under the indictment or information on which the defendant is tried, or cannot determine from it on what count or counts the jurors intended to acquit or convict the defendant, the court shall, with proper instructions, direct the jurors to reconsider the verdict, and the verdict shall not be received until it shall clearly appear therefrom whether the jurors intended to convict or acquit the defendant and on what count or counts they intended to acquit or convict the defendant. If the jury persists in rendering a defective verdict, the court shall declare a mistrial.

Committee Notes

1968 Adoption. Same as section 919.18, Florida Statutes.

1972 Amendment. Same as prior rule.

RULE 3.540. WHEN VERDICT MAY BE RENDERED

A verdict may be rendered and additional or corrective instructions given on any day, including Sunday or any legal holiday.

Committee Notes

1968 Adoption. Same as section 919.19, Florida Statutes.

1972 Amendment. Same as prior rule.

RULE 3.550. DISPOSITION OF DEFENDANT

If a verdict of guilty is rendered the defendant shall, if in custody, be remanded. If the defendant is at large on bail, the defendant may be taken into custody and committed to the proper official or remain at liberty on the same or additional bail as the court may direct.

Committee Notes

1968 Adoption. Same as section 919.20, Florida Statutes.

RULE 3.560. DISCHARGE OF JURORS

After the jurors have retired to consider their verdict, the court shall discharge them from the cause when:

(a)   their verdict has been received;

(b)   on the expiration of such time as the court deems proper, if the court finds there is no reasonable probability that the jurors can agree on a verdict; or

(c)   a necessity exists for their discharge.

The court may in any event discharge the jurors from the cause if the prosecuting attorney and the defendant consent to the discharge.

Committee Notes

1968 Adoption. Same as section 919.21, Florida Statutes, except   (4) omitted.

1972 Amendment. Same as prior rule.

RULE 3.570. IRREGULARITY IN RENDITION, RECEPTION, AND RECORDING OF VERDICT

No irregularity in the rendition or reception of a verdict may be raised unless it is raised before the jury is discharged. No irregularity in the recording of a verdict shall affect its validity unless the defendant was in fact prejudiced by the irregularity.

Committee Notes

1968 Adoption. Rule 3.570 is same as section 919.22, Florida Statutes.

Section 919.23, Florida Statutes, was not included in the rules. This deals with the recommendation of mercy and it was felt that this was not procedural but substantive and not within the scope of the rulemaking power of the supreme court.

1972 Amendment. Same as prior rule.

RULE 3.575. MOTION TO INTERVIEW JUROR

A party who has reason to believe that the verdict may be subject to legal challenge may move the court for an order permitting an interview of a juror or jurors to so determine. The motion shall be filed within 10 days after the rendition of the verdict, unless good cause is shown for the failure to make the motion within that time. The motion shall state the name of any juror to be interviewed and the reasons that the party has to believe that the verdict may be subject to challenge. After notice and hearing, the trial judge, upon a finding that the verdict may be subject to challenge, shall enter an order permitting the interview, and setting therein a time and a place for the interview of the juror or jurors, which shall be conducted in the presence of the court and the parties. If no reason is found to believe that the verdict may be subject to challenge, the court shall enter its order denying permission to interview.

Court Commentary

2004 Amendment. This rule does not abrogate Rule Regulating The Florida Bar 4-3.5(d) (4), which allows an attorney to interview a juror to determine whether the verdict may be subject to legal challenge after filing a notice of intention to interview.

XII. POST-TRIAL MOTIONS

RULE 3.580. COURT MAY GRANT NEW TRIAL

When a verdict has been rendered against the defendant or the defendant has been found guilty by the court, the court on motion of the defendant, or on its own motion, may grant a new trial or arrest judgment.

Committee Notes

1968 Adoption. Same as section 920.01, Florida Statutes, except arrest of judgment is added.

1972 Amendment. Same as prior rule.

RULE 3.590. TIME FOR AND METHOD OF MAKING MOTIONS; PROCEDURE; CUSTODY PENDING HEARING

(a)   **Time for Filing in Noncapital Cases.** A motion for new trial or in arrest of judgment, or both, in cases in which the state does not seek the death penalty, may be made within 10 days after the rendition of the verdict or the finding of the court. A timely motion may be amended to state new grounds without leave of court prior to expiration of the 10-day period and in the discretion of the court at any other time before the motion is determined.

(b)   **Time for Filing in Capital Cases Where the Death Penalty Is an Issue.** A motion for new trial or arrest of judgment, or both, or for a new penalty phase hearing may be made within 10 days after written final judgment of conviction and sentence of life imprisonment or death is filed. The motion may address grounds which arose in the guilt phase and the penalty phase of the trial. Separate motions for the guilt phase and the penalty phase may be filed. The motion or motions may be amended without leave of court prior to the expiration of the 10 day period, and in the discretion of the court, at any other time before the motion is determined.

(c)   **Oral Motions.** When the defendant has been found guilty by a jury or by the court, the motion may be dictated into the record, if a court reporter is present, and may be argued immediately after the return of the verdict or the finding of the court. The court may immediately rule on the motion.

(d)   **Written Motions.** The motion may be in writing, filed with the clerk; it shall state the grounds on which it is based. A copy of a written motion shall be served on the prosecuting attorney. When the court sets a time for the hearing thereon, the clerk may notify counsel for the respective parties or the attorney for the defendant may serve notice of hearing on the prosecuting officer.

(e)   **Custody Pending Motion.** Until the motion is disposed of, a defendant who is not already at liberty on bail shall remain in custody and not be allowed liberty on bail unless the court on good cause shown (if the offense for which the defendant is convicted is bailable) permits the defendant to be released on bail until the motion is disposed of. If the defendant is already at liberty on bail that is deemed by the court to be good and sufficient, it may permit the defendant to continue at large on such bail until the motion for new trial is heard and disposed of.

Committee Notes

1968 Adoption. (a) The same as the first part of section 920.02(3), Florida Statutes, except that the statutory word "further" is changed to "greater" in the rule and provision for motion in arrest of judgment is added.

(b)   Substantially the same as first part of section 920.02 (2),   Florida Statutes. The rule omits the requirement that the defendant be sentenced immediately on the denial of a motion for new trial (the court might wish to place the defendant on probation or might desire to call for a presentence investigation). The rule also omits the statute's requirement that an order of denial be dictated to the court reporter, because the clerk is supposed to be taking minutes at this stage.

NOTE: The provisions of the last part of section 920.02(2), Florida Statutes, as to supersedeas and appeal are not incorporated into this rule; such provisions are not germane to motions for new trial or arrest of judgment.

(c)   Substantially same as section 920.03, Florida Statutes.

(d)   Substantially same as last part of section 920.02   (3), Florida Statutes, except that the last sentence of the rule is new.

NOTE: The provisions of section 920.02(4), Florida Statutes, relating to supersedeas on appeal and the   steps that are necessary to obtain one, are not incorporated into a rule. The provisions of section 920.02(4) do   not belong in a group of rules dealing with motions for new trial.

1972 Amendment. Substantially the same as prior rule.

1980 Amendment. This brings rule 3.590(a) into conformity with Florida Rule of Civil Procedure   1.530(b) as it relates to the time within which a motion for new trial or in arrest of judgment may be filed. It also allows the defendant in a criminal case the opportunity to amend the motion. The opportunity to amend already exists in a civil case. No sound reason exists to justify the disparities in the rules.

2006 Amendment. This amendment provides the time limitations and procedures for moving for new   trial, arrest of judgment or a new penalty phase in capital cases in which the death penalty is an issue. The motion may be made within ten days after written final judgment of conviction and sentence of life imprisonment or death is filed.

RULE 3.600. GROUNDS FOR NEW TRIAL

(a)   **Grounds for Granting.** The court shall grant a new trial if any of the following grounds is established.

(1)   The jurors decided the verdict by lot.

(2)   The verdict is contrary to law or the weight of the evidence.

(3)   New and material evidence, which, if introduced at the trial would probably have changed the verdict or finding of the court, and which the defendant could not with reasonable diligence have discovered and produced at the trial, has been discovered.

(b)   **Grounds for Granting if Prejudice Established.** The court shall grant a new trial if any of the following grounds is established, providing substantial rights of the defendant were prejudiced thereby.

(1)   The defendant was not present at any proceeding at which the defendant's presence is required by these rules.

(2)   The jury received any evidence out of court, other than that resulting from an authorized view of the premises.

(3)   The jurors, after retiring to deliberate upon the verdict,

separated without leave of court.

> (4)   Any juror was guilty of misconduct.

> (5)   The prosecuting attorney was guilty of misconduct.

> (6)   The court erred in the decision of any matter of law arising during the course of the trial.

> (7)   The court erroneously instructed the jury on a matter of law or refused to give a proper instruction requested by the defendant.

> (8)   For any other cause not due to the defendant's own fault, the defendant did not receive a fair and impartial trial.

(c)   **Evidence.** When a motion for new trial calls for a decision on any question of fact, the court may consider evidence on the motion by affidavit or otherwise.

Committee Notes

1968 Adoption. Same as sections 920.04 and 920.05, Florida Statutes, except that the last paragraph of section 920.05 is omitted from the rule. The provision of the omitted paragraph that a new trial shall be granted to a defendant who has not received a fair and impartial trial through no personal fault is inserted in the rule as subdivision (b)   (8).
The provision of the omitted paragraph of the statute which requires a new trial when the sentence exceeds the penalty provided by law is omitted from the rule because no defendant is entitled to a new trial merely because an excessive sentence has been pronounced. The standing committee on Florida court rules questioned whether this rule is procedural or substantive and directed the subcommittee to call this fact to the attention of the supreme court.

(c)   Same as second paragraph of section 920.07, Florida Statutes.

1972 Amendment. Same as prior rule.

RULE 3.610. MOTION FOR ARREST OF JUDGMENT; GROUNDS

The court shall grant a motion in arrest of judgment only on 1 or more of the following grounds:

(a)   The indictment or information on which the defendant was tried is so defective that it will not support a judgment of conviction.

(b)   The court is without jurisdiction of the cause.

(c)   The verdict is so uncertain that it does not appear therefrom that the jurors intended to convict the defendant of an offense of which the defendant could be convicted under the indictment or information under which the defendant was tried.

(d)   The defendant was convicted of an offense for which the defendant could not be convicted under the indictment or information under which the defendant was tried.

Committee Notes

1968 Adoption. Note that (a) (1) of the rule revamps section 920.05 (2)(a) through (d), Florida Statutes, in an effort to better take into account the fact that an accusatorial writ that would not withstand a motion to quash (dismiss) might well support a judgment of conviction if no such motion is filed. See Sinclair v. State, 46 So.2d 453 (1950).

Note also that, where appropriate, the rule mentions "affidavit" in addition to "indictment" and "information." The standing committee on Florida court rules questioned whether this rule is procedural or substantive and directed the subcommittee to call this fact to the attention of the supreme court.

1972 Amendment. Same as prior rule. References to trial affidavit deleted.

RULE 3.620. WHEN EVIDENCE SUSTAINS ONLY CONVICTION OF LESSER OFFENSE

When the offense is divided into degrees or necessarily includes lesser offenses and the court, on a motion for new trial, is of the opinion that the evidence does not sustain the verdict but is sufficient to sustain a finding of guilt of a lesser degree or of a lesser offense necessarily included in the one charged, the court shall not grant a new trial but shall find or adjudge the defendant guilty of the lesser degree or lesser offense necessarily included in the charge, unless a new trial is granted by reason of some other prejudicial error.

Committee Notes

1968 Adoption. Substantially the same as section 920.06, Florida Statutes.

1972 Amendment. Same as prior rule.

RULE 3.630. SENTENCE BEFORE OR AFTER MOTION FILED

The court in its discretion may sentence the defendant either before or after the filing of a motion for new trial or arrest of judgment.

Committee Notes

1968 Adoption. Same as first paragraph of section 920.07, Florida Statutes. Provision for arrest of judgment is added.

1972 Amendment. Same as prior rule.

RULE 3.640. EFFECT OF GRANTING NEW TRIAL

When a new trial is granted, the new trial shall proceed in all respects as if no former trial had occurred except that when an offense is divided into degrees or the charge includes a lesser offense, and the defendant has been found guilty of a lesser degree or lesser included offense, the defendant cannot thereafter be prosecuted for a higher degree of the same offense or for a higher offense than that of which the defendant was convicted.

1968 Adoption. Based on section 920.09, Florida Statutes. The second paragraph of the existing statute allows the testimony of an absent witness, given at a former trial, to be used only if the witness is absent from the state or dead. This has been enlarged to include absent witnesses who are physically incapacitated to attend court or who have become mentally incapacitated to testify since the former trial.

1972 Committee Note. Same as prior rule.

XIII. JUDGMENT

RULE 3.650. JUDGMENT DEFINED

The term "judgment" means the adjudication by the court that the defendant is guilty or not guilty.

Committee Notes

1968 Adoption. Substantially the same as section 921.01, Florida Statutes.

1972 Amendment. Same as prior rule.

RULE 3.670. RENDITION OF JUDGMENT

If the defendant is found guilty, a judgment of guilty and, if the defendant has been acquitted, a judgment of not guilty shall be rendered in open court and in writing, signed by the judge, filed, and recorded. However, where allowed by law, the judge may withhold an adjudication of guilt if the judge places the defendant on probation.

When a judge renders a final judgment of conviction, withholds adjudication of guilt after a verdict of guilty, imposes a sentence, grants probation, or revokes probation, the judge shall forthwith inform the defendant concerning the rights of appeal therefrom, including the time allowed by law for taking an appeal. Within 15 days after the signed written judgment and sentence is filed with the clerk of court, the clerk of the court shall serve on counsel for the defendant and counsel for the state a copy of the judgment of conviction and sentence entered, noting thereon the date of service by a certificate of service. If it is the practice of the trial court or the clerk of court to hand deliver copies of the judgment and sentence at the time of sentencing and copies are in fact hand delivered at that time, hand delivery shall be noted in the court file, but no further service shall be required and the certificate of service need not be included on the hand-delivered copy.

Committee Notes

1968 Adoption. To the same effect as section 921.02, Florida Statutes, except the portion reading "in writing, signed by the judge" which was added. Last sentence was added to permit the judge to operate under section 948.01 (3), Florida Statutes.

The Florida law forming the basis of this proposal is found in article V, sections 4 and 5, Constitution of Florida, concerning the right of appeal from a judgment of conviction; section 924.06, Florida Statutes, specifying when a defendant may take an appeal; section 924.09, Florida Statutes, and Florida Criminal Appellate Rule 6.2 concerning the time for taking appeals by a defendant in criminal cases; and section 948.011, Florida Statutes, providing for a sentence of a fine and probation as to imprisonment.

The purpose of the proposed rule is to provide assurance that a defendant, represented or unrepresented by counsel, will have authoritative and timely notice of the right to appeal.

1972 Amendment. Same as prior rule [but some terminology has been changed].

2005 Amendment. Amended to conform with section 775.08435, Florida Statutes (2004), effective July 1, 2004 (ch. 2004-60, Laws of Fla.).

RULE 3.680. JUDGMENT ON INFORMAL VERDICT

If a verdict is rendered from which it can be clearly understood that the jurors intended to acquit the defendant, a judgment of not guilty shall be rendered thereon even though the verdict is defective. No judgment of guilty shall be rendered on a verdict unless the jurors clearly express in it a finding of guilt of the defendant.

Committee Notes

1968 Adoption. Same as section 921.02, Florida Statutes.

1972 Amendment. Same as prior rule.

RULE 3.690. JUDGMENT OF NOT GUILTY; DEFENDANT DISCHARGED AND SURETIES EXONERATED

When a judgment of not guilty is entered, the defendant, if in custody, shall be immediately discharged unless the defendant is in custody on some other charge. If the defendant is at large on bail, the defendant's sureties shall be exonerated and, if money or bonds have been deposited as bail, the money or bonds shall be refunded.

Committee Notes

1968 Adoption. Same as section 921.04, Florida Statutes.

1972 Amendment. Same as prior rule.

RULE 3.691. POST-TRIAL RELEASE

(a) **When Authorized.** All persons who have been adjudicated guilty of the commission of any offense, not capital, may be released, pending review of the conviction, at the discretion of either the trial or appellate court, applying the principles enunciated in Younghans v. State, 90 So.2d 308 (Fla. 1956), provided that no person may be admitted to bail on appeal from a conviction of a felony unless the defendant establishes that the appeal is taken in good faith, on grounds fairly debatable, and not frivolous. However, in no case shall bail be granted if such person has previously been convicted of a felony, the commission of which occurred prior to the commission of the subsequent felony, and the person's civil rights have not been restored or if other felony charges are pending against the person and probable cause has been found that the person has committed the felony or felonies at the time the request for bail is made.

(b)   Written Findings. In any case in which the court has the discretion to release the defendant pending review of the conviction and, after the defendant's conviction, denies release, it shall state in writing its reasons for the denial.

(c)   Review of Denial. An order by a trial court denying bail to a person pursuant to the provisions of subdivision (a) may be reviewed by motion to the appellate court and the motion shall be advanced on the calendar of the appellate court for expeditious review.

(d)   Conditions of Release. If the defendant is released after conviction and on appeal, the condition shall be: (1) the defendant will duly prosecute the appeal;   (2) the defendant will surrender himself or herself in execution of the judgment or sentence on its being affirmed or modified or on the appeal being dismissed; or in case the judgment is reversed and the cause remanded for a new trial, the defendant will appear in the court to which the cause may be remanded for a new trial, that the defendant will appear in the court to which the cause may be remanded and submit to the orders and process thereof and will not depart the jurisdiction of the court without leave.

(e)   Approval of Bond. The court shall approve the sufficiency and adequacy of the bond, its security, and sureties, prior to the release of the defendant.

Committee Notes

1977 Amendment. Chapter 76 138, section 2, Laws of Florida, by appropriate vote, repealed the provisions of rule 3.691, insofar as they were inconsistent with the legislative act. This rule has been amended to include the provisions of Chapter 76-138, Laws of Florida.

RULE 3.692. PETITION TO SEAL OR EXPUNGE

(a)   Requirements of Petition. All relief sought by reason of sections 943.0585–943.059, Florida Statutes, shall be by written petition, filed with the clerk. The petition shall state the grounds on which it is based and the official records to which it is directed and shall be supported by an affidavit of the party seeking relief, which affidavit shall state with particularity the statutory grounds and the facts in support of the motion. A petition seeking to seal or expunge nonjudicial criminal history records must be accompanied by a certificate of eligibility issued to the petitioner by the Florida Department of Law Enforcement. A copy of the completed petition and affidavit shall be served on the prosecuting attorney and the arresting authority. Notice and hearing shall be as provided in rule 3.590(c).

(b)   State's Response; Evidence. The state may traverse or demur to the petition and affidavit. The court may receive evidence on any issue of fact necessary to the decision of the petition.

(c)   Written Order. If the petition is granted, the court shall enter its written order so stating and further setting forth the records and agencies or departments to which it is directed.

(d) **Copies of Order.** On the receipt of an order sealing or expunging nonjudicial criminal history records, the clerk shall furnish a certified copy thereof to each agency or department named therein except the court.

(e) **Clerk's Duties.** In regard to the official records of the court, including the court file of the cause, the clerk shall:

(1) remove from the official records of the court, excepting the court file, all entries and records subject to the order, provided that, if it is not practical to remove the entries and records, the clerk shall make certified copies thereof and then expunge by appropriate means the original entries and records;

(2) seal the entries and records, or certified copies thereof, together with the court file and retain the same in a nonpublic index, subject to further order of the court (see Johnson v. State, 336 So.2d 93 (Fla. 1976));

(3) in multi-defendant cases, make a certified copy of the contents of the court file that shall be sealed under subdivision (2). Thereafter, all references to the petitioner shall be expunged from the original court file.

(f) **Costs.** All costs of certified copies involved herein shall be borne by the movant, unless the movant is indigent.

Committee Notes

1984 Amendment. Substantially the same as the former rule. The statutory reference in (1) was changed to cite the current statute and terminology was changed accordingly. Subdivision (f) of the former rule was deleted because it dealt with substantive matters covered by section 943.058, Florida Statutes (1981).

2000 Amendment. Substantially the same as the former rule, but references to certificate of eligibility for obtaining nonjudicial criminal history records were added pursuant to *State v. D.H.W.*, 686 So. 2d 1331 (Fla. 1996).

XIV. SENTENCE

RULE 3.700. SENTENCE DEFINED; PRONOUNCEMENT AND ENTRY; SENTENCING JUDGE

(a) **Sentence Defined.** The term sentence means the pronouncement by the court of the penalty imposed on a defendant for the offense of which the defendant has been adjudged guilty.

(b) **Pronouncement and Entry.** Every sentence or other final disposition of the case shall be pronounced in open court, including, if available at the time of sentencing, the amount of jail time credit the defendant is to receive. The final disposition of every case shall be entered in the minutes in courts in which minutes are kept and shall be docketed in courts that do not maintain minutes.

[Editor's Note: See Grossman v. State, 525 So.2d 833 (Fla. 1988), for pronouncement procedure when defendant is sentenced to death.]

(c)   **Sentencing Judge.**

(1)   **Noncapital Cases.** In any case, other than a capital case, in which it is necessary that sentence be pronounced by a judge other than the judge who presided at trial or accepted the plea, the sentencing judge shall not pass sentence until the judge becomes acquainted with what transpired at the trial, or the facts, including any plea discussions, concerning the plea and the offense.

(2)   **Capital Cases.** In any capital case in which it is necessary that sentence be pronounced by a judge other than the judge who presided at the capital trial, the sentencing judge shall conduct a new sentencing proceeding before a jury prior to passing sentence.

Committee Notes

1968 Adoption. This rule is a revamped version of section 921.05, Florida Statutes.

1972 Amendment. Subdivisions (a) and (b) are substantially the same as in former rule. Subdivision
(c)   was added to emphasize that the sentencing procedure should be conducted by the trial judge or the judge taking the plea. The rule makes provision for emergency situations when such judge is unavailable.

RULE 3.701. SENTENCING GUIDELINES

(a)   **Use with Forms.** This rule is to be used in conjunction with forms 3.988(a)–(i).

(b)   **Statement of Purpose.** The purpose of sentencing guidelines is to establish a uniform set of standards to guide the sentencing judge in the sentence decision-making process. The guidelines represent a synthesis of current sentencing theory and historic sentencing practices throughout the state. Sentencing guidelines are intended to eliminate unwarranted variation in the sentencing process by reducing the subjectivity in interpreting specific offense- related and offender-related criteria and in defining their relative importance in the sentencing decision. The sentencing guidelines embody the following principles:

(1)   Sentencing should be neutral with respect to race, gender, and social and economic status.

(2)   The primary purpose of sentencing is to punish the offender. Rehabilitation and other traditional considerations continue to be desired goals of the criminal justice system but must assume a subordinate role.

(3)   The penalty imposed should be commensurate with the severity of the convicted offense and the circumstances surrounding the offense.

(4)   The severity of the sanction should increase with the length and nature of the offender's criminal history.

(5)   The sentence imposed by the sentencing judge should reflect

155

the length of time to be served, shortened only by the application of gain time.

(6)   While the sentencing guidelines are designed to aid the judge in the sentencing decision and are not intended to usurp judicial discretion, departures from the presumptive sentences established in the guidelines shall be articulated in writing and made when circumstances or factors reasonably justify the aggravation or mitigation of the sentence. The level of proof necessary to establish facts supporting a departure from a sentence under the guidelines is a preponderance of the evidence.

(7)   Because the capacities of state and local correctional facilities are finite, use of incarcerative sanctions should be limited to those persons convicted of more serious offenses or those who have longer criminal histories. To ensure such usage of finite resources, sanctions used in sentencing convicted felons should be the least restrictive necessary to achieve the purposes of the sentence.

(c)   **Offense Categories.** Offenses have been grouped into 9 offense categories encompassing the following statutes:

Category 1: Murder, manslaughter: Chapter 782 (except subsection 782.04(1)(a)), subsection 316.193 (3)(c)3, and subsection 327.351(2).

Category 2: Sexual offenses: Section 775.22, chapters 794 and 800, section 826.04, and section 491.0112.

Category 3: Robbery: Section 812.13, and sections 812.133 and 812.135.

Category 4: Violent personal crimes: Section 231.06, chapters 784 and 836, section 843.01, and subsection 381.411 (4).

Category 5: Burglary: Chapter 810, section 817.025, and subsection 806.13(3).

Category 6: Thefts, forgery, fraud: Sections 192.037 and 206.56, chapters 322 and 409, section 370.142, section 415.111, chapter 443, section 493.3175, sections 494.0018, 496.413, and 496.417, chapter 509, subsection 517.301(1)(a), subsections 585.145(3) and 585.85   (2), section 687.146, and chapters 812 (except section 812.13), 815, 817, 831, and 832.

Category 7: Drugs: Section 499.005 and chapter 893.

Category 8: Weapons: Chapter 790 and section 944.40. Category 9: All other felony offenses.

(d)   **General Rules and Definitions.**

(1)   One guideline scoresheet shall be utilized for each defendant covering all offenses pending before the court for sentencing. The state attorney's office will prepare the scoresheets and present them to defense counsel for review as to accuracy in all cases unless the judge directs otherwise. The sentencing judge shall approve all scoresheets.

(2)   "Conviction" means a determination of guilt resulting from plea or trial, regardless of whether adjudication was withheld or whether imposition of

156

sentence was suspended.

        (3)   "Primary offense" is defined as the offense at conviction that, when scored on the guidelines scoresheet, recommends the most severe sanction. In the case of multiple offenses, the primary offense is determined in the following manner:

        (A)   A separate guidelines scoresheet shall be prepared scoring each offense at conviction as the "primary offense at conviction" with the other offenses at conviction scored as "additional offenses at conviction."

        (B)   The guidelines scoresheet that recommends the most severe sentence range shall be the scoresheet to be utilized by the sentencing judge pursuant to these guidelines.

        (4)   All other offenses for which the offender is convicted and that are pending before the court for sentencing at the same time shall be scored as additional offenses based on their degree and the number of counts of each.

        (5)   "Prior record" refers to any past criminal conduct on the part of the offender, resulting in conviction, prior to the commission of the primary offense. Prior record includes all prior Florida, federal, out-of-state, military, and foreign convictions, as well as convictions for violation of municipal or county ordinances that bring within the municipal or county code the violation of a state statute or statutes. Provided, however, that:

        (A)   Entries in criminal histories that show no disposition, disposition unknown, arrest only, or other nonconviction disposition shall not be scored.

        (B)   When scoring federal, foreign, military, or out-of-state convictions, assign the score for the analogous or parallel Florida statute.

        (C)   When unable to determine whether an offense at conviction is a felony or a misdemeanor, the offense should be scored as a misdemeanor. When the degree of the felony is ambiguous or impossible to determine, score the offense as a third-degree felony.

        (D)   Prior record shall include criminal traffic offenses, which shall be scored as misdemeanors.

        (E)   Convictions that do not constitute violations of a parallel or analogous state criminal statute shall not be scored.

        (F)   An offender's prior record shall not be scored if the offender has maintained a conviction-free record for a period of 10 consecutive years from the most recent date of release from confinement, supervision, or sanction, whichever is later, to the date of the primary offense.

        (G)   All prior juvenile dispositions that are the equivalent of convictions as defined in subdivision (d) (2), occurring within 3 years of the commission of the primary offense and that would have been criminal if committed by an adult, shall be included in prior record.

(6) "Legal status at time of offense" is defined as follows: Offenders on parole, probation, or community control; offenders in custody serving a sentence; escapees; fugitives who have fled to avoid prosecution or who have failed to appear for a criminal judicial proceeding or who have violated conditions of a supersedeas bond; and offenders in pretrial intervention or diversion programs. Legal status points are to be assessed where these forms of legal constraint existed at the time of the commission of offenses scored as primary or additional offenses at conviction. Legal status points are to be assessed only once whether there are one or more offenses at conviction.

(7) Victim injury shall be scored for each victim physically injured during a criminal episode or transaction, and for each count resulting in such injury whether there are one or more victims.

(8) The recommended sentences provided in the guideline grids are assumed to be appropriate for the composite score of the offender. A range is provided to permit some discretion. The permitted ranges allow the sentencing judge additional discretion when the particular circumstances of a crime or defendant make it appropriate to increase or decrease the recommended sentence without the requirement of finding reasonable justification to do so and without the requirement of a written explanation.

(9) For those offenses having a mandatory penalty, a scoresheet should be completed and the guideline sentence calculated. If the recommended sentence is less than the mandatory penalty, the mandatory sentence takes precedence. If the guideline sentence exceeds the mandatory sentence, the guideline sentence should be imposed.

(10) If the composite score for a defendant charged with a single offense indicates a guideline sentence that exceeds the maximum sentence provided by statute for that offense, the statutory maximum sentence should be imposed.

(11) Departures from the recommended or permitted guideline sentence should be avoided unless there are circumstances or factors that reasonably justify aggravating or mitigating the sentence. Any sentence outside the permitted guideline range must be accompanied by a written statement delineating the reasons for the departure. Reasons for deviating from the guidelines shall not include factors relating to prior arrests without conviction or the instant offenses for which convictions have not been obtained.

(12) A sentence must be imposed for each offense. However, the total sentence cannot exceed the total guideline sentence unless a written reason is given. Where the offender is being sentenced for a capital felony and other noncapital felonies that arose out of the same criminal episode or transaction, the sentencing court may impose any sentence authorized by law for the noncapital felonies.

(13) Community control is a form of intensive supervised custody in the community involving restriction of the freedom of the offender. When community control is imposed, it shall not exceed the term provided by general law.

(14) Sentences imposed after revocation of probation or community control must be in accordance with the guidelines. The sentence imposed after revocation of probation or community control may be included within the original cell (guidelines range) or may be increased to the next higher cell (guidelines range) without requiring a reason for departure.

(15)   Categories 3, 5, and 6 contain an additional factor to be scored under the heading of Prior Record: Prior convictions for similar offenses. Prior convictions scored under this factor should be calculated in addition to the general prior record score. Scoring is limited to prior felony convictions included within the category.

Sentencing Guidelines Commission Notes

1988 Amendments.

(a)   The operation of this rule is not intended to change the law or requirements of proof as regards sentencing.

(b)   These principles are binding on the sentencing court.

(c)   Only 1 category is proper in any particular case. Category 9, "All Other Felony Offenses," should be used only when the primary offense at conviction is not included in another, more specific category. The guidelines do not apply to capital felonies.

Inchoate offenses are included within the category of the offense attempted, solicited, or conspired to, as modified by chapter 777.

The form appearing at Florida Rule of Criminal Procedure 3.988(a) has been revised to incorporate a point value for inclusion in the prior record factor utilized in the determination of recommended sentence by scoring each prior conviction under section 316.193, Florida Statutes (Supp. 1984), or section 316.1931, Florida Statutes (Supp. 1984), or section 327.351, Florida Statutes (Supp. 1984), at a value of 32 points. This point value will be applied only if the offender is convicted for a violation of section 316.193(3)(c)3, Florida Statutes (Supp. 1986), or section 327.351, Florida Statutes (Supp. 1984), if the operation of a motor vehicle or vessel by the offender while intoxicated as defined in section 316.193 (1), Florida Statutes (Supp. 1986), or section 327.351(1), Florida Statutes (Supp. 1984), results in the death of any human being and the scoresheet utilized in sentencing is the form appearing at Florida Rule of Criminal Procedure 3.988(a). For purposes of determining a prior conviction for a violation of the above enumerated statute, a prior conviction for violation of section 316.1931 or section 316.193 or former section 860.01 or former section 316.028, or a previous conviction for any substantially similar alcohol-related or drug-related traffic offense outside this state shall also be considered a prior conviction.

(d)(1)   Ultimate responsibility for ensuring that scoresheets are accurately prepared rests with the sentencing court. Due to ethical considerations, defense counsel may not be compelled to submit a scoresheet. Probation and parole officers may be directed to compile guidelines scoresheets only when a presentence investigation has been ordered. The forms for calculating the guidelines are forms 3.988(a)–(i).

(d)(2)   This definition applies to both instant offense and prior record scoring.

(d)(3)   The proper offense category is identified on determination of the primary offense. When the defendant is convicted of violations of more than 1 unique statute, the offenses are to be sorted by statutory degree.

(d)(4)   No points shall be scored for lesser and included offenses. In the event of multiple counts of the same distinct offense and degree of felony being scored as primary offense, it shall be scored as additional counts of the primary offense. All other offenses for which the defendant is convicted that are pending before the court for sentencing shall be scored as additional offenses.

(d)(5)   Each separate prior felony and misdemeanor conviction in an offender's prior record that amounts to a violation of Florida law shall be scored, unless discharged by the passage of time. Any uncertainty in the scoring of the defendant's prior record shall be resolved in favor of the defendant, and disagreement as to the propriety of scoring specific entries in the prior record should be resolved by the trial judge.

Prior record includes all offenses for which the defendant has been found guilty, regardless of whether adjudication was withheld or the record has been expunged.

Juvenile dispositions, with the exclusion of status offenses, are included and considered along with adult convictions by operation of this provision. However, each separate adjudication is discharged from consideration if 3 years have passed between the date of disposition and the commission of the instant offense.

For any offense where sentence was previously suspended pursuant to the imposition of probation and such offense is now before the court for sentencing, upon a revocation of that probation based upon a subsequent criminal offense (which subsequent offense is also before the court for sentencing at the same time), the earlier offense shall be scored as "prior record" and not as "additional offense."

(d)(7)   This provision implements the intention of the commission that points for victim injury be added for each victim injured during a criminal transaction or episode. The injury need not be an element of the crime for which the defendant is convicted, but is limited to physical trauma. However, if the victim injury is the result of a crime for which the defendant has been acquitted, it shall not be scored.

(d)(8)   The first guideline cell in each category (any nonstate prison sanction) allows the court the flexibility to impose any lawful term of probation with or without a period of incarceration as a condition of probation, a county jail term alone, or any nonincarcerative disposition. Any sentence may include the requirement that a fine be paid. The sentences are found in forms 3.988(a)(i).

(d)(10)   If an offender is convicted under an enhancement statute, the reclassified degree should be used as the basis for scoring the primary offense in the appropriate category. If the offender is sentenced under section 775.084 (habitual offender), the maximum allowable sentence is increased as provided by the operation of that statute. If the sentence imposed departs from the recommended sentence, the provisions of (d)(11) shall apply.

(d)(11)   A sentencing judge may depart from the recommended sentence and impose a sentence within the permitted range without giving reasons therefor. If a sentencing judge departs from the permitted range, reasons for departure shall be articulated at the time sentence is imposed. The written statement shall be made a part of the record, with sufficient specificity to inform all parties, as well as the public, of the reasons for departure. The court is prohibited from considering offenses for which the defendant has not been convicted. Other factors, consistent and not in conflict with the statement of purpose, may be considered and utilized by the sentencing judge.

(d)(12)   The sentencing court shall impose or suspend sentence for each separate count, as convicted.   The total sentence shall not exceed the guideline sentence, unless the provisions of subdivision (d)(11) are   complied with.

If a split sentence is imposed (i.e., a combination of state prison and probation supervision), the   incarcerative portion imposed shall not be less than the minimum of the guideline range nor exceed the   maximum of the range. The total sanction (incarceration and probation) shall not exceed the term provided by   general law.

(d)   (13)   Community control is a viable alternative for any state prison sentence less than 24 months   without requiring a reason for departure. It is appropriate to impose a sentence of community control to be   followed by a term of probation. The total sanction (community control and probation) shall not exceed the term   provided by general law.

Community control is not an alternative sanction from the recommended range of any nonstate prison   sanction unless the provisions of rule 3.701(d)(11) are applied.

1991 Amendment. The purpose of the 1991 revision to rule 3.701(d)   (6) is to clarify the original intent   that legal constraint is a status consideration and is not to be considered a function of the number of offenses at   conviction.

1991 Amendment. The purpose of the 1991 revision to rule 3.701(d)(7) is to provide consistency in   the scoring of victim injury by scoring each offense at conviction for which victim injury can appropriately be   scored, whether committed against a single or multiple victims.

1993 Amendments. Inchoate offenses are included within the category of the offense attempted,   solicited, or conspired to, as modified by chapter 777. An attempt, solicitation, or conspiracy to commit first-   degree murder as defined in subsection 782.04(1)(a) shall be scored in category 1. An attempt, solicitation, or   conspiracy to commit capital sexual battery as defined in subsection 794.011(2) shall be scored in category 2.

RULE 3.702. SENTENCING GUIDELINES (1994)

(a)   **Use.** This rule is to be used in conjunction with the forms located at rule 3.990. This rule is intended to implement the 1994 revised sentencing guidelines in strict accordance with chapter 921, Florida Statutes, as revised by chapter 93-406, Laws of Florida.

(b)   **Purpose and Construction.** The purpose of the 1994 revised sentencing guidelines and the principles they embody are set out in subsection 921.001 (4). Existing caselaw construing the application of sentencing guidelines that is in conflict with the provisions of this rule or the statement of purpose or the principles embodied by the 1994 sentencing guidelines set out in subsection 921.001   (4)   is superseded by the operation of this rule.

(c)   **Offense Severity Ranking.** Felony offenses subject to the 1994 revised sentencing guidelines are listed in a single offense severity ranking chart located at section 921.0012. The offense severity ranking chart employs 10 offense levels, ranked from least severe to most severe. Each felony offense is assigned to a level according to the severity of the offense, commensurate with the harm or potential for harm to the community that is caused by the offense. Felony offenses not listed in section 921.0012 are to be assigned a severity level as described in section 921.0013.

(d) **General Rules and Definitions.**

(1)   A comprehensive guidelines scoresheet shall be prepared for each defendant covering all offenses pending before the court for sentencing, including offenses for which the defendant has been adjudicated an habitual felony offender or an habitual violent felony offender. The office of the state attorney or the probation services office, or both where appropriate, will prepare the scoresheets and present them to defense counsel for review as to accuracy. Where the defendant is alleged to have violated probation or community control and probation services will recommend revocation, probation services shall prepare a comprehensive guidelines scoresheet for use at sentencing after revocation of probation or community control. The sentencing judge shall review the scoresheet for accuracy.

(2)   "Conviction" means a determination of guilt resulting from plea or trial, regardless of whether adjudication was withheld or whether imposition of sentence was suspended.

(3)   "Primary offense" is the offense pending for sentencing that results in the highest number of total sentence points. Only one offense may be scored as the primary offense.

(4)   "Additional offense" is any offense, other than the primary offense, pending before the court for sentencing. Sentence points for additional offenses are determined by the severity level and the number of offenses at a particular severity level. Misdemeanors are scored at level "M" regardless of degree.

(5)   "Victim injury" is scored for physical injury or death suffered by a person as a direct result of any offense pending before the court for sentencing. If an offense pending before the court for sentencing involves sexual penetration, victim injury is to be scored. If an offense pending before the court for sentencing involves sexual contact, but no penetration, victim injury shall be scored. If the victim of an offense involving sexual penetration or sexual contact without penetration suffers any physical injury as a direct result of an offense pending before the court for sentencing, that physical injury is to be scored separately and in addition to any points scored for the sexual contact or sexual penetration.

Victim injury shall be scored for each victim physically injured and for each offense resulting in physical injury whether there are one or more victims. However, if the victim injury is the result of a crime of which the defendant has been acquitted, it shall not be scored.

(6)   Attempts, conspiracies, and solicitations charged under chapter 777 are scored at severity levels below the level at which the completed offense is located. Attempts and solicitations are scored 2 severity levels below the completed offense. Criminal conspiracies are scored 1 severity level below the completed offense.

(7)   "Total offense score" results from adding the sentence points for primary offense, additional offense, and victim injury.

162

(8)   "Prior record" refers to any conviction for an offense committed by the defendant prior to the commission of the primary offense. Prior record shall include convictions for offenses committed by the defendant as an adult or as a juvenile, convictions by federal, out-of-state, military, or foreign courts, and convictions for violations of county or municipal ordinances that incorporate by reference a penalty under state law. Federal, out-of-state, military, or foreign convictions are scored at the severity level at which the analogous or parallel Florida crime is located.

(A)   Convictions for offenses committed more than 10 years prior to the date of the commission of the primary offense are not scored as prior record if the defendant has not been convicted of any other crime for a period of 10 consecutive years from the most recent date of release from confinement, supervision, or other sanction, which-ever is later, to the date of the commission of the primary offense.

(B)   Juvenile dispositions of offenses committed by the defendant within 3 years prior to the date of the commission of the primary offense are scored as prior record if the offense would have been a crime if committed by an adult. Juvenile dispositions of sexual offenses committed by the defendant more than 3 years prior to the date of the primary offense are to be scored as prior record if the defendant has not maintained a conviction-free record, either as an adult or as a juvenile, for a period of 3 consecutive years from the most recent date of release from confinement, supervision, or sanction, whichever is later, to the date of commission of the primary offense.

(C)   Entries in criminal histories that show no disposition, disposition unknown, arrest only, or a disposition other than conviction shall not be scored. Criminal history records expunged or sealed under section 943.058 or other provisions of law, including former sections 893.14 and 901.33, shall be scored as prior record where the defendant whose record has been expunged or sealed is before the court for sentencing.

(D)   Any uncertainty in the scoring of the defendant's prior record shall be resolved in favor of the defendant, and disagreement as to the propriety of scoring specific entries in the prior record shall be resolved by the sentencing judge.

(E)   When unable to determine whether the conviction to be scored as prior record is a felony or a misdemeanor, the conviction should be scored as a misdemeanor. When the degree of felony is ambiguous or the severity level cannot be determined, the conviction should be scored at severity level 1.

(9)   "Legal status violations" occur when a defendant, while under any of the forms of legal status listed in subsection 921.0011(3), commits an offense that results in conviction. Legal status violations receive a score of 4 sentence points and are scored when the offense committed while under legal status is before the court for sentencing. Points for a legal status violation are to be assessed only once regardless of the existence of more than one form of legal status at the time an offense is committed or the number of offenses committed while under any form of legal status.

(10)   "Release program violations" occur when the defendant is found to have violated a condition of a release program designated in subsection 921.0011 (6). Six points shall be assessed for each violation up to a maximum of 18 points

in the case of multiple violations. Where there are multiple violations, points in excess of 6 may be assessed only for each successive violation that follows the reinstatement or modification of the release program and are not to be assessed for violation of several conditions of a single release program order.

(11)   "Total prior record score" results from adding sentence points for prior record, legal status violations, and release program violations.

(12)   Possession of a firearm, destructive device, semiautomatic weapon, or a machine gun during the commission or attempt to commit a crime will result in additional sentence points. Eighteen sentence points shall be assessed where the defendant is convicted of committing or attempting to commit any felony other than those enumerated in subsection 775.087(2) while having in his or her possession a firearm as defined in subsection 790.001 (6) or a destructive device as defined in subsection 790.001(4). Twenty-five sentence points shall be assessed where the offender is convicted of committing or attempting to commit any felony other than those enumerated in subsection 775.087 (2) while having in his or her possession a semiautomatic weapon as defined in subsection 775.087 (2) or a machine gun as defined in subsection 790.001(9).

(13)   "Subtotal sentence points" result from adding the total offense score, the total prior record score, and any additional points for possession of a firearm, destructive device, semiautomatic weapon, or machine gun.

(14)   If the primary offense is drug trafficking under section 893.135, the subtotal sentence points may be multiplied, at the discretion of the sentencing court, by a factor of 1.5. If the primary offense is a violation of the Law Enforcement Protection Act under subsections 775.0823   (2), (3), (4), or (5), the subtotal sentence points shall be multiplied by a factor of 2. If the primary offense is a violation of subsection 775.087(2)(a)(2) or subsections 775.0823(6) or (7), the subtotal sentence points shall be multiplied by a factor of 1.5. If both enhancements are applicable, only the enhancement with the higher multiplier is to be used.

(15)   "Total sentence points" result from the enhancement, if applicable, of the subtotal sentence points. If no enhancement is applicable, the subtotal sentence points are the total sentence points.

(16)   "Presumptive sentence" is determined by the total sentence points. If the total sentence points are less than or equal to 40, the recommended sentence, absent a departure, shall not be state prison. However, the sentencing court may increase sentence points less than or equal to 40 by up to and including 15 percent to arrive at total sentence points in excess of 40. If the total sentence points are greater than 40 but less than or equal to 52, the decision to sentence the defendant to state prison or a nonstate prison sanction is left to the discretion of the sentencing court. If the total sentence points are greater than 52, the sentence, absent a departure, must be to state prison.

A state prison sentence is calculated by deducting 28 points from the total sentence points where total sentence points exceed 40. The resulting number represents state prison months. State prison months may be increased or decreased by up to and including 25 percent at the discretion of the sentencing court. State prison months may not be increased where the sentencing court has exercised discretion to increase total sentence points under 40 points to achieve a state prison sentence. The sentence imposed must be entered on the score- sheet.

(17)   For those offenses having a mandatory penalty, a scoresheet should be completed and the guidelines presumptive sentence calculated. If the presumptive sentence is less than the mandatory penalty, the mandatory sentence takes precedence. If the presumptive sentence exceeds the mandatory sentence, the presumptive sentence should be imposed.

(18)   Departure from the recommended guidelines sentence provided by the total sentence points should be avoided unless there are circumstances or factors that reasonably justify aggravating or mitigating the sentence. A state prison sentence that deviates from the recommended prison sentence by more than 25 percent, a state prison sentence where the total sentence points are equal to or less than 40, or a sentence other than state prison where the total sentence points are greater than 52 must be accompanied by a written statement delineating the reasons for departure. Circumstances or factors that can be considered include, but are not limited to, those listed in subsections 921.0016 (3) and (4). Reasons for departing from the recommended guidelines sentence shall not include circumstances or factors relating to prior arrests without conviction or charged offenses for which convictions have not been obtained.

(A)   If a sentencing judge imposes a sentence that departs from the recommended guidelines sentence, the reasons for departure shall be orally articulated at the time sentence is imposed. Any departure sentence must be accompanied by a written statement, signed by the sentencing judge, delineating the reasons for departure. The written statement shall be filed in the court file within 15 days of the date of sentencing. A written transcription of orally stated reasons for departure articulated at the time sentence was imposed is sufficient if it is signed by the sentencing judge and filed in the court file within 15 days of the date of sentencing. The sentencing judge may also list the written reasons for departure in the space provided on the guidelines scoresheet and shall sign the scoresheet.

(B)   The written statement delineating the reasons for departure shall be made a part of the record. The written statement, if it is a separate document, must accompany the guidelines scoresheet required to be provided to the Department of Corrections pursuant to subsection 921.0014 (5).

(19)   The sentencing court shall impose or suspend sentence for each separate count, as convicted. The total sentence shall be within the guidelines sentence unless a departure is ordered.

If a split sentence is imposed, the incarcerative portion of the sentence must not deviate more than 25 percent from the recommended guidelines prison sentence. The total sanction (incarceration and community control or probation) shall not exceed the term provided by general law or the guidelines recommended sentence where the provisions of subsection 921.001 (5) apply.

(20)   Sentences imposed after revocation of probation or community control must be in accordance with the guidelines. Cumulative incarceration imposed after revocation of probation or community control is subject to limitations imposed by the guidelines. A violation of probation or community control may not be the basis for a departure sentence.

Committee Notes

1993 Adoption. (d)(1) If sentences are imposed under section 775.084 and the sentencing guidelines, a scoresheet listing only those offenses sentenced under the sentencing guidelines must be prepared and utilized in lieu of the comprehensive scoresheet.

Due to ethical considerations, defense counsel may not be compelled to submit or sign a scoresheet.

(d)(3) The primary offense need not be the highest ranked offense pending for sentencing where scoring the less severe offense as the primary offense will result in higher total sentence points. This can occur where the multipliers for drug trafficking or violations of the Law Enforcement Protection Act are applied or where past convictions can be included as prior record that could not be scored if the offense ranked at a higher severity level was the primary offense.

(d)(16) The presumptive sentence is assumed to be appropriate for the composite score of the defendant. Where the total sentence points do not exceed 40, the court has the flexibility to impose any lawful term of probation with or without a period of incarceration as a condition of probation, a county jail term alone, or any nonincarcerative disposition. Any sentence may include a requirement that a fine be paid.

RULE 3.703. SENTENCING GUIDELINES (1994 AS AMENDED)

(a) **Use.** This rule is to be used in conjunction with the forms located at rule 3.991. This rule implements the 1994 sentencing guidelines, as amended, in strict accordance with chapter 921, Florida Statutes. This rule applies to offenses committed on or after October 1, 1995, or as otherwise indicated.

(b) **Purpose and Construction.** The purpose of the 1994 sentencing guidelines and the principles they embody are set out in subsection 921.001 (4). Existing caselaw construing the application of sentencing guidelines that is in conflict with the provisions of this rule or the statement of purpose or the principles embodied by the 1994 sentencing guidelines set out in subsection 921.001(4) is superseded by the operation of this rule.

(c) **Offense Severity Ranking.**

(1) Felony offenses subject to the 1994 sentencing guidelines, as amended, are listed in a single offense severity ranking chart located at section 921.0012. The offense severity ranking chart employs 10 offense levels, ranked from least severe to most severe. Each felony offense is assigned to a level according to the severity of the offense, commensurate with the harm or potential for harm to the community that is caused by the offense. The numerical statutory reference in the left column of the chart and the felony degree designations in the middle column of the chart determine whether felony offenses are specifically listed in the offense severity ranking chart and the appropriate severity level. The language in the right column is merely descriptive.

(2) Felony offenses not listed in section 921.0012 are to be assigned a severity level in accordance with section 921.0013, as follows:

(A)   A felony of the third degree within offense level 1.

(B)   A felony of the second degree within offense level
4.

(C)   A felony of the first degree within offense level 7.

(D)   A felony of the first degree punishable by life within
offense level 9.

(E)   A life felony within offense level 10.

An offense does not become unlisted and subject to the provisions of section 921.0013, because of a reclassification of the degree of felony pursuant to section 775.0845, section 775.087, section 775.0875 or section 794.023.

(d)   General Rules and Definitions.

(1)   One or more sentencing guidelines scoresheets shall be prepared for each offender covering all offenses pending before the court for sentencing, including offenses for which the offender has been adjudicated an habitual felony offender, an habitual violent felony offender or violent career criminal. The office of the state attorney or the Department of Corrections, or both where appropriate, will prepare the scoresheets and present them to defense counsel for review as to accuracy. The Department of Corrections shall prepare sentencing guidelines scoresheets if the offender is alleged to have violated probation or community control and revocation is recommended.

(2)   One scoresheet shall be prepared for all offenses committed under any single version or revision of the guidelines, pending before the court for sentencing.

(3)   If an offender is before the court for sentencing for more than one felony and the felonies were committed under more than one version or revision of the guidelines, separate scoresheets must be prepared and used at sentencing. The sentencing court may impose such sentence concurrently or consecutively.

(4)   The sentencing judge shall review the scoresheet for accuracy and sign it.

(5)   Felonies, except capital felonies, with continuing dates of enterprise are to be sentenced under the guidelines in effect on the beginning date of the criminal activity.

(6)   "Conviction" means a determination of guilt resulting from plea or trial, regardless of whether adjudication was withheld or whether imposition of sentence was suspended.

(7)   "Primary offense" is the offense pending for sentencing that results in the highest number of total sentence points. Only one offense may be scored as the primary offense.

(8)   "Additional offense" is any offense, other than the primary

167

offense, pending before the court for sentencing. Sentence points for additional offenses are determined by the severity level and the number of offenses at a particular severity level. Misdemeanors are scored at level "M" regardless of degree.

(9) "Victim injury" is scored for physical injury or death suffered by a person as a direct result of any offense pending before the court for sentencing. Except as otherwise provided by law, the sexual penetration and sexual contact points will be scored as follows. Sexual penetration points are scored if an offense pending before the court for sentencing involves sexual penetration. Sexual contact points are scored if an offense pending before the court for sentencing involves sexual contact, but no penetration. If the victim of an offense involving sexual penetration or sexual contact without penetration suffers any physical injury as a direct result of an offense pending before the court for sentencing, that physical injury is to be scored in addition to any points scored for the sexual contact or sexual penetration.

Victim injury shall be scored for each victim physically injured and for each offense resulting in physical injury whether there are one or more victims. However, victim injury shall not be scored for an offense for which the offender has not been convicted.

Victim injury resultant from one or more capital felonies before the court for sentencing is not to be included upon any scoresheet prepared for non- capital felonies also pending before the court for sentencing. This in no way prohibits the scoring of victim injury as a result from the non-capital felonies before the court for sentencing.

(10) Unless specifically provided otherwise by statute, attempts, conspiracies, and solicitations are indicated in the space provided on the guidelines scoresheet and are scored at one severity level below the completed offense.

Attempts, solicitations, and conspiracies of third-degree felonies located in offense severity levels 1 and 2 are to be scored as misdemeanors. Attempts, solicitations, and conspiracies of third-degree felonies located in offense severity levels 3, 4, 5, 6, 7, 8, 9, and 10 are to be scored as felonies one offense level beneath the incomplete or inchoate offense.

(11) An increase in offense severity level may result from a reclassification of felony degrees pursuant to sections 775.0845, 775.087, 775.0875, or 794.023. Any such increase should be indicated in the space provided on the sentencing guidelines scoresheet.

(12) A single assessment of thirty prior serious felony points is added if the offender has a primary offense or any additional offense ranked in level 8, 9, or 10 and one or more prior serious felonies. A "prior serious felony" is an offense in the offender's prior record ranked in level 8, 9, or 10 and for which the offender is serving a sentence of confinement, supervision or other sanction or for which the offender's date of release from confinement, supervision or other sanction, whichever is later is within 3 years before the date the primary offense or any additional offenses were committed. Out of state convictions wherein the analogous or parallel Florida offenses are located in offense severity level 8, 9, or 10 are to be considered prior serious felonies.

(13) If the offender has one or more prior capital felonies, points shall be added to the subtotal sentence points of the offender equal to twice the number of points the offender receives for the primary offense and any additional offense. Out-of-state

convictions wherein the analogous or parallel Florida offenses are capital offenses are to be considered capital offenses for purposes of operation of this section.

(14)   "Total offense score" is the sum of the sentence points for primary offense, any additional offenses and victim injury.

(15)   "Prior record" refers to any conviction for an offense committed by the offender prior to the commission of the primary offense, excluding any additional offenses pending before the court for sentencing. Prior record shall include convictions for offenses committed by the offender as an adult or as a juvenile, convictions by federal, out-of-state, military, or foreign courts and convictions for violations of county or municipal ordinances that incorporate by reference a penalty under state law. Federal, out-of-state, military, or foreign convictions are scored at the severity level at which the analogous or parallel Florida crime is located.

(A)   Convictions for offenses committed more than 10 years prior to the date of the commission of the primary offense are not scored as prior record if the offender has not been convicted of any other crime for a period of 10 consecutive years from the most recent date of release from confinement, supervision, or other sanction, whichever is later, to the date of the commission of the primary offense.

(B)   Juvenile dispositions of offenses committed by the offender within 3 years prior to the date of the commission of the primary offense are scored as prior record if the offense would have been a crime if committed by an adult. Juvenile dispositions of sexual offenses committed by the offender more than 3 years prior to the date of the primary offense are to be scored as prior record if the offender has not maintained a conviction-free record, either as an adult or as a juvenile, for a period of 3 consecutive years from the most recent date of release from confinement, supervision, or sanction, whichever is later, to the date of commission of the primary offense.

(C)   Entries in criminal histories that show no disposition, disposition unknown, arrest only, or a disposition other than conviction are not scored. Criminal history records expunged or sealed under section 943.058 or other provisions of law, including former sections 893.14 and 901.33, are scored as prior record where the offender whose record has been expunged or sealed is before the court for sentencing.

(D)   Any uncertainty in the scoring of the offender's prior record shall be resolved in favor of the offender and disagreement as to the propriety of scoring specific entries in the prior record shall be resolved by the sentencing judge.

(E)   When unable to determine whether the conviction to be scored as prior record is a felony or a misdemeanor, the conviction should be scored as a misdemeanor. When the degree of felony is ambiguous or the severity level cannot be determined, the conviction should be scored at severity level 1.

(16)   "Legal status points" are assessed when an offender:

(A)   Escapes from incarceration;

(B)   Flees to avoid prosecution;

    (C)   Fails to appear for a criminal proceeding;

    (D)   Violates any condition of a supersedeas bond;

    (E)   Is incarcerated;

    (F)   Is under any form of a pretrial intervention or diversion program; or

    (G)   Is under any form of court-imposed or post-prison release community supervision and commits an offense that results in conviction. Legal status violations receive a score of 4 sentence points and are scored when the offense committed while under legal status is before the court for sentencing. Points for a legal status violation are to be assessed only once regardless of the existence of more than one form of legal status at the time an offense is committed or the number of offenses committed while under any form of legal status.

    (17)   Community sanction violation points occur when the offender is found to have violated a condition of:

    (A)   Probation;

    (B)   Community Control; or

    (C)   Pretrial Intervention or diversion.

    Community sanction violation points are assessed when a community sanction violation is before the court for sentencing. Six community sanction violation points shall be assessed for each violation or if the violation results from a new felony conviction, 12 community sanction violation points shall be assessed. Where there are multiple violations, points may be assessed only for each successive violation that follows a continuation of supervision, or modification or revocation of the community sanction before the court for sentencing and are not to be assessed for violation of several conditions of a single community sanction. Multiple counts of community sanction violations before the sentencing court shall not be the basis for multiplying the assessment of community sanction violation points.

    (18)   "Total prior record score" is the sum of all sentence points for prior record.

    (19)   Possession of a firearm, semiautomatic firearm, or a machine gun during the commission or attempt to commit a crime will result in additional sentence points. Eighteen sentence points are assessed if the offender is convicted of committing or attempting to commit any felony other than those enumerated in subsection 775.087(2) while having in his or her possession a firearm as defined in subsection 790.001(6). Twenty-five sentence points are assessed if the offender is convicted of committing or attempting to commit any felony other than those enumerated in subsection 775.087(3) while having in his or her possession a semiautomatic firearm as defined in subsection 775.087 (3) or a machine gun as defined in subsection 790.001(9). Only one assessment of either 18 or 25 points shall apply.

    (20)   "Subtotal sentence points" are the sum of the total offense

score, the total prior record score, any legal status points, community sanction points, prior serious felony points, prior capital felony points or points for possession of a firearm or semi-automatic weapon.

(21)   If the primary offense is drug trafficking under section 893.135 ranked in offense severity level 7 or 8, the subtotal sentence points may be multiplied, at the discretion of the sentencing court, by a factor of 1.5.

(22)   If the primary offense is a violation of the Law Enforcement Protection Act under subsection 775.0823(2), the subtotal sentence points are multiplied by a factor of 2.5. If the primary offense is a violation of subsection 775.0823(3), (4), (5), (6), (7), or (8) the subtotal sentence points are multiplied by a factor of 2.0. If the primary offense is a violation of the Law Enforcement Protection Act under subsection 775.0823(9) or (10) or section 784.07(3) or section 775.0875 (1), the subtotal sentence points are multiplied by a factor of 1.5.

(23)   If the primary offense is grand theft of the third degree of a motor vehicle and the offender's prior record includes three or more grand thefts of the third degree of a motor vehicle, the subtotal sentence points are multiplied by 1.5.

(24)   If the offender is found to be a member of a criminal street gang pursuant to section 874.04, at the time of the commission of the primary offense, the subtotal sentence points are multiplied by 1.5.

(25)   If the primary offense is determined to be a crime of domestic violence as defined in section 741.28 and to have been committed in the presence of a child who is related by blood or marriage to the victim or perpetrator and who is under the age of 16, the subtotal sentence points are multiplied, at the discretion of the court, by 1.5.

(26)   "Total sentence points" are the subtotal sentence points or the enhanced subtotal sentence points.

(27)   "Presumptive sentence" is determined by the total sentence points. A person sentenced for a felony committed on or after July 1, 1997, who has at least one prior felony conviction and whose recommended sentence is any nonstate prison sanction may be sentenced to community control or a term of incarceration not to exceed 22 months. A person sentenced for a felony committed on or after July 1, 1997, who has at least one prior felony conviction and whose minimum recommended sentence is less than 22 months in state prison may be sentenced to a term of incarceration not to exceed 22 months.

In all other cases, if the total sentence points are less than or equal to 40, the recommended sentence, absent a departure, shall not be state prison. The court may impose any nonstate prison sanction authorized by law, including community control. However, the sentencing court may increase sentence points less than or equal to 40 by up to and including 15% to arrive at total sentence points in excess of 40. If the total sentence points are greater than 40 but less than or equal to 52, the decision to sentence the defendant to state prison or a nonstate prison sanction is left to the discretion of the sentencing court. If the total sentence points are greater than 52, the sentence, absent a departure, must be to state prison.

A state prison sentence is calculated by deducting 28 points from the total sentence points where total sentence points exceed 40. The resulting number represents state prison months. State prison months may be increased or decreased by up to and including 25% at the discretion of the sentencing court. State prison months may not be increased where the sentencing court has exercised discretion to increase total sentence points under 40 points to achieve a state prison sentence. The sentence imposed must be entered on the scoresheet.

If the total sentence points are equal to or greater than 363, the court may sentence the offender to life imprisonment.

(28)   If the recommended sentence under the sentencing guidelines exceeds the maximum sentence authorized for the pending felony offenses, the guidelines sentence must be imposed, absent a departure. Such downward departure must be equal to or less than the maximum sentence authorized by section 775.082.

(29)   For those offenses having a mandatory penalty, a scoresheet should be completed and the guidelines presumptive sentence calculated. If the presumptive sentence is less than the mandatory penalty, the mandatory sentence takes precedence. If the presumptive sentence exceeds the mandatory sentence, the presumptive sentence should be imposed.

(30)   Departure from the recommended guidelines sentence provided by the total sentence points should be avoided unless there are circumstances or factors that reasonably justify aggravating or mitigating the sentence. A state prison sentence that deviates from the recommended prison sentence by more than 25%, a state prison sentence where the total sentence points are equal to or less than 40, or a sentence other than state prison where the total sentence points are greater than 52 must be accompanied by a written statement delineating the reasons for departure. Circumstances or factors that can be considered include, but are not limited to, those listed in subsections 921.0016 (3) and   (4). Reasons for departing from the recommended guidelines sentence shall not include circumstances or factors relating to prior arrests without conviction or charged offenses for which convictions have not been obtained.

(A)   If a sentencing judge imposes a sentence that departs from the recommended guidelines sentence, the reasons for departure shall be orally articulated at the time sentence is imposed. Any departure sentence must be accompanied by a written statement, signed by the sentencing judge, delineating the reasons for departure. The written statement shall be filed in the court file within 7 days after the date of sentencing. A written transcription of orally stated reasons for departure articulated at the time sentence was imposed is sufficient if it is signed by the sentencing judge and filed in the court file within 7 days after the date of sentencing. The sentencing judge may also list the written reasons for departure in the space provided on the guidelines scoresheet and shall sign the scoresheet.

(B)   The written statement delineating the reasons for departure shall be made a part of the record. The written statement, if it is a separate document, must accompany the guidelines scoresheet required to be provided to the Department of Corrections pursuant to subsection 921.0014 (5).

(31)   The sentencing court shall impose or suspend sentence for each separate count, as convicted. The total sentence shall be within the guidelines sentence unless a departure is ordered.

If a split sentence is imposed, the incarcerative portion of the sentence must not deviate more than 25 percent from the recommended guidelines prison sentence. The total sanction (incarceration and community control or probation) shall not exceed the term provided by general law or the guidelines recommended sentence where the provisions of subsection 921.001 (5) apply.

(32) Sentences imposed after revocation of probation or community control must be in accordance with the guidelines. Cumulative incarceration imposed after revocation of probation or community control is subject to limitations imposed by the guidelines. A violation of probation or community control may not be the basis for a departure sentence.

Committee Notes

1996 Amendments.

(a) This portion was amended to show that the earliest offense date to which this rule applies is October 1, 1995 and that all subsequent changes are incorporated. It is intended that Committee Notes will be used to indicate effective dates of changes.

(c) This amendment applies to offenses committed on or after October 1, 1996.

(d)(9) The 1996 Legislature created two crimes for which sexual penetration or sexual contact points are not scored. That exception applies to offenses committed on or after October 1, 1996 pursuant to section 872.06, Florida Statutes or section 944.35 (3)(b)2, Florida Statutes.

(d)(12) The amendment applies to offenses committed on or after October 1, 1996.

(d)(13) The amendment applies on or after October 1, 1996.

(d)(17) This amendment, which applies on or after October 1, 1996, clarifies when points may be assessed for multiple violations. It also incorporates legislative changes that indicate that multiple assessments may not be made for multiple counts of community sanction violations.

(d)(24) The amendment applies to crimes committed on or after October 1, 1996.

1997 Amendments.

(d)(25) The amendment applies to crimes committed on or after October 1, 1997.

RULE 3.704. THE CRIMINAL PUNISHMENT CODE

(a) **Use.** This rule is to be used in conjunction with the forms located at rule 3.992. This rule implements the 1998 Criminal Punishment Code, in compliance with chapter 921, Florida Statutes. This rule applies to offenses committed on or after October 1,

173

1998, or as otherwise required by law.

(b) **Purpose and Construction.** The purpose of the 1998 Criminal Punishment Code and the principles it embodies are set out in subsection 921.002 (1), Florida Statutes. Existing case law construing the application of sentencing guidelines will continue as precedent unless in conflict with the provisions of this rule or the 1998 Criminal Punishment Code.

(c) **Offense Severity Ranking.**

(1) Felony offenses subject to the 1998 Criminal Punishment Code are listed in a single offense severity ranking chart located at section 921.0022, Florida Statutes. The offense severity ranking chart employs 10 offense levels, ranked from least severe to most severe. Each felony offense is assigned to a level according to the severity of the offense, commensurate with the harm or potential for harm to the community that is caused by the offense, as determined by statute. The numerical statutory reference in the left column of the chart and the felony degree designations in the middle column of the chart determine whether felony offenses are specifically listed in the offense severity ranking chart and the appropriate severity level. The language in the right column is merely descriptive.

(2) Felony offenses not listed in section 921.0022 are assigned a severity level in accordance with section 921.0023, Florida Statutes, as follows:

(A) A felony of the third degree within offense level 1.

(B) A felony of the second degree within offense level 4.

(C) A felony of the first degree within offense level 7.

(D) A felony of the first degree punishable by life within offense level 9.

(E) A life felony within offense level 10.

An offense does not become unlisted and subject to the provisions of section 921.0023 because of a reclassification of the degree of felony under section 775.0845, section 775.087, section 775.0875 or section 794.023, Florida Statutes, or any other law that provides an enhanced penalty for a felony offense.

(d) **General Rules and Definitions.**

(1) One or more Criminal Punishment Code scoresheets must be prepared for each offender covering all offenses pending before the court for sentencing, including offenses for which the offender may qualify as an habitual felony offender, an habitual violent felony offender, a violent career criminal, or a prison releasee reoffender. The office of the state attorney must prepare the scoresheets and present them to defense counsel for review as to accuracy. If sentences are imposed under section 775.084, or section 775.082(9), Florida Statutes, and the Criminal Punishment Code, a scoresheet listing only those offenses sentenced under the Criminal Punishment Code must be filed in addition to any sentencing documents filed under section 775.084 or section 775.082(9).

(2)   One scoresheet must be prepared for all offenses committed under any single version or revision of the guidelines or Criminal Punishment Code pending before the court for sentencing.

(3)   If an offender is before the court for sentencing for more than one felony and the felonies were committed under more than one version or revision of the guidelines or Criminal Punishment Code, separate scoresheets must be prepared and used at sentencing. The sentencing court may impose such sentence concurrently or consecutively.

(4)   The sentencing judge must review the scoresheet for accuracy and sign it.

(5)   Felonies, except capital felonies, with continuing dates of enterprise are to be sentenced under the guidelines or Criminal Punishment Code in effect on the beginning date of the criminal activity.

(6)   "Conviction" means a determination of guilt that is the result of a plea or trial, regardless of whether adjudication is withheld.

(7)   "Primary offense" means the offense at conviction pending before the court for sentencing for which the total sentence points recommend a sanction that is as severe as, or more severe than, the sanction recommended for any other offense committed by the offender and pending before the court at sentencing. Only one count of one offense before the court for sentencing shall be classified as the primary offense.

(8)   "Additional offense" means any offense other than the primary offense for which an offender is convicted and which is pending before the court for sentencing at the time of the primary offense.

(9)   "Victim injury" is scored for physical injury or death suffered by a person as a direct result of any offense pending before the court for sentencing. Except as otherwise provided by law, the sexual penetration and sexual contact points will be scored as follows. Sexual penetration points are scored if an offense pending before the court for sentencing involves sexual penetration. Sexual contact points are scored if an offense pending before the court for sentencing involves sexual contact, but no penetration. If the victim of an offense involving sexual penetration or sexual contact without penetration suffers any physical injury as a direct result of an offense pending before the court for sentencing, that physical injury must be scored in addition to any points scored for the sexual contact or sexual penetration.

Victim injury must be scored for each victim physically injured and for each offense resulting in physical injury whether there are one or more victims. However, victim injury must not be scored for an offense for which the offender has not been convicted.

Victim injury resulting from one or more capital offenses before the court for sentencing must not be included upon any scoresheet prepared for non-capital offenses also pending before the court for sentencing. This does not prohibit the scoring of victim injury as a result of the non-capital offense or offenses before the court for sentencing.

(10)   Unless specifically provided otherwise by statute, attempts, conspiracies, and solicitations must be indicated in the space provided on the Criminal

Punishment Code scoresheet and must be scored at one severity level below the completed offense.

Attempts, solicitations, and conspiracies of third-degree felonies located in offense severity levels 1 and 2 must be scored as misdemeanors. Attempts, solicitations, and conspiracies of third-degree felonies located in offense severity levels 3, 4, 5, 6, 7, 8, 9, and 10 must be scored as felonies one offense level beneath the incomplete or inchoate offense.

(11)　　An increase in offense severity level may result from a reclassification of felony degrees under sections 775.0845, 775.087, 775.0875, or 794.023. Any such increase must be indicated in the space provided on the Criminal Punishment Code score-sheet.

(12)　　A single assessment of thirty prior serious felony points is added if the offender has a primary offense or any additional offense ranked in level 8, 9, or 10 and one or more prior serious felonies. A "prior serious felony" is an offense in the offender's prior record ranked in level 8, 9, or 10 and for which the offender is serving a sentence of confinement, supervision or other sanction or for which the offender's date of release from confinement, supervision, or other sanction, whichever is later, is within 3 years before the date the primary offense or any additional offenses were committed. Out of state convictions wherein the analogous or parallel Florida offenses are located in offense severity level 8, 9, or 10 must be considered prior serious felonies.

(13)　　If the offender has one or more prior capital felonies, points must be added to the subtotal sentence points of the offender equal to twice the number of points the offender receives for the primary offense and any additional offense. Out-of-state convictions wherein the analogous or parallel Florida offenses are capital offenses must be considered capital offenses for purposes of operation of this section.

(14)　　"Prior record" refers to any conviction for an offense committed by the offender prior to the commission of the primary offense. Prior record includes convictions for offenses committed by the offender as an adult or as a juvenile, convictions by federal, out of state, military, or foreign courts and convictions for violations of county or municipal ordinances that incorporate by reference a penalty under state law. Federal, out of state, military or foreign convictions are scored at the severity level at which the analogous or parallel Florida crime is located.

(A)　　Convictions for offenses committed more than 10 years before the date of the commission of the primary offense must not be scored as prior record if the offender has not been convicted of any other crime for a period of 10 consecutive years from the most recent date of release from confinement, supervision, or other sanction, whichever is later, to the date of the commission of the primary offense.

(B)　　Juvenile dispositions of offenses committed by the offender within 5 years before the date of the commission of the primary offense must be scored as prior record if the offense would have been a crime if committed by an adult. Juvenile dispositions of sexual offenses committed by the offender more than 5 years before the date of the primary offense must be scored as prior record if the offender has not maintained a conviction-free record, either as an adult or as a juvenile, for a period of 5 consecutive years from the most recent date of release from confinement, supervision, or sanction, whichever is later, to the date of commission of the primary offense.

(C)   Entries in criminal histories that show no disposition, disposition unknown, arrest only, or a disposition other than conviction must not be scored. Criminal history records expunged or sealed under section 943.058, Florida Statutes, or other provisions of law, including former sections 893.14 and 901.33, Florida Statutes, must be scored as prior record where the offender whose record has been expunged or sealed is before the court for sentencing.

(D)   Any uncertainty in the scoring of the offender's prior record must be resolved in favor of the offender and disagreement as to the propriety of scoring specific entries in the prior record must be resolved by the sentencing judge.

(E)   When unable to determine whether the conviction to be scored as prior record is a felony or a misdemeanor, the conviction must be scored as a misdemeanor. When the degree of felony is ambiguous or the severity level cannot be determined, the conviction must be scored at severity level 1.

(15)   "Legal status points" are assessed when an offender:

(A)   Escapes from incarceration;

(B)   Flees to avoid prosecution;

(C)   Fails to appear for a criminal proceeding;

(D)   Violates any condition of a supersedeas bond;

(E)   Is incarcerated;

(F)   Is under any form of a pretrial intervention or diversion program; or

(G)   Is under any form of court-imposed or post-prison release community supervision and commits an offense that results in conviction. Legal status violations receive a score of 4 sentence points and are scored when the offense committed while under legal status is before the court for sentencing. Points for a legal status violation must only be assessed once regardless of the existence of more than one form of legal status at the time an offense is committed or the number of offenses committed while under any form of legal status.

(16)   Community sanction violation points occur when the offender is found to have violated a condition of:

(A)   Probation;

(B)   Community Control; or

(C)   Pretrial intervention or diversion.

Community sanction violation points are assessed when a community sanction violation is before the court for sentencing. Six community sanction violation points must be assessed for each violation or if the violation results from a new felony conviction, 12 community sanction violation points must be assessed. For violations occurring on or after March 12, 2007, if the community sanction violation that is not based upon a failure to pay fines, costs, or restitution is committed by a violent felony offender of special concern as defined in s. 948.06, twelve community sanction violation points must be assessed or if the violation results from a new felony conviction, 24 community sanction points must be assessed. Where there are multiple violations, points may be assessed only for each successive violation that follows a continuation of supervision, or modification or revocation of the community sanction before the court for sentencing and are not to be assessed for violation of several conditions of a single community sanction. Multiple counts of community sanction violations before the sentencing court may not be the basis for multiplying the assessment of community sanction violation points.

        (17)   Possession of a firearm, semiautomatic firearm, or a machine gun during the commission or attempt to commit a crime will result in additional sentence points. Eighteen sentence points are assessed if the offender is convicted of committing or attempting to commit any felony other than those enumerated in subsection 775.087(2) while having in his or her possession a firearm as defined in subsection 790.001(6), Florida Statutes. Twenty-five sentence points are assessed if the offender is convicted of committing or attempting to commit any felony other than those enumerated in subsection 775.087(3) while having in his or her possession a semiautomatic firearm as defined in subsection 775.087 (3) or a machine gun as defined in subsection 790.001(9). Only one assessment of either 18 or 25 points can be made.

        (18)   "Subtotal sentence points" are the sum of the primary offense points, the total additional offense points, the total victim injury points, the total prior record points, any legal status points, community sanction points, prior serious felony points, prior capital felony points and points for possession of a firearm or semiautomatic weapon.

        (19)   If the primary offense is drug trafficking under section 893.135, Florida Statutes, ranked in offense severity level 7 or 8, the subtotal sentence points may be multiplied, at the discretion of the sentencing court, by a factor of 1.5.

        (20)   If the primary offense is a violation of the Law Enforcement Protection Act under subsection 775.0823(2), (3), or (4), Florida Statutes, the subtotal sentence points are multiplied by 2.5. If the primary offense is a violation of subsection 775.0823 (5), (6), (7), (8), or (9), the subtotal sentence points are multiplied by 2.0. If the primary offense is a violation of section 784.07(3) or 775.0875(1) or the Law Enforcement Protection Act under subsection 775.0823(10) or (11), the subtotal sentence points are multiplied by 1.5.

        (21)   If the primary offense is grand theft of the third degree of a motor vehicle and the offender's prior record includes three or more grand thefts of the third degree of a motor vehicle, the subtotal sentence points are multiplied by 1.5.

        (22)   If the offender is found to have committed the offense for the purpose of benefitting, promoting, or furthering the interests of a criminal gang under section 874.04, Florida Statutes, at the time of the commission of the primary offense, the subtotal sentence points are multiplied by 1.5.

        (23)   If the primary offense is a crime of domestic violence as defined in section 741.28, Florida Statutes, which was committed in the presence of a child under 16 years of age who is a family household member as defined in section 741.28(2)

with the victim or perpetrator, the subtotal sentence points are multiplied by 1.5.

(24)   "Total sentence points" are the subtotal sentence points or the enhanced subtotal sentence points.

(25)   The lowest permissible sentence is the minimum sentence that may be imposed by the trial court, absent a valid reason for departure. The lowest permissible sentence is any nonstate prison sanction in which the total sentence points equals or is less than 44 points, unless the court determines within its discretion that a prison sentence, which may be up to the statutory maximums for the offenses committed, is appropriate. When the total sentence points exceeds 44 points, the lowest permissible sentence in prison months must be calculated by subtracting 28 points from the total sentence points and decreasing the remaining total by 25 percent. The total sentence points must be calculated only as a means of determining the lowest permissible sentence. The permissible range for sentencing must be the lowest permissible sentence up to and including the statutory maximum, as defined in section 775.082, for the primary offense and any additional offenses before the court for sentencing. The sentencing court may impose such sentences concurrently or consecutively. However, any sentence to state prison must exceed 1 year. If the lowest permissible sentence under the Code exceeds the statutory maximum sentence as provided in section 775.082, the sentence required by the Code must be imposed. If the total sentence points are greater than or equal to 363, the court may sentence the offender to life imprisonment. The sentence imposed must be entered on the scoresheet.

(26)   For those offenses having a mandatory minimum sentence, a scoresheet must be completed and the lowest permissible sentence under the Code calculated. If the lowest permissible sentence is less than the mandatory minimum sentence, the mandatory minimum sentence takes precedence. If the lowest permissible sentence exceeds the mandatory sentence, the requirements of the Criminal Punishment Code and any mandatory minimum penalties apply. Mandatory minimum sentences must be recorded on the scoresheet.

(27)   Any downward departure from the lowest permissible sentence, as calculated according to the total sentence points under section 921.0024, Florida Statutes, is prohibited unless there are circumstances or factors that reasonably justify the downward departure. Circumstances or factors that can be considered include, but are not limited to, those listed in subsection 921.0026(2), Florida Statutes.

(A)   If a sentencing judge imposes a sentence that is below the lowest permissible sentence, it is a departure sentence and must be accompanied by a written statement by the sentencing court delineating the reasons for the departure, filed within 7 days after the date of sentencing. A written transcription of orally stated reasons for departure articulated at the time sentence was imposed is sufficient if it is filed by the court within 7 days after the date of sentencing. The sentencing judge may also list the written reasons for departure in the space provided on the Criminal Punishment Code scoresheet.

(B)   The written statement delineating the reasons for departure must be made a part of the record. The written statement, if it is a separate document, must accompany the scoresheet required to be provided to the Department of Corrections under subsection 921.0024 (6).

If a split sentence is imposed, the total sanction (incarceration and community control or probation) must not exceed the term provided by general law or the maximum sentence under the Criminal Punishment Code.

(28)   If the lowest permissible sentence under the criminal punishment code is a state prison sanction but the total sentencing points do not exceed 48 points (or 54 points if six of those points are for a violation of probation, community control, or other community supervision that does not involve a new crime), the court may sentence the defendant to probation, community control, or community supervision with mandatory participation in a prison diversion program, as provided for in s. 921.00241, Florida Statutes, if the defendant meets the requirements for that program as set forth in section 921.00241.

(29)   If the total sentence points equal 22 or less, the court must sentence the offender to a nonstate prison sanction unless it makes written findings that a nonstate prison sanction could present a danger to the public.

(30)   Sentences imposed after revocation of probation or community control must be imposed according to the sentencing law applicable at the time of the commission of the original offense.

Committee Note

The terms must and shall, as used in this rule, are mandatory and not permissive.

2001 Amendment. 3.704(d)(14)(B). The definition of "prior record" was amended to include juvenile   dispositions of offenses committed within 5 years prior to the date of the commission of the primary offense.   "Prior record" was previously defined to include juvenile disposition of offenses committed within 3 years prior   to the date of the commission of the primary offense. This amendment reflects the legislative change to section   921.0021, Florida Statutes, effective July 1, 2001. This new definition of prior record applies to primary   offenses committed on or after July 1, 2001.

RULE 3.710. PRESENTENCE REPORT

(a)   **Cases In Which Court Has Discretion.** In all cases in which the court has discretion as to what sentence may be imposed, the court may refer the case to the Department of Corrections for investigation and recommendation. No sentence or sentences other than probation shall be imposed on any defendant found guilty of a first felony offense or found guilty of a felony while under the age of 18 years, until after such investigation has first been made and the recommendations of the Department of Corrections received and considered by the sentencing judge.

(b)   **Capital Defendant Who Refuses To Present Mitigation Evidence.** Should a defendant in a capital case choose not to challenge the death penalty and refuse to present mitigation evidence, the court shall refer the case to the Department of Corrections for the preparation of a presentence report. The report shall be comprehensive and should include information such as previous mental health problems (including hospitalizations), school records, and relevant family background.

Committee Notes

1972 Adoption. The rule provides for the utilization of a pre-sentence report as part of the sentencing process. While use of the report is discretionary in all cases, it is mandatory in two instances, the sentencing of a first felony offender and of a defendant under 18 years of age. Of course, no report is necessary where the specific sentence is mandatory, e.g., the sentence of death or life imprisonment in a verdict of first degree murder.

1988 Amendment. This amendment changes wording to conform with current responsibility of the Department of Corrections to prepare the presentence investigation and report.

2004 Amendment. The amendment adds subdivision (b). Section 948.015, Florida Statutes, is by its own terms inapplicable to those cases described in this new subdivision. Nonetheless, subdivision (b) requires a report that is "comprehensive." Accordingly, the report should include, if reasonably available, in addition to those matters specifically listed in *Muhammad v. State*, 782 So.2d 343, 363 (Fla. 2000), a description of the status of all of the charges in the indictment as well as any other pending offenses; the defendant's medical history; and those matters listed in sections 948.015 (3)–(8) and (13), Florida Statutes. The Department of Corrections should not recommend a sentence.

RULE 3.711. PRESENTENCE REPORT: WHEN PREPARED

(a)   Except as provided in subdivision (b), the sentencing court shall not authorize the commencement of the presentence investigation until there has been a finding of guilt.

(b)   The sentencing court may authorize the commencement of the presentence investigation prior to finding of guilt if:

(1)   the defendant has consented to such action; and

(2)   nothing disclosed by the presentence investigation comes to the attention of the prosecution, the court, or the jury prior to an adjudication of guilt. Upon motion of the defense and prosecution, the court may examine the presentence investigation prior to the entry of a plea.

Committee Notes

1972 Adoption. The rule permits presentence investigations to be initiated prior to finding of guilt. Its purpose is to reduce unwarranted jail time by a defendant who expects to plead guilty and who may well merit probation or commitment to facilities other than prison.

RULE 3.712. PRESENTENCE REPORT: DISCLOSURE

The presentence investigation shall not be a public record and shall be available only to the following persons under the following stated conditions:

(a)   To the sentencing court to assist it in determining an appropriate sentence.

(b)   To persons or agencies having a legitimate professional interest in the information that it would contain.

(c)   To reviewing courts if relevant to an issue on which an appeal has been taken.

(d)   To the parties as rule 3.713 provides.

Committee Notes

1972 Amendment. Provides for disclosure of the report to the trial court, appropriate agencies of the state, and appellate courts, if needed.

RULE 3.713. PRESENTENCE INVESTIGATION DISCLOSURE: PARTIES

(a)   The trial judge may disclose any of the contents of the presentence investigation to the parties prior to sentencing. Any information so disclosed to one party shall be disclosed to the opposing party.

(b)   The trial judge shall disclose all factual material, including but not limited to the defendant's education, prior occupation, prior arrests, prior convictions, military service, and the like, to the defendant and the state a reasonable time prior to sentencing. If any physical or mental evaluations of the defendant have been made and are to be considered for the purposes of sentencing or release, such reports shall be disclosed to counsel for both parties.

(c)   On motion of the defendant or the prosecutor or on its own motion, the sentencing court may order the defendant to submit to a mental or physical examination that would be relevant to the sentencing decision. Copies of the examination or any other examination to be considered for the purpose of sentencing shall be disclosed to counsel for the parties subject to the limitation of rule 3.713(b).

Committee Notes

1972 Adoption. This rule represents a compromise between the philosophy that presentence investigations should be fully disclosed to a defendant and the objection that such disclosure would dry up sources of confidential information and render such report virtually useless. (a) gives the trial judge discretion to disclose any or all of the report to the parties. (b) makes mandatory the disclosure of factual and physical and mental evaluation material only. In this way, it is left to the discretion of the trial judge to disclose to a defendant or defendant's counsel any other evaluative material. The judicial discretion should amply protect the confidentiality of those sources who do not wish to be disclosed, while the availability of all factual material will permit the defendant to discover and make known to the sentencing court any errors that may appear in the report.

RULE 3.720. SENTENCING HEARING

As soon as practicable after the determination of guilt and after the examination of any presentence reports, the sentencing court shall order a sentencing hearing. At the hearing:

(a)   The court shall inform the defendant of the finding of guilt against the defendant and of the judgment and ask the defendant whether there is any legal cause to show why sentence should not be pronounced. The defendant may allege and show as legal cause why sentence should not be pronounced only:

      (1)   that the defendant is insane;

      (2)   that the defendant has been pardoned of the offense for which he or she is about to be sentenced;

      (3)   that the defendant is not the same person against whom the verdict or finding of the court or judgment was rendered; or

      (4)   if the defendant is a woman and sentence of death is to be pronounced, that she is pregnant.

(b)   The court shall entertain submissions and evidence by the parties that are relevant to the sentence.

(c)   In cases where guilt was determined by plea, the court shall inform itself, if not previously informed, of the existence of plea discussions or agreements and the extent to which they involve recommendations as to the appropriate sentence.

(d)   (1) If the accused was represented by a public defender or other court appointed counsel, the court shall notify the accused of the imposition of a lien pursuant to section 938.29, Florida Statutes. The amount of the lien shall be given and a judgment entered in that amount against the accused. Notice of the accused's right to a hearing to contest the amount of the lien shall be given at the time of sentence.

      (2)   If the accused requests a hearing to contest the amount of the lien, the court shall set a hearing date within 30 days of the date of sentencing.

Committee Notes

1968 Adoption (of Rule 3.730). A revamped version of section 921.08, Florida Statutes.

1972 Amendment. 3.720(a): Substantially the same as former rule 3.730. 3.720(b): The defendant is to be permitted to challenge factual bases for the sentence that the defendant believes to be incorrect. When possible, submissions should be done informally, but the rule does not preclude an evidentiary hearing if it should be necessary. 3.720(c): Provides for plea discussions to be made a part of the record.

1980 Amendment. Modification of the rule by the addition of (d)(1) and (d)(2) requires a trial judge to adequately inform a defendant of the imposition of a lien for public defender services. A uniform procedure for scheduling hearings to contest liens would reduce the number of postsentence petitions from incarcerated defendants at times remote from sentencing. The procedure is designed to complete all lien requirements established by section 27.56, Florida Statutes, before defendants are removed from the jurisdiction of the trial court.

RULE 3.721. RECORD OF THE PROCEEDINGS

The sentencing court shall ensure that a record of the entire sentencing proceeding is made and preserved in such a manner that it can be transcribed as needed.

Committee Notes

1972 Adoption. New, providing for a record of the sentencing proceeding.

RULE 3.730. ISSUANCE OF CAPIAS WHEN NECESSARY TO BRING DEFENDANT BEFORE COURT

Whenever the court deems it necessary to do so in order to procure the presence of the defendant before it for the adjudication of guilt or the pronouncement of sentence, or both, when the defendant is not in custody, it shall direct the clerk to issue immediately or when directed by the prosecuting attorney a capias for the arrest of the defendant. Subsequent capiases may be issued from time to time by direction of the court or the prosecuting attorney.

Committee Notes

1968 Adoption (of Rule 3.710). A revamped version of section 921.06, Florida Statutes, adding provision that defendant be required to be present at the adjudication of guilt.

1972 Amendment. Same as prior rule 3.710.

RULE 3.750. PROCEDURE WHEN PARDON IS ALLEGED AS CAUSE FOR NOT PRONOUNCING SENTENCE

When the cause alleged for not pronouncing sentence is that the defendant has been pardoned for the offense for which the defendant is about to be sentenced, the court, if necessary, shall postpone the pronouncement of sentence for the purpose of hearing evidence on the allegation. If the court decides that the allegation is true, it shall discharge the defendant from custody unless the defendant is in custody on some other charge. If, however, it decides that the allegation is not true, it shall proceed to pronounce sentence.

Committee Notes

1968 Adoption. A revamped version of section 921.10, Florida Statutes.

1972 Amendment. Same as prior rule.

RULE 3.760. PROCEDURE WHEN NONIDENTITY IS ALLEGED AS CAUSE FOR NOT PRONOUNCING SENTENCE

When the cause alleged for not pronouncing sentence is that the person brought before the court to be sentenced is not the same person against whom the verdict, finding of the court, or judgment was rendered, the court, if necessary, shall postpone the pronouncement of sentence for the purpose of hearing evidence on the allegation. If the court decides that the allegation is true, it shall discharge the person from custody unless the person is in custody on some other charge. If, however, it decides that the allegation is not true, it shall proceed to pronounce sentence.

Committee Notes

1968 Adoption. A revamped version of section 921.11, Florida Statutes.

1972 Amendment. Same as prior rule.

RULE 3.770. PROCEDURE WHEN PREGNANCY IS ALLEGED AS CAUSE FOR NOT PRONOUNCING DEATH SENTENCE

When pregnancy of a female defendant is alleged as the cause for not pronouncing the death sentence, the court shall postpone the pronouncement of sentence until after it has decided the truth of that allegation. If necessary in order to arrive at such a decision, it shall immediately fix a time for a hearing to determine whether the defendant is pregnant and shall appoint not exceeding 3 competent disinterested physicians to examine the defendant as to her alleged pregnancy and to testify at the hearing as to whether she is pregnant. Other evidence regarding whether the defendant is pregnant may be introduced at the hearing by either party. If the court decides that the defendant is not pregnant, it shall proceed to pronounce sentence. If it decides that she is pregnant, it shall commit her to prison until it appears that she is not pregnant and shall then pronounce sentence upon her.

Committee Notes

1968 Adoption. A revamped version of section 921.12, Florida Statutes.

Note that the rule omits the statutory provisions for the payment of fees to the examining physicians. The supreme court probably does not have the power to make rules governing such matters.

1972 Amendment. Same as prior rule.

RULE 3.780. SENTENCING HEARING FOR CAPITAL CASES

(a) **Evidence.** In all proceedings based on section 921.141, Florida Statutes, the state and defendant will be permitted to present evidence of an aggravating or mitigating nature, consistent with the requirements of the statute. Each side will be permitted to cross-examine the witnesses presented by the other side. The state will present evidence first.

(b) **Rebuttal.** The trial judge shall permit rebuttal testimony.

(c) **Opening Statement and Closing Argument.** Both the state and the defendant will be given an equal opportunity for one opening statement and one closing argument. The state will proceed first.

Committee Notes

1977 Adoption. This is a new rule designed to create a uniform procedure that will be consistent with both section 921.141, Florida Statutes, and *State v. Dixon*, 283 So.2d 1 (Fla. 1973).

RULE 3.790. PROBATION AND COMMUNITY CONTROL

(a) **Suspension of the Pronouncement and Imposition of Sentence; Probation or Community Control.** Pronouncement and imposition of sentence of imprisonment shall not be made on a defendant who is to be placed on probation, regardless of whether the defendant has been adjudicated guilty. An order of the court placing a person on probation or community control shall place the probationer under the authority of the Department of Corrections to be supervised as provided by law. The court shall specify the length of time during which the defendant is to be supervised.

(b) **Revocation of Probation or Community Control; Judgment; Sentence.**

(1) **Generally.** Except as otherwise provided in subdivisions (b)(2) and (b)(3) below, when a probationer or a community controllee is brought before a court of competent jurisdiction charged with a violation of probation or community control, the court shall advise the person of the charge and, if the charge is admitted to be true, may immediately enter an order revoking, modifying, or continuing the probation or community control. If the violation of probation or community control is not admitted by the probationer or community controllee, the court may commit the person or release the person with or without bail to await further hearing or it may dismiss the charge of violation of probation or community control. If the charge is not admitted by the probationer or community controllee and if it is not dismissed, the court, as soon as practicable, shall give the probationer or community controllee an opportunity to be fully heard in person, by counsel, or both. After the hearing, the court may enter an order revoking, modifying, or continuing the probation or community control. Following a revocation of probation or community control, the trial court shall adjudicate the defendant guilty of the crime forming the basis of the probation or community control if no such adjudication has been made previously. Pronouncement and imposition of sentence then shall be made on the defendant.

(2) **Lunsford Act Proceedings.** When a probationer or community controllee is arrested for violating his or her probation or community control in a material respect and is under supervision for any criminal offense proscribed in chapter 794, Florida Statutes, section 800.04(4), Florida Statutes, section 800.04(5), Florida Statutes, section 800.04(6), Florida Statutes, section 827.071, Florida Statutes, or section 847.0145, Florida Statutes, or is a registered sexual predator or a registered sexual offender, or is under supervision for a criminal offense for which, but for the effective date, he or she would meet the registration criteria of section 775.21, Florida Statutes, section 943.0435, Florida Statutes, or section 944.607, Florida Statutes, the court must make a finding that the probationer or community controllee is not a danger to the public prior to release with or without bail.

(A) The hearing to determine whether the defendant is a danger to the public shall be conducted by a court of competent jurisdiction no sooner than 24 hours after arrest. The time for conducting the hearing may be extended at the request of the accused, or at the request of the state upon a showing of good cause.

(B) At the hearing, the defendant shall have the right to be heard in person or through counsel, to present witnesses and evidence, and to cross-examine witnesses.

(C) In determining the danger posed by the defendant's

186

release, the court may consider:

(i)   the nature and circumstances of the violation and any new offenses charged;

(ii)   the defendant's past and present conduct, including convictions of crimes;

(iii)   any record of arrests without conviction for crimes involving violence or sexual crimes;

(iv)   any other evidence of allegations of unlawful sexual conduct or the use of violence by the defendant;

(v)   the defendant's family ties, length of residence in the community, employment history, and mental condition;

(vi)   the defendant's history and conduct during the probation or community control supervision from which the violation arises and any other previous supervisions, including disciplinary records of previous incarcerations;

(vii)   the likelihood that the defendant will engage again in a criminal course of conduct;

(viii) the weight of the evidence against the defendant; and

(ix)   any other facts the court considers relevant.

(3)   **Anti-Murder Act Proceedings.** The provisions of this subdivision shall control over any conflicting provisions in subdivision (b)(2). When a probationer or community controllee is arrested for violating his or her probation or community control in a material respect and meets the criteria for a violent felony offender of special concern, or for certain other related categories of offender, as set forth in section 948.06(8), Florida Statutes, the defendant shall be brought before the court that granted the probation or community control and, except when the alleged violation is based solely on the defendant's failure to pay costs, fines, or restitution, shall not be granted bail or any other form of pretrial release prior to the resolution of the probation or community control violation hearing.

(A)   The court shall not dismiss the probation or community control violation warrant pending against the defendant without holding a recorded violation hearing at which both the state and the accused are represented.

(B)   If, after conducting the hearing, the court determines that the defendant has committed a violation of probation or community control other than a failure to pay costs, fines, or restitution, the court shall make written findings as to whether the defendant poses a danger to the community. In determining the danger to the community posed by the defendant's release, the court shall base its findings on one or more of the following:

(i) The nature and circumstances of the violation and any new offenses charged;

(ii) The defendant's present conduct, including criminal convictions;

(iii) The defendant's amenability to nonincarcerative sanctions based on his or her history and conduct during the probation or community control supervision from which the violation hearing arises and any other previous supervisions, including disciplinary records of previous incarcerations;

(iv) The weight of the evidence against the defendant; and

(v) Any other facts the court considers relevant.

(C) If the court finds that the defendant poses a danger to the community, the court shall revoke probation or community control and sentence the defendant up to the statutory maximum, or longer if permitted by law.

(D) If the court finds that the defendant does not pose a danger to the community, the court may revoke, modify, or continue the probation or community control or may place the probationer into community control as provided in section 948.06, Florida Statutes.

Committee Notes

1968 Adoption. Subdivisions (a) and (b) contain the procedural aspects of section 948.01(1), (2), and (3), Florida Statutes. It should be noted that in (b) provision is made for no pronouncements in addition to no imposition of sentence prior to the granting of probation. The terminology in section 948.01(3), Florida Statutes, is that the trial court shall "withhold the imposition of sentence." The selected terminology is deemed preferable to the present statutory language since the latter is apparently subject to misconstruction whereby a sentence may be pronounced and merely the execution of the sentence is suspended.

The Third District Court of Appeal has indicated that the proper procedure to be followed is that probation be granted prior to sentencing. A sentence, therefore, is not a prerequisite of probation. See *Yates v. Buchanan*, 170 So.2d 72 (Fla. 3d DCA 1964); also see *Bateh v. State*, 101 So.2d 869 (Fla. 1st DCA 1958), decided by the First District Court of Appeal to the same effect.

While a trial court initially can set a probationary period at less than the maximum allowed by law, this period may be extended to the maximum prior to the expiration of the initially-set probationary period. *Pickman v. State*, 155 So.2d 646 (Fla. 1st DCA 1963). This means, therefore, that any specific time set by the court as to the probationary period is not binding if the court acts timely in modifying it. It is clear, in view of the foregoing, that if a trial judge pronounces a definite sentence and then purports to suspend its execution and place the defendant on probation for the period of time specified in the sentence, matters may become unduly complicated.

If such procedure is considered to be nothing more than an informal manner of suspending the imposition of sentence and thus adhering to present statutory requirements, it should be noted that the time specified in the "sentence" is not binding on the court with reference to subsequent modification, if timely action follows. On the other hand, if the action of the trial court is considered strictly, it would be held to be void as not in conformity with statutory requirements.

A probationary period is not a sentence, and any procedure that tends to mix them is undesirable, even if this mixture is accomplished by nothing more than the terminology used by the trial court in its desire to place a person on probation. See sections 948.04 and 948.06(1), Florida Statutes, in which clear distinctions are drawn between the period of a sentence and the period of probation.

(c) Contains the procedural aspects of section 948.06(1), Florida Statutes.

1972 Amendment. (a) of former rule deleted, as its substance is now contained in rules 3.710, 3.711, and 3.713. Former subdivisions (b) and (c) are now renumbered (a) and (b) respectively.

1988 Amendment. This amendment changes wording to conform with current responsibilities of the Department of Corrections to supervise a person placed on either probation or community control and brings community control within the scope of the rule.

RULE 3.800. CORRECTION, REDUCTION, AND MODIFICATION OF SENTENCES

(a) **Correction.** A court may at any time correct an illegal sentence imposed by it, or an incorrect calculation made by it in a sentencing scoresheet, when it is affirmatively alleged that the court records demonstrate on their face an entitlement to that relief, provided that a party may not file a motion to correct an illegal sentence under this subdivision during the time allowed for the filing of a motion under subdivision (b)(1) or during the pendency of a direct appeal. A defendant may seek correction of an allegedly erroneous sexual predator designation under this subdivision, but only when it is apparent from the face of the record that the defendant did not meet the criteria for designation as a sexual predator. All orders denying motions under this subdivision shall include a statement that the movant has the right to appeal within 30 days of rendition of the order.

(b) **Motion to Correct Sentencing Error.** A motion to correct any sentencing error, including an illegal sentence, may be filed as allowed by this subdivision. This subdivision shall not be applicable to those cases in which the death sentence has been imposed and direct appeal jurisdiction is in the Supreme Court under article V, section 3(b)
(1) of the Florida Constitution. The motion must identify the error with specificity and provide a proposed correction. A response to the motion may be filed within 15 days, either admitting or contesting the alleged error. Motions may be filed by the state under this subdivision only if the correction of the sentencing error would benefit the defendant or to correct a scrivener's error.

(1) Motion Before Appeal. During the time allowed for the filing of a notice of appeal of a sentence, a defendant or the state may file a motion to correct a sentencing error.

(A) This motion shall stay rendition under Florida Rule of Appellate Procedure 9.020(i).

(B)	Unless the trial court determines that the motion can be resolved as a matter of law without a hearing, it shall hold a calendar call no later than 20 days from the filing of the motion, with notice to all parties, for the express purpose of either ruling on the motion or determining the need for an evidentiary hearing. If an evidentiary hearing is needed, it shall be set no more than 20 days from the date of the calendar call. Within 60 days from the filing of the motion, the trial court shall file an order ruling on the motion. If no order is filed within 60 days, the motion shall be considered denied. A party may file a motion for rehearing of any order entered under subdivisions (a) and (b) of this rule within 15 days of the date of service of the order or within 15 days of the expiration of the time period for filing an order if no order is filed. A response may be filed within 10 days of service of the motion. The trial court's order disposing of the motion for rehearing shall be filed within 15 days of the response but not later than 40 days from the date of the order of which rehearing is sought. If no order is filed within 40 days, the motion is deemed denied. A timely filed motion for rehearing shall toll rendition of the order subject to appellate review and the order shall be deemed rendered 40 days from the order of which rehearing is sought, or upon the filing of a written order denying the motion for rehearing, whichever is earlier.

(2)	**Motion Pending Appeal.** If an appeal is pending, a defendant or the state may file in the trial court a motion to correct a sentencing error. The motion may be filed by appellate counsel and must be served before the party's first brief is served. A notice of pending motion to correct sentencing error shall be filed in the appellate court, which notice automatically shall extend the time for the filing of the brief until 10 days after the clerk of circuit court transmits the supplemental record under Florida Rule of Appellate Procedure 9.140(f)(6).

(A)	The motion shall be served on the trial court and on all trial and appellate counsel of record. Unless the motion expressly states that appellate counsel will represent the movant in the trial court, trial counsel will represent the movant on the motion under Florida Rule of Appellate Procedure 9.140(d). If the state is the movant, trial counsel will represent the defendant unless appellate counsel for the defendant notifies trial counsel and the trial court that he or she will represent the defendant on the state's motion.

(B)	The trial court shall resolve this motion in accordance with the procedures in subdivision (b)(1)(B).

(C)	In accordance with Florida Rule of Appellate Procedure 9.140(f)(6), the clerk of circuit court shall supplement the appellate record with the motion, the order, any amended sentence, and, if designated, a transcript of any additional portion of the proceedings.

(c)	**Reduction and Modification.** A court may reduce or modify to include any of the provisions of chapter 948, Florida Statutes, a legal sentence imposed by it, sua sponte, or upon motion filed, within 60 days after the imposition, or within 60 days after receipt by the court of a mandate issued by the appellate court on affirmance of the judgment and/or sentence on an original appeal, or within 60 days after receipt by the court of a certified copy of an order of the appellate court dismissing an original appeal from the judgment and/or sentence, or, if further appellate review is sought in a higher court or in successively higher courts, within 60 days after the highest state or federal court to which a timely appeal has been taken under authority of law, or in which a petition for certiorari has been timely filed under authority of law, has entered an order of affirmance or an order dismissing the appeal and/or denying certiorari. If review is upon motion, the trial court shall have 90 days from the date the motion is filed or such time as agreed by the parties or as extended by the trial court to enter an order ruling on the motion. If no order is entered on the motion within 90 days or such time as extended by the parties or the trial court, the motion shall be deemed denied. This subdivision shall not be applicable to those cases in which the death sentence is imposed or those cases in which the trial judge has imposed the minimum mandatory sentence or has no sentencing discretion.

Committee Notes

1968 Adoption. Same as sections 921.24 and 921.25, Florida Statutes. Similar to Federal Rule of Criminal Procedure 35.

1972 Amendment. Same as prior rule.

1977 Amendment. This amendment provides a uniform time within which a defendant may seek a reduction in sentence and excludes death and minimum mandatory sentences from its operation.

1980 Amendment. Permits the sentencing judge, within the 60-day time period, to modify as well as to reduce the sentence originally imposed. Such modification would permit the judge to impose, in the modification, any sentence which could have been imposed initially, including split sentence or probation. The trial judge may not, in such modification, increase the original sentence.

1996 Amendments. Subdivision (b) was added and existing subdivision (b) was renumbered as subdivision (c) in order to authorize the filing of a motion to correct a sentence or order of probation, thereby providing a vehicle to correct sentencing errors in the trial court and to preserve the issue should the motion be denied. A motion filed under subdivision (b) is an authorized motion which tolls the time for filing the notice of appeal. The presence of a defendant who is represented by counsel would not be required at the hearing on the disposition of such a motion if it only involved a question of law.

2000 Amendment. The amendment to subdivision (a) is intended to conform the rule with *State v. Mancino*, 714 So.2d 429 (Fla. 1998).

Court Commentary

1999 Amendments. Rule 3.800(b) was substantially rewritten to accomplish the goals of the Criminal Appeal Reform Act of 1996 (Ch. 96-248, Laws of Fla.). As revised, this rule permits the filing of a motion during the initial stages of an appeal. A motion pursuant to this rule is needed only if the sentencing error has not been adequately preserved for review at an earlier time in the trial court.

The State may file a motion to correct a sentencing error pursuant to rule 3.800(b) only if the correction of that error will benefit the defendant or correct a scrivener's error. This amendment is not intended to alter the substantive law of the State concerning whether a change to the defendant's sentence violates the constitutional prohibition against double jeopardy. *See, e.g., Cheshire v. State*, 568 So. 2d 908 (Fla. 1990); *Goene v. State*, 577 So. 2d 1306, 1309 (Fla. 1991); *Troupe v. Rowe*, 283 So. 2d 857, 859 (Fla. 1973).

A scrivener's error in this context describes clerical or ministerial errors in a criminal case that occur in the written sentence, judgment, or order of probation or restitution. The term scrivener's error refers to a mistake in the written sentence that is at variance with the oral pronouncement of sentence or the record but not those errors that are the result of a judicial determination or error. See, e.g., *Allen v. State*, 739 So.2d 166 (Fla. 3d DCA 1999) (correcting a "scrivener's error" in the written order that adjudicated the appellant in contempt for "jailing polygraph exam"); *Pressley v. State*, 726 So. 2d 403 (Fla. 2d DCA 1999) (correcting scrivener's error in the sentencing documents that identified the defendant as a habitual offender when he was not sentenced as a habitual offender); *Ricks v. State*, 725 So.2d 1205 (Fla. 2d DCA 1999) (correcting scrivener's error that resulted from the written sentence not identifying the defendant as a habitual offender although the court had orally pronounced a habitual offender sentence), review denied, 732 So.2d 328 (Fla. 1999); *McKee v. State*, 712 So.2d 837 (Fla. 2d DCA 1998) (remanding for the trial court to determine whether a scrivener's error occurred where the written order of probation imposed six years' probation, which conflicted with the written sentence and the trial court minutes that reflected only five years' probation had been imposed); *Florczak v. State*, 712 So.2d 467, 467 (Fla. 4th DCA 1998) (correcting a scrivener's error in the judgment of conviction where the defendant was acquitted of grand theft but the written judgment stated otherwise); *Stombaugh v. State*, 704 So.2d 723, 725B26 (Fla. 5th DCA 1998) (finding a scrivener's error occurred where the State had nol prossed a count of the information as part of plea bargain but the written sentence reflected that the defendant was sentenced under that count). But see *Carridine v. State*, 721 So.2d 818, 819 (Fla. 4th DCA 1998) (trial court's failure to sign written reasons for imposing an upward departure sentence did not constitute a scrivener's error that could be corrected nunc pro tunc by the trial court), and cases cited therein.

When a trial court determines that an evidentiary hearing is necessary to resolve a factual issue, it is possible that the court will need to utilize the entire 60-day period authorized by this rule. However, trial courts and counsel are strongly encouraged to cooperate to resolve these motions as expeditiously as possible because they delay the appellate process. For purposes of this rule, sentencing errors include harmful errors in orders entered as a result of the sentencing process. This includes errors in orders of probation, orders of community control, cost and restitution orders, as well as errors within the sentence itself.

RULE 3.801. CORRECTION OF JAIL CREDIT

(a) **Correction of Jail Credit.** A court may correct a sentence that fails to allow a defendant credit for all of the time he or she spent in the county jail before sentencing as provided in section 921.161, Florida Statutes.

(b) **Time Limitations.** No motion shall be filed or considered pursuant to this rule if filed more than 1 year after the sentence becomes final. For sentences imposed prior to July 1, 2013, a motion under this rule may be filed on or before July 1, 2014.

(c) **Contents of Motion.** The motion shall be under oath and include:

(1) a brief statement of the facts relied on in support of the motion;

(2) the dates, location of incarceration and total time for credit already provided;

(3)   the dates, location of incarceration and total time for credit the defendant contends was not properly awarded;

(4)   whether any other criminal charges were pending at the time of the incarceration noted in subdivision (c)(3), and if so, the location, case number and resolution of the charges; and

(5)   whether the defendant waived any county jail credit at the time of sentencing, and if so, the number of days waived.

(d)   Successive Motions. No successive motions for jail credit will be considered.

(e)   Incorporation of Portions of Florida Rule of Criminal Procedure 3.850. The following subdivisions of Florida Rule of Criminal Procedure 3.850 apply to proceedings under this rule: 3.850(e), (f), (j), (k), and (n).

Court Commentary

2013 Adoption. All jail credit issues must be handled pursuant to this rule. The rule is intended to require that jail credit issues be dealt with promptly, within 1 year of the sentence becoming final. No successive motions for jail credit will be allowed.

XV.   EXECUTION OF SENTENCE

RULE 3.810. COMMITMENT OF DEFENDANT; DUTY OF SHERIFF

On pronouncement of a sentence imposing a penalty other than a fine only or death, the court shall, unless the execution of the sentence is suspended or stayed, and, in such case, on termination of the suspension or stay, forthwith commit the defendant to the custody of the sheriff under a commitment to which shall be attached a certified copy of the sentence and, unless both are contained in the same instrument if the sentence is imprisonment in the state prison, a certified copy of the judgment of conviction and a certified copy of the indictment or information, and the sheriff shall thereupon, within a reasonable time, if the sheriff is not the proper official to execute the sentence, transfer the defendant, together with the commitment and attached certified copies, to the custody of the official whose duty it is to execute the sentence and shall take from that person a receipt for the defendant and make a return thereof to the court.

Committee Notes

1968 Adoption. Substantially the same as section 922.01, Florida Statutes. There has been added to the rule the requirement that, if the commitment is to the state prison, it shall be accompanied by a certified copy of the judgment of conviction and a certified copy of the indictment or information. (Section 944.18, Florida Statutes, requires a certified copy of the indictment or information to be transmitted to the Division of Corrections; the Division of Corrections should also have a certified copy of the judgment.)

1972 Amendment. Same as prior rule.

RULE 3.811. INSANITY AT TIME OF EXECUTION: CAPITAL CASES

(a) **Insanity to Be Executed.** A person under sentence of death shall not be executed while insane to be executed.

(b) **Insanity Defined.** A person under sentence of death is insane for purposes of execution if the person lacks the mental capacity to understand the fact of the impending execution and the reason for it.

(c) **Stay of Execution.** No motion for a stay of execution pending hearing, based on grounds of the prisoner's insanity to be executed, shall be entertained by any court until such time as the Governor of Florida shall have held appropriate proceedings for determining the issue pursuant to the appropriate Florida Statutes.

(d) **Motion for Stay after Governor's Determination of Sanity to Be Executed.** On determination of the Governor of Florida, subsequent to the signing of a death warrant for a prisoner under sentence of death and pursuant to the applicable Florida Statutes relating to insanity at time of execution, that the prisoner is sane to be executed, counsel for the prisoner may move for a stay of execution and a hearing based on the prisoner's insanity to be executed.

(1) The motion shall be filed in the circuit court of the circuit in which the execution is to take place and shall be heard by one of the judges of that circuit or such other judge as shall be assigned by the chief justice of the supreme court to hear the motion. The state attorney of the circuit shall represent the State of Florida in any proceedings held on the motion.

(2) The motion shall be in writing and shall contain a certificate of counsel that the motion is made in good faith and on reasonable grounds to believe that the prisoner is insane to be executed.

(3) Counsel for the prisoner shall file, along with the motion, all reports of experts that were submitted to the governor pursuant to the statutory procedure for executive determination of sanity to be executed. If any of the evidence is not available to counsel for the prisoner, counsel shall attach to the motion an affidavit so stating, with an explanation of why the evidence is unavailable.

(4) Counsel for the prisoner and the state may submit such other evidentiary material and written submissions including reports of experts on behalf of the prisoner as shall be relevant to determination of the issue.

(5) A copy of the motion and all supporting documents shall be served on the Florida Department of Legal Affairs and the state attorney of the circuit in which the motion has been filed.

(e) **Order Granting.** If the circuit judge, upon review of the motion and submissions, has reasonable grounds to believe that the prisoner is insane to be executed, the judge shall grant a stay of execution and may order further proceedings which may include a hearing pursuant to rule 3.812.

Committee Notes

1988 Adoption. This rule is not intended to preclude the Office of the Attorney

General or the state attorney of the circuit in which the trial was held from appearing on behalf of the State of Florida under circumstances when permitted by law.

RULE 3.812. HEARING ON INSANITY AT TIME OF EXECUTION: CAPITAL CASES

(a) **Hearing on Insanity to Be Executed.** The hearing on the prisoner's insanity to be executed shall not be a review of the governor's determination, but shall be a hearing de novo.

(b) **Issue at Hearing.** At the hearing the issue shall be whether the prisoner presently meets the criteria for insanity at time of execution, that is, whether the prisoner lacks the mental capacity to understand the fact of the pending execution and the reason for it.

(c) **Procedure.** The court may do any of the following as may be appropriate and adequate for a just resolution of the issues raised:

(1) require the presence of the prisoner at the hearing;

(2) appoint no more than 3 disinterested mental health experts to examine the prisoner with respect to the criteria for insanity to be executed and to report their findings and conclusions to the court; or

(3) enter such other orders as may be appropriate to effectuate a speedy and just resolution of the issues raised.

(d) **Evidence.** At hearings held pursuant to this rule, the court may admit such evidence as the court deems relevant to the issues, including but not limited to the reports of expert witnesses, and the court shall not be strictly bound by the rules of evidence.

(e) **Order.** If, at the conclusion of the hearing, the court shall find, by clear and convincing evidence, that the prisoner is insane to be executed, the court shall enter its order continuing the stay of the death warrant; otherwise, the court shall deny the motion and enter its order dissolving the stay of execution.

RULE 3.820. HABEAS CORPUS

(a) **Custody Pending Appeal of Order of Denial.** When a defendant has been sentenced, and is actually serving the sentence, and has not appealed from the judgment or sentence, but seeks a release from imprisonment by habeas corpus proceedings, and the writ has been discharged after it has been issued, the custody of the prisoner shall not be disturbed, pending review by the appellate court.

(b) **Custody Pending Appeal of Order Granting.** Pending review of a decision discharging a prisoner on habeas corpus, the prisoner shall be discharged on bail, with sureties to be approved as other bail bonds are approved for the prisoner's appearance to answer and abide by the judgment of the appellate court.

Committee Notes

1968 Adoption. Same as section 922.03, Florida Statutes.

1972 Amendment. Same as prior rule, but some terminology has been changed.

XVI.   CRIMINAL CONTEMPT

RULE 3.830. DIRECT CRIMINAL CONTEMPT

A criminal contempt may be punished summarily if the court saw or heard the conduct constituting the contempt committed in the actual presence of the court. The judgment of guilt of contempt shall include a recital of those facts on which the adjudication of guilt is based. Prior to the adjudication of guilt the judge shall inform the defendant of the accusation against the defendant and inquire as to whether the defendant has any cause to show why he or she should not be adjudged guilty of contempt by the court and sentenced therefor. The defendant shall be given the opportunity to present evidence of excusing or mitigating circumstances. The judgment shall be signed by the judge and entered of record. Sentence shall be pronounced in open court.

Committee Notes

1968 Adoption. This proposal is consistent with present Florida practice in authorizing summary proceedings in direct criminal contempt cases. See *Ballengee v. State*, 144 So.2d 68 (Fla. 2d DCA 1962); *Baumgartner v. Joughin*, 105 Fla. 334, 141 So. 185 (1932); also see *State v. Lehman*, 100 Fla. 481, 129 So. 818 (1930), holding that the defendant is not entitled to notice of the accusation or a motion for attachment. Fairness dictates that the defendant be allowed to present excusing or mitigating evidence even in direct criminal contempt cases.

Much of the terminology of the proposal is patterned after Federal Rule of Criminal Procedure 42(a) with variations for purposes of clarity. What may be considered a significant change from the terminology of the federal rule is that the proposal provides for a "judgment" of contempt, whereas the term "order" of contempt is used in the federal rule. Both terms have been used in Florida appellate cases. The term "judgment" is preferred here since it is consistent with the procedure of adjudicating guilt and is more easily reconciled with a "conviction" of contempt, common terminology on the trial and appellate levels in Florida. It also is consistent with appeals in contempt cases. See, e.g., *State ex rel. Shotkin v. Buchanan*, 149 So.2d 574, 98 A.L.R.2d 683 (Fla. 3d DCA 1963), for the use of the term "judgment".

1972 Amendment. Same as prior rule.

RULE 3.840. INDIRECT CRIMINAL CONTEMPT

A criminal contempt, except as provided in rule 3.830 concerning direct contempts, shall be prosecuted in the following manner:

(a)   **Order to Show Cause.** The judge, on the judge's own motion or on affidavit of any person having knowledge of the facts, may issue and sign an order directed to the defendant, stating the essential facts constituting the criminal contempt charged and requiring the defendant to appear before the court to show cause why the defendant should not be held in contempt of court. The order shall specify the time and place of the hearing, with a reasonable time allowed for preparation of the defense after service of the order on the defendant.

(b)   Motions; Answer. The defendant, personally or by counsel, may move to dismiss the order to show cause, move for a statement of particulars, or answer the order by way of explanation or defense. All motions and the answer shall be in writing unless specified otherwise by the judge. A defendant's omission to file motions or answer shall not be deemed as an admission of guilt of the contempt charged.

(c)   Order of Arrest; Bail. The judge may issue an order of arrest of the defendant if the judge has reason to believe the defendant will not appear in response to the order to show cause. The defendant shall be admitted to bail in the manner provided by law in criminal cases.

(d)   Arraignment; Hearing. The defendant may be arraigned at the time of the hearing, or prior thereto at the defendant's request. A hearing to determine the guilt or innocence of the defendant shall follow a plea of not guilty. The judge may conduct a hearing without assistance of counsel or may be assisted by the prosecuting attorney or by an attorney appointed for that purpose. The defendant is entitled to be represented by counsel, have compulsory process for the attendance of witnesses, and testify in his or her own defense. All issues of law and fact shall be heard and determined by the judge.

(e)   Disqualification of Judge. If the contempt charged involves disrespect to or criticism of a judge, the judge shall disqualify himself or herself from presiding at the hearing. Another judge shall be designated by the chief justice of the supreme court.

(f)   Verdict; Judgment. At the conclusion of the hearing the judge shall sign and enter of record a judgment of guilty or not guilty. There should be included in a judgment of guilty a recital of the facts constituting the contempt of which the defendant has been found and adjudicated guilty.

(g)   Sentence; Indirect Contempt. Prior to the pronouncement of sentence, the judge shall inform the defendant of the accusation and judgment against the defendant and inquire as to whether the defendant has any cause to show why sentence should not be pronounced. The defendant shall be afforded the opportunity to present evidence of mitigating circumstances. The sentence shall be pronounced in open court and in the presence of the defendant.

Committee Notes

1968 Adoption.

(a)(1)   Order to Show Cause. The courts have used various and, at times, misleading terminology with reference to this phase of the procedure, viz. "citation," "rule nisi," "rule," "rule to show cause," "information," "indicted," and "order to show cause." Although all apparently have been used with the same connotation the terminology chosen probably is more readily understandable than the others. This term is used in Federal Rule of Criminal Procedure 42(b) dealing with indirect criminal contempts.

In proceedings for indirect contempt, due process of law requires that the accused be given notice of the charge and a reasonable opportunity to meet it by way of defense or explanation. *State ex rel. Giblin v. Sullivan*, 157 Fla. 496, 26 So.2d 509 (1946); *State ex rel. Geary v. Kelly*, 137 So.2d 262, 263 (Fla. 3d DCA1962).

The petition (affidavit is used here) must be filed by someone having actual knowledge of the facts and must be under oath. *Phillips v. State*, 147 So.2d 163 (Fla. 3d DCA 1962); see also *Croft v. Culbreath*, 150 Fla. 60, 6 So.2d 638 (1942); *Ex parte Biggers*, 85 Fla. 322, 95 So. 763 (1923).

(2) **Motions; Answer.** The appellate courts of Florida, while apparently refraining from making motions and answers indispensable parts of the procedure, seem to regard them with favor in appropriate situations. Regarding motions to quash and motion for bill of particulars, see *Geary v. State*, 139 So.2d 891 (Fla. 3d DCA 1962); regarding the answer, see State ex rel. *Huie v. Lewis*, 80 So.2d 685 (Fla. 1955).

Elsewhere in these rules is a recommended proposal that a motion to dismiss replace the present motion to quash; hence, the motion to dismiss is recommended here.

The proposal contains no requirement that the motions or answer be under oath. Until section 38.22, Florida Statutes, was amended in 1945 there prevailed in Florida the common law rule that denial under oath is conclusive and requires discharge of the defendant in indirect contempt cases; the discharge was considered as justified because the defendant could be convicted of perjury if the defendant had sworn falsely in the answer or in a motion denying the charge. The amendment of section 38.22, Florida Statutes, however, has been construed to no longer justify the discharge of the defendant merely because the defendant denies the charge under oath. See *Ex parte Earman*, 85 Fla. 297, 95 So. 755 (1923), re the common law; see *Dodd v. State*, 110 So.2d 22 (Fla. 3d DCA 1959) re the construction of section 38.22, Florida Statutes, as amended. There appears, therefore, no necessity of requiring that a pleading directed to the order to show cause be under oath, except as a matter of policy of holding potential perjury prosecutions over the heads of defendants. It is recommended, therefore, that no oath be required at this stage of the proceeding.

Due process of law in the prosecution for indirect contempt requires that the defendant have the right to assistance by counsel. *Baumgartner v. Joughin*, 105 Fla. 335, 141 So. 185 (1932), adhered to, 107 Fla. 858,143 So. 436 (1932).

(3) **Order of Arrest; Bail.** Arrest and bail, although apparently used only rarely, were permissible at common law and, accordingly, are unobjectionable under present Florida law. At times each should serve a useful purpose in contempt proceedings and should be included in the rule. As to the common law, see *Ex parte Biggers*, supra.

(4) **Arraignment; Hearing.** Provision is made for a pre-hearing arraignment in case the defendant wishes to plead guilty to the charge prior to the date set for the hearing. The defendant has a constitutional right to a hearing under the due process clauses of the state and federal constitutions. *State ex rel. Pipia v. Buchanan*, 168 So.2d 783 (Fla. 3d DCA 1964). This right includes the right to assistance of counsel and the right to call witnesses. *Baumgartner v. Joughin*, supra. The defendant cannot be compelled to testify against himself. *Demetree v. State, ex rel.* Marsh, 89 So.2d 498 (Fla. 1956).

Section 38.22, Florida Statutes, as amended in 1945, provides that all issues of law or fact shall be heard and determined by the judge. Apparently under this statute the defendant is not only precluded from considering a jury trial as a right but also the judge has no discretion to allow the defendant a jury trial. See *State ex rel. Huie v. Lewis*, supra, and *Dodd v. State*, supra, in which the court seems to assume this, such assumption seemingly being warranted by the terminology of the statute.

There is no reason to believe that the statute is unconstitutional as being in violation of section 11 of the Declaration of Rights of the Florida Constitution which provides, in part, that the accused in all criminal prosecutions shall have the right to a public trial by an impartial jury. Criminal contempt is not a crime; consequently, no criminal prosecution is involved. *Neering v. State*, 155 So.2d 874 (Fla. 1963); *State ex rel. Saunders v. Boyer*, 166 So.2d 694 (Fla. 2d DCA 1964); *Ballengee v. State*, 144 So.2d 68 (Fla. 2d DCA 1962).

Section 3 of the Declaration of Rights, providing that the right of trial by jury shall be secured to all and remain inviolate forever, also apparently is not violated. This provision has been construed many times as guaranteeing a jury trial in proceedings at common law, as practiced at the time of the adoption of the constitution (see, e.g., *Hawkins v. Rellim Inv. Co.*, 92 Fla. 784, 110 So. 350 (1926)), i.e., it is applicable only to cases in which the right existed before the adoption of the constitution (see, e.g., *State ex rel. Sellers v. Parker*, 87 Fla. 181, 100 So. 260 (1924)). Section 3 was never intended to extend the right of a trial by jury beyond this point. *Boyd v. Dade County*, 123 So.2d 323 (Fla. 1960).

There is some authority that trial by jury in indirect criminal contempt existed in the early common law, but this practice was eliminated by the Star Chamber with the result that for centuries the common law courts have punished indirect contempts without a jury trial. See 36 Mississippi Law Journal 106. The practice in Florida to date apparently has been consistent with this position. No case has been found in this state in which a person was tried by a jury for criminal contempt. See Justice Terrell's comment adverse to such jury trials in *State ex rel. Huie v. Lewis*, supra.

The United States Supreme Court has assumed the same position with reference to the dictates of the common law. Quoting from *Eilenbecker v. District Court*, 134 U.S. 31, 36, 10 S.Ct. 424, 33 L.Ed. 801 (1890), the Court stated, "If it has ever been understood that proceedings according to the common law for contempt of court have been subject to the right of trial by jury, we have been unable to find any instance of it." *United States v. Barnett*, 376 U.S. 681, 696, 84 S.Ct. 984, 12 L.Ed.2d 23 (1964). In answer to the contention that contempt proceedings without a jury were limited to trivial offenses, the Court stated, "[W]e find no basis for a determination that, at the time the Constitution was adopted, contempt was generally regarded as not extending to cases of serious misconduct." 376 U.S. at 701. There is little doubt, therefore, that a defendant in a criminal contempt case in Florida has no constitutional right to a trial by jury.

Proponents for such trials seemingly must depend on authorization by the legislature or Supreme Court of Florida to attain their objective. By enacting section 38.22, Florida Statutes, which impliedly prohibits trial by jury the legislature exhibited a legislative intent to remain consistent with the common law rule. A possible alternative is for the Supreme Court of Florida to promulgate a rule providing for such trials and assume the position that under its constitutional right to govern practice and procedure in the courts of Florida such rule would supersede section 38.22, Florida Statutes. It is believed that the supreme court has such authority. Accordingly, alternate proposals are offered for the court's consideration; the first provides for a jury trial unless waived by the defendant and the alternate is consistent with present practice.

(5) **Disqualification of Judge.** Provision for the disqualification of the judge is made in federal rule 42(b). The proposal is patterned after this rule.

Favorable comments concerning disqualification of judges in appropriate cases may be found in opinions of the Supreme Court of Florida. See *Pennekamp v. State*, 156 Fla. 227, 22 So.2d 875 (1945), and concurring opinion in *State ex rel Huie v. Lewis*, supra.

(6) **Verdict; Judgment.** "Judgment" is deemed preferable to the term "order," since the proper procedure involves an adjudication of guilty. The use of "judgment" is consistent with present Florida practice. E.g., Dinnen v. State, 168 So.2d 703 (Fla. 2d DCA 1964); State ex rel. Byrd v. Anderson, 168 So.2d 554 (Fla. 1st DCA 1964).

The recital in the judgment of facts constituting the contempt serves to preserve for postconviction purposes a composite record of the offense by the person best qualified to make such recital: the judge. See *Ryals v. United States,* 69 F.2d 946 (5th Cir. 1934), in which such procedure is referred to as "good practice."

(7) **Sentence; Indirect Contempt.** The substance of this subdivision is found in present sections 921.05 (2), 921.07 and 921.13, Florida Statutes. While these sections are concerned with sentences in criminal cases, the First District Court of Appeal in 1964 held that unless a defendant convicted of criminal contempt is paid the same deference the defendant is not being accorded due process of law as provided in section 12 of the Declaration of Rights of the Florida Constitution and the Fourteenth Amendment of the Constitution of the United States. *Neering v. State*, 164 So.2d 29 (Fla. 1st DCA 1964).

Statement concerning the effect the adoption of this proposed rule will have on contempt statutes:

This rule is not concerned with the source of the power of courts to punish for contempt. It is concerned with desirable procedure to be employed in the implementation of such power. Consequently, its adoption will in no way affect the Florida statutes purporting to be legislative grants of authority to the courts to punish for contempt, viz., sections 38.22 (dealing with "all" courts), 932.03 (dealing with courts having original jurisdiction in criminal cases), and 39.13 (dealing with juvenile courts). This is true regardless of whether the source of power is considered to lie exclusively with the courts as an inherent power or is subject, at least in part, to legislative grant.

The adoption of the rule also will leave unaffected the numerous Florida statutes concerned with various situations considered by the legislature to be punishable as contempt (e.g., section 38.23, Florida Statutes), since these statutes deal with substantive rather than procedural law.

Section 38.22, Florida Statutes, as discussed in the preceding notes, is concerned with procedure in that it requires the court to hear and determine all questions of law or fact. Insofar, therefore, as criminal contempts are concerned the adoption of the alternate proposal providing for a jury trial will mean that the rule supersedes this aspect of the statute and the statute should be amended accordingly.

1972 Amendment. Same as prior rule.

XVII.   POSTCONVICTION RELIEF

RULE 3.850. MOTION TO VACATE, SET ASIDE, OR CORRECT SENTENCE

(a)   **Grounds for Motion.** The following grounds may be claims for relief from judgment or release from custody by a person who has been tried and found guilty or has entered a plea of guilty or nolo contendere before a court established by the laws of Florida:

(1)   The judgment was entered or sentence was imposed in violation of the Constitution or laws of the United States or the State of Florida.

(2)   The court did not have jurisdiction to enter the judgment.

(3)   The court did not have jurisdiction to impose the sentence.

(4)   The sentence exceeded the maximum authorized by law.

(5)   The plea was involuntary.

(6)   The judgment or sentence is otherwise subject to collateral attack.

(b)   **Time Limitations.** A motion to vacate a sentence that exceeds the limits provided by law may be filed at any time. No other motion shall be filed or considered pursuant to this rule if filed more than 2 years after the judgment and sentence become final unless it alleges that

(1)   the facts on which the claim is predicated were unknown to the movant or the movant's attorney and could not have been ascertained by the exercise of due diligence, and the claim is made within 2 years of the time the new facts were or could have been discovered with the exercise of due diligence, or

(2)   the fundamental constitutional right asserted was not established within the period provided for herein and has been held to apply retroactively, and the claim is made within 2 years of the date of the mandate of the decision announcing the retroactivity, or

(3)   the defendant retained counsel to timely file a 3.850 motion and counsel, through neglect, failed to file the motion. A claim based on this exception shall not be filed more than 2 years after the expiration of the time for filing a motion for postconviction relief.

(c)   **Contents of Motion.** The motion must be under oath stating that the defendant has read the motion or that it has been read to him or her, that the defendant understands its content, and that all of the facts stated therein are true and correct. The motion must also include an explanation of:

(1)   the judgment or sentence under attack and the court that rendered the same;

(2)   whether the judgment resulted from a plea or a trial;

          (3)   whether there was an appeal from the judgment or sentence and the disposition thereof;

          (4)   whether a previous postconviction motion has been filed, and if so, how many;

          (5)   if a previous motion or motions have been filed, the reason or reasons the claim or claims in the present motion were not raised in the former motion or motions;

          (6)   the nature of the relief sought; and

          (7)   a brief statement of the facts and other conditions relied on in support of the motion.

This rule does not authorize relief based on grounds that could have or should have been raised at trial and, if properly preserved, on direct appeal of the judgment and sentence. If the defendant is filing a newly discovered evidence claim based on recanted trial testimony or on a newly discovered witness, the defendant shall include an affidavit from that person as an attachment to his or her motion. For all other newly discovered evidence claims, the defendant shall attach an affidavit from any person whose testimony is necessary to factually support the defendant's claim for relief. If the affidavit is not attached to the motion, the defendant shall provide an explanation why the required affidavit could not be obtained.

      (d)   **Form of Motion.** Motions shall be typewritten or hand-written in legible printed lettering, in blue or black ink, double-spaced, with margins no less than 1 inch on white 8 1/2-by-11 inch paper. No motion, including any memorandum of law, shall exceed 50 pages without leave of the court upon a showing of good cause.

      (e)   **Amendments to Motion.** When the court has entered an order under subdivision (f)(2) or (f) (3), granting the defendant an opportunity to amend the motion, any amendment to the motion must be served within 60 days. A motion may otherwise be amended at any time prior to either the entry of an order disposing of the motion or the entry of an order pursuant to subdivision (f) (5) or directing that an answer to the motion be filed pursuant to (f)(6), whichever occurs first. Leave of court is required for the filing of an amendment after the entry of an order pursuant to subdivision (f) (5) or (f)(6). Notwithstanding the timeliness of an amendment, the court need not consider new factual assertions contained in an amendment unless the amendment is under oath. New claims for relief contained in an amendment need not be considered by the court unless the amendment is filed within the time frame specified in subdivision (b).

      (f)   **Procedure; Evidentiary Hearing; Disposition.** On filing of a motion under this rule, the clerk shall forward the motion and file to the court. Disposition of the motion shall be in accordance with the following procedures, which are intended to result in a single, final, appealable order that disposes of all claims raised in the motion.

          (1)   **Untimely and Insufficient Motions.** If the motion is insufficient on its face, and the time to file a motion under this rule has expired prior to the filing of the motion, the court shall enter a final appealable order summarily denying the motion with prejudice.

   (2) **Timely but Insufficient Motions.** If the motion is insufficient on its face, and the motion is timely filed under this rule, the court shall enter a nonfinal, nonappealable order allowing the defendant 60 days to amend the motion. If the amended motion is still insufficient or if the defendant fails to file an amended motion within the time allowed for such amendment, the court, in its discretion, may permit the defendant an additional opportunity to amend the motion or may enter a final, appealable order summarily denying the motion with prejudice.

   (3) **Timely Motions Containing Some Insufficient Claims.** If the motion sufficiently states one or more claims for relief and it also attempts but fails to state additional claims, and the motion is timely filed under this rule, the court shall enter a nonappealable order granting the defendant 60 days to amend the motion to sufficiently state additional claims for relief. Any claim for which the insufficiency has not been cured within the time allowed for such amendment shall be summarily denied in an order that is a nonfinal, nonappealable order, which may be reviewed when a final, appealable order is entered.

   (4) **Motions Partially Disposed of by the Court Record.** If the motion sufficiently states one or more claims for relief but the files and records in the case conclusively show that the defendant is not entitled to relief as to one or more claims, the claims that are conclusively refuted shall be summarily denied on the merits without a hearing. A copy of that portion of the files and records in the case that conclusively shows that the defendant is not entitled to relief as to one or more claims shall be attached to the order summarily denying these claims. The files and records in the case are the documents and exhibits previously filed in the case and those portions of the other proceedings in the case that can be transcribed. An order that does not resolve all the claims is a nonfinal, nonappealable order, which may be reviewed when a final, appealable order is entered.

   (5) **Motions Conclusively Resolved by the Court Record.** If the motion is legally sufficient but all grounds in the motion can be conclusively resolved either as a matter of law or by reliance upon the records in the case, the motion shall be denied without a hearing by the entry of a final order. If the denial is based on the records in the case, a copy of that portion of the files and records that conclusively shows that the defendant is entitled to no relief shall be attached to the final order.

   (6) **Motions Requiring a Response from the State Attorney.** Unless the motion, files, and records in the case conclusively show that the defendant is entitled to no relief, the court shall order the state attorney to file, within the time fixed by the court, an answer to the motion. The answer shall respond to the allegations contained in the defendant's sufficiently pleaded claims, describe any matters in avoidance of the sufficiently pleaded claims, state whether the defendant has used any other available state postconviction remedies including any other motion under this rule, and state whether the defendant has previously been afforded an evidentiary hearing.

   (7) **Appointment of Counsel.** The court may appoint counsel to represent the defendant under this rule. The factors to be considered by the court in making this determination include: the adversary nature of the proceeding, the complexity of the proceeding, the complexity of the claims presented, the defendant's apparent level of intelligence and education, the need for an evidentiary hearing, and the need for substantial legal research.

   (8) **Disposition by Evidentiary Hearing.**

(A)   If an evidentiary hearing is required, the court shall grant a prompt hearing and shall cause notice to be served on the state attorney and the defendant or defendant's counsel, and shall determine the issues, and make findings of fact and conclusions of law with respect thereto.

(B)   At an evidentiary hearing, the defendant shall have the burden of presenting evidence and the burden of proof in support of his or her motion, unless otherwise provided by law.

(C)   The order issued after the evidentiary hearing shall resolve all the claims raised in the motion and shall be considered the final order for purposes of appeal.

(g)   Defendant's Presence Not Required. The defendant's presence shall not be required at any hearing or conference held under this rule except at the evidentiary hearing on the merits of any claim.

(h)   Successive Motions.

(1)   A second or successive motion must be titled: "Second or Successive Motion for Postconviction Relief."

(2)   A second or successive motion is an extraordinary pleading. Accordingly, a court may dismiss a second or successive motion if the court finds that it fails to allege new or different grounds for relief and the prior determination was on the merits or, if new and different grounds are alleged, the judge finds that the failure of the defendant or the attorney to assert those grounds in a prior motion constituted an abuse of the procedure or there was no good cause for the failure of the defendant or defendant's counsel to have asserted those grounds in a prior motion. When a motion is dismissed under this subdivision, a copy of that portion of the files and records necessary to support the court's ruling shall accompany the order denying the motion.

(i)   Service on Parties. The clerk of the court shall promptly serve on the parties a copy of any order entered under this rule, noting thereon the date of service by an appropriate certificate of service.

(j)   Rehearing. Any party may file a motion for rehearing of any order addressing a motion under this rule within 15 days of the date of service of the order. A motion for rehearing is not required to preserve any issue for review in the appellate court. A timely filed motion for rehearing shall toll finality of any final order addressing a motion under this rule. A motion for rehearing must be based on a good faith belief that the court has overlooked a previously argued issue of fact or law or an argument based on a legal precedent or statute not available prior to the court's ruling. A response may be filed within 10 days of service of the motion. The trial court's order disposing of the motion for rehearing shall be filed within 15 days of the response but not later than 40 days from the date of the order of which rehearing is sought. If no order is filed within 40 days, the motion is deemed denied.

(k)   Appeals. An appeal may be taken to the appropriate appellate court only from the final order disposing of the motion. All final orders denying motions for postconviction relief shall include a statement that the defendant has the right to appeal within 30 days of the rendition of the order. All nonfinal, nonappelable orders entered pursuant to subdivision (f) should include a statement that the defendant has no right to appeal the order until entry of the final order.

      (l)   **Belated Appeals and Discretionary Review.** Pursuant to the procedures outlined in Florida Rule of Appellate Procedure 9.141, a defendant may seek a belated appeal or discretionary review.

      (m)   **Habeas Corpus.** An application for writ of habeas corpus on behalf of a prisoner who is authorized to apply for relief by motion pursuant to this rule shall not be entertained if it appears that the applicant has failed to apply for relief, by motion, to the court that sentenced the applicant or that the court has denied the applicant relief, unless it also appears that the remedy by motion is inadequate or ineffective to test the legality of the applicant's detention.

      (n)   **Certification of Defendant; Sanctions.** No motion may be filed pursuant to this rule unless it is filed in good faith and with a reasonable belief that it is timely, has potential merit, and does not duplicate previous motions that have been disposed of by the court.

      (1)   By signing a motion pursuant to this rule, the defendant certifies that: the defendant has read the motion or that it has been read to the defendant and that the defendant understands its content; the motion is filed in good faith and with a reasonable belief that it is timely filed, has potential merit, and does not duplicate previous motions that have been disposed of by the court; and, the facts contained in the motion are true and correct.

      (2)   The defendant shall either certify that the defendant can understand English or, if the defendant cannot understand English, that the defendant has had the motion translated completely into a language that the defendant understands. The motion shall contain the name and address of the person who translated the motion and that person shall certify that he or she provided an accurate and complete translation to the defendant. Failure to include this information and certification in a motion shall be grounds for the entry of an order dismissing the motion pursuant to subdivision (f)   (1), (f)(2), or (f)(3).

      (3)   Conduct prohibited under this rule includes, but is not limited to, the following: the filing of frivolous or malicious claims; the filing of any motion in bad faith or with reckless disregard for the truth; the filing of an application for habeas corpus subject to dismissal pursuant to subdivision (m); the willful violation of any provision of this rule; and the abuse of the legal process or procedures governed by this rule.

      The court, upon its own motion or on the motion of a party, may determine whether a motion has been filed in violation of this rule. The court shall issue an order setting forth the facts indicating that the defendant has or may have engaged in prohibited conduct. The order shall direct the defendant to show cause, within a reasonable time limit set by the court, why the court should not find that the defendant has engaged in prohibited conduct under this rule and impose an appropriate sanction. Following the issuance of the order to show cause and the filing of any response by the defendant, and after such further hearing as the court may deem appropriate, the court shall make a final determination of whether the defendant engaged in prohibited conduct under this subsection.

(4)   If the court finds by the greater weight of the evidence that the defendant has engaged in prohibited conduct under this rule, the court may impose one or more sanctions, including:

(A)   contempt as otherwise provided by law;

(B)   assessing the costs of the proceeding against the defendant;

(C)   dismissal with prejudice of the defendant's motion;

(D)   prohibiting the filing of further pro se motions under this rule and directing the clerk of court to summarily reject any further pro se motion under this rule;

(E)   requiring that any further motions under this rule be signed by a member in good standing of The Florida Bar, who shall certify that there is a good faith basis for each claim asserted in the motion; and/or

(F)   if the defendant is a prisoner, a certified copy of the order be forwarded to the appropriate institution or facility for consideration of disciplinary action against the defendant, including forfeiture of gain time pursuant to Chapter 944, Florida Statutes.

(5)   If the court determines there is probable cause to believe that a sworn motion contains a false statement of fact constituting perjury, the court may refer the matter to the state attorney.

Committee Notes

1972 Amendment. Same as prior rule. Former rule 3.860, previously deleted, now found in article 18, The Florida Bar Integration Rules.

1977 Amendment. Nothing has been taken from proposed rule 3.850. Additions have been made. The committee proceeded on the theory that generally the motions coming under the purview of the rule were filed by prisoners and will be considered ex parte.

The proposed amendment contemplates that in those cases where the trial court found the movant entitled to some relief, the state attorney would be noticed and given an opportunity to be heard. The rule further contemplates that if the appellate court reverses, it would do so with directions to conduct a hearing with notice to all parties.

(a), (b), (c), (d), (e)

The committee was of the opinion that the motion should contain the minimum prerequisites indicated in the lettered portions to permit the trial court to quickly ascertain whether or not the motion was entitled to consideration and, if not, provide for its return to the movant as unacceptable. This procedure is similar to federal rules dealing with postconviction motions.

The committee perceives that denial of a motion will either be based on the insufficiency of the motion itself or on the basis of the file or record which the trial court will have before it. The proposal provides for a simplified expeditious disposition of appeals in such cases. It is to be noted, however, that in those cases where the record is relied on as a basis for denial of the motion, it may in exceptional cases involve a substantial record, but the advantages of this procedure seem to justify coping with the unusual or exceptional case. It is the opinion of the committee that, in any order of denial based on the insufficiency of the motion or on the face of the record, trial courts will set forth specifically the basis of the court's ruling with sufficient specificity to delineate the issue for the benefit of appellate courts.

The committee thought that the provision permitting ex parte denial of a motion based on the face of the record was appropriate inasmuch as the movant was granted an opportunity for rehearing in which to point out any errors the court may have made, thus providing sufficient safeguards to ensure consideration of the prisoner's contentions.

The prisoner or movant's motion for rehearing will be a part of the record on appeal, thereby alerting the appellate court to the movant's dissatisfaction with the trial court's ruling.

1984 Amendment. The committee felt that provisions should be added to allow the court to consider why a subsequent motion was being filed and whether it was properly filed, similar to Federal Rule of Criminal Procedure 9(b) or 35.

The committee also felt that the court should have the authority to order the state to respond to a 3.850 motion by answer or other pleading as the court may direct.

The committee felt that even if a motion filed under rule 3.850 does not substantially comply with the requirements of the rule, the motion should still be filed and ruled on by the court. Hence the former provision authorizing the court to refuse to receive such a nonconforming motion has been removed and words allowing the presiding judge to summarily deny a noncomplying motion have been satisfied.

1992 Amendment. Pursuant to *State v. District Court of Appeal of Florida*, First District, 569 So.2d 439 (Fla. 1990), motions seeking a belated direct appeal based on the ineffective assistance of counsel should be filed in the trial court under rule 3.850. Also, see rule 3.111(e) regarding trial counsel's duties before
withdrawal after judgment and sentence.

1993 Amendment. This amendment is necessary to make this rule consistent with rule 3.851.

Court Commentary

1996 Court Commentary. Florida Rule of Judicial Administration 2.071(b) allows for telephonic and teleconferencing communication equipment to be utilized "for a motion hearing, a pretrial conference, or a status conference." Teleconferencing sites have been established by the Department of Management Services, Division of Communications at various metropolitan locations in the state. The "Shevin Study"[1] examined, at this Court's request, the issue of delays in capital postconviction relief proceedings and noted that travel problems of counsel cause part of those delays. The Court strongly encourages the use of the new telephonic and teleconferencing technology for postconviction relief proceedings that do not require evidentiary hearings.

[1] Letter from Robert L. Shevin "Re: Study of the Capital Collateral Representative" to Chief Justice Stephen H. Grimes (Feb. 26, 1996) (on file with the Supreme Court of Florida in No. 87,688).

2013 Amendment.

Rule 3.850 has been revised to address several issues identified by the Postconviction Rules Workgroup in 2006 and by the Criminal Court Steering Committee and the Subcommittee on Postconviction Relief in 2011.

Rule 3.850(d).   New subdivision (d) is derived from the final two sentences formerly contained in subdivision (c).

Rule 3.850(e).   Subdivision (e) was added to codify existing case law on amendments to postconviction motions and to comport with subdivision (f).

Rule 3.850(f).   Subdivision (f) attempts to set out each of the different options that a trial judge has when considering a motion under this rule. It reflects the timeframe requirement of subdivision (b) and codifies existing case law regarding timely but facially insufficient motions, partial orders of denial, and the appointment of counsel. *See*, e.g., *Spera v. State*, 971 So. 2d 754 (Fla. 2007).

Rule 3.850(g).   Subdivision (g) was previously contained in subdivision (e), but the language is largely derived from rule 3.851(c)(3).

Rule 3.850(h).   Subdivision (h), formerly rule 3.850(f), was substantially rewritten.

Rule 3.850(i).   Subdivision (i) is substantially the same as former subdivision (g).

Rule 3.850(j).   Subdivision (j) allows both the state and the defendant the right to rehearing and is intended to allow the court to correct an obvious error without the expense and delay of a state appeal. *See King v. State*, 870 So. 2d 69 (Fla. 2d DCA 2003). The statement regarding finality is consistent with Florida Rule of Appellate Procedure 9.020(h) and is intended to clarify the date of rendition of the final order disposing of any motion under this rule.

Rule 3.850(k).   Subdivision (k), formerly rule 3.850(i), was substantially rewritten to simplify the review process in both the trial and appellate courts and to provide for the efficient disposition of all claims in both courts. The requirement of a statement indicating whether the order is a nonfinal or final order subject to appeal is intended to ensure that all claims will be disposed of by the trial court and addressed in a single appeal.

Rule 3.850(*l*).   Subdivision (*l*), formerly rule 3.850(j), reflects the consolidation of the subdivision with former rule 3.850(k).

Rule 3.850(n).   Subdivision (n) is a substantial rewrite of former subdivision (m).

RULE 3.851. COLLATERAL RELIEF AFTER DEATH SENTENCE HAS BEEN IMPOSED AND AFFIRMED ON DIRECT APPEAL

(a)　**Scope.** This rule shall apply to all motions and petitions for any type of postconviction or collateral relief brought by a prisoner in state custody who has been sentenced to death and whose conviction and death sentence have been affirmed on direct appeal. It shall apply to all postconviction motions filed on or after October 1, 2001, by prisoners who are under sentence of death. Motions pending on that date are governed by the version of this rule in effect immediately prior to that date.

(b)　**Appointment of Postconviction Counsel.**

(1)　Upon the issuance of the mandate affirming a judgment and sentence of death on direct appeal, the Supreme Court of Florida shall at the same time issue an order appointing the appropriate office of the Capital Collateral Regional Counsel or directing the trial court to immediately appoint counsel from the Registry of Attorneys maintained by the Justice Administrative Commission. The name of Registry Counsel shall be filed with the Supreme Court of Florida.

(2)　Within 30 days of the issuance of the mandate, the Capital Collateral Regional Counsel or Registry Counsel shall file a notice of appearance in the trial court or a motion to withdraw based on a conflict of interest or some other legal ground. Motions to withdraw filed more than 30 days after the issuance of the mandate shall not be entertained unless based on a specific conflict of interest as set forth in section 27.703, Florida Statutes.

(3)　Within 15 days after Capital Collateral Regional Counsel or Registry Counsel files a motion to withdraw, the chief judge or assigned judge shall rule on the motion and appoint new postconviction counsel if necessary. The appointment of new collateral counsel shall be from the Registry of attorneys maintained by the Justice Administrative Commission unless the case is administratively transferred to another Capital Collateral Regional Counsel.

(c)　**Preliminary Procedures.**

(1)　**Judicial Assignment.** Within 30 days of the issuance of mandate affirming a judgment and sentence of death on direct appeal, the chief judge shall assign the case to a judge qualified under the Rules of Judicial Administration to conduct capital proceedings.

(2)　**Status Conferences.** The assigned judge shall conduct a status conference not later than 90 days after the judicial assignment, and shall hold status conferences at least every 90 days thereafter until the evidentiary hearing has been completed or the motion has been ruled on without a hearing. The attorneys, with leave of the trial court, may appear electronically at the status conferences. Requests to appear electronically shall be liberally granted. Pending motions, disputes involving public records, or any other matters ordered by the court shall be heard at the status conferences.

(3)　**Prisoner's Presence Not Required.** The prisoner's presence shall not be required at any hearing or conference held under this rule, except at the evidentiary hearing on the merits of any claim and at any hearing involving conflict with or removal of collateral counsel.

(4)   **Duties of Defense Counsel.** Within 45 days of appointment of postconviction counsel, the defendant's trial counsel shall provide to postconviction counsel all information pertaining to the defendant's capital case which was obtained during the representation of the defendant. Postconviction counsel shall maintain the confidentiality of all confidential information received.

(5)   **Record on Appeal.** The Clerk of the Supreme Court of Florida shall promptly deliver the record on appeal to the records repository after the appointment of postconviction counsel.

(d)   Time Limitation.

(1)   Any motion to vacate judgment of conviction and sentence of death shall be filed by the prisoner within 1 year after the judgment and sentence become final. For the purposes of this rule, a judgment is final:

(A)   on the expiration of the time permitted to file in the United States Supreme Court a petition for writ of certiorari seeking review of the Supreme Court of Florida decision affirming a judgment and sentence of death (90 days after the opinion becomes final); or

(B)   on the disposition of the petition for writ of certiorari by the United States Supreme Court, if filed.

(2)   No motion shall be filed or considered pursuant to this rule if filed beyond the time limitation provided in subdivision (d) (1) unless it alleges:

(A)   the facts on which the claim is predicated were unknown to the movant or the movant's attorney and could not have been ascertained by the exercise of due diligence, or

(B)   the fundamental constitutional right asserted was not established within the period provided for in subdivision (d) (1) and has been held to apply retroactively, or

(C)   postconviction counsel, through neglect, failed to file the motion.

(3)   All petitions for extraordinary relief in which the Supreme Court of Florida has original jurisdiction, including petitions for writs of habeas corpus, shall be filed simultaneously with the initial brief filed on behalf of the death sentenced prisoner in the appeal of the circuit court's order on the initial motion for postconviction relief filed under this rule.

(4)   The time limitation in subdivision (d) (1) is established with the understanding that each death-sentenced prisoner will have counsel assigned and available to begin addressing the prisoner's postconviction issues within the time specified in this rule. Should the governor sign a death warrant before the expiration of the time limitation in sub-division (d) (1), the Supreme Court of Florida, on a defendant's request, will grant a stay of execution to allow any postconviction relief motions to proceed in a timely and orderly manner. Furthermore, this time limitation shall not preclude the right to

amend or to supplement pending pleadings under these rules.

(5)   An extension of time may be granted by the Supreme Court of Florida for the filing of postconviction pleadings if the prisoner's counsel makes a showing of good cause for counsel's inability to file the postconviction pleadings within the 1 year period established by this rule.

(e)   **Contents of Motion.**

(1)   **Initial Motion.** A motion filed under this rule is an initial postconviction motion if no state court has previously ruled on a postconviction motion challenging the same judgment and sentence. An initial motion and memorandum of law filed under this rule shall not exceed 75 pages exclusive of the attachments. Attachments shall include, but are not limited to, the judgment and sentence. The memorandum of law shall set forth the applicable case law supporting the granting of relief as to each separately pled claim. This rule does not authorize relief based upon claims that could have or should have been raised at trial and, if properly preserved, on direct appeal of the judgment and sentence. If claims that were raised on appeal or should have been raised on appeal are contained in the motion, the memorandum of law shall contain a brief statement explaining why these claims are being raised on postconviction relief. The motion shall be under oath and shall include:

(A)   a description of the judgment and sentence under attack and the name of the court that rendered the same;

(B)   a statement of each issue raised on appeal and the disposition thereof;

(C)   the nature of the relief sought;

(D)   a detailed allegation of the factual basis for any claim for which an evidentiary hearing is sought; and

(E)   a detailed allegation as to the basis for any purely legal or constitutional claim for which an evidentiary hearing is not required and the reason that this claim could not have been or was not raised on direct appeal.

(2)   **Successive Motion.** A motion filed under this rule is successive if a state court has previously ruled on a postconviction motion challenging the same judgment and sentence. A successive motion shall not exceed 25 pages, exclusive of attachments, and shall include:

(A)   all of the pleading requirements of an initial motion under subdivision (e)(1);

(B)   the disposition of all previous claims raised in postconviction proceedings and the reason or reasons the claim or claims raised in the present motion were not raised in the former motion or motions;

(C)   if based upon newly discovered evidence, Brady v. Maryland, 373 U.S. 83 (1963), or Giglio v. United States, 405 U.S. 150 (1972), the following:

(i)   the names, addresses, and telephone numbers of all witnesses supporting the claim;

(ii)   a statement that the witness will be available, should an evidentiary hearing be scheduled, to testify under oath to the facts alleged in the motion or affidavit;

(iii)   if evidentiary support is in the form of documents, copies of all documents shall be attached, including any affidavits obtained; and

(iv)   as to any witness or document listed in the motion or attachment to the motion, a statement of the reason why the witness or document was not previously available.

(f)   Procedure; Evidentiary Hearing; Disposition.

Text of rule effective prior to amendment by Florida Supreme Court Opinion No. SC11-399. See also text of rule as amended by Florida Supreme Court Opinion SC11-399.

(1)   **Filing and Service.** All pleadings in the postconviction proceeding shall be filed with the clerk of the trial court and served on the assigned judge, opposing party, and the attorney general. Upon the filing of any original court paper in the post-conviction proceeding, the clerk of the trial court shall determine that the assigned judge has received a copy. All motions other than the postconviction motion itself shall be accompanied by a notice of hearing.

(f)   Procedure; Evidentiary Hearing; Disposition.

Text of rule as amended by Florida Supreme Court Opinion SC11-399. See also text of rule prior to amendment by Florida Supreme Court Opinion SC11-399.

(1)   **Filing and Service.** All pleadings in the postconviction proceeding shall be filed with the clerk of the trial court and served on the assigned judge, opposing party, and the attorney general. Upon the filing of any original court document in the postconviction proceeding, the clerk of the trial court shall determine that the assigned judge has received a copy. All motions other than the postconviction motion itself shall be accompanied by a notice of hearing.

(2)   **Duty of Clerk.** A motion filed under this rule shall be immediately delivered to the chief judge or the assigned judge along with the court file.

(3)   **Answer.**

(A)   **Answer to the Initial Motion.** Within 60 days of the filing of an initial motion, the state shall file its answer. The answer and accompanying memorandum of law shall not exceed 75 pages, exclusive of attachments and exhibits. The answer shall address the legal insufficiency of any claim in the motion, respond to the allegations of the motion, and address any procedural bars. As to any claims of legal insufficiency or procedural bar, the state shall include a short statement of any applicable case law.

(B)   Answer to a Successive Motion. Within 20 days of the filing of a successive motion, the state shall file its answer. The answer shall not exceed 25 pages, exclusive of attachments and exhibits. The answer shall specifically respond to each claim in the motion and state the reason(s) that an evidentiary hearing is or is not required.

(4)   Amendments. A motion filed under this rule may be amended up to 30 days prior to the evidentiary hearing upon motion and good cause shown. The trial court may in its discretion grant a motion to amend provided that the motion sets forth the reason the claim was not raised earlier and attaches a copy of the claim sought to be added. Granting a motion under this subdivision shall not be a basis for granting a continuance of the evidentiary hearing unless a manifest injustice would occur if a continuance was not granted. If amendment is allowed, the state shall file an amended answer within 20 days after the amended motion is filed.

(5)   Case Management Conference; Evidentiary Hearing.

(A)   Initial Postconviction Motion. No later than 90 days after the state files its answer to an initial motion, the trial court shall hold a case management conference. At the case management conference, the defendant shall disclose all documentary exhibits that he or she intends to offer at the evidentiary hearing and shall file and serve an exhibit list of all such exhibits and a witness list with the names and addresses of any potential witnesses. All expert witnesses shall be specifically designated on the witness list and copies of all expert reports shall be attached. Within 60 days after the case management conference, the state shall disclose all documentary exhibits that it intends to offer at the evidentiary hearing and shall file and serve an exhibit list of all such exhibits and a witness list with the names and addresses of any potential witnesses. All expert witnesses shall be specifically designated on the witness list, and copies of all expert reports shall be attached. At the case management conference, the trial court shall:

(i)   schedule an evidentiary hearing, to be held within 150 days, on claims listed by the defendant as requiring a factual determination;

(ii)   hear argument on any purely legal claims not based on disputed facts; and

(iii)   resolve disputes arising from the exchange of information under this subdivision.

(B)   Successive Postconviction Motion. Within 30 days after the state files its answer to a successive motion for postconviction relief, the trial court shall hold a case management conference. At the case management conference, the trial court also shall determine whether an evidentiary hearing should be held and hear argument on any purely legal claims not based on disputed facts. If the motion, files, and records in the case conclusively show that the movant is entitled to no relief, the motion may be denied without an evidentiary hearing. If the trial court determines that an evidentiary hearing should be held, the court shall schedule the hearing to be held within 60 days. If a death warrant has been signed, the trial court shall expedite these time periods in accordance with subdivision (h) of this rule.

(C)   Extension of Time to Hold Evidentiary Hearing. The trial court also may for good cause extend the time for holding an evidentiary hearing for up to 90 days.

(D)   Procedures   After   Evidentiary   Hearing.
Immediately following an evidentiary hearing, the trial court shall order a transcript of the hearing which shall be filed within 30 days. Within 30 days of receipt of the transcript, the court shall render its order, ruling on each claim considered at the evidentiary hearing and all other claims raised in the motion, making detailed findings of fact and conclusions of law with respect to each claim, and attaching or referencing such portions of the record as are necessary to allow for meaningful appellate review. The order issued after the evidentiary hearing shall resolve all the claims raised in the motion and shall be considered the final order for purposes of appeal. The clerk of the trial court shall promptly serve upon the parties and the attorney general a copy of the final order, with a certificate of service.

(6)   Mental Health Expert. If the defendant intends to offer expert testimony of his or her mental status, the state shall be entitled to have the defendant examined by its own mental health expert. If the defendant fails to cooperate with the state's expert, the trial court may, in its discretion, proceed as provided in rule 3.202(e). Reports provided to either party by an expert witness shall be disclosed to opposing counsel upon receipt.

(7)   Rehearing. Motions for rehearing shall be filed within 15 days of the rendition of the trial court's order and a response thereto filed within 10 days thereafter. The trial court's order disposing of the motion for rehearing shall be rendered not later than 15 days thereafter.

(8)   Appeals. Any party may appeal a final order entered on a defendant's motion for rule 3.851 relief by filing a notice of appeal with the clerk of the lower tribunal within 30 days of the rendition of the order to be reviewed. Pursuant to the procedures outlined in Florida Rule of Appellate Procedure 9.142, a prisoner under sentence of death may petition for a belated appeal.

(g)   Incompetence to Proceed in Capital Collateral Proceedings.

(1)   A death-sentenced prisoner pursuing collateral relief under this rule who is found by the court to be mentally incompetent shall not be proceeded against if there are factual matters at issue, the development or resolution of which require the prisoner's input. However, all collateral relief issues that involve only matters of record and claims that do not require the prisoner's input shall proceed in collateral proceedings notwithstanding the prisoner's incompetency.

(2)   Collateral counsel may file a motion for competency determination and an accompanying certificate of counsel that the motion is made in good faith and on reasonable grounds to believe that the death- sentenced prisoner is incompetent to proceed. The motion and certificate shall replace the signed oath by the prisoner that otherwise must accompany a motion filed under this rule.

(3)   If, at any stage of a postconviction proceeding, the court determines that there are reasonable grounds to believe that a death-sentenced prisoner is incompetent to proceed and that factual matters are at issue, the development or resolution of which require the prisoner's input, a judicial determination of incompetency is required.

(4)   The motion for competency examination shall be in writing and shall allege with specificity the factual matters at issue and the reason that competent consultation with the prisoner is necessary with respect to each factual matter specified. To the extent that it does not invade the lawyer-client privilege with collateral counsel, the motion shall contain a recital of the specific observations of, and conversations with, the death-sentenced prisoner that have formed the basis of the motion.

(5)   If the court finds that there are reasonable grounds to believe that a death-sentenced prisoner is incompetent to proceed in a postconviction proceeding in which factual matters are at issue, the development or resolution of which require the prisoner's input, the court shall order the prisoner examined by no more than 3, nor fewer than 2, experts before setting the matter for a hearing. The court may seek input from the death-sentenced prisoner's counsel and the state attorney before appointment of the experts.

(6)   The order appointing experts shall:

(A)   identify the purpose of the evaluation and specify the area of inquiry that should be addressed;

(B)   specify the legal criteria to be applied; and

(C)   specify the date by which the report shall be submitted and to whom it shall be submitted.

(7)   Counsel for both the death-sentenced prisoner and the state may be present at the examination, which shall be conducted at a date and time convenient for all parties and the Department of Corrections.

(8)   On appointment by the court, the experts shall examine the death-sentenced prisoner with respect to the issue of competence to proceed, as specified by the court in its order appointing the experts to evaluate the prisoner, and shall evaluate the prisoner as ordered.

(A)   The experts first shall consider factors related to the issue of whether the death-sentenced prisoner meets the criteria for competence to proceed, that is, whether the prisoner has sufficient present ability to consult with counsel with a reasonable degree of rational understanding and whether the prisoner has a rational as well as factual understanding of the pending collateral proceedings.

(B)   In considering the issue of competence to proceed, the experts shall consider and include in their report:

(i)   the prisoner's capacity to understand the adversary nature of the legal process and the collateral proceedings;

(ii)   the prisoner's ability to disclose to collateral counsel facts pertinent to the postconviction proceeding at issue; and

(iii)   any other factors considered relevant by the experts and the court as specified in the order appointing the experts.

(C)   Any written report submitted by an expert shall:

     (i) identify the specific matters referred for evaluation;

     (ii) describe the evaluative procedures, techniques, and tests used in the examination and the purpose or purposes for each;

     (iii) state the expert's clinical observations, findings, and opinions on each issue referred by the court for evaluation, and indicate specifically those issues, if any, on which the expert could not give an opinion; and

     (iv) identify the sources of information used by the expert and present the factual basis for the expert's clinical findings and opinions.

   (9) If the experts find that the death-sentenced prisoner is incompetent to proceed, the experts shall report on any recommended treatment for the prisoner to attain competence to proceed. In considering the issues relating to treatment, the experts shall report on:

     (A) the mental illness or intellectual disability causing the incompetence;

     (B) the treatment or treatments appropriate for the mental illness or intellectual disability of the prisoner and an explanation of each of the possible treatment alternatives in order of choices; and

     (C) the likelihood of the prisoner attaining competence under the treatment recommended, an assessment of the probable duration of the treatment required to restore competence, and the probability that the prisoner will attain competence to proceed in the foreseeable future.

   (10) Within 30 days after the experts have completed their examinations of the death-sentenced prisoner, the court shall schedule a hearing on the issue of the prisoner's competence to proceed.

   (11) If, after a hearing, the court finds the prisoner competent to proceed, or, after having found the prisoner incompetent, finds that competency has been restored, the court shall enter its order so finding and shall proceed with a postconviction motion. The prisoner shall have 60 days to amend his or her rule 3.851 motion only as to those issues that the court found required factual consultation with counsel.

   (12) If the court does not find the prisoner incompetent, the order shall contain:

     (A) findings of fact relating to the issues of competency;

     (B) copies of the reports of the examining experts; and

     (C) copies of any other psychiatric, psychological, or social work reports submitted to the court relative to the mental state of the death-sentenced prisoner.

(13) If the court finds the prisoner incompetent or finds the prisoner competent subject to the continuation of appropriate treatment, the court shall follow the procedures set forth in rule 3.212(c), except that, to the extent practicable, any treatment shall take place at a custodial facility under the direct supervision of the Department of Corrections.

(h) **After Death Warrant Signed.**

(1) **Judicial Assignment.** The chief judge of the circuit shall assign the case to a judge qualified under the Rules of Judicial Administration to conduct capital cases as soon as notification of the death warrant is received.

(2) **Calendar Advancement.** Proceedings after a death warrant has been issued shall take precedence over all other cases. The assigned judge shall make every effort to resolve scheduling conflicts with other cases including cancellation or rescheduling of hearings or trials and requesting senior judge assistance.

(3) **Schedule of Proceedings.** The time limitations in this rule shall not apply after a death warrant has been signed. All motions shall be heard expeditiously considering the time limitations set by the date of execution and the time required for appellate review.

(4) **Location of Hearings.** The location of hearings after a death warrant is signed shall be determined by the trial judge considering the availability of witnesses or evidence, the security problems involved in the case, and any other factor determined by the trial court.

(5) **Postconviction Motions.** All motions filed after a death warrant is issued shall be considered successive motions and subject to the content requirement of subdivision (e)(2) of this rule.

(6) **Case Management Conference.** The assigned judge shall schedule a case management conference as soon as reasonably possible after receiving notification that a death warrant has been signed. During the case management conference the court shall set a time for filing a postconviction motion and shall schedule a hearing to determine whether an evidentiary hearing should be held and hear argument on any purely legal claims not based on disputed facts. If the motion, files, and records in the case conclusively show that the movant is entitled to no relief, the motion may be denied without an evidentiary hearing. If the trial court determines that an evidentiary hearing should be held, the court shall schedule the hearing to be held as soon as reasonably possible considering the time limitations set by the date of execution and the time required for appellate review.

(7) **Reporting.** The assigned judge shall require the proceedings conducted under death warrant to be reported using the most advanced and accurate technology available in general use at the location of the hearing. The proceedings shall be transcribed expeditiously considering the time limitations set by the execution date.

(8) **Procedures After Hearing.** The court shall obtain a transcript of all proceedings and shall render its order in accordance with subdivision (f)(5)(D) of this rule as soon as possible after the hearing is concluded. A copy of the final order shall be electronically transmitted to the Supreme Court of Florida and to the attorneys of record.

(9) **Transmittal of Record.** The record shall be immediately delivered to the clerk of the Supreme Court of Florida by the clerk of the trial court or as ordered by the assigned judge. The record shall also be electronically transmitted if the technology is available. A notice of appeal shall not be required to transmit the record.

(i) **Dismissal of Postconviction Proceedings.**

(1) This subdivision applies only when a prisoner seeks both to dismiss pending postconviction proceedings and to discharge collateral counsel.

(2) If the prisoner files the motion pro se, the Clerk of the Court shall serve copies of the motion on counsel of record for both the prisoner and the state. Counsel of record may file responses within 10 days.

(3) The trial judge shall review the motion and the responses and schedule a hearing. The prisoner, collateral counsel, and the state shall be present at the hearing.

(4) The judge shall examine the prisoner at the hearing and shall hear argument of the prisoner, collateral counsel, and the state. No fewer than 2 or more than 3 qualified experts shall be appointed to examine the prisoner if the judge concludes that there are reasonable grounds to believe the prisoner is not mentally competent for purposes of this rule. The experts shall file reports with the court setting forth their findings. Thereafter, the court shall conduct an evidentiary hearing and enter an order setting forth findings of competency or incompetency.

(5) If the prisoner is found to be incompetent for purposes of this rule, the court shall deny the motion without prejudice.

(6) If the prisoner is found to be competent for purposes of this rule, the court shall conduct a complete (Durocher/Faretta) inquiry to determine whether the prisoner knowingly, freely and voluntarily wants to dismiss pending postconviction proceedings and discharge collateral counsel.

(7) If the court determines that the prisoner has made the decision to dismiss pending postconviction proceedings and discharge collateral counsel knowingly, freely, and voluntarily, the court shall enter an order dismissing all pending postconviction proceedings and discharging collateral counsel. But if the court determines that the prisoner has not made the decision to dismiss pending postconviction proceedings and discharge collateral counsel knowingly, freely, and voluntarily, the court shall enter an order denying the motion without prejudice.

(8) If the court grants the motion:

(A) a copy of the motion, the order, and the transcript of the hearing or hearings conducted on the motion shall be forwarded to the Clerk of the Supreme Court of Florida within 30 days; and

(B) discharged counsel shall, within 10 days after issuance of the order, file with the clerk of the circuit court 2 copies of a notice seeking review in the Supreme Court of Florida, and shall, within 20 days after the filing of the transcript, serve an initial brief. Both the prisoner and the state may serve responsive briefs. Briefs shall be served as prescribed by rule 9.210.

(9)   If the court denies the motion, the prisoner may seek review as prescribed by Florida Rule of Appellate Procedure 9.142(b).

Court Commentary

1993 Adoption. This rule is consistent with the recommendation of the Supreme Court Committee on Postconviction Relief in Capital Cases, which was created because of the substantial delays in the death penalty postconviction relief process. The committee was created because of the inability of the capital collateral representative to properly represent all death penalty inmates in postconviction relief cases and because of the resulting substantial delays in those cases. That committee recognized that, to make the process work properly, each death row prisoner should have counsel available to represent him or her in postconviction relief proceedings. The committee found that one of the major problems with the process was that the triggering mechanism to start or assure movement of the postconviction relief proceedings was the signing of a death warrant. In a number of instances, the courts were not aware of the problems concerning representation of a defendant until a death warrant was signed. In other instances, the committee found that, when postconviction relief motions had been filed, they clearly had not moved at an orderly pace and the signing of a death warrant was being used as a means to expedite the process. The committee recommended that specific named counsel should be designated to represent each prisoner not later than 30 days after the defendant's judgment and sentence of death becomes final. To assure that representation, the committee's report noted that it was essential that there be adequate funding of the capital collateral representative and sought temporary assistance from The Florida Bar in providing pro bono representation for some inmates.

There is a justification for the reduction of the time period for a capital prisoner as distinguished from a noncapital prisoner, who has two years to file a postconviction relief proceeding. A capital prisoner will have counsel immediately available to represent him or her in a postconviction relief proceeding, while counsel is not provided or constitutionally required for noncapital defendants to whom the two-year period applies.

In the event the capital collateral representative is not fully funded and available to provide proper representation for all death penalty defendants, the reduction in the time period would not be justified and would necessarily have to be repealed, and this Court will forthwith entertain a petition for the repeal of the rule. In this context, it is important to emphasize that the governor agrees that absent the circumstance where a competent death sentenced individual voluntarily requests that a death warrant be signed, no death warrants will be issued during the initial round of federal and state review, provided that counsel for death penalty defendants is proceeding in a timely and diligent manner. This Court agrees that the initial round of postconviction proceedings should proceed in a deliberate but timely manner without the pressure of a pending death warrant. Subdivision 3.851(b)(4) above addresses concerns of The Florida Bar and The Florida Bar Foundation.

The provisions of the present rule 3.851 providing for time periods where a 60 day warrant is signed by the governor are abolished because they are unnecessary if the guidelines are followed. The proceedings and grounds for postconviction relief remain as provided under Florida Rule of Criminal Procedure 3.850, which include, as one of the grounds, the opportunity for a defendant to present newly discovered evidence in accordance with *Scott v. Dugger*, 604 So.2d 465 (Fla. 1992), *Jones v. State*, 591 So.2d 911 (Fla. 1991), and *Richardson v. State*, 546 So.2d 1037 (Fla. 1989).

1996 Amendment. Subdivision (c) is added to make the Court's decision in *Huff v. State*, 622 So.2d 982 (Fla. 1993), applicable to all rule 3.850 motions filed by a prisoner who has been sentenced to death. Florida Rule of Judicial Administration 2.071(b) allows for telephonic and teleconferencing communication equipment to be utilized "for a motion hearing, pretrial conference, or a status conference." Teleconferencing sites have been established by the Department of Management Services, Division of Communications at various metropolitan locations in the state. The "Shevin Study" examined, at this Court's request, the issue of delays in capital postconviction relief proceedings and noted that travel problems of counsel cause part of those delays. The Court strongly encourages the use of the new telephonic and teleconferencing technology for postconviction relief proceedings that do not require evidentiary hearings, such as the hearing required under subdivision (c) of this rule. Only the attorneys need be involved in a hearing held under subdivision (c) of this rule; attendance of the postconviction defendant is not required.

2001 Amendment. Several new procedures are added to rule 3.851. New subdivision (b), Appointment of Postconviction Counsel, is added to ensure appointment of postconviction counsel upon the Supreme Court of Florida's issuance of mandate on direct appeal. New subdivision (c), Preliminary Procedures, provides for, among other things, the assignment of a qualified judge within 30 days after mandate issues on direct appeal and status conferences every 90 days after the assignment until the evidentiary hearing has been completed or the motion has been ruled on without a hearing. These status conferences are intended to provide a forum for the timely resolution of public records issues and other preliminary matters. New subdivision (f), Procedure; Evidentiary Hearing; Disposition, sets forth general procedures. Most significantly, that subdivision requires an evidentiary hearing on claims listed in an initial motion as requiring a factual determination. The Court has identified the failure to hold evidentiary hearings on initial motions as a major cause of delay in the capital postconviction process and has determined that, in most cases, requiring an evidentiary hearing on initial motions presenting factually based claims will avoid this cause of delay. See *Amendments to Florida Rules of Criminal Procedure 3.851, 3.852 and 3.993*, 772 So.2d 488, 491 (Fla. 2000).

2006 Amendment. The amendments provide for the appointment of Registry Counsel in areas of the state that are not served by a Capital Collateral Regional Counsel. Counsel are allowed to appear at status conferences electronically to authorize both telephonic and video appearances.

2013 Amendment. Only minor amendments are made to rule 3.851.

Editor's Note

On October 18, 2012, the Supreme Court of Florida issued a revised opinion in case number SC11- 399, which was originally issued on June 21, 2012. See *In re Amendments to the Florida Rules of Judicial Administration*, 102 So. 3d 451(Fla. 2012). The opinion provides in relevant part:

"First, the new electronic filing requirements the Courts adopts will become effective in the civil, probate, small claims, and family law divisions of the trial courts, as well as for appeals to the circuit courts in these categories of cases, on April 1, 2013, at

12:01 a.m., except as may be otherwise provided by administrative order. Electronic filing will be mandatory in these divisions pursuant to rule 2.525 on that date. However, until the new rules take effect in these divisions, any clerk who is already accepting documents filed by electronic transmission under the current rules should continue to do so; attorneys in these counties are encouraged to file documents electronically under the current rules.

"Next, the new electronic filing requirements the Court adopts will become effective in the criminal, traffic, and juvenile divisions of the trial courts, as well as for appeals to the circuit court in these categories of cases, on October 1, 2013, at 12:01 a.m., except as may be otherwise provided by administrative order. Electronic filing will be mandatory in these divisions under rule 2.525 on that date. The new e-filing requirements, as they apply in proceedings brought pursuant to the Florida Mental Health Act (Baker Act), Chapter 394, Part I, Florida Statutes, and the Involuntary Commitment of Sexually Violent Predators Act (Jimmy Ryce), Chapter 394, Part V, Florida Statutes, will also not be mandatory in these cases until October 1, 2013. As stated above, until the new rules take effect in these divisions and proceedings, any clerk who is already accepting electronically filed documents under the current rules should continue to do so; attorneys are again encouraged to utilize existing electronic filing procedures under the current rules.

"However, until the new rules and procedures take effect in the district courts, any clerk who is already accepting documents filed by electronic transmission may continue to do so; attorneys in these districts are encouraged to file documents electronically. Clerks will not be required to electronically transmit the record on appeal until July 1, 2013, at 12:01 a.m. Until July 1, we encourage clerks, whenever possible, to electronically transmit the record under the new rules and requirements.

"(W)e note that, in all types of cases, pursuant to amended rule 2.525(d) self-represented parties and self-represented nonparties, including nonparty governmental or public agencies, and attorneys excused from e-mail service under Florida Rule of Judicial Administration 2.516 will be permitted, but nor required, to file documents electronically.

By order of November 28, 2012, in case number SC11-399, the Court released a revised implementation schedule, which provides, in pertinent part: "The e-filing rules adopted in the October 2012 opinion will be mandatory in this (Supreme) Court on February 27, 2013, at 12:01 a.m.; and effective earlier on a voluntary basis as will be indicated by further administrative order of the chief justice.

"Thereafter, the e-filing rules will be mandatory in the Second District Court of Appeal on July 22, 2013, at 12:01 a.m.; in the Third District Court of Appeal on September 27, 2013, at 12:01 a.m.; in the Fourth District Court of Appeal on October 31, 2013, at 12:01 a.m.; in the Fifth District Court of Appeal on November 27, 2013 at 12:01 a.m.; and in the First District Court of Appeal on December 27, 2013, at 12:01 a.m., unless made mandatory earlier by the chief judge of the applicable district court of appeal. The e-filing rules will be effective earlier on a voluntary trial basis in the district courts of appeal as will be indicated by further administrative order by the chief judge of the applicable district court."

[Editor's Note: Email service, which becomes mandatory for criminal cases on October 1, 2013, is governed by this rule.]

RULE 3.852. CAPITAL POSTCONVICTION PUBLIC RECORDS PRODUCTION

Florida Rules of Criminal Procedure 2014

(a) **Applicability and Scope.**

(1) This rule is applicable only to the production of public records for capital postconviction defendants and does not change or alter the time periods specified in Florida Rule of Criminal Procedure 3.851. Furthermore, this rule does not affect, expand, or limit the production of public records for any purposes other than use in a proceeding held pursuant to rule 3.850 or rule 3.851.

(2) This rule shall not be a basis for renewing requests that have been initiated previously or for relitigating issues pertaining to production of public records upon which a court has ruled prior to October 1, 1998.

(3) This rule is to be used in conjunction with the forms found at Florida Rule of Criminal Procedure 3.993.

(b) **Definitions.**

(1) "Public records" has the meaning set forth in section 119.011, Florida Statutes.

(2) "Trial court" means:

(A) the judge who entered the judgment and imposed the sentence of death; or

(B) the judge assigned by the chief judge.

(3) "Records repository" means the location designated by the secretary of state pursuant to section 27.7081, Florida Statutes, for archiving capital postconviction public records.

(4) "Collateral counsel" means a capital collateral regional counsel from one of the three regions in Florida; a private attorney who has been appointed to represent a capital defendant for postconviction litigation; or a private attorney who has been hired by the capital defendant or who has agreed to work pro bono for a capital defendant for postconviction litigation.

(5) "Agency" means an entity or individual as defined in section 119.011, Florida Statutes, that is subject to the requirements of producing public records for inspection under section 119.07, Florida Statutes.

(6) "Index" means a list of the public records included in each container of public records sent to the records repository.

(c) **Filing and Service.**

(1) The original of all notices, requests, or objections filed under this rule must be filed with the clerk of the trial court. Copies must be served on the trial court, the attorney general, the state attorney, collateral counsel, and any affected person or agency, unless otherwise required by this rule.

(2) Service shall be made pursuant to Florida Rule of Criminal

Procedure 3.030.

(3)   In all instances requiring written notification or request, the party who has the obligation of providing a notification or request shall provide proof of receipt.

(4)   Persons and agencies receiving postconviction public records notifications or requests pursuant to this rule are not required to furnish records filed in a trial court prior to the receipt of the notice.

(d)   Action Upon Issuance of Mandate.

(1)   Within 15 days after receiving written notification of the Supreme Court of Florida's mandate affirming the sentence of death, the attorney general shall file with the trial court a written notice of the mandate and serve a copy of it upon the state attorney who prosecuted the case, the Department of Corrections, and the defendant's trial counsel. The notice to the state attorney shall direct the state attorney to submit public records to the records repository within 90 days after receipt of written notification and to notify each law enforcement agency involved in the investigation of the capital offense to submit public records to the records repository within 90 days after receipt of written notification. The notice to the Department of Corrections shall direct the department to submit public records to the records repository within 90 days after receipt of written notification.

(2)   Within 90 days after receiving written notification of issuance of the Supreme Court of Florida's mandate affirming a death sentence, the state attorney shall provide written notification to the attorney general of the name and address of any additional person or agency that has public records pertinent to the case.

(3)   Within 90 days after receiving written notification of issuance of the Supreme Court of Florida's mandate affirming a death sentence, the defendant's trial counsel shall provide written notification to the attorney general of the name and address of any person or agency with information pertinent to the case which has not previously been provided to collateral counsel.

(4)   Within 15 days after receiving written notification of any additional person or agency pursuant to subdivision (d)   (2) or (d) (3) of this rule, the attorney general shall notify all persons or agencies identified pursuant to subdivisions (d)(2) or (d)(3) that these persons or agencies are required by law to copy, index, and deliver to the records repository all public records pertaining to the case that are in their possession. The person or agency shall bear the costs related to copying, indexing, and delivering the records.

(e)   Action Upon Receipt of Notice of Mandate.

(1)   Within 15 days after receipt of a written notice of the mandate from the attorney general, the state attorney shall provide written notification to each law enforcement agency involved in the specific case to submit public records to the records repository within 90 days after receipt of written notification. A copy of the notice shall be served upon the defendant's trial counsel.

(2)   Within 90 days after receipt of a written notice of the

mandate from the attorney general, the state attorney shall copy, index, and deliver to the records repository all public records that were produced in the state attorney's investigation or prosecution of the case. The state attorney shall bear the costs. The state attorney shall also provide written notification to the attorney general of compliance with this section, including certifying that, to the best of the state attorney's knowledge or belief, all public records in the state attorney's possession have been copied, indexed, and delivered to the records repository as required by this rule.

(3) Within 90 days after receipt of written notification of the mandate from the attorney general, the Department of Corrections shall copy, index, and deliver to the records repository all public records determined by the department to be relevant to the subject matter of a proceeding under rule 3.851, unless such copying, indexing, and delivering would be unduly burdensome. The department shall bear the costs. The secretary of the department shall provide written notification to the attorney general of compliance with this section certifying that, to the best of the secretary of the department's knowledge or belief, all such public records in the possession of the secretary of the department have been copied, indexed, and delivered to the records repository.

(4) Within 90 days after receipt of written notification of the mandate from the state attorney, a law enforcement agency shall copy, index, and deliver to the records repository all public records which were produced in the investigation or prosecution of the case. Each agency shall bear the costs. The chief law enforcement officer of each law enforcement agency shall provide written notification to the attorney general of compliance with this section including certifying that, to the best of the chief law enforcement officer's knowledge or belief, all such public records in possession of the agency or in possession of any employee of the agency, have been copied, indexed, and delivered to the records repository.

(5) Within 90 days after receipt of written notification of the mandate from the attorney general, each additional person or agency identified pursuant to subdivision (d) (2) or (d) (3) of this rule shall copy, index, and deliver to the records repository all public records which were produced during the prosecution of the case. The person or agency shall bear the costs. The person or agency shall provide written notification to the attorney general of compliance with this subdivision and shall certify, to the best of the person or agency's knowledge and belief, all such public records in the possession of the person or agency have been copied, indexed, and delivered to the records repository.

(f) **Exempt or Confidential Public Records.**

(1) Any public records delivered to the records repository pursuant to these rules that are confidential or exempt from the requirements of section 119.07, Florida Statutes, or article I, section 24(a), Florida Constitution, must be separately contained, without being redacted, and sealed. The outside of the container must clearly identify that the public record is confidential or exempt and that the seal may not be broken without an order of the trial court. The outside of the container must identify the nature of the public records and the legal basis for the exemption.

(2) Upon the entry of an appropriate court order, sealed containers subject to an inspection by the trial court shall be shipped to the clerk of court. The containers may be opened only for inspection by the trial court in camera. The moving party shall bear all costs associated with the transportation and inspection of such records by

the trial court. The trial court shall perform the unsealing and inspection without ex parte communications and in accord with procedures for reviewing sealed documents.

(g) Demand for Additional Public Records.

(1) Within 240 days after collateral counsel is appointed, retained, or appears pro bono, such counsel shall send a written demand for additional public records to each person or agency submitting public records or identified as having information pertinent to the case under subdivision (d) of this rule. However, if collateral counsel was appointed prior to October 1, 2001, then within 90 days after collateral counsel is appointed, retained, or appears pro bono, such counsel shall send a written demand for additional public records to each person or agency submitting public records or identified as having information pertinent to the case under subdivision (d) of this rule.

(2) Within 90 days of receipt of the written demand, each person or agency notified under this subdivision shall deliver to the records repository any additional public records in the possession of the person or agency that pertain to the case and shall certify to the best of the person or agency's knowledge and belief that all additional public records have been delivered to the records repository or, if no additional public records are found, shall recertify that the public records previously delivered are complete.

(3) Within 60 days of receipt of the written demand, any person or agency may file with the trial court an objection to the written demand described in subdivision (g) (1). The trial court shall hold a hearing and issue a ruling within 30 days after the filing of any objection, ordering a person or agency to produce additional public records if the court determines each of the following exists:

(A) Collateral counsel has made a timely and diligent search as provided in this rule.

(B) Collateral counsel's written demand identifies, with specificity, those additional public records that are not at the records repository.

(C) The additional public records sought are relevant to the subject matter of a proceeding under rule 3.851, or appear reasonably calculated to lead to the discovery of admissible evidence.

(D) The additional public records request is not overly broad or unduly burdensome.

(h) Cases in Which Mandate was Issued Prior to Effective Date of Rule.

(1) If the mandate affirming a defendant's conviction and sentence of death was issued prior to October 1, 1998, and no initial public records requests have been made by collateral counsel by that date, the attorney general and the state attorney shall file notifications with the trial court as required by subdivisions (d) and (e) of this rule.

(2) If on October 1, 1998, a defendant is represented by collateral counsel and has initiated the public records process, collateral counsel shall, within 90 days after October 1, 1998, or within 90 days after the production of records which were

225

requested prior to October 1, 1998, whichever is later, file with the trial court and serve a written demand for any additional public records that have not previously been the subject of a request for public records. The request for these records shall be treated the same as a request pursuant to subdivisions (d)   (3) and (d)(4) of this rule, and the records shall be copied, indexed, and delivered to the repository as required in subdivision (e) (5) of this rule.

(3)   Within 10 days of the signing of a defendant's death warrant, collateral counsel may request in writing the production of public records from a person or agency from which collateral counsel has previously requested public records. A person or agency shall copy, index, and deliver to the repository any public record:

(A)   that was not previously the subject of an objection;

(B)   that was received or produced since the previous request; or

(C)   that was, for any reason, not produced previously.

The person or agency providing the records shall bear the costs of copying, indexing, and delivering such records. If none of these circumstances exist, the person or agency shall file with the trial court and the parties an affidavit stating that no other records exist and that all public records have been produced previously. A person or agency shall comply with this subdivision within 10 days from the date of the written request or such shorter time period as is ordered by the court.

(4)   In all instances in subdivision (h) which require written notification the receiving party shall provide proof of receipt by return mail or other carrier.

(i)   Limitation on Postproduction Request for Additional Records.

(1)   In order to obtain public records in addition to those provided under subdivisions (e), (f), (g), and (h) of this rule, collateral counsel shall file an affidavit in the trial court which:

(A) attests that collateral counsel has made a timely and diligent search of the records repository; and

(B)   identifies with specificity those public records not at the records repository; and

(C)   establishes that the additional public records are either relevant to the subject matter of the postconviction proceeding or are reasonably calculated to lead to the discovery of admissible evidence; and

(D)   shall be served in accord with subdivision (c)(1) of this rule.

(2)   Within 30 days after the affidavit of collateral counsel is filed, the trial court may order a person or agency to produce additional public records only upon finding each of the following:

226

           (A)   collateral counsel has made a timely and diligent search of the records repository;

           (B)   collateral counsel's affidavit identifies with specificity those additional public records that are not at the records repository;

           (C)   the additional public records sought are either relevant to the subject matter of a proceeding under rule 3.851 or appear reasonably calculated to lead to the discovery of admissible evidence; and

           (D)   the additional records request is not overly broad or unduly burdensome.

        (j)   **Copying of Public Records.** Collateral counsel shall provide the personnel, supplies, and any necessary equipment to copy records held at the records repository.

        (k)   **Authority of the Court.** In proceedings under this rule the trial court may:

           (1)   compel or deny disclosure of records;

           (2)   conduct an in-camera inspection;

           (3)   extend the times in this rule upon a showing of good cause;

           (4)   impose sanctions upon any party, person, or agency affected by this rule including initiating contempt proceedings, taxing expenses, extending time, ordering facts to be established, and granting other relief; and

           (5)   resolve any dispute arising under this rule unless jurisdiction is in an appellate court.

        (l)   **Scope of Production and Resolution of Production Issues.**

           (1)   Unless otherwise limited, the scope of production under any part of this rule shall be that the public records sought are not privileged or immune from production and are either relevant to the subject matter of the proceeding under rule 3.851 or are reasonably calculated to lead to the discovery of admissible evidence.

           (2)   Any objections or motions to compel production of public records pursuant to this rule shall be filed within 30 days after the end of the production time period provided by this rule. Counsel for the party objecting or moving to compel shall file a copy of the objection or motion directly with the trial court. The trial court shall hold a hearing on the objection or motion on an expedited basis.

           (3)   The trial court may order mediation for any controversy as to public records production pursuant to this rule in accord with Florida Rules of Civil Procedure 1.700, 1.710, 1.720, 1.730, or the trial court may refer any such controversy to a magistrate in accord with Florida Rule of Civil Procedure 1.490.

        (m)   **Destruction of Records Repository Records.** Sixty days after a capital sentence is carried out, after a defendant is released from incarceration following the granting of a pardon or reversal of the sentence, or after a defendant has been resentenced to a term of years, the attorney general shall provide written notification of this occurrence to the secretary of state with service in accord with subdivision (c)(1). After the expiration of the 60 days, the secretary of state may then destroy the copies of the records held by the records repository that pertain to that case, unless an objection to the destruction is filed in the trial court and served upon the secretary of state and in accord with subdivision (c)(1). If no objection has been served within the 60-day period, the records may then be destroyed. If an objection is served, the records shall not be destroyed until a final disposition of the objection.

RULE 3.853. MOTION FOR POSTCONVICTION DNA TESTING

(a) **Purpose.** This rule provides procedures for obtaining DNA (deoxyribonucleic acid) testing under sections 925.11 and 925.12, Florida Statutes.

(b) **Contents of Motion.** The motion for postconviction DNA testing must be under oath and must include the following:

(1) a statement of the facts relied upon in support of the motion, including a description of the physical evidence containing DNA to be tested and, if known, the present location or last known location of the evidence and how it originally was obtained;

(2) a statement that the evidence was not previously tested for DNA, or a statement that the results of previous DNA testing were inconclusive and that subsequent scientific developments in DNA testing techniques likely would produce a definitive result establishing that the movant is not the person who committed the crime;

(3) a statement that the movant is innocent and how the DNA testing requested by the motion will exonerate the movant of the crime for which the movant was sentenced, or a statement how the DNA testing will mitigate the sentence received by the movant for that crime;

(4) a statement that identification of the movant is a genuinely disputed issue in the case and why it is an issue or an explanation of how the DNA evidence would either exonerate the defendant or mitigate the sentence that the movant received;

(5) a statement of any other facts relevant to the motion; and

(6) a certificate that a copy of the motion has been served on the prosecuting authority.

(c) **Procedure.**

(1) Upon receipt of the motion, the clerk of the court shall file it and deliver the court file to the assigned judge.

(2) The court shall review the motion and deny it if it is facially insufficient. If the motion is facially sufficient, the prosecuting authority shall be ordered to respond to the motion within 30 days or such other time as may be ordered by the court.

(3)   Upon receipt of the response of the prosecuting authority, the court shall review the response and enter an order on the merits of the motion or set the motion for hearing.

(4)   In the event that the motion shall proceed to a hearing, the court may appoint counsel to assist the movant if the court determines that assistance of counsel is necessary and upon a determination of indigency pursuant to section 27.52, Florida Statutes.

(5)   The court shall make the following findings when ruling on the motion:

(A)   Whether it has been shown that physical evidence that may contain DNA still exists.

(B)   Whether the results of DNA testing of that physical evidence likely would be admissible at trial and whether there exists reliable proof to establish that the evidence containing the tested DNA is authentic and would be admissible at a future hearing.

(C)   Whether there is a reasonable probability that the movant would have been acquitted or would have received a lesser sentence if the DNA evidence had been admitted at trial.

(6)   If the court orders DNA testing of the physical evidence, the cost of the testing may be assessed against the movant, unless the movant is indigent. If the movant is indigent, the state shall bear the cost of the DNA testing ordered by the court.

(7)   The court-ordered DNA testing shall be ordered to be conducted by the Department of Law Enforcement or its designee, as provided by statute. However, the court, upon a showing of good cause, may order testing by another laboratory or agency certified by the American Society of Crime Laboratory Directors/Laboratory Accreditation Board (ASCLD/LAB) or Forensic Quality Services, Inc. (FQS) if requested by a movant who can bear the cost of such testing.

(8)   The results of the DNA testing ordered by the court shall be provided in writing to the court, the movant, and the prosecuting authority.

(d)   Time Limitations. The motion for postconviction DNA testing may be filed or considered at any time following the date that the judgment and sentence in the case becomes final.

(e)   Rehearing. The movant may file a motion for rehearing of any order denying relief within 15 days after service of the order denying relief. The time for filing an appeal shall be tolled until an order on the motion for rehearing has been entered.

(f)   Appeal. An appeal may be taken by any adversely affected party within 30 days from the date the order on the motion is rendered. All orders denying relief must include a statement that the movant has the right to appeal within 30 days after the order denying relief is rendered.

XVIII. FORMS

RULE 3.992. **CRIMINAL PUNISHMENT CODE SCORESHEET**

(a) Criminal Punishment Code Scoresheet

The Criminal Punishment Code Scoresheet Preparation Manual is available at:
http://www.dc.state.fl.us/pub/sen_cpcm/index.html

1. DATE OF SENTENCE	2. PREPARER'S NAME	3. COUNTY	4. SENTENCING JUDGE	
5. Name (last, First, M.I.)	6. DOB	8. RACE ☐B ☐W ☐OTHER	10. PRIMARY OFF. DATE	12. PLEA ☐
	7. DC #	9. GENDER ☐ M ☐ F	11. PRIMARY DOCKET #	TRIAL ☐

I. PRIMARY OFFENSE: If Qualifier, please check   A   S   C   R (A=Attempt, S=Solicitation, C=Conspiracy, R=Reclassification

FELONY DEGREE	F.S. #	DESCRIPTION	OFFENSE LEVEL	**POINTS**
_____ /	_____ /	_____ /	_____ /	

(Level - Points: 1=4, 2=10, 3=16, 4=22, 5=28, 6=36, 7=56, 8=74, 9=92, 10=116)

Prior capital felony triples Primary Offense points ☐   **I.** _____

II. ADDITIONAL OFFENSE(S): Supplemental page attached ☐

DOCKET #	FEL/MM DEGREE	F.S. #	OFFENSE LEVEL	QUALIFY A S C R	COUNTS	POINTS	TOTAL
_____ /	_____ /	____ /	_____	☐☐☐☐	_____ X	_____ =	_____
DESCRIPTION _____							
_____ /	_____ /	____ /	_____	☐☐☐☐	_____ X	_____ =	_____
DESCRIPTION _____							

Florida Rules of Criminal Procedure 2014

_____ / _____ / _____/ _____ _____ X _____ = _____
DESCRIPTION _____

_____ / _____ / _____/ _____ _____ X _____ = _____
DESCRIPTION _____

(Level - Points: M=0.2, 1=0.7, 2=1.2, 3=2.4, 4=3.6, 5=5.4, 6=18, 7=28, 8=37, 9=46, 10=58)

Prior capital felony triples Additional Offense points ☐   Supplemental page points _____

II. _____

III. VICTIM INJURY:

	Number	Total		Number	Total
2nd Degree Murder	240 x	=	Slight	4 x	=
Death	120 x	=	Sex Penetration	80 x	=
Severe	40 x	=	Sex Contact	40 x	=
Moderate	18 x	=			

III. _____

IV. PRIOR RECORD: Supplemental page attached ☐

FEL/MM DEGREE	F.S. #	OFFENSE LEVEL	QUALIFY: A S C R	DESCRIPTION	NUMBER	POINTS	TOTAL
_____	_/	_____	☐☐☐☐	_____	_____	X _____	= _____
_____	_/	_____	☐☐☐☐	_____	_____	X _____	= _____
_____	_/	_____	☐☐☐☐	_____	_____	X _____	= _____
_____	_/	_____	☐☐☐☐	_____	_____	X _____	= _____
_____	_/	_____	☐☐☐☐	_____	_____	X _____	= _____
_____	_/	_____	☐☐☐☐	_____	_____	X _____	= _____

(Level = Points: M=0.2, 1=0.5, 2=0.8, 3=1.6, 4=2.4, 5=3.6, 6=9, 7=14, 8=19, 9=23, 10=29)

Supplemental page points _____

IV.   _____

Page 1 Subtotal: _____

Effective Date: For offenses committed under the Criminal Punishment Code effective for offenses committee on or after October 1, 1998 and subsequent revisions.

NAME (LAST, FIRST, MI)	DOCKET #

Page 1 Subtotal: _____

V.　　Legal Status violation = 4 Points

☐ Escape　☐ Fleeing　☐ Failure to appear　☐ Supersedeas bond　☐ Incarceration　☐ Pretrial intervention or diversion program

☐ Court imposed or post prison release community supervision resulting in a conviction

V. _____

VI.　Community Sanction violation before the court for sentencing
☐ Probation　☐ Community Control　☐ Pretrial Intervention or diversion

VI. _____

☐　6 points for any violation other than new felony conviction　x _____ each successive violation　OR

☐　New felony conviction = 12 points x _____ each successive violation if new offense results in conviction before or at same time as sentence for violation of probation OR

☐　12 points x _____ each successive violation for a violent felony offender of special concern when the violation is not based solely on failure to pay costs, fines, or restitution OR

☐　New felony conviction = 24 points x _____ each successive violation for a violent felony offender of special concern if new offense results in a conviction before or at the same time for violation of probation

VII.　Firearm/Semi-Automatic or Machine Gun = 18 or 25 Points

VII. _____

VIII.　Prior Serious Felony - 30 Points

VIII. _____

Subtotal Sentence Points _____

IX.　Enhancements (only if the primary offense qualifies for enhancement)

Law Enf. Protect.	Drug Trafficker	Motor Vehicle Theft	Criminal Gang Offense	Domestic Violence in the Presence of Related Child

(offenses committed on
or after 3/12/07)

___ x 1.5 ___ x 2.0 ___ x 2.5 _____ x 1.5   _____ x 1.5   _____ x 1.5   ___ x 1.5

                                                         Enhanced Subtotal Sentence Points   IX. _____

                                          TOTAL SENTENCE POINTS   _____

SENTENCE COMPUTATION

If the total sentence points are less than or equal to 44, the lowest permissible sentence is any non-state prison sanction. If the total sentence points are 22 points or less, see Section 775.082(10), Florida Statues, to determine if the court must sentence the offender to a non-state prison sanction.

If total sentence points are greater than 44:

_____ minus 28 = _____ x .75

= _____

            total sentence points   lowest permissible prison

sentence in months

If total sentence points are 60 points or less and court makes findings pursuant to both Florida Statutes 948.20 and 397.334(3), the court may place the defendant into a treatment-based drug court program.

The maximum sentence is up to the statutory maximum for the primary and any additional offenses as provided in s. 775.082, F.S., unless the lowest permissible sentence under the Code exceeds the statutory maximum. Such sentences may be imposed concurrently or consecutively. If total sentence points are greater than or equal to 363, a life sentence may be imposed.

_____

                               maximum sentence in years

TOTAL SENTENCE IMPOSED

                                     Years   Months   Days

☐ State Prison   ☐ Life

_____   _____   _____

☐ County Jail   ☐ Time Served

_____   _____   _____

☐ Community Control

_____   _____   _____

☐ Probation   ☐ Modified

_____   _____   _____

Please check if sentenced as ☐ habitual offender, ☐ habitual violent offender, ☐ violent career criminal, ☐ prison releasee reoffender,
or a ☐ mandatory minimum applies.

☐ Mitigated Departure   ☐ Plea Bargain   ☐ Prison Diversion Program

Other Reason: _____

JUDGE'S SIGNATURE	

Effective Date: For offenses committed under the Criminal Punishment Code effective for offenses committed on or after October 1, 1998, and subsequent revisions.

(b)   Supplemental Criminal Punishment Code Scoresheet

NAME (LAST, FIRST, MI.I)	DOCKET #	DATE OF SENTENCE

II.   ADDITIONAL OFFENSES(S):

DOCKET #	FEL/MM DEGREE	F.S. #	OFFENSE LEVEL	QUALIFY A S C R	COUNTS	POINTS	TOTAL
____ /	____ /	____ /	_____	□□ □□	_____ X	_____ =	_____
DESCRIPTION _____							
____ /	____ /	____ /	_____	□□ □□	_____ X	_____ =	_____
DESCRIPTION _____							
____ /	____ /	____ /	_____	□□ □□	_____ X	_____ =	_____
DESCRIPTION _____							
____ /	____ /	____ /	_____	□□ □□	_____ X	_____ =	_____
DESCRIPTION _____							
____ /	____ /	____ /	_____	□□ □□	_____ X	_____ =	_____
DESCRIPTION _____							

(Level - Points: M=0.2, 1=0.7, 2=1.2, 3=2.4, 4=3.6, 5=5.4, 6=18, 7=28, 8=37, 9=46, 10=58)

II. ____

IV.   PRIOR RECORD

FEL/MM DEGREE	F.S. #	OFFENSE LEVEL	QUALIFY: A S C R	DESCRIPTION	NUMBER	POINTS	TOTAL
_____	___ /	_____	□□ □□	_____	_____ X	_____ =	_____
_____	___ /	_____	□□ □□	_____	_____ X	_____ =	_____
_____	___ /	_____	□□ □□	_____	_____ X	_____ =	_____
_____	___ /	_____	□□ □□	_____	_____ X	_____ =	_____
_____	___ /	_____	□□ □□	_____	_____ X	_____ =	_____
_____	___ /	_____	□□ □□	_____	_____ X	_____ =	_____

(Level = Points: M=0.2, 1=0.5, 2=0.8, 3=1.6, 4=2.4, 5=3.6, 6=9, 7=14, 8=19, 9=23, 10=29)

IV. ____

REASONS FOR DEPARTURE - MITIGATING CIRCUMSTANCES

(reasons may be checked here or written on the scoresheet)

☐ Legitimate, uncoerced plea bargain.

☐ The defendant was an accomplice to the offense and was a relatively minor participant in the criminal conduct.

☐ The capacity of the defendant to appreciate the criminal nature of the conduct or to conform that   conduct to the requirements of law was substantially impaired.

☐ The defendant requires specialized treatment for a mental disorder that is unrelated to substance abuse or addiction, or for a physical disability, and the defendant is amenable to treatment.

☐ The need for payment of restitution to the victim outweighs the need for a prison sentence.

☐ The victim was an initiator, willing participant, aggressor, or provoker of the incident.

☐ The defendant acted under extreme duress or under the domination of another person.

☐ Before the identity of the defendant was determined, the victim was substantially compensated.

☐ The defendant cooperated with the State to resolve the current offense or any other offense.

☐ The offense was committed in an unsophisticated manner and was an isolated incident for which the defendant has shown remorse.

☐ At the time of the offense the defendant was too young to appreciate the consequences of the offense.

☐ The defendant is to be sentenced as a youthful offender.

☐ The defendant is amenable to the services of a postadjudicatory treatment-based drug court program and is otherwise qualified to participate in the program.

☐ The defendant was making a good faith effort to obtain or provide medical assistance for an individual experiencing a drug-related overdose.

Pursuant to 921.0026(3) the defendant's substance abuse or addiction does not justify a downward departure from the lowest permissible sentence, except for the provisions of s. 921.0026(2)(m).

Effective Date: For offenses committed under the Criminal Punishment Code effective for offenses committed on or after October 1, 1998 and subsequent revisions

End of Florida Rules of Criminal Procedure

Florida Evidence Code 2014

Florida Evidence Code

TITLE VII

EVIDENCE

CHAPTER 90

EVIDENCE CODE

90.101   Short title.—This chapter shall be known and may be cited as the "Florida Evidence Code."

History.—s. 1, ch. 76-237; s. 1, ch. 77-77; s. 22, ch. 78-361; s. 1, ch. 78-379.

90.102   Construction.—This chapter shall replace and supersede existing statutory or common law in conflict with its provisions.

History.—s. 1, ch. 76-237; s. 1, ch. 77-77; s. 22, ch. 78-361; s. 1, ch. 78-379.

90.103   Scope; applicability.—

(1)   Unless otherwise provided by statute, this code applies to the same proceedings that the general law of evidence applied to before the effective date of this code.

(2)   This act shall apply to criminal proceedings related to crimes committed after the effective date of this code and to civil actions and all other proceedings pending on or brought after October 1, 1981.

(3)   Nothing in this act shall operate to repeal or modify the parol evidence rule.

History.—ss. 1, 5, 7, ch. 76-237; s. 1, ch. 77-77; ss. 1, 22, ch. 78-361; ss. 1, 2, ch. 78-379; s. 1, ch. 81-93.

90.104   Rulings on evidence.—

(1)   A court may predicate error, set aside or reverse a judgment, or grant a new trial on the basis of admitted or excluded evidence when a substantial right of the party is adversely affected and:

(a)   When the ruling is one admitting evidence, a timely objection or motion to strike appears on the record, stating the specific ground of objection if the specific ground was not apparent from the context; or

(b)   When the ruling is one excluding evidence, the substance of the evidence was made known to the court by offer of proof or was apparent from the context within which the questions were asked.

If the court has made a definitive ruling on the record admitting or excluding evidence, either at or before trial, a party need not renew an objection or offer of proof to preserve a claim of error for appeal.

 Florida Evidence Code

(2) In cases tried by a jury, a court shall conduct proceedings, to the maximum extent practicable, in such a manner as to prevent inadmissible evidence from being suggested to the jury by any means.

(3) Nothing in this section shall preclude a court from taking notice of fundamental errors affecting substantial rights, even though such errors were not brought to the attention of the trial judge.

History.—s. 1, ch. 76-237; s. 1, ch. 77-77; s. 1, ch. 77-174; s. 22, ch. 78-361; s. 1, ch. 78-379; s. 1, ch. 2003-259.

90.105   Preliminary questions.—

(1) Except as provided in subsection (2), the court shall determine preliminary questions concerning the qualification of a person to be a witness, the existence of a privilege, or the admissibility of evidence.

(2) When the relevancy of evidence depends upon the existence of a preliminary fact, the court shall admit the proffered evidence when there is prima facie evidence sufficient to support a finding of the preliminary fact. If prima facie evidence is not introduced to support a finding of the preliminary fact, the court may admit the proffered evidence subject to the subsequent introduction of prima facie evidence of the preliminary fact.

(3) Hearings on the admissibility of confessions shall be conducted out of the hearing of the jury. Hearings on other preliminary matters shall be similarly conducted when the interests of justice require or when an accused is a witness, if he or she so requests.

History.—s. 1, ch. 76-237; s. 1, ch. 77-77; s. 22, ch. 78-361; s. 1, ch. 78-379; s. 471, ch. 95-147.

90.106   Summing up and comment by judge.—A judge may not sum up the evidence or comment to the jury upon the weight of the evidence, the credibility of the witnesses, or the guilt of the accused.

History.—s. 1, ch. 76-237; s. 1, ch. 77-77; s. 22, ch. 78-361; s. 1, ch. 78-379.

90.107   Limited admissibility.—When evidence that is admissible as to one party or for one purpose, but inadmissible as to another party or for another purpose, is admitted, the court, upon request, shall restrict such evidence to its proper scope and so inform the jury at the time it is admitted.

History.—s. 1, ch. 76-237; s. 1, ch. 77-77; s. 22, ch. 78-361; s. 1, ch. 78-379.

90.108   Introduction of related writings or recorded statements.—

(1) When a writing or recorded statement or part thereof is introduced by a party, an adverse party may require him or her at that time to introduce any other part or any other writing or recorded statement that in fairness ought to be considered contemporaneously. An adverse party is not bound by evidence introduced under this section.

244

(2)   The report of a court reporter, when certified to by the court reporter as being a correct transcript of the testimony and proceedings in the case, is prima facie a correct statement of such testimony and proceedings.

History.—s. 1, ch. 76-237; s. 1, ch. 77-77; ss. 2, 22, ch. 78-361; ss. 1, 2, ch. 78-379; s. 472, ch. 95-147; s. 5, ch. 95-286.

90.201   Matters which must be judicially noticed.—A court shall take judicial notice of:

(1)   Decisional, constitutional, and public statutory law and resolutions of the Florida Legislature and the Congress of the United States.

(2)   Florida rules of court that have statewide application, its own rules, and the rules of United States courts adopted by the United States Supreme Court.

(3)   Rules of court of the United States Supreme Court and of the United States Courts of Appeal.

History.—s. 1, ch. 76-237; s. 1, ch. 77-77; ss. 21, 22, ch. 78-361; ss. 1, 2, ch. 78-379.

90.202   Matters which may be judicially noticed.—A court may take judicial notice of the following matters, to the extent that they are not embraced within s. 90.201:

(1)   Special, local, and private acts and resolutions of the Congress of the United States and of the Florida Legislature.

(2)   Decisional, constitutional, and public statutory law of every other state, territory, and jurisdiction of the United States.

(3)   Contents of the Federal Register.

(4)   Laws of foreign nations and of an organization of nations.

(5)   Official actions of the legislative, executive, and judicial departments of the United States and of any state, territory, or jurisdiction of the United States.

(6)   Records of any court of this state or of any court of record of the United States or of any state, territory, or jurisdiction of the United States.

(7)   Rules of court of any court of this state or of any court of record of the United States or of any other state, territory, or jurisdiction of the United States.

(8)   Provisions of all municipal and county charters and charter amendments of this state, provided they are available in printed copies or as certified copies.

(9)   Rules promulgated by governmental agencies of this state which are published in the Florida Administrative Code or in bound written copies.

(10)   Duly enacted ordinances and resolutions of municipalities and counties located in Florida, provided such ordinances and resolutions are available in printed copies or as certified copies.

(11)   Facts that are not subject to dispute because they are generally known within the territorial jurisdiction of the court.

(12)   Facts that are not subject to dispute because they are capable of accurate and ready determination by resort to sources whose accuracy cannot be questioned.

(13)   Official seals of governmental agencies and departments of the United States and of any state, territory, or jurisdiction of the United States.

History.—s. 1, ch. 76-237; s. 1, ch. 77-77; s. 1, ch. 77-174; ss. 3, 22, ch. 78-361; ss. 1, 2, ch. 78-379.

90.203   Compulsory judicial notice upon request.—A court shall take judicial notice of any matter in s. 90.202 when a party requests it and:

(1)   Gives each adverse party timely written notice of the request, proof of which is filed with the court, to enable the adverse party to prepare to meet the request.

(2)   Furnishes the court with sufficient information to enable it to take judicial notice of the matter.

History.—s. 1, ch. 76-237; s. 1, ch. 77-77; s. 22, ch. 78-361; s. 1, ch. 78-379.

90.204   Determination of propriety of judicial notice and nature of matter noticed.—

(1)   When a court determines upon its own motion that judicial notice of a matter should be taken or when a party requests such notice and shows good cause for not complying with s. 90.203(1), the court shall afford each party reasonable opportunity to present information relevant to the propriety of taking judicial notice and to the nature of the matter noticed.

(2)   In determining the propriety of taking judicial notice of a matter or the nature thereof, a court may use any source of pertinent and reliable information, whether or not furnished by a party, without regard to any exclusionary rule except a valid claim of privilege and except for the exclusions provided in s. 90.403.

(3)   If a court resorts to any documentary source of information not received in open court, the court shall make the information and its source a part of the record in the action and shall afford each party reasonable opportunity to challenge such information, and to offer additional information, before judicial notice of the matter is taken.

History.—s. 1, ch. 76-237; s. 1, ch. 77-77; s. 22, ch. 78-361; s. 1, ch. 78-379.

90.205   Denial of a request for judicial notice.—Upon request of counsel, when a court denies a request to take judicial notice of any matter, the court shall inform the parties at the earliest practicable time and shall indicate for the record that it has denied the request.

History.—s. 1, ch. 76-237; s. 1, ch. 77-77; s. 22, ch. 78-361; s. 1, ch. 78-379.

90.206   Instructing jury on judicial notice.—The court may instruct the jury during the trial to accept as a fact a matter judicially noticed.

History.—s. 1, ch. 76-237; s. 1, ch. 77-77; ss. 4, 22, ch. 78-361; ss. 1, 2, ch. 78-379.

90.207   Judicial notice by trial court in subsequent proceedings.—The failure or refusal of a court to take judicial notice of a matter does not preclude a court from taking judicial notice of the matter in subsequent proceedings, in accordance with the procedure specified in ss. 90.201-90.206.

History.—s. 1, ch. 76-237; s. 1, ch. 77-77; s. 22, ch. 78-361; s. 1, ch. 78-379.

90.301   Presumption defined; inferences.—

(1)   For the purposes of this chapter, a presumption is an assumption of fact which the law makes from the existence of another fact or group of facts found or otherwise established.

(2)   Except for presumptions that are conclusive under the law from which they arise, a presumption is rebuttable.

(3)   Nothing in this chapter shall prevent the drawing of an inference that is appropriate.

(4)   Sections 90.301-90.304 are applicable only in civil actions or proceedings.

History.—s. 1, ch. 76-237; s. 1, ch. 77-77; ss. 5, 22, ch. 78-361; ss. 1, 2, ch. 78-379.

90.302   Classification of rebuttable presumptions.—Every rebuttable presumption is either:

(1)   A presumption affecting the burden of producing evidence and requiring the trier of fact to assume the existence of the presumed fact, unless credible evidence sufficient to sustain a finding of the nonexistence of the presumed fact is introduced, in which event, the existence or nonexistence of the presumed fact shall be determined from the evidence without regard to the presumption; or

(2)   A presumption affecting the burden of proof that imposes upon the party against whom it operates the burden of proof concerning the nonexistence of the presumed fact.

History.—s. 1, ch. 76-237; s. 1, ch. 77-77; s. 22, ch. 78-361; s. 1, ch. 78-379.

90.303   Presumption affecting the burden of producing evidence defined.—In a civil action or proceeding, unless otherwise provided by statute, a presumption established primarily to facilitate the determination of the particular action in which the presumption is applied, rather than to implement public policy, is a presumption affecting the burden of producing evidence.

History.—s. 1, ch. 76-237; s. 1, ch. 77-77; s. 22, ch. 78-361; s. 1, ch. 78-379.

90.304	**Presumption affecting the burden of proof defined.**—In civil actions, all rebuttable presumptions which are not defined in s. 90.303 are presumptions affecting the burden of proof.

History.—s. 1, ch. 76-237; s. 1, ch. 77-77; s. 22, ch. 78-361; s. 1, ch. 78-379.

90.401	**Definition of relevant evidence.**—Relevant evidence is evidence tending to prove or disprove a material fact.

History.—s. 1, ch. 76-237; s. 1, ch. 77-77; s. 22, ch. 78-361; s. 1, ch. 78-379.

90.402	**Admissibility of relevant evidence.**—All relevant evidence is admissible, except as provided by law.

History.—s. 1, ch. 76-237; s. 1, ch. 77-77; s. 22, ch. 78-361; s. 1, ch. 78-379.

90.4025	**Admissibility of paternity determination in certain criminal prosecutions.**—If a person less than 18 years of age gives birth to a child and the paternity of that child is established under chapter 742, such evidence of paternity is admissible in a criminal prosecution under ss. 794.011, 794.05, 800.04, and 827.04(3).

History.—s. 8, ch. 96-215; s. 2, ch. 96-409; s. 27, ch. 99-2.

90.4026	**Statements expressing sympathy; admissibility; definitions.**—

(1)	As used in this section:

(a)	"Accident" means an occurrence resulting in injury or death to one or more persons which is not the result of willful action by a party.

(b)	"Benevolent gestures" means actions that convey a sense of compassion or commiseration emanating from human impulses.

(c)	"Family" means the spouse, parent, grandparent, stepmother, stepfather, child, grandchild, brother, sister, half-brother, half-sister, adopted child of parent, or spouse's parent of an injured party.

(2)	The portion of statements, writings, or benevolent gestures expressing sympathy or a general sense of benevolence relating to the pain, suffering, or death of a person involved in an accident and made to that person or to the family of that person shall be inadmissible as evidence in a civil action. A statement of fault, however, which is part of, or in addition to, any of the above shall be admissible pursuant to this section.

History.—s. 1, ch. 2001-132.

90.403	**Exclusion on grounds of prejudice or confusion.**—Relevant evidence is inadmissible if its probative value is substantially outweighed by the danger of unfair prejudice, confusion of issues, misleading the jury, or needless presentation of cumulative evidence. This section shall not be construed to mean that evidence of the existence of available third-party benefits is inadmissible.

History.—s. 1, ch. 76-237; s. 1, ch. 77-77; ss. 6, 22, ch. 78-361; ss. 1, 2, ch. 78-379.

90.404   **Character evidence; when admissible.—**

(1)   CHARACTER EVIDENCE GENERALLY.—Evidence of a person's character or a trait of character is inadmissible to prove action in conformity with it on a particular occasion, except:

(a)   Character of accused.—Evidence of a pertinent trait of character offered by an accused, or by the prosecution to rebut the trait.

(b)   Character of victim.—

1.   Except as provided in s. 794.022, evidence of a pertinent trait of character of the victim of the crime offered by an accused, or by the prosecution to rebut the trait; or

2.   Evidence of a character trait of peacefulness of the victim offered by the prosecution in a homicide case to rebut evidence that the victim was the aggressor.

(c)   Character of witness.—Evidence of the character of a witness, as provided in ss. 90.608-90.610.

(2)   OTHER CRIMES, WRONGS, OR ACTS.—

(a)   Similar fact evidence of other crimes, wrongs, or acts is admissible when relevant to prove a material fact in issue, including, but not limited to, proof of motive, opportunity, intent, preparation, plan, knowledge, identity, or absence of mistake or accident, but it is inadmissible when the evidence is relevant solely to prove bad character or propensity.

(b)   1.   In a criminal case in which the defendant is charged with a crime involving child molestation, evidence of the defendant's commission of other crimes, wrongs, or acts of child molestation is admissible and may be considered for its bearing on any matter to which it is relevant.

2.   For the purposes of this paragraph, the term "child molestation" means conduct proscribed by s. 787.025(2)(c), s. 787.06(3)(g) and (h), s. 794.011, excluding s. 794.011(10), s. 794.05, s. 796.03, s. 796.035, s. 800.04, s. 827.071, s. 847.0135(5), s. 847.0145, or s. 985.701(1) when committed against a person 16 years of age or younger.

(c)   1.   In a criminal case in which the defendant is charged with a sexual offense, evidence of the defendant's commission of other crimes, wrongs, or acts involving a sexual offense is admissible and may be considered for its bearing on any matter to which it is relevant.

2.   For the purposes of this paragraph, the term "sexual offense" means conduct proscribed by s. 787.025(2)(c),s. 787.06(3)(b), (d), (f), (g), or (h), s. 794.011, excluding s. 794.011(10), s. 794.05, s. 796.03, s. 796.035, s. 825.1025(2)(b), s. 827.071, s. 847.0135(5), s. 847.0145, or s. 985.701(1).

(d) 1. When the state in a criminal action intends to offer evidence of other criminal offenses under paragraph (a), paragraph (b), or paragraph (c), no fewer than 10 days before trial, the state shall furnish to the defendant or to the defendant's counsel a written statement of the acts or offenses it intends to offer, describing them with the particularity required of an indictment or information. No notice is required for evidence of offenses used for impeachment or on rebuttal.

2. When the evidence is admitted, the court shall, if requested, charge the jury on the limited purpose for which the evidence is received and is to be considered. After the close of the evidence, the jury shall be instructed on the limited purpose for which the evidence was received and that the defendant cannot be convicted for a charge not included in the indictment or information.

(3) Nothing in this section affects the admissibility of evidence under s. 90.610.

History.—s. 1, ch. 76-237; s. 1, ch. 77-77; s. 22, ch. 78-361; s. 1, ch. 78-379; s. 2, ch. 90-40; s. 26, ch. 93-156; s. 473, ch. 95-147; s. 1, ch. 2001-221; s. 9, ch. 2008-172; s. 2, ch. 2011-220; s. 14, ch. 2012-97.

90.405   Methods of proving character.—

(1)   REPUTATION.—When evidence of the character of a person or of a trait of that person's character is admissible, proof may be made by testimony about that person's reputation.

(2)   SPECIFIC INSTANCES OF CONDUCT.—When character or a trait of character of a person is an essential element of a charge, claim, or defense, proof may be made of specific instances of that person's conduct.

History.—s. 1, ch. 76-237; s. 1, ch. 77-77; ss. 7, 22, ch. 78-361; ss. 1, 2, ch. 78-379; s. 474, ch. 95-147.

90.406   Routine practice.—Evidence of the routine practice of an organization, whether corroborated or not and regardless of the presence of eyewitnesses, is admissible to prove that the conduct of the organization on a particular occasion was in conformity with the routine practice.

History.—s. 1, ch. 76-237; s. 1, ch. 77-77; s. 22, ch. 78-361; s. 1, ch. 78-379.

90.407   Subsequent remedial measures.—Evidence of measures taken after an injury or harm caused by an event, which measures if taken before the event would have made injury or harm less likely to occur, is not admissible to prove negligence, the existence of a product defect, or culpable conduct in connection with the event. This rule does not require the exclusion of evidence of subsequent remedial measures when offered for another purpose, such as proving ownership, control, or the feasibility of precautionary measures, if controverted, or impeachment.

History.—s. 1, ch. 76-237; s. 1, ch. 77-77; s. 1, ch. 77-174; s. 22, ch. 78-361; s. 1, ch. 78-379; s. 13, ch. 99-225.

90.408   Compromise and offers to compromise.—Evidence of an offer to compromise a claim which was disputed as to validity or amount, as well as any relevant conduct or statements made in negotiations concerning a compromise, is inadmissible to prove liability or absence of liability for the claim or its value.

History.—s. 1, ch. 76-237; s. 1, ch. 77-77; s. 22, ch. 78-361; s. 1, ch. 78-379.

90.409   Payment of medical and similar expenses.—Evidence of furnishing, or offering or promising to pay, medical or hospital expenses or other damages occasioned by an injury or accident is inadmissible to prove liability for the injury or accident.

History.—s. 1, ch. 76-237; s. 1, ch. 77-77; s. 22, ch. 78-361; s. 1, ch. 78-379.

90.410   Offer to plead guilty; nolo contendere; withdrawn pleas of guilty.— Evidence of a plea of guilty, later withdrawn; a plea of nolo contendere; or an offer to plead guilty or nolo contendere to the crime charged or any other crime is inadmissible in any civil or criminal proceeding. Evidence of statements made in connection with any of the pleas or offers is inadmissible, except when such statements are offered in a prosecution under chapter 837.

History.—s. 1, ch. 76-237; s. 1, ch. 77-77; ss. 8, 22, ch. 78-361; ss. 1, 2, ch. 78-379.

90.501   Privileges recognized only as provided.—Except as otherwise provided by this chapter, any other statute, or the Constitution of the United States or of the State of Florida, no person in a legal proceeding has a privilege to:

(1)   Refuse to be a witness.

(2)   Refuse to disclose any matter.

(3)   Refuse to produce any object or writing.

(4)   Prevent another from being a witness, from disclosing any matter, or from producing any object or writing.

History.—s. 1, ch. 76-237; s. 1, ch. 77-77; ss. 9, 22, ch. 78-361; ss. 1, 2, ch. 78-379.

90.5015   Journalist's privilege.—

(1)   DEFINITIONS.—For purposes of this section, the term:

(a)   "Professional journalist" means a person regularly engaged in collecting, photographing, recording, writing, editing, reporting, or publishing news, for gain or livelihood, who obtained the information sought while working as a salaried employee of, or independent contractor for, a newspaper, news journal, news agency, press association, wire service, radio or television station, network, or news magazine. Book authors and others who are not professional journalists, as defined in this paragraph, are not included in the provisions of this section.

(b)   "News" means information of public concern relating to local, statewide, national, or worldwide issues or events.

(2)   PRIVILEGE.—A professional journalist has a qualified privilege not to be a witness concerning, and not to disclose the information, including the identity of any

source, that the professional journalist has obtained while actively gathering news. This privilege applies only to information or eyewitness observations obtained within the normal scope of employment and does not apply to physical evidence, eyewitness observations, or visual or audio recording of crimes. A party seeking to overcome this privilege must make a clear and specific showing that:

      (a)   The information is relevant and material to unresolved issues that have been raised in the proceeding for which the information is sought;

      (b)   The information cannot be obtained from alternative sources; and

      (c)   A compelling interest exists for requiring disclosure of the information.

      (3)   DISCLOSURE.—A court shall order disclosure pursuant to subsection (2) only of that portion of the information for which the showing under subsection (2) has been made and shall support such order with clear and specific findings made after a hearing.

      (4)   WAIVER.—A professional journalist does not waive the privilege by publishing or broadcasting information.

      (5)   CONSTRUCTION.—This section must not be construed to limit any privilege or right provided to a professional journalist under law.

      (6)   AUTHENTICATION.—Photographs, diagrams, video recordings, audio recordings, computer records, or other business records maintained, disclosed, provided, or produced by a professional journalist, or by the employer or principal of a professional journalist, may be authenticated for admission in evidence upon a showing, by affidavit of the professional journalist, or other individual with personal knowledge, that the photograph, diagram, video recording, audio recording, computer record, or other business record is a true and accurate copy of the original, and that the copy truly and accurately reflects the observations and facts contained therein.

      (7)   ACCURACY OF EVIDENCE.—If the affidavit of authenticity and accuracy, or other relevant factual circumstance, causes the court to have clear and convincing doubts as to the authenticity or accuracy of the proffered evidence, the court may decline to admit such evidence.

      (8)   SEVERABILITY.—If any provision of this section or its application to any particular person or circumstance is held invalid, that provision or its application is severable and does not affect the validity of other provisions or applications of this section.

History.—s. 1, ch. 98-48.

90.502   Lawyer-client privilege.—

      (1)   For purposes of this section:

      (a)   A "lawyer" is a person authorized, or reasonably believed by the client to be authorized, to practice law in any state or nation.

(b)   A "client" is any person, public officer, corporation, association, or other organization or entity, either public or private, who consults a lawyer with the purpose of obtaining legal services or who is rendered legal services by a lawyer.

(c)   A communication between lawyer and client is "confidential" if it is not intended to be disclosed to third persons other than:

1.   Those to whom disclosure is in furtherance of the rendition of legal services to the client.

2.   Those reasonably necessary for the transmission of the communication.

(2)   A client has a privilege to refuse to disclose, and to prevent any other person from disclosing, the contents of confidential communications when such other person learned of the communications because they were made in the rendition of legal services to the client.

(3)   The privilege may be claimed by:

(a)   The client.

(b)   A guardian or conservator of the client.

(c)   The personal representative of a deceased client.

(d)   A successor, assignee, trustee in dissolution, or any similar representative of an organization, corporation, or association or other entity, either public or private, whether or not in existence.

(e)   The lawyer, but only on behalf of the client. The lawyer's authority to claim the privilege is presumed in the absence of contrary evidence.

(4)   There is no lawyer-client privilege under this section when:

(a)   The services of the lawyer were sought or obtained to enable or aid anyone to commit or plan to commit what the client knew was a crime or fraud.

(b)   A communication is relevant to an issue between parties who claim through the same deceased client.

(c)   A communication is relevant to an issue of breach of duty by the lawyer to the client or by the client to the lawyer, arising from the lawyer-client relationship.

(d)   A communication is relevant to an issue concerning the intention or competence of a client executing an attested document to which the lawyer is an attesting witness, or concerning the execution or attestation of the document.

(e)   A communication is relevant to a matter of common interest between two or more clients, or their successors in interest, if the communication was made by any of them to a lawyer retained or consulted in common when offered in a civil action between the clients or their successors in interest.

Florida Evidence Code

(5) Communications made by a person who seeks or receives services from the Department of Revenue under the child support enforcement program to the attorney representing the department shall be confidential and privileged as provided for in this section. Such communications shall not be disclosed to anyone other than the agency except as provided for in this section. Such disclosures shall be protected as if there were an attorney-client relationship between the attorney for the agency and the person who seeks services from the department.

(6) A discussion or activity that is not a meeting for purposes of s. 286.011 shall not be construed to waive the attorney-client privilege established in this section. This shall not be construed to constitute an exemption to either s. 119.07 or s. 286.011.

History.—s. 1, ch. 76-237; s. 1, ch. 77-77; s. 22, ch. 78-361; s. 1, ch. 78-379; s. 16, ch. 92-138; s. 12, ch. 94-124; s. 1378, ch. 95-147; s. 1, ch. 2000-316.

90.5021   Fiduciary lawyer-client privilege.—

(1) For the purpose of this section, a client acts as a fiduciary when serving as a personal representative or a trustee as defined in ss. 731.201 and 736.0103, an administrator ad litem as described in s. 733.308, a curator as described in s. 733.501, a guardian or guardian ad litem as defined in s. 744.102, a conservator as defined in s. 710.102, or an attorney in fact as described in chapter 709.

(2) A communication between a lawyer and a client acting as a fiduciary is privileged and protected from disclosure under s. 90.502 to the same extent as if the client were not acting as a fiduciary. In applying s. 90.502 to a communication under this section, only the person or entity acting as a fiduciary is considered a client of the lawyer.

(3) This section does not affect the crime or fraud exception to the lawyer-client privilege provided in s. 90.502(4)(a).

History.—s. 1, ch. 2011-183.

90.503   Psychotherapist-patient privilege.—

(1) For purposes of this section:

(a) A "psychotherapist" is:

1. A person authorized to practice medicine in any state or nation, or reasonably believed by the patient so to be, who is engaged in the diagnosis or treatment of a mental or emotional condition, including alcoholism and other drug addiction;

2. A person licensed or certified as a psychologist under the laws of any state or nation, who is engaged primarily in the diagnosis or treatment of a mental or emotional condition, including alcoholism and other drug addiction;

3. A person licensed or certified as a clinical social worker, marriage and family therapist, or mental health counselor under the laws of this state, who is engaged primarily in the diagnosis or treatment of a mental or emotional condition, including alcoholism and other drug addiction;

4. Treatment personnel of facilities licensed by the state pursuant to chapter 394, chapter 395, or chapter 397, of facilities designated by the Department of Children and Family Services pursuant to chapter 394 as treatment facilities, or of facilities defined as community mental health centers pursuant to s. 394.907(1), who are engaged primarily in the diagnosis or treatment of a mental or emotional condition, including alcoholism and other drug addiction; or

5. An advanced registered nurse practitioner certified under s. 464.012, whose primary scope of practice is the diagnosis or treatment of mental or emotional conditions, including chemical abuse, and limited only to actions performed in accordance with part I of chapter 464.

(b) A "patient" is a person who consults, or is interviewed by, a psychotherapist for purposes of diagnosis or treatment of a mental or emotional condition, including alcoholism and other drug addiction.

(c) A communication between psychotherapist and patient is "confidential" if it is not intended to be disclosed to third persons other than:

1. Those persons present to further the interest of the patient in the consultation, examination, or interview.

2. Those persons necessary for the transmission of the communication.

3. Those persons who are participating in the diagnosis and treatment under the direction of the psychotherapist.

(2) A patient has a privilege to refuse to disclose, and to prevent any other person from disclosing, confidential communications or records made for the purpose of diagnosis or treatment of the patient's mental or emotional condition, including alcoholism and other drug addiction, between the patient and the psychotherapist, or persons who are participating in the diagnosis or treatment under the direction of the psychotherapist. This privilege includes any diagnosis made, and advice given, by the psychotherapist in the course of that relationship.

(3) The privilege may be claimed by:

(a) The patient or the patient's attorney on the patient's behalf.

(b) A guardian or conservator of the patient.

(c) The personal representative of a deceased patient.

(d) The psychotherapist, but only on behalf of the patient. The authority of a psychotherapist to claim the privilege is presumed in the absence of evidence to the contrary.

(4) There is no privilege under this section:

(a) For communications relevant to an issue in proceedings to compel hospitalization of a patient for mental illness, if the psychotherapist in the course of diagnosis or treatment has reasonable cause to believe the patient is in need of hospitalization.

(b)   For communications made in the course of a court-ordered examination of the mental or emotional condition of the patient.

(c)   For communications relevant to an issue of the mental or emotional condition of the patient in any proceeding in which the patient relies upon the condition as an element of his or her claim or defense or, after the patient's death, in any proceeding in which any party relies upon the condition as an element of the party's claim or defense.

History.—s. 1, ch. 76-237; s. 1, ch. 77-77; s. 22, ch. 78-361; s. 1, ch. 78-379; s. 40, ch. 90-347; s. 1, ch. 92-57; s. 19, ch. 93-39; s. 475, ch. 95-147; s. 28, ch. 99-2; s. 5, ch. 99-8; s. 1, ch. 2006-204.

90.5035   Sexual assault counselor-victim privilege.—

(1)   For purposes of this section:

(a)   A "rape crisis center" is any public or private agency that offers assistance to victims of sexual assault or sexual battery and their families.

(b)   A "sexual assault counselor" is any employee of a rape crisis center whose primary purpose is the rendering of advice, counseling, or assistance to victims of sexual assault or sexual battery.

(c)   A "trained volunteer" is a person who volunteers at a rape crisis center, has completed 30 hours of training in assisting victims of sexual violence and related topics provided by the rape crisis center, is supervised by members of the staff of the rape crisis center, and is included on a list of volunteers that is maintained by the rape crisis center.

(d)   A "victim" is a person who consults a sexual assault counselor or a trained volunteer for the purpose of securing advice, counseling, or assistance concerning a mental, physical, or emotional condition caused by a sexual assault or sexual battery, an alleged sexual assault or sexual battery, or an attempted sexual assault or sexual battery.

(e)   A communication between a sexual assault counselor or trained volunteer and a victim is "confidential" if it is not intended to be disclosed to third persons other than:

1.   Those persons present to further the interest of the victim in the consultation, examination, or interview.

2.   Those persons necessary for the transmission of the communication.

3.   Those persons to whom disclosure is reasonably necessary to accomplish the purposes for which the sexual assault counselor or the trained volunteer is consulted.

(2)   A victim has a privilege to refuse to disclose, and to prevent any other person from disclosing, a confidential communication made by the victim to a sexual assault counselor or trained volunteer or any record made in the course of advising, counseling, or assisting the victim. Such confidential communication or record may be disclosed only with

the prior written consent of the victim. This privilege includes any advice given by the sexual assault counselor or trained volunteer in the course of that relationship.

(3)   The privilege may be claimed by:

(a)   The victim or the victim's attorney on his or her behalf.

(b)   A guardian or conservator of the victim.

(c)   The personal representative of a deceased victim.

(d)   The sexual assault counselor or trained volunteer, but only on behalf of the victim. The authority of a sexual assault counselor or trained volunteer to claim the privilege is presumed in the absence of evidence to the contrary.

History.—s. 1, ch. 83-284; s. 476, ch. 95-147; s. 1, ch. 2002-246.

90.5036   Domestic violence advocate-victim privilege.—

(1)   For purposes of this section:

(a)   A "domestic violence center" is any public or private agency that offers assistance to victims of domestic violence, as defined in s. 741.28, and their families.

(b)   A "domestic violence advocate" means any employee or volunteer who has 30 hours of training in assisting victims of domestic violence and is an employee of or volunteer for a program for victims of domestic violence whose primary purpose is the rendering of advice, counseling, or assistance to victims of domestic violence.

(c)   A "victim" is a person who consults a domestic violence advocate for the purpose of securing advice, counseling, or assistance concerning a mental, physical, or emotional condition caused by an act of domestic violence, an alleged act of domestic violence, or an attempted act of domestic violence.

(d)   A communication between a domestic violence advocate and a victim is "confidential" if it relates to the incident of domestic violence for which the victim is seeking assistance and if it is not intended to be disclosed to third persons other than:

1.   Those persons present to further the interest of the victim in the consultation, assessment, or interview.

2.   Those persons to whom disclosure is reasonably necessary to accomplish the purpose for which the domestic violence advocate is consulted.

(2)   A victim has a privilege to refuse to disclose, and to prevent any other person from disclosing, a confidential communication made by the victim to a domestic violence advocate or any record made in the course of advising, counseling, or assisting the victim. The privilege applies to confidential communications made between the victim and the domestic violence advocate and to records of those communications only if the advocate is registered under s. 39.905 at the time the communication is made. This privilege includes any advice given by the domestic violence advocate in the course of that relationship.

(3)   The privilege may be claimed by:

(a)   The victim or the victim's attorney on behalf of the victim.

(b)   A guardian or conservator of the victim.

(c)   The personal representative of a deceased victim.

(d)   The domestic violence advocate, but only on behalf of the victim. The authority of a domestic violence advocate to claim the privilege is presumed in the absence of evidence to the contrary.

History.—s. 7, ch. 95-187; s. 127, ch. 98-403.

90.504   Husband-wife privilege.—

(1)   A spouse has a privilege during and after the marital relationship to refuse to disclose, and to prevent another from disclosing, communications which were intended to be made in confidence between the spouses while they were husband and wife.

(2)   The privilege may be claimed by either spouse or by the guardian or conservator of a spouse. The authority of a spouse, or guardian or conservator of a spouse, to claim the privilege is presumed in the absence of contrary evidence.

(3)   There is no privilege under this section:

(a)   In a proceeding brought by or on behalf of one spouse against the other spouse.

(b)   In a criminal proceeding in which one spouse is charged with a crime committed at any time against the person or property of the other spouse, or the person or property of a child of either.

(c)   In a criminal proceeding in which the communication is offered in evidence by a defendant-spouse who is one of the spouses between whom the communication was made.

History.—s. 1, ch. 76-237; s. 1, ch. 77-77; ss. 10, 22, ch. 78-361; ss. 1, 2, ch. 78-379.

90.505   Privilege with respect to communications to clergy.—

(1)   For the purposes of this section:

(a)   A "member of the clergy" is a priest, rabbi, practitioner of Christian Science, or minister of any religious organization or denomination usually referred to as a church, or an individual reasonably believed so to be by the person consulting him or her.

(b)   A communication between a member of the clergy and a person is "confidential" if made privately for the purpose of seeking spiritual counsel and advice from the member of the clergy in the usual course of his or her practice or discipline and not intended for further disclosure except to other persons present in furtherance of the communication.

(2)   A person has a privilege to refuse to disclose, and to prevent another from disclosing, a confidential communication by the person to a member of the clergy in his or her capacity as spiritual adviser.

(3)   The privilege may be claimed by:

(a)   The person.

(b)   The guardian or conservator of a person.

(c)   The personal representative of a deceased person.

(d)   The member of the clergy, on behalf of the person. The member of the clergy's authority to do so is presumed in the absence of evidence to the contrary.

History.—s. 1, ch. 76-237; s. 1, ch. 77-77; s. 1, ch. 77-174; ss. 11, 22, ch. 78-361; ss. 1, 2, ch. 78-379; s. 477, ch. 95-147.

90.5055   Accountant-client privilege.—

(1)   For purposes of this section:

(a)   An "accountant" is a certified public accountant or a public accountant.

(b)   A "client" is any person, public officer, corporation, association, or other organization or entity, either public or private, who consults an accountant with the purpose of obtaining accounting services.

(c)   A communication between an accountant and the accountant's client is "confidential" if it is not intended to be disclosed to third persons other than:

1.   Those to whom disclosure is in furtherance of the rendition of accounting services to the client.

2.   Those reasonably necessary for the transmission of the communication.

(2)   A client has a privilege to refuse to disclose, and to prevent any other person from disclosing, the contents of confidential communications with an accountant when such other person learned of the communications because they were made in the rendition of accounting services to the client. This privilege includes other confidential information obtained by the accountant from the client for the purpose of rendering accounting advice.

(3)   The privilege may be claimed by:

(a)   The client.

(b)   A guardian or conservator of the client.

(c)   The personal representative of a deceased client.

(d) A successor, assignee, trustee in dissolution, or any similar representative of an organization, corporation, or association or other entity, either public or private, whether or not in existence.

(e) The accountant, but only on behalf of the client. The accountant's authority to claim the privilege is presumed in the absence of contrary evidence.

(4) There is no accountant-client privilege under this section when:

(a) The services of the accountant were sought or obtained to enable or aid anyone to commit or plan to commit what the client knew or should have known was a crime or fraud.

(b) A communication is relevant to an issue of breach of duty by the accountant to the accountant's client or by the client to his or her accountant.

(c) A communication is relevant to a matter of common interest between two or more clients, if the communication was made by any of them to an accountant retained or consulted in common when offered in a civil action between the clients.

History.—s. 12, ch. 78-361; s. 2, ch. 78-379; s. 478, ch. 95-147.

90.506 Privilege with respect to trade secrets.—A person has a privilege to refuse to disclose, and to prevent other persons from disclosing, a trade secret owned by that person if the allowance of the privilege will not conceal fraud or otherwise work injustice. When the court directs disclosure, it shall take the protective measures that the interests of the holder of the privilege, the interests of the parties, and the furtherance of justice require. The privilege may be claimed by the person or the person's agent or employee.

History.—s. 1, ch. 76-237; s. 1, ch. 77-77; s. 22, ch. 78-361; s. 1, ch. 78-379; s. 479, ch. 95-147.

90.507 Waiver of privilege by voluntary disclosure.—A person who has a privilege against the disclosure of a confidential matter or communication waives the privilege if the person, or the person's predecessor while holder of the privilege, voluntarily discloses or makes the communication when he or she does not have a reasonable expectation of privacy, or consents to disclosure of, any significant part of the matter or communication. This section is not applicable when the disclosure is itself a privileged communication.

History.—s. 1, ch. 76-237; s. 1, ch. 77-77; ss. 13, 22, ch. 78-361; ss. 1, 2, ch. 78-379; s. 480, ch. 95-147.

90.508 Privileged matter disclosed under compulsion or without opportunity to claim privilege.—Evidence of a statement or other disclosure of privileged matter is inadmissible against the holder of the privilege if the statement or disclosure was compelled erroneously by the court or made without opportunity to claim the privilege.

History.—s. 1, ch. 76-237; s. 1, ch. 77-77; s. 22, ch. 78-361; s. 1, ch. 78-379.

90.509 Application of privileged communication.—Nothing in this act shall abrogate a privilege for any communication which was made prior to July 1, 1979, if such communication was privileged at the time it was made.

History.—s. 1, ch. 76-237; s. 1, ch. 77-77; s. 22, ch. 78-361; s. 1, ch. 78-379; s. 41, ch. 81-259.

90.510   Privileged communication necessary to adverse party.—In any civil case or proceeding in which a party claims a privilege as to a communication necessary to an adverse party, the court, upon motion, may dismiss the claim for relief or the affirmative defense to which the privileged testimony would relate. In making its determination, the court may engage in an in camera inquiry into the privilege.

History.—s. 1, ch. 76-237; s. 1, ch. 77-77; s. 22, ch. 78-361; s. 1, ch. 78-379.

90.601   General rule of competency.—Every person is competent to be a witness, except as otherwise provided by statute.

History.—s. 1, ch. 76-237; s. 1, ch. 77-77; s. 22, ch. 78-361, s. 1, ch. 78-379.

90.603   Disqualification of witness.—A person is disqualified to testify as a witness when the court determines that the person is:

(1)   Incapable of expressing himself or herself concerning the matter in such a manner as to be understood, either directly or through interpretation by one who can understand him or her.

(2)   Incapable of understanding the duty of a witness to tell the truth.

History.—s. 1, ch. 76-237; s. 1, ch. 77-77; s. 22, ch. 78-361; s. 1, ch. 78-379; s. 482, ch. 95-147.

90.604   Lack of personal knowledge.—Except as otherwise provided in s. 90.702, a witness may not testify to a matter unless evidence is introduced which is sufficient to support a finding that the witness has personal knowledge of the matter. Evidence to prove personal knowledge may be given by the witness's own testimony.

History.—s. 1, ch. 76-237; s. 1, ch. 77-77; s. 22, ch. 78-361; s. 1, ch. 78-379; s. 483, ch. 95-147.

90.605   Oath or affirmation of witness.—

(1)   Before testifying, each witness shall declare that he or she will testify truthfully, by taking an oath or affirmation in substantially the following form: "Do you swear or affirm that the evidence you are about to give will be the truth, the whole truth, and nothing but the truth?" The witness's answer shall be noted in the record.

(2)   In the court's discretion, a child may testify without taking the oath if the court determines the child understands the duty to tell the truth or the duty not to lie.

History.—s. 1, ch. 76-237; s. 1, ch. 77-77; s. 22, ch. 78-361; s. 1, ch. 78-379; s. 3, ch. 85-53; s. 484, ch. 95-147.

90.606   Interpreters and translators.—

(1)   (a)   When a judge determines that a witness cannot hear or understand the English language, or cannot express himself or herself in English sufficiently to be understood, an interpreter who is duly qualified to interpret for the witness shall be sworn to do so.

(b)   This section is not limited to persons who speak a language other than English, but applies also to the language and descriptions of any person, such as a child or a person who is mentally or developmentally disabled, who cannot be reasonably understood, or who cannot understand questioning, without the aid of an interpreter.

(2)   A person who serves in the role of interpreter or translator in any action or proceeding is subject to all the provisions of this chapter relating to witnesses.

(3)   An interpreter shall take an oath that he or she will make a true interpretation of the questions asked and the answers given and that the interpreter will make a true translation into English of any writing which he or she is required by his or her duties to decipher or translate.

History.—s. 1, ch. 76-237; s. 1, ch. 77-77; s. 22, ch. 78-361; s. 1, ch. 78-379; s. 2, ch. 85-53; s. 485, ch. 95-147.

90.6063   Interpreter services for deaf persons.—

(1)   The Legislature finds that it is an important concern that the rights of deaf citizens be protected. It is the intent of the Legislature to ensure that appropriate and effective interpreter services be made available to Florida's deaf citizens.

(2)   In all judicial proceedings and in sessions of a grand jury wherein a deaf person is a complainant, defendant, witness, or otherwise a party, or wherein a deaf person is a juror or grand juror, the court or presiding officer shall appoint a qualified interpreter to interpret the proceedings or deliberations to the deaf person and to interpret the deaf person's testimony, statements, or deliberations to the court, jury, or grand jury. A qualified interpreter shall be appointed, or other auxiliary aid provided as appropriate, for the duration of the trial or other proceeding in which a deaf juror or grand juror is seated.
(3)(a) "Deaf person" means any person whose hearing is so seriously impaired as to prohibit the person from understanding oral communications when spoken in a normal, conversational tone.

(b)   For the purposes of this section, the term "qualified interpreter" means an interpreter certified by the National Registry of Interpreters for the Deaf or the Florida Registry of Interpreters for the Deaf or an interpreter whose qualifications are otherwise determined by the appointing authority.

(4)   Every deaf person whose appearance before a proceeding entitles him or her to an interpreter shall notify the appointing authority of his or her disability not less than 5 days prior to any appearance and shall request at such time the services of an interpreter. Whenever a deaf person receives notification of the time of an appearance before a proceeding less than 5 days prior to the proceeding, the deaf person shall provide his or her notification and request as soon thereafter as practicable. In any case, nothing in this subsection shall operate to relieve an appointing authority's duty to provide an interpreter

for a deaf person so entitled, and failure to strictly comply with the notice requirement will not be deemed a waiver of the right to an interpreter. An appointing authority may require a person requesting the appointment of an interpreter to furnish reasonable proof of the person's disability when the appointing authority has reason to believe that the person is not so disabled.

(5)   The appointing authority may channel requests for qualified interpreters through:

(a)   The Florida Registry of Interpreters for the Deaf;

(b)   The Division of Vocational Rehabilitation of the Department of Education; or

(c)   Any other resource wherein the appointing authority knows that qualified interpreters can be found.

(6)   No qualified interpreter shall be appointed unless the appointing authority and the deaf person make a preliminary determination that the interpreter is able to communicate readily with the deaf person and is able to repeat and translate statements to and from the deaf person accurately.

(7)   Before a qualified interpreter may participate in any proceedings subsequent to an appointment under the provisions of this act, such interpreter shall make an oath or affirmation that he or she will make a true interpretation in an understandable manner to the deaf person for whom the interpreter is appointed and that he or she will repeat the statements of the deaf person in the English language to the best of his or her skill and judgment. Whenever a deaf person communicates through an interpreter to any person under such circumstances that the communication would be privileged, and the recipient of the communication could not be compelled to testify as to the communication, this privilege shall apply to the interpreter.

(8)   An interpreter appointed by the court in a criminal matter or in a civil matter shall be entitled to a reasonable fee for such service, in addition to actual expenses for travel, to be paid out of general county funds.

History.—ss. 1, 2, 3, 4, 5, 7, 8, 9, ch. 80-155; s. 42, ch. 81-259; s. 1, ch. 90-123; s. 2, ch. 93-125; s. 486, ch. 95-147; s. 6, ch. 99-8; s. 18, ch. 2002-22.

90.607   Competency of certain persons as witnesses.—
(1)   (a)   Except as provided in paragraph (b), the judge presiding at the trial of an action is not competent to testify as a witness in that trial. An objection is not necessary to preserve the point.

(b)   By agreement of the parties, the trial judge may give evidence on a purely formal matter to facilitate the trial of the action.

(2)   (a)   A member of the jury is not competent to testify as a witness in a trial when he or she is sitting as a juror. If the juror is called to testify, the opposing party shall be given an opportunity to object out of the presence of the jury.

(b)   Upon an inquiry into the validity of a verdict or indictment, a juror is not competent to testify as to any matter which essentially inheres in the verdict or indictment.

History.—s. 1, ch. 76-237; s. 1, ch. 77-77; s. 22, ch. 78-361; s. 1, ch. 78-379; s. 487, ch. 95-147.

90.608   Who may impeach.—Any party, including the party calling the witness, may attack the credibility of a witness by:

(1)   Introducing statements of the witness which are inconsistent with the witness's present testimony.

(2)   Showing that the witness is biased.

(3)   Attacking the character of the witness in accordance with the provisions of s. 90.609 or s. 90.610.

(4)   Showing a defect of capacity, ability, or opportunity in the witness to observe, remember, or recount the matters about which the witness testified.

(5)   Proof by other witnesses that material facts are not as testified to by the witness being impeached.

History.—s. 1, ch. 76-237; s. 1, ch. 77-77; ss. 14, 22, ch. 78-361; ss. 1, 2, ch. 78-379; s. 1, ch. 90-174; s. 488, ch. 95-147.

90.609   Character of witness as impeachment.—A party may attack or support the credibility of a witness, including an accused, by evidence in the form of reputation, except that:

(1)   The evidence may refer only to character relating to truthfulness.

(2)   Evidence of a truthful character is admissible only after the character of the witness for truthfulness has been attacked by reputation evidence.

History.—s. 1, ch. 76-237; s. 1, ch. 77-77; ss. 15, 22, ch. 78-361; ss. 1, 2, ch. 78-379.

90.610   Conviction of certain crimes as impeachment.—

(1)   A party may attack the credibility of any witness, including an accused, by evidence that the witness has been convicted of a crime if the crime was punishable by death or imprisonment in excess of 1 year under the law under which the witness was convicted, or if the crime involved dishonesty or a false statement regardless of the punishment, with the following exceptions:

(a)   Evidence of any such conviction is inadmissible in a civil trial if it is so remote in time as to have no bearing on the present character of the witness.

(b)   Evidence of juvenile adjudications are inadmissible under this subsection.

Florida Evidence Code

(2)   The pendency of an appeal or the granting of a pardon relating to such crime does not render evidence of the conviction from which the appeal was taken or for which the pardon was granted inadmissible. Evidence of the pendency of the appeal is admissible.

(3)   Nothing in this section affects the admissibility of evidence under s. 90.404 or s. 90.608.

History.—s. 1, ch. 76-237; s. 1, ch. 77-77; ss. 16, 22, ch. 78-361; ss. 1, 2, ch. 78-379; s. 489, ch. 95-147.

90.611   Religious beliefs or opinions.—Evidence of the beliefs or opinions of a witness on matters of religion is inadmissible to show that the witness's credibility is impaired or enhanced thereby.

History.—s. 1, ch. 76-237; s. 1, ch. 77-77; s. 22, ch. 78-361; s. 1, ch. 78-379; s. 490, ch. 95-147.

90.612   Mode and order of interrogation and presentation.—

(1)   The judge shall exercise reasonable control over the mode and order of the interrogation of witnesses and the presentation of evidence, so as to:

(a)   Facilitate, through effective interrogation and presentation, the discovery of the truth.

(b)   Avoid needless consumption of time.

(c)   Protect witnesses from harassment or undue embarrassment.

(2)   Cross-examination of a witness is limited to the subject matter of the direct examination and matters affecting the credibility of the witness. The court may, in its discretion, permit inquiry into additional matters.

(3)   Leading questions should not be used on the direct examination of a witness except as may be necessary to develop the witness's testimony. Ordinarily, leading questions should be permitted on cross-examination. When a party calls a hostile witness, an adverse party, or a witness identified with an adverse party, interrogation may be by leading questions.

The judge shall take special care to protect a witness under age 14 from questions that are in a form that cannot reasonably be understood by a person of the age and understanding of the witness, and shall take special care to restrict the unnecessary repetition of questions.

History.—s. 1, ch. 76-237; s. 1, ch. 77-77; s. 22, ch. 78-361; s. 1, ch. 78-379; s. 1, ch. 95-179; s. 2, ch. 2000-316.

90.613   Refreshing the memory of a witness.—When a witness uses a writing or other item to refresh memory while testifying, an adverse party is entitled to have such writing or other item produced at the hearing, to inspect it, to cross-examine the witness thereon, and to introduce it, or, in the case of a writing, to introduce those portions which relate to the testimony of the witness, in evidence. If it is claimed that the writing contains matters not related to the subject matter of the testimony, the judge shall examine the writing in camera, excise any portions not so related, and order delivery of the remainder to the party entitled thereto. Any portion withheld over objection shall be preserved and made available to the appellate court in the event of an appeal. If a writing or other item is not produced or delivered pursuant to order under this section, the testimony of the witness concerning those matters shall be stricken.

History.—s. 1, ch. 76-237; s. 1, ch. 77-77; s. 22, ch. 78-361; s. 1, ch. 78-379; s. 491, ch. 95-147.

90.614   Prior statements of witnesses.—

(1)   When a witness is examined concerning the witness's prior written statement or concerning an oral statement that has been reduced to writing, the court, on motion of the adverse party, shall order the statement to be shown to the witness or its contents disclosed to him or her.

(2)   Extrinsic evidence of a prior inconsistent statement by a witness is inadmissible unless the witness is first afforded an opportunity to explain or deny the prior statement and the opposing party is afforded an opportunity to interrogate the witness on it, or the interests of justice otherwise require. If a witness denies making or does not distinctly admit making the prior inconsistent statement, extrinsic evidence of such statement is admissible. This subsection is not applicable to admissions of a party-opponent as defined in s. 90.803(18).

History.—s. 1, ch. 76-237; s. 1, ch. 77-77; ss. 17, 22, ch. 78-361; ss. 1, 2, ch. 78-379; s. 492, ch. 95-147.

90.615   Calling witnesses by the court.—

(1)   The court may call witnesses whom all parties may cross-examine.

(2)   When required by the interests of justice, the court may interrogate witnesses, whether called by the court or by a party.

History.—s. 1, ch. 76-237; s. 1, ch. 77-77; s. 22, ch. 78-361; s. 1, ch. 78-379.

90.616   Exclusion of witnesses.—

(1)   At the request of a party the court shall order, or upon its own motion the court may order, witnesses excluded from a proceeding so that they cannot hear the testimony of other witnesses except as provided in subsection (2).

(2)   A witness may not be excluded if the witness is:

(a)   A party who is a natural person.

(b)   In a civil case, an officer or employee of a party that is not a natural person. The party's attorney shall designate the officer or employee who shall be the party's representative.

(c)   A person whose presence is shown by the party's attorney to be essential to the presentation of the party's cause.

(d)   In a criminal case, the victim of the crime, the victim's next of kin, the parent or guardian of a minor child victim, or a lawful representative of such person, unless, upon motion, the court determines such person's presence to be prejudicial.

History.—s. 2, ch. 90-174; s. 1, ch. 92-107; s. 493, ch. 95-147.

90.701   Opinion testimony of lay witnesses.—If a witness is not testifying as an expert, the witness's testimony about what he or she perceived may be in the form of inference and opinion when:

(1)   The witness cannot readily, and with equal accuracy and adequacy, communicate what he or she has perceived to the trier of fact without testifying in terms of inferences or opinions and the witness's use of inferences or opinions will not mislead the trier of fact to the prejudice of the objecting party; and

(2)   The opinions and inferences do not require a special knowledge, skill, experience, or training.

History.—s. 1, ch. 76-237; s. 1, ch. 77-77; s. 22, ch. 78-361; s. 1, ch. 78-379; s. 494, ch. 95-147.

90.702   Testimony by experts.—If scientific, technical, or other specialized knowledge will assist the trier of fact in understanding the evidence or in determining a fact in issue, a witness qualified as an expert by knowledge, skill, experience, training, or education may testify about it in the form of an opinion or otherwise, if:

(1)   The testimony is based upon sufficient facts or data;

(2)   The testimony is the product of reliable principles and methods; and

(3)   The witness has applied the principles and methods reliably to the facts of the case.

History.—s. 1, ch. 76-237; s. 1, ch. 77-77; s. 22, ch. 78-361; s. 1, ch. 78-379; s. 1, ch. 2013-107.

90.703   Opinion on ultimate issue.—Testimony in the form of an opinion or inference otherwise admissible is not objectionable because it includes an ultimate issue to be decided by the trier of fact.

History.—s. 1, ch. 76-237; s. 1, ch. 77-77; s. 22, ch. 78-361; s. 1, ch. 78-379.

90.704   Basis of opinion testimony by experts.—The facts or data upon which an expert bases an opinion or inference may be those perceived by, or made known to, the expert at or before the trial. If the facts or data are of a type reasonably relied upon by experts in the subject to support the opinion expressed, the facts or data need not be admissible in evidence. Facts or data that are otherwise inadmissible may not be disclosed to the jury by the proponent of the opinion or inference unless the court determines that their probative value in assisting the jury to evaluate the expert's opinion substantially outweighs their prejudicial effect.

History.—s. 1, ch. 76-237; s. 1, ch. 77-77; s. 22, ch. 78-361; s. 1, ch. 78-379; s. 495, ch. 95-147; s. 2, ch. 2013-107.

90.705   Disclosure of facts or data underlying expert opinion.—

(1)   Unless otherwise required by the court, an expert may testify in terms of opinion or inferences and give reasons without prior disclosure of the underlying facts or data. On cross-examination the expert shall be required to specify the facts or data.

(2)   Prior to the witness giving the opinion, a party against whom the opinion or inference is offered may conduct a voir dire examination of the witness directed to the underlying facts or data for the witness's opinion. If the party establishes prima facie evidence that the expert does not have a sufficient basis for the opinion, the opinions and inferences of the expert are inadmissible unless the party offering the testimony establishes the underlying facts or data.

History.—s. 1, ch. 76-237; s. 1, ch. 77-77; s. 22, ch. 78-361; s. 1, ch. 78-379; s. 496, ch. 95-147.

90.706   Authoritativeness of literature for use in cross-examination.—Statements of facts or opinions on a subject of science, art, or specialized knowledge contained in a published treatise, periodical, book, dissertation, pamphlet, or other writing may be used in cross-examination of an expert witness if the expert witness recognizes the author or the treatise, periodical, book, dissertation, pamphlet, or other writing to be authoritative, or, notwithstanding nonrecognition by the expert witness, if the trial court finds the author or the treatise, periodical, book, dissertation, pamphlet, or other writing to be authoritative and relevant to the subject matter.

History.—s. 18, ch. 78-361; s. 2, ch. 78-379.

90.801   Hearsay; definitions; exceptions.—

(1)   The following definitions apply under this chapter:

(a)   A "statement" is:

1.   An oral or written assertion; or

2.   Nonverbal conduct of a person if it is intended by the person as an assertion.

(b)   A "declarant" is a person who makes a statement.

(c)   "Hearsay" is a statement, other than one made by the declarant while testifying at the trial or hearing, offered in evidence to prove the truth of the matter asserted.

(2)   A statement is not hearsay if the declarant testifies at the trial or hearing and is subject to cross-examination concerning the statement and the statement is:

(a)   Inconsistent with the declarant's testimony and was given under oath subject to the penalty of perjury at a trial, hearing, or other proceeding or in a deposition;

Florida Evidence Code

(b) Consistent with the declarant's testimony and is offered to rebut an express or implied charge against the declarant of improper influence, motive, or recent fabrication; or

(c) One of identification of a person made after perceiving the person.

History.—s. 1, ch. 76-237; s. 1, ch. 77-77; ss. 19, 22, ch. 78-361; ss. 1, 2, ch. 78-379; s. 2, ch. 81-93; s. 497, ch. 95-147.

90.802   Hearsay rule.—Except as provided by statute, hearsay evidence is inadmissible.

History.—s. 1, ch. 76-237; s. 1, ch. 77-77; s. 22, ch. 78-361; s. 1, ch. 78-379.

90.803   Hearsay exceptions; availability of declarant immaterial.—The provision of s. 90.802 to the contrary notwithstanding, the following are not inadmissible as evidence, even though the declarant is available as a witness:

(1) SPONTANEOUS STATEMENT.—A spontaneous statement describing or explaining an event or condition made while the declarant was perceiving the event or condition, or immediately thereafter, except when such statement is made under circumstances that indicate its lack of trustworthiness.

(2) EXCITED UTTERANCE.—A statement or excited utterance relating to a startling event or condition made while the declarant was under the stress of excitement caused by the event or condition.

(3) THEN-EXISTING MENTAL, EMOTIONAL, OR PHYSICAL CONDITION.—

(a) A statement of the declarant's then-existing state of mind, emotion, or physical sensation, including a statement of intent, plan, motive, design, mental feeling, pain, or bodily health, when such evidence is offered to:

1. Prove the declarant's state of mind, emotion, or physical sensation at that time or at any other time when such state is an issue in the action.

2. Prove or explain acts of subsequent conduct of the declarant.

(b) However, this subsection does not make admissible:

1. An after-the-fact statement of memory or belief to prove the fact remembered or believed, unless such statement relates to the execution, revocation, identification, or terms of the declarant's will.

2. A statement made under circumstances that indicate its lack of trustworthiness.

(4) STATEMENTS FOR PURPOSES OF MEDICAL DIAGNOSIS OR TREATMENT.—Statements made for purposes of medical diagnosis or treatment by a person seeking the diagnosis or treatment, or made by an individual who has knowledge of the facts and is legally responsible for the person who is unable to communicate the facts,

which statements describe medical history, past or present symptoms, pain, or sensations, or the inceptions or general character of the cause or external source thereof, insofar as reasonably pertinent to diagnosis or treatment.

(5)   RECORDED RECOLLECTION.—A memorandum or record concerning a matter about which a witness once had knowledge, but now has insufficient recollection to enable the witness to testify fully and accurately, shown to have been made by the witness when the matter was fresh in the witness's memory and to reflect that knowledge correctly. A party may read into evidence a memorandum or record when it is admitted, but no such memorandum or record is admissible as an exhibit unless offered by an adverse party.

(6)   RECORDS OF REGULARLY CONDUCTED BUSINESS ACTIVITY.—

(a)   A memorandum, report, record, or data compilation, in any form, of acts, events, conditions, opinion, or diagnosis, made at or near the time by, or from information transmitted by, a person with knowledge, if kept in the course of a regularly conducted business activity and if it was the regular practice of that business activity to make such memorandum, report, record, or data compilation, all as shown by the testimony of the custodian or other qualified witness, or as shown by a certification or declaration that complies with paragraph (c) and s. 90.902(11), unless the sources of information or other circumstances show lack of trustworthiness. The term "business" as used in this paragraph includes a business, institution, association, profession, occupation, and calling of every kind, whether or not conducted for profit.

(b)   Evidence in the form of an opinion or diagnosis is inadmissible under paragraph (a) unless such opinion or diagnosis would be admissible under ss. 90.701-90.705 if the person whose opinion is recorded were to testify to the opinion directly.

(c)   A party intending to offer evidence under paragraph (a) by means of a certification or declaration shall serve reasonable written notice of that intention upon every other party and shall make the evidence available for inspection sufficiently in advance of its offer in evidence to provide to any other party a fair opportunity to challenge the admissibility of the evidence. If the evidence is maintained in a foreign country, the party intending to offer the evidence must provide written notice of that intention at the arraignment or as soon after the arraignment as is practicable or, in a civil case, 60 days before the trial. A motion opposing the admissibility of such evidence must be made by the opposing party and determined by the court before trial. A party's failure to file such a motion before trial constitutes a waiver of objection to the evidence, but the court for good cause shown may grant relief from the waiver.

(7)   ABSENCE OF ENTRY IN RECORDS OF REGULARLY CONDUCTED ACTIVITY.—Evidence that a matter is not included in the memoranda, reports, records, or data compilations, in any form, of a regularly conducted activity to prove the nonoccurrence or nonexistence of the matter, if the matter was of a kind of which a memorandum, report, record, or data compilation was regularly made and preserved, unless the sources of information or other circumstances show lack of trustworthiness.

(8)   PUBLIC RECORDS AND REPORTS.—Records, reports, statements reduced to writing, or data compilations, in any form, of public offices or agencies, setting forth the activities of the office or agency, or matters observed pursuant to duty imposed by law as to matters which there was a duty to report, excluding in criminal cases matters observed by a police officer or other law enforcement personnel, unless the sources of information or

other circumstances show their lack of trustworthiness. The criminal case exclusion shall not apply to an affidavit otherwise admissible under s. 316.1934 or s. 327.354.

(9) RECORDS OF VITAL STATISTICS.—Records or data compilations, in any form, of births, fetal deaths, deaths, or marriages, if a report was made to a public office pursuant to requirements of law. However, nothing in this section shall be construed to make admissible any other marriage of any party to any cause of action except for the purpose of impeachment as set forth in s. 90.610.

(10) ABSENCE OF PUBLIC RECORD OR ENTRY.—Evidence, in the form of a certification in accord with s. 90.902, or in the form of testimony, that diligent search failed to disclose a record, report, statement, or data compilation or entry, when offered to prove the absence of the record, report, statement, or data compilation or the nonoccurrence or nonexistence of a matter of which a record, report, statement, or data compilation would regularly have been made and preserved by a public office and agency.

(11) RECORDS OF RELIGIOUS ORGANIZATIONS.—Statements of births, marriages, divorces, deaths, parentage, ancestry, relationship by blood or marriage, or other similar facts of personal or family history contained in a regularly kept record of a religious organization.

(12) MARRIAGE, BAPTISMAL, AND SIMILAR CERTIFICATES.—Statements of facts contained in a certificate that the maker performed a marriage or other ceremony or administered a sacrament, when such statement was certified by a member of the clergy, public official, or other person authorized by the rules or practices of a religious organization or by law to perform the act certified, and when such certificate purports to have been issued at the time of the act or within a reasonable time thereafter.

(13) FAMILY RECORDS.—Statements of fact concerning personal or family history in family Bibles, charts, engravings in rings, inscriptions on family portraits, engravings on urns, crypts, or tombstones, or the like.

(14) RECORDS OF DOCUMENTS AFFECTING AN INTEREST IN PROPERTY.—The record of a document purporting to establish or affect an interest in property, as proof of the contents of the original recorded or filed document and its execution and delivery by each person by whom it purports to have been executed, if the record is a record of a public office and an applicable statute authorized the recording or filing of the document in the office.

(15) STATEMENTS IN DOCUMENTS AFFECTING AN INTEREST IN PROPERTY.—A statement contained in a document purporting to establish or affect an interest in property, if the matter stated was relevant to the purpose of the document, unless dealings with the property since the document was made have been inconsistent with the truth of the statement or the purport of the document.

(16) STATEMENTS IN ANCIENT DOCUMENTS.—Statements in a document in existence 20 years or more, the authenticity of which is established.

(17) MARKET REPORTS, COMMERCIAL PUBLICATIONS.—Market quotations, tabulations, lists, directories, or other published compilations, generally used and relied upon by the public or by persons in particular occupations if, in the opinion of the

court, the sources of information and method of preparation were such as to justify their admission.

(18) ADMISSIONS.—A statement that is offered against a party and is:

(a)   The party's own statement in either an individual or a representative capacity;

(b)   A statement of which the party has manifested an adoption or belief in its truth;

(c)   A statement by a person specifically authorized by the party to make a statement concerning the subject;

(d)   A statement by the party's agent or servant concerning a matter within the scope of the agency or employment thereof, made during the existence of the relationship; or

(e)   A statement by a person who was a coconspirator of the party during the course, and in furtherance, of the conspiracy. Upon request of counsel, the court shall instruct the jury that the conspiracy itself and each member's participation in it must be established by independent evidence, either before the introduction of any evidence or before evidence is admitted under this paragraph.

(19) REPUTATION CONCERNING PERSONAL OR FAMILY HISTORY.— Evidence of reputation:

(a)   Among members of a person's family by blood, adoption, or marriage;

(b)   Among a person's associates; or

(c)   In the community,
concerning a person's birth, adoption, marriage, divorce, death, relationship by blood, adoption, or marriage, ancestry, or other similar fact of personal or family history.

(20) REPUTATION CONCERNING BOUNDARIES OR GENERAL HISTORY.—Evidence of reputation:

(a)   In a community, arising before the controversy about the boundaries of, or customs affecting lands in, the community.

(b)   About events of general history which are important to the community, state, or nation where located.

(21) REPUTATION AS TO CHARACTER.—Evidence of reputation of a person's character among associates or in the community.

(22) FORMER TESTIMONY.—Former testimony given by the declarant which testimony was given as a witness at another hearing of the same or a different proceeding, or in a deposition taken in compliance with law in the course of the same or another proceeding, if the party against whom the testimony is now offered, or, in a civil action or proceeding, a predecessor in interest, or a person with a similar interest, had an opportunity

Florida Evidence Code

and similar motive to develop the testimony by direct, cross, or redirect examination; provided, however, the court finds that the testimony is not inadmissible pursuant to s. 90.402 or s. 90.403.

(23) HEARSAY EXCEPTION; STATEMENT OF CHILD VICTIM.—

[1](a) Unless the source of information or the method or circumstances by which the statement is reported indicates a lack of trustworthiness, an out-of-court statement made by a child victim with a physical, mental, emotional, or developmental age of 16 or less describing any act of child abuse or neglect, any act of sexual abuse against a child, the offense of child abuse, the offense of aggravated child abuse, or any offense involving an unlawful sexual act, contact, intrusion, or penetration performed in the presence of, with, by, or on the declarant child, not otherwise admissible, is admissible in evidence in any civil or criminal proceeding if:

1. The court finds in a hearing conducted outside the presence of the jury that the time, content, and circumstances of the statement provide sufficient safeguards of reliability. In making its determination, the court may consider the mental and physical age and maturity of the child, the nature and duration of the abuse or offense, the relationship of the child to the offender, the reliability of the assertion, the reliability of the child victim, and any other factor deemed appropriate; and

2. The child either:

a. Testifies; or

b. Is unavailable as a witness, provided that there is other corroborative evidence of the abuse or offense. Unavailability shall include a finding by the court that the child's participation in the trial or proceeding would result in a substantial likelihood of severe emotional or mental harm, in addition to findings pursuant to s. 90.804(1).

(b) In a criminal action, the defendant shall be notified no later than 10 days before trial that a statement which qualifies as a hearsay exception pursuant to this subsection will be offered as evidence at trial. The notice shall include a written statement of the content of the child's statement, the time at which the statement was made, the circumstances surrounding the statement which indicate its reliability, and such other particulars as necessary to provide full disclosure of the statement.

(c) The court shall make specific findings of fact, on the record, as to the basis for its ruling under this subsection.

(24) HEARSAY EXCEPTION; STATEMENT OF ELDERLY PERSON OR DISABLED ADULT.—

(a) Unless the source of information or the method or circumstances by which the statement is reported indicates a lack of trustworthiness, an out-of-court statement made by an elderly person or disabled adult, as defined in s. 825.101, describing any act of abuse or neglect, any act of exploitation, the offense of battery or aggravated battery or assault or aggravated assault or sexual battery, or any other violent act on the declarant elderly person or disabled adult, not otherwise admissible, is admissible in evidence in any civil or criminal proceeding if:

         1.   The court finds in a hearing conducted outside the presence of the jury that the time, content, and circumstances of the statement provide sufficient safeguards of reliability. In making its determination, the court may consider the mental and physical age and maturity of the elderly person or disabled adult, the nature and duration of the abuse or offense, the relationship of the victim to the offender, the reliability of the assertion, the reliability of the elderly person or disabled adult, and any other factor deemed appropriate; and

         2.   The elderly person or disabled adult either:

         a.   Testifies; or

         b.   Is unavailable as a witness, provided that there is corroborative evidence of the abuse or offense. Unavailability shall include a finding by the court that the elderly person's or disabled adult's participation in the trial or proceeding would result in a substantial likelihood of severe emotional, mental, or physical harm, in addition to findings pursuant to s. 90.804(1).

        (b)   In a criminal action, the defendant shall be notified no later than 10 days before the trial that a statement which qualifies as a hearsay exception pursuant to this subsection will be offered as evidence at trial. The notice shall include a written statement of the content of the elderly person's or disabled adult's statement, the time at which the statement was made, the circumstances surrounding the statement which indicate its reliability, and such other particulars as necessary to provide full disclosure of the statement.

        (c)   The court shall make specific findings of fact, on the record, as to the basis for its ruling under this subsection.

History.—s. 1, ch. 76-237; s. 1, ch. 77-77; s. 1, ch. 77-174; ss. 20, 22, ch. 78-361; ss. 1, 2, ch. 78-379; s. 4, ch. 85-53; s. 11, ch. 87-224; s. 2, ch. 90-139; s. 3, ch. 90-174; s. 12, ch. 91-255; s. 498, ch. 95-147; s. 1, ch. 95-158; s. 2, ch. 96-330; s. 1, ch. 98-2; s. 2, ch. 2003-259; s. 1, ch. 2013-98.

[1]Note.—Section 8, ch. 2013-98, provides in part that "before March 1, 2014, the Department of Law Enforcement or any other criminal justice agency is not required to comply with an order to expunge a criminal history record as required by this act."

90.804   Hearsay exceptions; declarant unavailable.—

        (1)   DEFINITION OF UNAVAILABILITY.—"Unavailability as a witness" means that the declarant:

        (a)   Is exempted by a ruling of a court on the ground of privilege from testifying concerning the subject matter of the declarant's statement;

        (b)   Persists in refusing to testify concerning the subject matter of the declarant's statement despite an order of the court to do so;

        (c)   Has suffered a lack of memory of the subject matter of his or her statement so as to destroy the declarant's effectiveness as a witness during the trial;

(d)   Is unable to be present or to testify at the hearing because of death or because of then-existing physical or mental illness or infirmity; or

(e)   Is absent from the hearing, and the proponent of a statement has been unable to procure the declarant's attendance or testimony by process or other reasonable means.

However, a declarant is not unavailable as a witness if such exemption, refusal, claim of lack of memory, inability to be present, or absence is due to the procurement or wrongdoing of the party who is the proponent of his or her statement in preventing the witness from attending or testifying.

(2)   HEARSAY EXCEPTIONS.—The following are not excluded under s. 90.802, provided that the declarant is unavailable as a witness:

(a)   Former testimony.—Testimony given as a witness at another hearing of the same or a different proceeding, or in a deposition taken in compliance with law in the course of the same or another proceeding, if the party against whom the testimony is now offered, or, in a civil action or proceeding, a predecessor in interest, had an opportunity and similar motive to develop the testimony by direct, cross, or redirect examination.

(b)   Statement under belief of impending death.—In a civil or criminal trial, a statement made by a declarant while reasonably believing that his or her death was imminent, concerning the physical cause or instrumentalities of what the declarant believed to be impending death or the circumstances surrounding impending death.

(c)   Statement against interest.—A statement which, at the time of its making, was so far contrary to the declarant's pecuniary or proprietary interest or tended to subject the declarant to liability or to render invalid a claim by the declarant against another, so that a person in the declarant's position would not have made the statement unless he or she believed it to be true. A statement tending to expose the declarant to criminal liability and offered to exculpate the accused is inadmissible, unless corroborating circumstances show the trustworthiness of the statement.

(d)   Statement of personal or family history.—A statement concerning the declarant's own birth, adoption, marriage, divorce, parentage, ancestry, or other similar fact of personal or family history, including relationship by blood, adoption, or marriage, even though the declarant had no means of acquiring personal knowledge of the matter stated.

(e)   Statement by deceased or ill declarant similar to one previously admitted.—In an action or proceeding brought against the personal representative, heir at law, assignee, legatee, devisee, or survivor of a deceased person, or against a trustee of a trust created by a deceased person, or against the assignee, committee, or guardian of a mentally incompetent person, when a declarant is unavailable as provided in paragraph (1)(d), a written or oral statement made regarding the same subject matter as another statement made by the declarant that has previously been offered by an adverse party and admitted in evidence.

(f)   Statement offered against a party that wrongfully caused the declarant's unavailability.—A statement offered against a party that wrongfully caused, or acquiesced

Florida Evidence Code

in wrongfully causing, the declarant's unavailability as a witness, and did so intending that result.

History.—s. 1, ch. 76-237; s. 1, ch. 77-77; s. 22, ch. 78-361; s. 1, ch. 78-379; s. 3, ch. 90-139; s. 4, ch. 90-174; s. 499, ch. 95-147; s. 2, ch. 2005-46; s. 1, ch. 2012-152.

90.805   Hearsay within hearsay.—Hearsay within hearsay is not excluded under s. 90.802, provided each part of the combined statements conforms with an exception to the hearsay rule as provided in s. 90.803 or s. 90.804.

History.—s. 1, ch. 76-237; s. 1, ch. 77-77; s. 22, ch. 78-361; s. 1, ch. 78-379.

90.806   Attacking and supporting credibility of declarant.—

(1)   When a hearsay statement has been admitted in evidence, credibility of the declarant may be attacked and, if attacked, may be supported by any evidence that would be admissible for those purposes if the declarant had testified as a witness. Evidence of a statement or conduct by the declarant at any time inconsistent with the declarant's hearsay statement is admissible, regardless of whether or not the declarant has been afforded an opportunity to deny or explain it.

(2)   If the party against whom a hearsay statement has been admitted calls the declarant as a witness, the party is entitled to examine the declarant on the statement as if under cross-examination.

History.—s. 1, ch. 76-237; s. 1, ch. 77-77; s. 22, ch. 78-361; s. 1, ch. 78-379; s. 500, ch. 95-147.

90.901   Requirement of authentication or identification.—Authentication or identification of evidence is required as a condition precedent to its admissibility. The requirements of this section are satisfied by evidence sufficient to support a finding that the matter in question is what its proponent claims.

History.—s. 1, ch. 76-237; s. 1, ch. 77-77; s. 22, ch. 78-361; s. 1, ch. 78-379.

90.902   Self-authentication.—Extrinsic evidence of authenticity as a condition precedent to admissibility is not required for:

(1)   A document bearing:

(a)   A seal purporting to be that of the United States or any state, district, commonwealth, territory, or insular possession thereof; the Panama Canal Zone; the Trust Territory of the Pacific Islands; or a court, political subdivision, department, officer, or agency of any of them; and

(b)   A signature by the custodian of the document attesting to the authenticity of the seal.

(2)   A document not bearing a seal but purporting to bear a signature of an officer or employee of any entity listed in subsection (1), affixed in the officer's or employee's official capacity.

(3)   An official foreign document, record, or entry that is:

(a)   Executed or attested to by a person in the person's official capacity authorized by the laws of a foreign country to make the execution or attestation; and

(b)   Accompanied by a final certification, as provided herein, of the genuineness of the signature and official position of:

1.   The executing person; or

2.   Any foreign official whose certificate of genuineness of signature and official position relates to the execution or attestation or is in a chain of certificates of genuineness of signature and official position relating to the execution or attestation.

The final certification may be made by a secretary of an embassy or legation, consul general, consul, vice consul, or consular agent of the United States or a diplomatic or consular official of the foreign country assigned or accredited to the United States. When the parties receive reasonable opportunity to investigate the authenticity and accuracy of official foreign documents, the court may order that they be treated as presumptively authentic without final certification or permit them in evidence by an attested summary with or without final certification.

(4)   A copy of an official public record, report, or entry, or of a document authorized by law to be recorded or filed and actually recorded or filed in a public office, including data compilations in any form, certified as correct by the custodian or other person authorized to make the certification by certificate complying with subsection (1), subsection (2), or subsection (3) or complying with any act of the Legislature or rule adopted by the Supreme Court.

(5)   Books, pamphlets, or other publications purporting to be issued by a governmental authority.

(6)   Printed materials purporting to be newspapers or periodicals.

(7)   Inscriptions, signs, tags, or labels purporting to have been affixed in the course of business and indicating ownership, control, or origin.

(8)   Commercial papers and signatures thereon and documents relating to them, to the extent provided in the Uniform Commercial Code.

(9)   Any signature, document, or other matter declared by the Legislature to be presumptively or prima facie genuine or authentic.

(10)   Any document properly certified under the law of the jurisdiction where the certification is made.

(11)   An original or a duplicate of evidence that would be admissible under s. 90.803(6), which is maintained in a foreign country or domestic location and is accompanied by a certification or declaration from the custodian of the records or another qualified person certifying or declaring that the record:

Florida Evidence Code

(a)   Was made at or near the time of the occurrence of the matters set forth by, or from information transmitted by, a person having knowledge of those matters;

(b)   Was kept in the course of the regularly conducted activity; and

(c)   Was made as a regular practice in the course of the regularly conducted activity,

provided that falsely making such a certification or declaration would subject the maker to criminal penalty under the laws of the foreign or domestic location in which the certification or declaration was signed.

History.—s. 1, ch. 76-237; s. 1, ch. 77-77; s. 1, ch. 77-174; s. 22, ch. 78-361; s. 1, ch. 78-379; s. 501, ch. 95-147; s. 3, ch. 2003-259.

90.903   Testimony of subscribing witness unnecessary.—The testimony of a subscribing witness is not necessary to authenticate a writing unless the statute requiring attestation requires it.

History.—s. 1, ch. 76-237; s. 1, ch. 77-77; s. 22, ch. 78-361; s. 1, ch. 78-379.

90.91   Photographs of property wrongfully taken; use in prosecution, procedure; return of property to owner.—In any prosecution for a crime involving the wrongful taking of property, a photograph of the property alleged to have been wrongfully taken may be deemed competent evidence of such property and may be admissible in the prosecution to the same extent as if such property were introduced as evidence. Such photograph shall bear a written description of the property alleged to have been wrongfully taken, the name of the owner of the property, the location where the alleged wrongful taking occurred, the name of the investigating law enforcement officer, the date the photograph was taken, and the name of the photographer. Such writing shall be made under oath by the investigating law enforcement officer, and the photograph shall be identified by the signature of the photographer. Upon the filing of such photograph and writing with the law enforcement authority or court holding such property as evidence, the property may be returned to the owner from whom the property was taken.

History.—s. 4, ch. 84-363.

90.951   Definitions.—For purposes of this chapter:

(1)   "Writings" and "recordings" include letters, words, or numbers, or their equivalent, set down by handwriting, typewriting, printing, photostating, photography, magnetic impulse, mechanical or electronic recording, or other form of data compilation, upon paper, wood, stone, recording tape, or other materials.

(2)   "Photographs" include still photographs, X-ray films, videotapes, and motion pictures.

(3)   An "original" of a writing or recording means the writing or recording itself, or any counterpart intended to have the same effect by a person executing or issuing it. An "original" of a photograph includes the negative or any print made from it. If data are stored in a computer or similar device, any printout or other output readable by sight and shown to reflect the data accurately is an "original."

Florida Evidence Code

(4) "Duplicate" includes:

(a) A counterpart produced by the same impression as the original, from the same matrix; by means of photography, including enlargements and miniatures; by mechanical or electronic rerecording; by chemical reproduction; or by other equivalent technique that accurately reproduces the original; or

(b) An executed carbon copy not intended by the parties to be an original.

History.—s. 1, ch. 76-237; s. 1, ch. 77-77; s. 22, ch. 78-361; s. 1, ch. 78-379.

90.952 Requirement of originals.—Except as otherwise provided by statute, an original writing, recording, or photograph is required in order to prove the contents of the writing, recording, or photograph.

History.—s. 1, ch. 76-237; s. 1, ch. 77-77; s. 1, ch. 77-174; s. 22, ch. 78-361; s. 1, ch. 78-379.

90.953 Admissibility of duplicates.—A duplicate is admissible to the same extent as an original, unless:

(1) The document or writing is a negotiable instrument as defined in s. 673.1041, a security as defined in s. 678.1021, or any other writing that evidences a right to the payment of money, is not itself a security agreement or lease, and is of a type that is transferred by delivery in the ordinary course of business with any necessary endorsement or assignment.

(2) A genuine question is raised about the authenticity of the original or any other document or writing.

(3) It is unfair, under the circumstance, to admit the duplicate in lieu of the original.

History.—s. 1, ch. 76-237; s. 1, ch. 77-77; s. 22, ch. 78-361; s. 1, ch. 78-379; s. 57, ch. 92-82; s. 29, ch. 99-2.

90.954 Admissibility of other evidence of contents.—The original of a writing, recording, or photograph is not required, except as provided in s. 90.953, and other evidence of its contents is admissible when:

(1) All originals are lost or destroyed, unless the proponent lost or destroyed them in bad faith.

(2) An original cannot be obtained in this state by any judicial process or procedure.

(3) An original was under the control of the party against whom offered at a time when that party was put on notice by the pleadings or by written notice from the adverse party that the contents of such original would be subject to proof at the hearing, and such original is not produced at the hearing.

(4) The writing, recording, or photograph is not related to a controlling issue.

History.—s. 1, ch. 76-237; s. 1, ch. 77-77; s. 1, ch. 77-174; s. 22, ch. 78-361; s. 1, ch. 78-379; s. 502, ch. 95-147.

90.955   Public records.—

(1)   The contents of an official record or of a document authorized to be recorded or filed, and actually recorded or filed, with a governmental agency, either federal, state, county, or municipal, in a place where official records or documents are ordinarily filed, including data compilations in any form, may be proved by a copy authenticated as provided in s. 90.902, if otherwise admissible.

(2)   If a party cannot obtain, by the exercise of reasonable diligence, a copy that complies with subsection (1), other evidence of the contents is admissible.

History.—s. 1, ch. 76-237; s. 1, ch. 77-77; s. 22, ch. 78-361; s. 1, ch. 78-379.

90.956   Summaries.—When it is not convenient to examine in court the contents of voluminous writings, recordings, or photographs, a party may present them in the form of a chart, summary, or calculation by calling a qualified witness. The party intending to use such a summary must give timely written notice of his or her intention to use the summary, proof of which shall be filed with the court, and shall make the summary and the originals or duplicates of the data from which the summary is compiled available for examination or copying, or both, by other parties at a reasonable time and place. A judge may order that they be produced in court.

History.—s. 1, ch. 76-237; s. 1, ch. 77-77; s. 22, ch. 78-361; s. 1, ch. 78-379; s. 503, ch. 95-147.

90.957   Testimony or written admissions of a party.—A party may prove the contents of writings, recordings, or photographs by the testimony or deposition of the party against whom they are offered or by that party's written admission, without accounting for the nonproduction of the original.

History.—s. 1, ch. 76-237; s. 1, ch. 77-77; s. 22, ch. 78-361; s. 1, ch. 78-379; s. 504, ch. 95-147.

90.958   Functions of court and jury.—

(1)   Except as provided in subsection (2), when the admissibility under this chapter of other evidence of the contents of writings, recordings, or photographs depends upon the existence of a preliminary fact, the question as to whether the preliminary fact exists is for the court to determine.

(2)   The trier of fact shall determine whether:

(a)   The asserted writing ever existed.

(b)   Another writing, recording, or photograph produced at the trial is the original.

(c)   Other evidence of the contents correctly reflects the contents.

History.—s. 1, ch. 76-237; s. 1, ch. 77-77; s. 22, ch. 78-361; s. 1, ch. 78-379.

Florida Evidence Code

TITLE VII

EVIDENCE

CHAPTER 92

WITNESSES, RECORDS, AND DOCUMENTS

92.05 **Final judgments and decrees of courts of record.**—All final judgments and decrees heretofore or hereafter rendered and entered in courts of record of this state, and certified copies thereof, shall be admissible as prima facie evidence in the several courts of this state of the entry and validity of such judgments and decrees. For the purposes of this section, a court of record shall be taken and construed to mean any court other than a municipal court or the Metropolitan Court of Miami-Dade County.

History.—s. 1, ch. 4723, 1899; GS 1522; RGS 2722; CGL 4390; s. 7, ch. 22858, 1945; s. 1, ch. 67-362; s. 15, ch. 73-334; s. 13, ch. 2008-4.

92.06 **Judgments and decrees of United States District Courts.**—All final judgments and decrees heretofore or hereafter to be rendered and entered in the United States District Courts of this state and certified copies thereof are declared to be admissible as prima facie evidence in the several courts of this state of the entry and validity of such judgments and decrees.

History.—s. 1, ch. 14748, 1931; CGL 1936 Supp. 4391(1).

92.07 **Judgments and decrees of this state.**—The recitals in all judgments and decrees of the Supreme Court and of the several circuit courts of this state, when such judgment or decree appears regular and has been recorded as provided by law for more than 20 years, shall be admissible in evidence as prima facie proof of the truth of the facts so recited. Either party to any suit at law or equity may offer a properly certified copy of such judgment or decree entered and recorded more than 20 years prior to the institution of the suit in which the same is offered, and such copy shall be admissible in evidence as prima facie proof of the facts in said judgment or decree set forth; provided, however, the party offering the same shall at least 10 days before the trial of the suit in which this copy is offered in evidence give notice to the opposite side of the intention to offer such copy in evidence and the purpose for which the same will be offered, and deliver with such notice a copy of the judgment or decree; provided, that nothing in this law shall render admissible in evidence any instrument of writing based on any judgment, deed of conveyance or power of attorney included in this law where any such instrument of writing has heretofore been brought in question in any action at law or in equity in any suit now pending or heretofore decided.

History.—s. 1, ch. 10111, 1925; CGL 4391.

92.08 **Deeds and powers of attorney of record for 20 years or more.**—The recitals in any deed of conveyance or power of attorney shall be admissible in evidence when offered in evidence by either party to any suit at law or in equity as prima facie proof of the truth of the facts therein recited, provided such deed of conveyance or power of attorney appears regular on its face and is a muniment in the chain of title under which the party offering the deed claims, and has been recorded as provided by law for more than 20 years prior to the institution of the suit in which it is offered; and provided further, that the party offering the deed of conveyance or power of attorney for such purposes shall at least 10 days before the trial of the suit in which the said copy is offered in evidence give notice to the opposite side of the intention to offer such copy in evidence and the purpose for which the same will be offered, and deliver with such notice a copy of the deed or power of attorney. The original deed or power of attorney shall be offered unless the party offering the certified copy shall show that the original is not within the custody or control of the party offering the copy.

History.—s. 2, ch. 10111, 1925; CGL 4392.

92.09   Effect of reversal, etc., of judgment or successful attack on deed.—No copy of a judgment or decree shall be admitted in evidence as aforesaid when it shall be made to appear that such decree has been reversed, annulled, vacated, or set aside, or that the same in collateral proceedings has been successfully attacked. No deed shall be admitted in evidence as hereinbefore provided if it shall appear that the execution or validity of said deed has been successfully attacked in any proceedings to which the grantee therein named or those or any of them holding under such grantee has been a party or parties.

History.—s. 3, ch. 10111, 1925; CGL 4393.

92.13   Certified copies of records of certified copies.—Certified copies of the record of certified copies of deeds, mortgages, powers of attorney and other instruments referred to in s. 695.19 shall have the same effect as to notice and all other purposes whatsoever as the record of the original has or can have; and certified copies of the record of such certified copies shall be admissible and may be used in evidence in the same manner and with like effect and under the same conditions as certified copies of the record of the original instrument.

History.—s. 2, ch. 11989, 1927; CGL 4388, 5718.

92.14   United States deeds and patents and copies thereof.—Deeds and patents issued by the United States Government and photographic copies made by authority of said government from its records thereof in the General Land Office, embracing lands in this state, and certified copies of the record thereof made in this state may be used in evidence in the courts of this state subject to the same rules that are applicable to the admission in evidence of other deeds and certified copies of the record thereof.

History.—s. 3, ch. 8565, 1921; CGL 5716.

92.141   Law enforcement employees; travel expenses; compensation as witness.—
Any employee of a law enforcement agency of a municipality or county or the state who appears as an official witness to testify at any hearing or law action in any court of this state as a direct result of his or her employment in the law enforcement agency is entitled to per diem and travel expenses at the same rate provided for state employees under s. 112.061, except that if the employee travels by privately owned vehicle he or she is entitled to such travel expenses for the actual distance traveled to and from court. In addition thereto, such employee is entitled to receive the daily witness pay, exclusive of the mileage allowance, provided by s. 92.142, except when the employee is appearing as a witness during time compensated as a part of his or her normal duties.

History.—s. 1, ch. 63-508; s. 1, ch. 67-427; s. 3, ch. 76-237; s. 1, ch. 77-77; s. 22, ch. 78-361; s. 1, ch. 78-379; s. 43, ch. 81-259; s. 1, ch. 84-153; s. 505, ch. 95-147.

Note.—Former s. 90.141.

92.142   Witnesses; pay.—

(1)   Witnesses in all cases, civil and criminal, in all courts, now or hereafter created, and witnesses summoned before any arbitrator or general or special magistrate appointed by the court shall receive for each day's actual attendance $5 and also 6 cents per mile for actual distance traveled to and from the courts. A witness in a criminal case required to appear in a county other than the county of his or her residence and residing more than 50 miles from the location of the trial shall be entitled to per diem and travel expenses at the same rate provided for state employees under s. 112.061, in lieu of any other witness fee.

(2)   An employee of the state who is required, as a direct result of employment, to appear as an official witness to testify in the course of any action in any court of this state, or before an administrative law judge, a hearing officer, hearing examiner, or any board or commission of the state or of its agencies, instrumentalities, or political subdivisions, shall be considered to be on duty during such appearance and shall be entitled to per diem and travel expenses as provided in s. 112.061. Except as provided in s. 92.141 and as provided in this subsection, such employee shall be required to tender to the employing agency any witness fee and other expense reimbursement received by the employee for such appearance.

(3)   Any witness subpoenaed to testify on behalf of the state in any action brought pursuant to s. 895.05 or chapter 542 who is required to travel outside his or her county of residence and more than 50 miles from his or her residence, or who is required to travel from out of state, shall be entitled to per diem and travel expenses at the same rate provided for state employees under s. 112.061 in lieu of any state witness fee.

History.—s. 5, ch. 3106, 1879; RS 1103; s. 1, ch. 4387, 1895; GS 1512; s. 2, ch. 5649, 1907; s. 1, ch. 6905, 1915; s. 1, ch. 7280, 1917; RGS 2712; CGL 4379; s. 1, ch. 29927, 1955; s. 8, ch. 65-483; s. 1, ch. 67-401; s. 15, ch. 73-334; s. 3, ch. 76-237; s. 1, ch. 77-77; s. 1, ch. 78-175; s. 22, ch. 78-361; ss. 1, 2, ch. 78-379; s. 1, ch. 83-36; s. 506, ch. 95-147; s. 9, ch. 96-410; s. 59, ch. 2004-11; s. 36, ch. 2005-236.

Note.—Former s. 90.14.

92.143   Compensation to traffic court witnesses.—Any party who secures the attendance of a witness in traffic court shall bear all costs of calling the witness, including witness fees. If the witness is required to testify on behalf of the prosecution, the office of the state attorney of the respective judicial circuit shall pay the fees and costs of calling the witness.

History.—s. 66, ch. 2005-236.

92.15   Receipts in cases involving title from United States.—A receipt of a receiver of a United States Land Office shall in all cases be prima facie evidence that the title to the land covered by said receipt has passed from the United States to the person named in the receipt as having paid for the said land.

History.—s. 1, ch. 3915, 1889; RS 1119; GS 1537; RGS 2737; CGL 4409.

92.151   Witness compensation; payment; overcharges.—Compensation shall be paid to the witness by the party in whose behalf the witness is summoned, and the prevailing party may tax the same as costs against the prevailing party's adversary; but no person shall be compelled to attend court as a witness in any civil cause unless the party in whose behalf the person is summoned shall first pay the person the amount of compensation to which he or she would be entitled for mileage and per diem for 1 day, or the same is deposited with the executive officer of said court, and the person shall not be compelled to attend thereafter unless paid in advance. But if any witness should serve without payment in advance, at the completion of his or her services the witness may exhibit his or her account for compensation, and when the same shall have been taxed and approved by the court wherein the services have been rendered, such bill shall have the force and effect of judgment and execution against the party in whose behalf the witness was summoned, and be collected by the sheriff as in other cases of execution. Any witness who shall charge and receive more than is really due shall forfeit and pay to the party injured 4 times the amount so unjustly claimed; and if the witness shall willfully make out the account for more than is lawfully due, the witness shall forfeit the compensation.

History.—s. 41, Nov. 11, 1828; RS 1104; s. 4, ch. 4387, 1895; GS 1513; RGS 2713; CGL 4380; s. 3, ch. 76-237; s. 1, ch. 77-77; s. 22, ch. 78-361; s. 1, ch. 78-379; s. 507, ch. 95-147.

Note.—Former s. 90.15.

92.153   Production of documents by witnesses; reimbursement of costs.—

(1)   DEFINITIONS.—As used in this section:

(a)   "Disinterested witness" means a person to whom a summons is issued with respect to documents involving or relating to transactions of others and who has not initiated a proceeding, is not a party to a proceeding, and is not the subject of investigation in a proceeding and who, at the time the summons is issued, is not an officer, employee, accountant, or attorney, or acting as such, for a person who has initiated, is a party to, or is the subject of investigation in a proceeding.

(b)   "Document" means any book, paper, record, or other data, or a reproduction thereof.

(c)   "Proceeding" means any civil or criminal action before a court; any investigation, inquiry, or proceeding before a grand jury, a state attorney, or a state, county, municipal, or other governmental department, division, bureau, commission or other body, or any officer thereof; any action before an officer or person authorized to issue a summons; or any administrative action authorized by law.

(d)   "Summons" means any subpoena, subpoena duces tecum, order, or other legal process which requires the production of documents.

(2)   REIMBURSEMENT OF A DISINTERESTED WITNESS.—

(a)   In any proceeding, a disinterested witness shall be paid for any costs the witness reasonably incurs either directly or indirectly in producing, searching for, reproducing, or transporting documents pursuant to a summons; however, the cost of documents produced pursuant to a subpoena or records request by a state attorney or public defender may not exceed 15 cents per page and $10 per hour for research or retrieval.

(b)　In a proceeding before a court or an administrative agency or officer, which is not an investigation or inquiry and which by law or rule includes the right to a public trial or hearing in the same proceeding and which involves adversary parties, responsibility for payment to the disinterested witness shall be fixed by the court, agency, or officer before which the proceeding is pending. Payment shall be enforced by the court, agency, or officer upon motion by the disinterested witness.

(c)　In all other proceedings, payment to the disinterested witness shall be made by the person or governmental authority requesting the summons. Any disinterested witness who desires reimbursement of such costs shall submit a request for reimbursement, supported by an affidavit, to the person or governmental authority responsible for payment. Payment shall be made within 30 days from the date the request is submitted. If payment is not made within such time, the witness may enforce payment by bringing a separate action in a court which has jurisdiction of the total amount of such costs and which is located in the judicial circuit where the witness resides.

History.—ss. 1, 2, ch. 81-196; s. 508, ch. 95-147; s. 77, ch. 2003-402.

92.16　Certificates of Board of Trustees of the Internal Improvement Trust Fund respecting the ownership, conveyance of, and other facts in connection with public lands.—A certificate of the Board of Trustees of the Internal Improvement Trust Fund under its official seal, with respect to the present or past ownership by the state or by the school, seminary or internal improvement funds of any lands in this state, or of the conveyance or transfer of any such lands by said Board of Trustees of the Internal Improvement Trust Fund or of the State Board of Education or other officers or boards of the state having power to convey any such lands, or any facts shown by the public records of his or her office with respect to any of such lands, or the transfer, ownership, or conveyance of the same, shall be prima facie evidence of the facts therein certified, and every such certificate shall be admissible in evidence in all of the courts of this state. All such certificates shall, without other or further proof, be admitted to record and recorded in the deed books of the respective counties of this state where the lands mentioned in such certificates lie, and the record of every such certificate shall have the same force and effect for all purposes as the record of deeds.

History.—s. 1, ch. 2063, 1875; RS 1112; GS 1524; s. 1, ch. 7381, 1917; RGS 2724; CGL 4395; s. 7, ch. 22858, 1945; s. 3, ch. 63-294; ss. 27, 35, ch. 69-106; s. 509, ch. 95-147.

92.17　Effect of seal of Board of Trustees of the Internal Improvement Trust Fund.—The impression of the seal of the Board of Trustees of the Internal Improvement Trust Fund upon any deed, agreement or contract, purporting to have been made by the Board of Trustees of the Internal Improvement Trust Fund, or by the members of the State Board of Education, shall entitle the same to be received in evidence in all courts and in all proceedings in this state.

History.—s. 1, ch. 3127, 1879; ss. 1, 2, ch. 3877, 1889; RS 1114; GS 1526; RGS 2726; CGL 4397; s. 4, ch. 63-294; ss. 27, 35, ch. 69-106.

92.18   Certificate of state officer.—The certificate of any state officer, under seal of office, as to any official act occurring in the course of the official business of the office in which the state officer presides, shall be prima facie evidence of such fact.

History.—s. 1, ch. 3250, 1881; RS 1113; GS 1525; RGS 2725; CGL 4396; s. 510, ch. 95-147.

92.19   Portions of records.—In all cases where any certified copy of any record, pleading, document, deed, conveyance, paper or instrument in writing, involving the title to real estate shall be lawfully admissible in evidence in any of the courts of this state, a certified copy of such portions of such instrument as shall contain the essential parts thereof and only such portion of the descriptive matter thereof as shall be involved in the case on trial, shall likewise be admissible in evidence; and in no case shall it be necessary to include in such certified copies descriptive matter not involved in the case in which such copy is offered in evidence.

History.—s. 1, ch. 10237, 1925; CGL 4400.

92.20   Certificates issued under authority of Congress.—Every certificate issued under authority of the Congress and every duly certified copy thereof under the seal of the United States governmental department having the authority to issue such certified copy, relating to the grade, classification, quality or condition of agricultural products shall be accepted in any court of this state as prima facie evidence of the true grade, classification, condition or quality of such agricultural product at the time of its inspection.

History.—s. 1, ch. 13568, 1929; CGL 1936 Supp. 4400(1).

92.21   Certificate as to sanitary condition of buildings.—Every owner, agent, or lessee of any building or buildings used for the purpose of providing board and lodgings for the entertainment of guests, containing 10 rooms or more, who shall have obtained and posted a certificate as provided by law, may present the same as evidence in the owner's, agent's, or lessee's defense in any suit in any of the courts in this state in which damages are claimed for injuries from alleged unsanitary conditions of said buildings and premises.

History.—s. 4, ch. 4606, 1899; GS 1527; RGS 2727; CGL 4398; s. 511, ch. 95-147.

92.23   Rule of evidence in suits on fire policies for loss or damage to building.—In all suits or proceedings brought upon policies of insurance on buildings against loss or damage by fire, hereafter issued or renewed, the insurer shall not be permitted to deny that the property insured was worth, at the time of insuring it by the policy, the full sum insured therein on such property.

History.—s. 2, ch. 4677, 1899; GS 1528; RGS 2728; CGL 4399.

92.231   Expert witnesses; fee.—

(1)   The term "expert witness" as used herein shall apply to any witness who offers himself or herself in the trial of any action as an expert witness or who is subpoenaed to testify in such capacity before a state attorney in the investigation of a criminal matter, or before a grand jury, and who is permitted by the court to qualify and testify as such, upon any matter pending before any court.

(2) Any expert or skilled witness who shall have testified in any cause shall be allowed a witness fee including the cost of any exhibits used by such witness in an amount agreed to by the parties, and the same shall be taxed as costs. In instances where services are provided for the state, including for state-paid private court-appointed counsel, payment from state funds shall be in accordance with standards adopted by the Legislature.

(3) In a criminal case in which the state or an indigent defendant requires the services of an expert witness whose opinion is relevant to the issues of the case, the expert witness shall be compensated in accordance with standards adopted by the Legislature.

History.—ss. 1, 2, ch. 25090, 1949; s. 19, ch. 29737, 1955; s. 1, ch. 59-201; s. 3, ch. 76-237; s. 1, ch. 77-77; s. 22, ch. 78-361; s. 1, ch. 78-379; s. 512, ch. 95-147; s. 78, ch. 2003-402; s. 37, ch. 2005-236.

Note.—Former s. 90.231.

92.233   Compensation of witness summoned in two or more criminal cases.—A witness subpoenaed in two or more criminal cases pending at the same time shall be paid one charge for per diem and mileage, but when the costs are taxed against the defendant, a witness may charge the full amount in each case.

History.—s. 4, ch. 159, 1848; RS 2865; s. 1, ch. 5133, 1903; GS 3921; RGS 6020; CGL 8314; s. 102, ch. 70-339; s. 79, ch. 2003-402.

Note.—Former s. 932.34; s. 914.09.

92.24   Certain tax deeds prima facie evidence of title.—All tax deeds issued under and pursuant to the provisions and in the form prescribed in and by the following acts and statutes of this state, to wit: s. 10, chapter 4888, Acts, 1901 and said section as amended by s. 1, chapter 5152, Acts, 1903; s. 577 of the General Statutes of Florida, 1906; s. 779 of the Revised General Statutes of Florida, 1920, and said section as amended by s. 12, chapter 14572, Acts, 1929; are declared to be prima facie evidence of the regularity of the proceedings from the valuation of the land described in such deeds respectively, by the assessors, to the date of the deed or deeds inclusive, and shall be so received in evidence in any and all the courts of this state, without regard to date of execution.

History.—s. 1, ch. 5150, 1903; GS 1521; RGS 2721; CGL 4389.

92.25   Records destroyed by fire; use of abstracts.—Whenever in the trial of any suit, or in any proceeding in any court of this state, it shall be made to appear that the original of any deed or other instrument of writing, or of any record of any court relating to any land, the title thereof or any interest therein being in controversy in such suit or proceeding, is lost or destroyed, or not within the power of the party to produce the same, and that the record thereof has been heretofore destroyed by fire, and that no certified copy of such record is in the possession or control of such party, it is lawful for such party, and the court shall receive as evidence, any abstract of title, or letter-press copy thereof made in the ordinary course of business prior to such loss or destruction; and it is also lawful for any such party to offer, and the court shall receive as evidence, any copy, extract or minutes from such destroyed records, or from the original thereof, which were at the date of such destruction in the possession of any person or persons then engaged in the business of making abstracts of titles for others for hire.

Florida Evidence Code

History.—s. 1, ch. 4951, 1901; GS 1529; RGS 2729; CGL 4401.

92.251   Uniform Foreign Depositions Law.—

(1)   This section may be cited as the "Uniform Foreign Depositions Law."

(2)   Whenever any mandate, writ or commission is issued out of any court of record in any other state, territory, district, or foreign jurisdiction, or whenever upon notice or agreement it is required to take the testimony of a witness or witnesses in this state, witnesses may be compelled to appear and testify in the same manner and by the same process and proceeding as may be employed for the purpose of taking testimony in proceedings pending in this state.

(3)   This section shall be so interpreted and construed as to effectuate its general purposes to make uniform the law of those states which enact it.

History.—ss. 1, 2, 3, ch. 59-250; s. 3, ch. 76-237; s. 1, ch. 77-77; s. 22, ch. 78-361; s. 1, ch. 78-379.

Note.—Former s. 90.25.

92.26   Records destroyed by fire; use of sworn copies.—A sworn copy of any writing admissible under s. 92.25 made by the person or persons having possession of such writing shall be admissible in evidence; provided, the party desiring to use such sworn copy, as aforesaid, shall have given the opposite party a reasonable opportunity to verify the correctness of such copy; and provided, that no abstract of title or letter-press copy thereof, extract or minutes or copy made admissible in evidence by this section, shall be so admitted by virtue hereof unless a copy thereof shall have been served on the opposite party, or the opposite party's attorney or counsel, at least 10 days before the same is offered in evidence. Nothing herein shall be construed to prevent the impeachment of such evidence, or its exclusion by the court for good and sufficient cause.

History.—s. 1, ch. 4951, 1901; GS 1530; RGS 2730; CGL 4402; s. 513, ch. 95-147; s. 12, ch. 95-280.

92.27   Records destroyed by fire; effect of abstracts in evidence.—In all cases in which any destroyed abstracts, copies, minutes, extracts, maps or plats, or copies thereof, purchased and placed in the clerk's office, as provided by law, or which are made admissible in evidence under any of the provisions of this revision, whether purchased or placed in such office or not, shall be received in evidence under this law, all deeds or other instruments of writing appearing thereby to have been executed by any person or persons, or in which they appear to have joined, shall (except as against any person or persons in actual possession of the land or lot described therein at the time of the destruction of the record of such county, claiming title thereto, otherwise than under sale for taxes or special assessments) be presumed to have been executed and acknowledged according to law; and all sales under powers, and all judgments, decrees and legal proceedings, and all sales thereunder (sale for taxes and assessments, and judgments and proceedings for the enforcement of taxes and assessments excepted) shall be presumed to be regular and correct, except as against the person or persons in this section above-mentioned and excepted.

History.—s. 4, ch. 4951, 1901; GS 1531; RGS 2731; CGL 4403.

92.28   Records destroyed by fire; land title suits; what may be received in evidence.—In all suits or proceedings concerning any land, or any estate, interest or right in, or any lien or encumbrance upon the same, when it shall be made to appear that the original of any deed, conveyance, map, plat or other written or record evidence has been lost or destroyed, or is not in the power, custody or control of the party wishing to use it on the trial to produce same, and the record thereof has been heretofore destroyed by fire, the court shall receive all such evidence as may have a bearing on the case to establish the execution or contents of any deed, conveyance, map, plat record, or other written evidence so lost or destroyed; provided, that the testimony of the parties themselves shall be received only in such cases, and subject to all the qualifications in respect to such testimony as now provided by law; and provided further, that any writing in the hands of any person or persons, which may become admissible in evidence under the provisions of this section, or any part of this law, shall be rejected and not admitted as evidence, unless the same appear upon the face thereof without erasure, blemish, alteration, interlineation or interpolation in any material part, unless the same shall be explained to the satisfaction of the court, and appear fairly and honestly made in the ordinary course of business.

History.—s. 5, ch. 4951, 1901; GS 1532; RGS 2732; CGL 4404.

92.29   Photographic or electronic copies.—Photographic reproductions or reproductions through electronic recordkeeping systems made by any federal, state, county, or municipal governmental board, department or agency, in the regular course of business, of any original record, document, paper or instrument in writing or in an electronic recordkeeping system, which is, or may be, required or authorized to be made, filed, or recorded with that board, department or agency shall in all cases and in all courts and places be admitted and received as evidence with a like force and effect as the original would be, whether the original record, document, paper, or instrument in writing or in an electronic recordkeeping system is in existence or not.

History.—s. 1, ch. 20866, 1941; s. 7, ch. 94-348.

92.295   Copies of voter registration records.—Any reproduction of an original voter registration record stored pursuant to s. 98.461, whether microfilmed or maintained digitally or on electronic, magnetic, or optic media, which reproduction is certified by the supervisor of elections who is the custodian of the record, is admissible as evidence in any judicial or administrative proceeding in this state with the same effect as the original voter registration record, whether the original voter registration record exists or not.

History.—s. 1, ch. 88-45; s. 7, ch. 90-315.

92.30   Presumption of death; official findings.—A written finding of presumed death, made by the Secretary of the Army, the Secretary of the Navy, or other officer or employee of the United States authorized to make such findings, pursuant to the [1]Federal Missing Persons Act (56 Stat. 143, 1092, and Pub. L. No. 408, Ch. 371, 2d Sess. 78th Cong.; 50 U.S.C. App. Supp. 1001-17), as now or hereafter amended, or a duly certified copy of such finding, shall be received in any court, office, or other place in this state as evidence of the death of the person therein found to be dead, and the date, circumstances, and place of the person's disappearance.

History.—s. 1, ch. 22866, 1945; s. 22, ch. 77-104; s. 514, ch. 95-147.

¹Note.—Repealed by Act Sept. 6, 1966, Pub. L. No. 89-554, s. 8(a), 80 Stat. 632, 651-654, 656, 657, 659, 662.

92.31   Missing persons and persons imprisoned or interned in foreign countries; official reports.—An official written report or record, or duly certified copy thereof, that a person is missing, missing in action, interned in a neutral country, or beleaguered, besieged, or captured by an enemy, or is dead, or is alive, made by any officer or employee of the United States authorized by the act referred to in s. 92.30, or by any other law of the United States to make same, shall be received in any court, office, or other place in this state as evidence that such person is missing, missing in action, interned in a neutral country, or beleaguered, besieged, or captured by an enemy, or is dead, or is alive, as the case may be.

History.—s. 2, ch. 22866, 1945.

92.32   Official findings and reports; presumption of authority to issue or execute.—For the purposes of this law, any finding, report, or record, or duly certified copy thereof, purporting to have been signed by such an officer or employee of the United States as is described above, shall prima facie be deemed to have been signed and issued by such an officer or employee pursuant to law, and the person signing same shall prima facie be deemed to have acted within the scope of the person's authority. If a copy purports to have been certified by a person authorized by law to certify the same, such certified copy shall be prima facie evidence of the person's authority so to certify.

History.—s. 3, ch. 22866, 1945; s. 515, ch. 95-147.

92.33   Written statement concerning injury to person or property; furnishing copies; admission as evidence.—Every person who shall take a written statement by any injured person with respect to any accident or with respect to any injury to person or property shall, at the time of taking such statement, furnish to the person making such statement a true and complete copy thereof. Any person having taken, or having possession of any written statement or a copy of such statement, by any injured person with respect to any accident or with respect to any injury to person or property shall, at the request of the person who made such statement or his or her personal representative, furnish the person who made such statement or his or her personal representative a true and complete copy thereof. No written statement by an injured person shall be admissible in evidence or otherwise used in any manner in any civil action relating to the subject matter thereof unless it shall be made to appear that a true and complete copy thereof was furnished to the person making such statement at the time of the making thereof, or, if it shall be made to appear that thereafter a person having possession of such statement refused, upon request of the person who made the statement or his or her personal representatives, to furnish him or her a true and complete copy thereof.

History.—s. 1, ch. 26482, 1951; s. 516, ch. 95-147.

92.351   Prohibition against prisoners submitting nondocumentary physical evidence without authorization of court; prisoner mailings to courts.—

(1)   No prisoner as defined by s. 57.085 who is a party to a judicial proceeding may submit evidence or any other item that is not in paper document form to a court or clerk of court without first obtaining authorization from the court. This prohibition includes, but is not limited to, all nondocumentary evidence or items offered in support of a motion, pleading, or other document filed with the court. This prohibition does not preclude a

prisoner who is appearing in person or through counsel before a court at a trial or hearing from submitting physical evidence to the court at the appropriate time.

(2) A corrections or detention facility for prisoners may conduct a cursory examination of the outside of any package or other mailing from a prisoner to a court or clerk of court of this state to determine whether the package or mailing contains materials other than paper documents. If such package or mailing appears to contain materials other than paper documents, the facility shall refuse to forward it until the sender presents a court order authorizing the mailing of such nondocumentary items or demonstrates that the contents are not prohibited by this section.

History.—s. 3, ch. 96-106.

92.38 Comparison of disputed writings.—Comparison of a disputed writing with any writing proved to the satisfaction of the judge to be genuine, shall be permitted to be made by the witnesses; and such writings, and the evidence of witnesses respecting the same, may be submitted to the jury, or to the court in case of a trial by the court, as evidence of the genuineness, or otherwise, of the writing in dispute.

History.—s. 55, ch. 1096, 1861; RS 1121; GS 1539; RGS 2739; CGL 4411.

Note.—Former s. 90.20.

92.39 Evidence of individual's claim against the state in suits between them.—In suits between the state and individuals, no claim for a credit shall be allowed upon trial, but such as shall appear to have been presented to the Chief Financial Officer for his or her examination, and by him or her disallowed in whole or in part, unless it shall be proved to the satisfaction of the court that the defendant is, at the time of the trial, in possession of vouchers not before in the defendant's power to procure, and that the defendant was prevented from exhibiting a claim for such credit at the Chief Financial Officer's office by unavoidable accident.

History.—s. 4, Feb. 10, 1837; RS 1122; GS 1540; RGS 2740; CGL 4412; s. 517, ch. 95-147; s. 108, ch. 2003-261.

Note.—Former s. 90.22.

92.40 Reports of building, housing, or health code violations; admissibility.—A copy of a report, notice, or citation of a violation of any building, housing, or health code by a governmental agency charged with the enforcement of such codes, certified by the agency, if otherwise material shall be admissible as evidence.

History.—s. 11, ch. 73-330.

92.50 Oaths, affidavits, and acknowledgments; who may take or administer; requirements.—

(1) IN THIS STATE.—Oaths, affidavits, and acknowledgments required or authorized under the laws of this state (except oaths to jurors and witnesses in court and such other oaths, affidavits and acknowledgments as are required by law to be taken or administered by or before particular officers) may be taken or administered by or before any judge, clerk, or deputy clerk of any court of record within this state, including federal

courts, or before any United States commissioner or any notary public within this state. The jurat, or certificate of proof or acknowledgment, shall be authenticated by the signature and official seal of such officer or person taking or administering the same; however, when taken or administered before any judge, clerk, or deputy clerk of a court of record, the seal of such court may be affixed as the seal of such officer or person.

(2) IN OTHER STATES, TERRITORIES, AND DISTRICTS OF THE UNITED STATES.—Oaths, affidavits, and acknowledgments required or authorized under the laws of this state, may be taken or administered in any other state, territory, or district of the United States, before any judge, clerk or deputy clerk of any court of record, within such state, territory, or district, having a seal, or before any notary public or justice of the peace, having a seal, in such state, territory, or district; provided, however, such officer or person is authorized under the laws of such state, territory, or district to take or administer oaths, affidavits and acknowledgments. The jurat, or certificate of proof or acknowledgment, shall be authenticated by the signature and official seal of such officer or person taking or administering the same; provided, however, when taken or administered by or before any judge, clerk, or deputy clerk of a court of record, the seal of such court may be affixed as the seal of such officer or person.

(3) IN FOREIGN COUNTRIES.—Oaths, affidavits, and acknowledgments, required or authorized by the laws of this state, may be taken or administered in any foreign country, by or before any judge or justice of a court of last resort, any notary public of such foreign country, any minister, consul general, charge d'affaires, or consul of the United States resident in such country. The jurat, or certificate of proof or acknowledgment, shall be authenticated by the signature and official seal of the officer or person taking or administering the same; provided, however, when taken or administered by or before any judge or justice of a court of last resort, the seal of such court may be affixed as the seal of such judge or justice.

History.—s. 1, ch. 48, 1845; RS 1299; GS 1730; RGS 2945; CGL 4669; s. 1, ch. 23156, 1945; s. 7, ch. 24337, 1947; s. 15, ch. 73-334; s. 3, ch. 76-237; s. 1, ch. 77-77; s. 22, ch. 78-361; s. 1, ch. 78-379.

Note.—Former s. 90.01.

92.51 Oaths, affidavits, and acknowledgments; taken or administered by commissioned officer of United States Armed Forces.—

(1) Oaths, affidavits, and acknowledgments required or authorized by the laws of this state may be taken or administered within or without the United States by or before any commissioned officer in active service of the Armed Forces of the United States with the rank of second lieutenant or higher in the Army, Air Force or Marine Corps or ensign or higher in the Navy or Coast Guard when the person required or authorized to make and execute the oath, affidavit, or acknowledgment is a member of the Armed Forces of the United States, the spouse of such member or a person whose duties require the person's presence with the Armed Forces of the United States.

(2) A certificate endorsed upon the instrument which shows the date of the oath, affidavit, or acknowledgment and which states in substance that the person appearing before the officer acknowledged the instrument as the person's act or made or signed the instrument under oath shall be sufficient for all intents and purposes. The instrument shall not be rendered invalid by the failure to state the place of execution or acknowledgment.

(3)   If the signature, rank, and branch of service or subdivision thereof of any commissioned officer appears upon such instrument, document or certificate no further proof of the authority of such officer so to act shall be required and such action by such commissioned officer shall be prima facie evidence that the person making such oath, affidavit or acknowledgment is within the purview of this act.

History.—ss. 1, 2, 3, ch. 61-196; s. 3, ch. 76-237; s. 1, ch. 77-77; s. 22, ch. 78-361; s. 1, ch. 78-379; s. 518, ch. 95-147.

Note.—Former s. 90.011.

92.52   Affirmation equivalent to oath.—Whenever an oath shall be required by any law of this state in any proceeding, an affirmation may be substituted therefor.

History.—RS 1300; GS 1731; RGS 2946; CGL 4670; s. 3, ch. 76-237; s. 1, ch. 77-77; s. 22, ch. 78-361; s. 1, ch. 78-379.

Note.—Former s. 90.02.

92.525   Verification of documents; perjury by false written declaration, penalty.—

(1)   When it is authorized or required by law, by rule of an administrative agency, or by rule or order of court that a document be verified by a person, the verification may be accomplished in the following manner:

(a)   Under oath or affirmation taken or administered before an officer authorized under s. 92.50 to administer oaths; or

(b)   By the signing of the written declaration prescribed in subsection (2).

(2)   A written declaration means the following statement: "Under penalties of perjury, I declare that I have read the foregoing [document] and that the facts stated in it are true," followed by the signature of the person making the declaration, except when a verification on information or belief is permitted by law, in which case the words "to the best of my knowledge and belief" may be added. The written declaration shall be printed or typed at the end of or immediately below the document being verified and above the signature of the person making the declaration.

(3)   A person who knowingly makes a false declaration under subsection (2) is guilty of the crime of perjury by false written declaration, a felony of the third degree, punishable as provided in s. 775.082, s. 775.083, or s. 775.084.

(4)   As used in this section:

(a)   The term "administrative agency" means any department or agency of the state or any county, municipality, special district, or other political subdivision.

(b)   The term "document" means any writing including, without limitation, any form, application, claim, notice, tax return, inventory, affidavit, pleading, or paper.

Florida Evidence Code

(c) The requirement that a document be verified means that the document must be signed or executed by a person and that the person must state under oath or affirm that the facts or matters stated or recited in the document are true, or words of that import or effect.

History.—s. 12, ch. 86-201.

92.53 Videotaping the testimony of a victim or witness under age 16 or who has an intellectual disability.—

(1) On motion and hearing in camera and a finding that there is a substantial likelihood that a victim or witness who is under the age of 16 or who has an intellectual disability as defined in s. 393.063 would suffer at least moderate emotional or mental harm due to the presence of the defendant if such victim or witness is required to testify in open court, or is unavailable as defined in s. 90.804(1), the trial court may order the videotaping of the testimony of the victim or witness in a case, whether civil or criminal in nature, in which videotaped testimony is to be used at trial in lieu of trial testimony in open court.

(2) The motion may be filed by:

(a) The victim or witness, or the victim's or witness's attorney, parent, legal guardian, or guardian ad litem;

(b) A trial judge on his or her own motion;

(c) Any party in a civil proceeding; or

(d) The prosecuting attorney or the defendant, or the defendant's counsel.

(3) The judge shall preside, or shall appoint a special master to preside, at the videotaping unless:

(a) The child or the person who has the intellectual disability is represented by a guardian ad litem or counsel;

(b) The representative of the victim or witness and the counsel for each party stipulate that the requirement for the presence of the judge or special master may be waived; and

(c) The court finds at a hearing on the motion that the presence of a judge or special master is not necessary to protect the victim or witness.

(4) The defendant and the defendant's counsel must be present at the videotaping unless the defendant has waived this right. The court may require the defendant to view the testimony from outside the presence of the child or the person who has an intellectual disability by means of a two-way mirror or another similar method that ensures that the defendant can observe and hear the testimony of the victim or witness in person, but the victim or witness cannot hear or see the defendant. The defendant and the attorney for the defendant may communicate by any appropriate private method.

(5) Any party, or the court on its own motion, may request the aid of an interpreter, as provided in s. 90.606, to aid the parties in formulating methods of questioning the child

295

or person who has the intellectual disability and in interpreting the answers of the child or person during proceedings conducted under this section.

(6) The motion referred to in subsection (1) may be made at any time with reasonable notice to each party to the cause, and videotaping of testimony may be made any time after the court grants the motion. The videotaped testimony is admissible as evidence in the trial of the cause; however, such testimony is not admissible in any trial or proceeding in which such witness testifies by use of closed circuit television pursuant to s. 92.54.

(7) The court shall make specific findings of fact, on the record, as to the basis for its ruling under this section.

History.—ss. 1, 2, ch. 79-69; s. 1, ch. 84-36; ss. 5, 9, ch. 85-53; s. 9, ch. 85-80; s. 1, ch. 93-131; s. 21, ch. 94-154; s. 1379, ch. 95-147; s. 30, ch. 99-2; s. 4, ch. 2000-338; s. 89, ch. 2004-267; s. 4, ch. 2013-162.

Note.—Former ss. 918.17, 90.90.

92.54   Use of closed circuit television in proceedings involving a victim or witness under the age of 16 or who has an intellectual disability.—

(1) Upon motion and hearing in camera and upon a finding that there is a substantial likelihood that a victim or witness under the age of 16 or who has an intellectual disability will suffer at least moderate emotional or mental harm due to the presence of the defendant if such victim or witness is required to testify in open court, or is unavailable as defined in s. 90.804(1), the trial court may order that the testimony of the victim or witness be taken outside of the courtroom and shown by means of closed circuit television.

(2) The motion may be filed by the victim or witness; the attorney, parent, legal guardian, or guardian ad litem of the victim or witness; the prosecutor; the defendant or the defendant's counsel; or the trial judge on his or her own motion.

(3) Only the judge, the prosecutor, the defendant, the attorney for the defendant, the operators of the videotape equipment, an interpreter, and some other person who, in the opinion of the court, contributes to the well-being of the child or the person who has an intellectual disability and who will not be a witness in the case may be in the room during the recording of the testimony.

(4) During the victim's or witness's testimony by closed circuit television, the court may require the defendant to view the testimony from the courtroom. In such a case, the court shall permit the defendant to observe and hear the testimony of the victim or witness, but must ensure that the victim or witness cannot hear or see the defendant. The defendant's right to assistance of counsel, which includes the right to immediate and direct communication with counsel conducting cross-examination, must be protected and, upon the defendant's request, such communication must be provided by any appropriate electronic method.

(5) The court shall make specific findings of fact, on the record, as to the basis for its ruling under this section.

History.—s. 6, ch. 85-53; s. 12, ch. 87-224; s. 2, ch. 93-131; s. 22, ch. 94-154; s. 1380, ch. 95-147; s. 5, ch. 2013-162.

92.55   Judicial or other proceedings involving victim or witness under the age of 16 or person who has an intellectual disability; special protections; use of registered service or therapy animals.—

(1)   Upon motion of any party, upon motion of a parent, guardian, attorney, or guardian ad litem for a victim or witness under the age of 16 or person who has an intellectual disability, or upon its own motion, the court may enter any order necessary to protect such victim or witness in any judicial proceeding or other official proceeding from severe emotional or mental harm due to the presence of the defendant if the victim or witness is required to testify in open court. Such orders must relate to the taking of testimony and include, but are not limited to:

(a)   Interviewing or the taking of depositions as part of a civil or criminal proceeding.

(b)   Examination and cross-examination for the purpose of qualifying as a witness or testifying in any proceeding.

(c)   The use of testimony taken outside of the courtroom, including proceedings under ss. 92.53 and 92.54.

(2)   In ruling upon the motion, the court shall consider:

(a)   The age of the child, the nature of the offense or act, the relationship of the child to the parties in the case or to the defendant in a criminal action, the degree of emotional trauma that will result to the child as a consequence of the defendant's presence, and any other fact that the court deems relevant; or

(b)   The age of the person who has an intellectual disability, the functional capacity of such person, the nature of the offenses or act, the relationship of the person to the parties in the case or to the defendant in a criminal action, the degree of emotional trauma that will result to the person as a consequence of the defendant's presence, and any other fact that the court deems relevant.

(3)   In addition to such other relief provided by law, the court may enter orders limiting the number of times that a child or a person who has an intellectual disability may be interviewed, prohibiting depositions of such child or person, requiring the submission of questions before the examination of the child or person, setting the place and conditions for interviewing the child or person or for conducting any other proceeding, or permitting or prohibiting the attendance of any person at any proceeding. The court shall enter any order necessary to protect the rights of all parties, including the defendant in any criminal action.

(4)   The court may set any other conditions it finds just and appropriate when taking the testimony of a child, including the use of a service or therapy animal that has been evaluated and registered according to national standards, in any proceeding involving a sexual offense. When deciding whether to permit a child to testify with the assistance of a registered service or therapy animal, the court shall consider the age of the child, the interests of the child, the rights of the parties to the litigation, and any other relevant factor that would facilitate the testimony by the child.

History.—s. 7, ch. 85-53; s. 3, ch. 93-131; s. 23, ch. 94-154; s. 8, ch. 2000-336; s. 3, ch. 2011-220; s. 6, ch. 2013-162.

92.56   Judicial proceedings and court records involving sexual offenses.—

(1)   (a)   The confidential and exempt status of criminal intelligence information or criminal investigative information made confidential and exempt pursuant to s. 119.071(2)(h) must be maintained in court records pursuant to s. 119.0714(1)(h) and in court proceedings, including testimony from witnesses.

(b)   If a petition for access to such confidential and exempt records is filed with the trial court having jurisdiction over the alleged offense, the confidential and exempt status of such information shall be maintained by the court if the state or the victim demonstrates that:

1.   The identity of the victim is not already known in the community;

2.   The victim has not voluntarily called public attention to the offense;

3.   The identity of the victim has not otherwise become a reasonable subject of public concern;

4.   The disclosure of the victim's identity would be offensive to a reasonable person; and

5.   The disclosure of the victim's identity would:

a.   Endanger the victim because the assailant has not been apprehended and is not otherwise known to the victim;

b.   Endanger the victim because of the likelihood of retaliation, harassment, or intimidation;

c.   Cause severe emotional or mental harm to the victim;

d.   Make the victim unwilling to testify as a witness; or

e.   Be inappropriate for other good cause shown.

(2)   A defendant charged with a crime described in chapter 794 or chapter 800, or with child abuse, aggravated child abuse, or sexual performance by a child as described in chapter 827, may apply to the trial court for an order of disclosure of information in court records held confidential and exempt pursuant to s. 119.0714(1)(h) or maintained as confidential and exempt pursuant to court order under this section. Such identifying information concerning the victim may be released to the defendant or his or her attorney in order to prepare the defense. The confidential and exempt status of this information may not be construed to prevent the disclosure of the victim's identity to the defendant; however, the defendant may not disclose the victim's identity to any person other than the defendant's attorney or any other person directly involved in the preparation of the defense. A willful and knowing disclosure of the identity of the victim to any other person by the defendant constitutes contempt.

(3)   The state may use a pseudonym instead of the victim's name to designate the victim of a crime described in chapter 794 or chapter 800, or of child abuse, aggravated child abuse, or sexual performance by a child as described in chapter 827, or any crime involving the production, possession, or promotion of child pornography as described in chapter 847, in all court records and records of court proceedings, both civil and criminal.

(4)   The protection of this section may be waived by the victim of the alleged offense in a writing filed with the court, in which the victim consents to the use or release of identifying information during court proceedings and in the records of court proceedings.

(5)   This section does not prohibit the publication or broadcast of the substance of trial testimony in a prosecution for an offense described in chapter 794 or chapter 800, or a crime of child abuse, aggravated child abuse, or sexual performance by a child, as described in chapter 827, but the publication or broadcast may not include an identifying photograph, an identifiable voice, or the name or address of the victim, unless the victim has consented in writing to the publication and filed such consent with the court or unless the court has declared such records not confidential and exempt as provided for in subsection (1).

(6)   A willful and knowing violation of this section or a willful and knowing failure to obey any court order issued under this section constitutes contempt.

History.—s. 3, ch. 95-207; s. 1, ch. 2008-172; s. 4, ch. 2008-234; s. 3, ch. 2011-83.

92.561   Prohibition on reproduction of child pornography.—

(1)   In a criminal proceeding, any property or material that portrays sexual performance by a child as defined in s. 827.071, or constitutes child pornography as defined in s. 847.001, must remain secured or locked in the care, custody, and control of a law enforcement agency, the state attorney, or the court.

(2)   Notwithstanding any law or rule of court, a court shall deny, in a criminal proceeding, any request by the defendant to copy, photograph, duplicate, or otherwise reproduce any property or material that portrays sexual performance by a child or constitutes child pornography so long as the state attorney makes the property or material reasonably available to the defendant.

(3)   For purposes of this section, property or material is deemed to be reasonably available to the defendant if the state attorney provides ample opportunity at a designated facility for the inspection, viewing, and examination of the property or material that portrays sexual performance by a child or constitutes child pornography by the defendant, his or her attorney, or any individual whom the defendant uses as an expert during the discovery process or at a court proceeding.

History.—s. 4, ch. 2011-220.

92.565   Admissibility of confession in sexual abuse cases.—

(1)   As used in this section, the term "sexual abuse" means an act of a sexual nature or sexual act that may be prosecuted under any law of this state, including those offenses specifically designated in subsection (2).

(2)   In any criminal action in which the defendant is charged with a crime against a victim under s. 794.011; s. 794.05; s. 800.04; s. 826.04; s. 827.03, involving sexual abuse; s. 827.04, involving sexual abuse; s. 827.071; or s. 847.0135(5), or any other crime involving sexual abuse of another, or with any attempt, solicitation, or conspiracy to commit any of these crimes, the defendant's memorialized confession or admission is admissible during trial without the state having to prove a corpus delicti of the crime if the court finds in a hearing conducted outside the presence of the jury that the state is unable to show the existence of each element of the crime, and having so found, further finds that the defendant's confession or admission is trustworthy. Factors which may be relevant in determining whether the state is unable to show the existence of each element of the crime include, but are not limited to, the fact that, at the time the crime was committed, the victim was:

(a)   Physically helpless, mentally incapacitated, or mentally defective, as those terms are defined in s. 794.011;

(b)   Physically incapacitated due to age, infirmity, or any other cause; or

(c)   Less than 12 years of age.

(3)   Before the court admits the defendant's confession or admission, the state must prove by a preponderance of evidence that there is sufficient corroborating evidence that tends to establish the trustworthiness of the statement by the defendant. Hearsay evidence is admissible during the presentation of evidence at the hearing. In making its determination, the court may consider all relevant corroborating evidence, including the defendant's statements.

(4)   The court shall make specific findings of fact, on the record, for the basis of its ruling.

History.—s. 1, ch. 2000-204; s. 10, ch. 2008-172.

92.57   Termination of employment of witness prohibited.—A person who testifies in a judicial proceeding in response to a subpoena may not be dismissed from employment because of the nature of the person's testimony or because of absences from employment resulting from compliance with the subpoena. In any civil action arising out of a violation of this section, the court may award attorney's fees and punitive damages to the person unlawfully dismissed, in addition to actual damages suffered by such person.

History.—s. 1, ch. 90-185.

92.60   Foreign records of regularly conducted business activity.—

(1)   For the purposes of this section:

(a)   "Foreign record of regularly conducted business activity" means a memorandum, report, record, or data compilation, in any form, of acts, events, conditions, opinions, or diagnoses, maintained in a foreign country.

(b)   "Foreign certification" means a written declaration made and signed in a foreign country by the custodian of a foreign record of regularly conducted business activity or another qualified person that, if falsely made, would subject the maker to criminal penalty under the laws of that country.

(c) "Business" means any business, institution, association, profession, occupation, or calling of any kind, whether or not conducted for profit.

(2) In a criminal or civil proceeding in a court of the State of Florida, a foreign record of regularly conducted business activity, or a copy of such record, shall not be excluded as evidence by the hearsay rule if a foreign certification attests that:

(a) Such record was made at or near the time of the occurrence of the matters set forth by, or from information transmitted by, a person with knowledge of those matters;

(b) Such record was kept in the course of a regularly conducted business activity;

(c) The business activity made such a record as a regular practice; and

(d) If such record is not the original, it is a duplicate of the original;

unless the source of information or the method or circumstances of preparation indicate lack of trustworthiness.

(3) A foreign certification under this section shall authenticate such record or duplicate.

(4) No evidence in such records in the form of opinion or diagnosis is admissible under subsection (2) unless such opinion or diagnosis would be admissible under ss. 90.701-90.705 if the person whose opinion is recorded were to testify to the opinion directly.

(5) At the arraignment or as soon after the arraignment as practicable, or 60 days prior to a civil trial, a party intending to offer in evidence under this section a foreign record of regularly conducted business activity shall provide written notice of that intention to each other party. A motion opposing admission in evidence of such record shall be made by the opposing party and determined by the court before trial. Failure by a party to file such motion before trial shall constitute a waiver of objection to such record or duplicate, but the court for cause shown may grant relief from the waiver.

History.—s. 17, ch. 88-381; s. 1, ch. 97-189.

92.605   Production of certain records by Florida businesses and out-of-state corporations.—

(1)   For the purposes of this section, the term:

(a) "Adverse result" includes one of the following consequences to notification of the existence of a court order, a subpoena, or a search warrant:

1.   Danger to the life or physical safety of an individual.

2.   A flight from prosecution.

3.   The destruction of or tampering with evidence.

4.   The intimidation of potential witnesses.

5.   Serious jeopardy to an investigation or undue delay of a trial.

(b)   "Applicant" means a law enforcement officer who is seeking a court order or subpoena under s. 16.56, s. 27.04, s. 905.185, or s. 914.04 or who is issued a search warrant under s. 933.01, or anyone who is authorized to issue a subpoena under the Florida Rules of Criminal Procedure.

(c)   "Business" means any business, institution, association, profession, occupation, or calling of any kind, whether or not conducted for profit.

(d)   "Electronic communication services" and "remote computing services" have the same meaning as provided in the Electronic Communications Privacy Act in chapter 121 (commencing with s. 2701) of part I of Title 18 of the United States Code Annotated. This section does not apply to corporations that do not provide those services to the public.

(e)   "Out-of-state corporation" means any corporation that is qualified to do business in this state under s. 607.1501.

(f)   "Out-of-state record of regularly conducted business activity" means a memorandum, report, record, or data compilation, in any form, of acts, events, conditions, opinions, or diagnoses, maintained in another state or country.

(g)   "Out-of-state certification" means a written declaration made and signed in another state or country by the custodian of an out-of-state record of regularly conducted business activity or another qualified person that, if falsely made, would subject the declarant to criminal penalty under the laws of another state or country.

(h)   "Properly served" means delivery by hand or in a manner reasonably allowing for proof of delivery if delivered by United States mail, overnight delivery service, or facsimile to a person or entity properly registered to do business in any state. In order for an out-of-state corporation to be properly served, the service described in this paragraph must be effected on the corporation's registered agent.

(2)   The following provisions apply to any subpoena, court order, or search warrant issued in compliance with the Electronic Communications Privacy Act in chapter 121 (commencing with s. 2701) of part I of Title 18 of the United States Code and that is subject to this chapter, which allows a search for records that are in the actual or constructive possession of an out-of-state corporation that provides electronic communication services or remote computing services to the public, when those records would reveal the identity of the customers using those services; data stored by, or on behalf of, the customers; the customers' usage of those services; or the recipients or destinations of communications sent to or from those customers.

(a)   Any subpoena, court order, or warrant issued under this subsection must contain the following language in bold type on the first page of the document: "This (subpoena, order, warrant) is issued pursuant to Florida Statute s. 92.605. A response is due within 20 business days of receipt of this (subpoena, order, warrant) unless a longer time period is stated herein."

(b)   When properly served with a subpoena, court order, or search warrant issued by a Florida court or other applicant, an out-of-state corporation subject to this section shall provide to the applicant all records sought pursuant to such subpoena, court order, or warrant within 20 business days after receipt, or the date indicated within the subpoena, if later, including those records maintained or located outside the State of Florida. If the records cannot be produced within the 20-day time period, the out-of-state corporation shall notify the applicant within the 20-day time period and agree to produce the documents at the earliest possible time. The applicant shall pay the out-of-state corporation the reasonable expenses associated with compliance.

(c)   When the applicant makes a showing and the court finds that failure to produce records within 20 business days would cause an adverse result, the subpoena, court order, or warrant may require production of records within less than 20 business days. A court may reasonably extend the time required for production of the records upon finding that the out-of-state corporation needs the extension and that an extension of time would not cause an adverse result.

(d)   An out-of-state corporation seeking to quash or object to the subpoena, court order, or warrant must seek relief from the court issuing such subpoena, court order, or warrant within the time required for production of records under this section. The issuing court shall hear and decide that motion within 5 court days after the motion is filed.

(e)   Upon written request from the applicant or if ordered by the court, the out-of-state corporation shall verify the authenticity of records that it produces by providing an affidavit that complies with the requirements set forth in this section. Records produced in compliance with this section are admissible in evidence as set forth in subsection (5).

(3)   A Florida business that provides electronic communication services or remote computing services to the public, when served with a subpoena, court order, or warrant issued by another state to produce records that would reveal the identity of the customers using those services; data stored by, or on behalf of, the customers; the customers' usage of those services; or the recipients or destinations of communications sent to or from those customers shall produce those records as if that subpoena, court order, or warrant had been issued by a Florida court.

(4)   A cause of action does not arise against any out-of-state corporation or Florida business subject to this section, or its officers, employees, agents, or other specified persons, for providing records, information, facilities, or assistance in accordance with the terms of a subpoena, court order, or warrant subject to this section.

(5)   In a criminal proceeding in a court of this state, an out-of-state record of regularly conducted business activity, or a copy of such record, shall not be excluded as hearsay evidence by s. 90.802, if an out-of-state certification attests that:

(a)   Such record was made at or near the time of the occurrence of the matters set forth by, or from information transmitted by, a person with knowledge of those matters.

(b)   Such record was kept in the course of a regularly conducted business activity.

(c)   The business activity made such a record as a regular practice.

(d)   If such record is not the original, it is a duplicate of the original, unless the source of information or the method or circumstances of preparation indicate lack of trustworthiness.

(6)   An out-of-state certification under this section shall authenticate such record or duplicate.

(7)   No evidence in such records in the form of opinion or diagnosis is admissible under subsection (5) unless such opinion or diagnosis would be admissible under ss. 90.701-90.705 if the person whose opinion is recorded were to testify to the opinion directly.

(8)   As soon after the arraignment as practicable, or 60 days prior to trial, a party intending to offer in evidence under this section an out-of-state record of regularly conducted business activity shall provide written notice of that intention to each other party. A motion opposing admission in evidence of such record shall be made by the opposing party and determined by the court before trial. Failure by a party to file such motion before trial shall constitute a waiver of objection to such record or duplicate, but the court for cause shown may grant relief from the waiver.

(9)   In any criminal case, the content of any electronic communication may be obtained under this section only by court order or by the issuance of a search warrant, unless otherwise provided under the Electronic Communications Privacy Act or other provision of law.

History.—s. 3, ch. 2003-71.

Made in the USA
San Bernardino, CA
28 August 2014